Indigenous Ethnographies of North East India

ABOUT THE EDITORS

Dr. Somenath Bhattacharjee is the M.Sc. Gold Medalist (1st Class, 1st) in Anthropology from the University of North Bengal (2004). His area of specialization is Social-Cultural Anthropology.

At present he is working as an Assistant Professor, in the Department of Anthropology of Assam University, Diphu Campus. His area of research interest is Tribal ethnography, Medical Anthropology, Folk and material culture. A number of his research papers and articles are published in different reputed National, International Journals and Conference proceedings.

Dr. Anup Kumar Dey did his post graduation in English and M. Phil. from Assam University, Silchar. He has also done his Ph.D. on the plays of Arthur Miller in the same university. He taught English Literature in two Government Degree Colleges in Tripura for more than 7 years and is currently working as an Assistant Professor in the Department of English, Assam University, Diphu Campus for more than 5 years. His research papers are published in many well reputed international journals. He has completed one Minor Research Project under UGC on the poetry of Margaret Atwood. Currently he is engaged with a National Security Council sponsored research project on the Zeme Naga tribe. His areas of interest include Drama Studies, Postcolonial Literature and Indian English Writings.

ABOUT THE COMPILORS

Dr. Subhajit Choudhury worked as Deputy Registrar, Assam University, Diphu Campus, (on lien from Indian Institute of Technology Guwahati). Did Ph.D. in Library and Information Science in 2007. Have published 30 papers in National & International conference proceeding and also contributed chapters in three edited books. His research areas are Information Literacy, E-Governance, ICT in LICs, Community Information Science, Indigenous people, Health Literacy etc. He is the life member of ILA, IASLIC.

Mr. Hemanta Dhing Mazumdar did his post graduation in History and also B.Ed. from Gauhati University. Instead of choosing any profession he prefers to dedicate his life for social cause and especially for ushering his mission to bring to light the true history of North East India hitherto unknown to the world. His mission leads him to associate himself with Akhil Bharatiya Itihas Sankalan Yojana, an organization dedicated to the cause of recording the real history of India. At present, he is shouldering the responsibility of Zonal Organizing Secretary, North East India as well as Akhil Bharatiya Sampark Pramukh of the organization.

Indigenous Ethnographies of North East India

A Study from EMIC Perspective

Edited by
Somenath Bhattacharjee
Anup Kumar Dey

Compiled by
Subhajit Choudhury
Hemanta Dhing Majumdar

CONCEPT PUBLISHING COMPANY PVT. LTD.
NEW DELHI-110059

ISBN-13: 978-93-88937-71-9

First Published 2021

Published and Printed by

Concept Since 1974

Concept Publishing Company Pvt. Ltd.
A/15-16, Commercial Block, Mohan Garden,
New Delhi-110059 (INDIA)
T: 91 11 25351460, 91 11 25351794
E: publishing@conceptpub.com *W*: www.conceptpub.com

Cataloging in Publication Data--Courtesy: D.K. Agencies (P) Ltd. <docinfo@dkagencies.com>

National Seminar on "Indigenous Ethnography, Emic Perspective and National Cultural Heritage: Focusing North East India" (2016 : Diphu, India)

Indigenous ethnographies of North East India : a study from emic perspective / edited by Somenath Bhattacharjee, Anup Kumar Dey ; compiled by Subhajit Choudhury, Hemanta Dhing Majumdar.

pages cm

"The present volume is an academic outcome of selected research papers presented in the ICSSR sponsored two days National Seminar on "Indigenous Ethnography, Emic Perspective and National Cultural Heritage: Focusing North East India", held on 6th-7thJanuary, 2016, in the Department of Anthropology, Assam University, Diphu Campus, in collaboration with Bharatiya Itihas Sankalan Samiti, Assam"—Introduction.

Includes bibliographical references and Index.

ISBN 9789388937719

1. Ethnology—India, Northeastern—Congresses. 2. Ethnoscience—India, Northeastern—Congresses. 3. Indigenous peoples—India, Northeastern—Social life and customs—Congresses. 4. India, Northeastern—Civilization—Congresses. I. Bhattacharjee, Somenath, editor. II. Assam University (Silchar, India). Diphu Campus. Department of Anthropology, organizer. III. Bharatiya Itihas Sankalan Samiti (Silchar, India), organizer. IV. Indian Council of Social Science Research, sponsoring body. V. Title.

LCC GN635.I4N38 2016 | DDC 305.8009541 23

Foreword

Social Anthropology, the other name for which is 'interpretative anthropology' is based on ethnography. The discourse of Ethnography began in the post-evolutionary anthropology which commenced towards the end of Nineteenth Century in England; in a way triggered by the first anthropological field-work in December, 1998 with the Cambridge University expedition led by Haddon, Rivers and Seligman to Torres Straits in New Guinea. This was a field-work of barely a fortnight's duration in the true fashion of ethnographic field-work which continues to this day.

What is ethnography? The term implies systematic and objective (to the extent possible) of cultural characteristics of a people and their description. This is the stuff on which analysis and interpretation of data depends.

In India, ethnographic field research contesting earlier methods of data generation began towards the end of the first decade of Twentieth Century. One should pay regard to late Sarat Chandra Roy, a Lawyer turned anthropologist of Ranchi, who is truly called the father of Indian Anthropology with the publication of his first of a series of monographic accounts on the tribes of Chotanagpur region. The tradition was continued by the Department of Anthropology, Calcutta University, established in 1921, which developed appropriate strategies and methodology of field-work.

In the north-eastern region, the tradition began in the work of a few missionaries and British civil servants who collected material for the tribes of what is today Assam, Meghalaya, Nagaland and Manipur. These were published by the Assam Government in the form of monographs which are like a valuable treasure house of authentic data on the tribes till today.

What, in a fact, we do today in a various University Departments of Anthropology and Sociology is elaboration of the same methods and analytical techniques, albeit with some refinements. The present edited volume is an attempt to document the ethnography of different indigenous perspectives from emic perspective and to find out their significance in the context of Indian civilization.

Prof. A.C. Bhagabati
Honorary Coordinator & Head of Division
North Eastern Regional Centre
Indira Gandhi National Centre for The Arts (IGNCA)
(Former Vice-Chancellor, Arunachal University, India)

Contents

Our Contributors

Professor Buddhadeb Chaudhuri, Chairperson, Commission on Human Rights, International Union of Anthropological and Ethnological Sciences; Former Dr. Ambedkar Chair Professor in Anthropology, Calcutta University, And Coordinator, Human Rights Programme, Calcutta University; 4A, Fort Royale, 28 Prince Anwar Shah Road, Kolkata-700033.
E-mail: buddhadebc@gmail.com

Prof. Birinchi K. Medhi, Formerly Professor, Department of Anthropology, Gauhati University, Guwahati, Assam.
E-mail: profbirinchimedhi@rediffmail.com

Prof. Rani Hazarika Kakaty, Department of Anthropology, Gauhati University. Guwahati (Assam).

Dr. Kh. Narendra Singh, Associate Professor, Department of Anthropology, Assam University, Diphu Campus.
E-mail: kh.singh@rediffmail.com

Dr. Dwipen Bezbaruah, Professor, Department of Anthropology, Gauhati University. Guwahati (Assam).

Dr. Nil Ratan Roy, Associate Professor, Department of Education, Visvabharati Santiniketan. (W.B.).
E-mail: nil_education@yahoo.co.in

Dr. Pinak Tarafdar, Associate Professor Department of Anthropology, University of North Bengal Rajarammohanpur, District- Darjeeling. Siliguri, West Bengal, 734013.
E-mail: pinaknbu@gmail.com

Dr. Arifur Zaman, Associate Professor, Department of Anthropology, Gauhati University, Guwahati, Assam.
E-mail: arifurzaman@gmail.com

Dr. Subhajit Choudhury, Deputy Registrar, Assam University, Diphu Campus, Diphu, Assam.
E-mail: subhajit.lib@gmail.com

Dr. Bhola Nath Ghosh, Assistant Professor, Sociological Research Unit, Indian Statistical Institute, Kolkata 700108.
E-mail: bholanathghosh@hotmail.com or bhola@isical.ac.in

Dr. Sangeeta Chakravarty, University of Science and Technology, Meghalaya, India.
E-mail: sangeeta0404@gmail.com

Arindita Goswami, Assistant Professor, Department of Anthropology, Dibrugarh University, Dibrugarh–786004, Assam.
E-mail: arindita25@gmail.com

Humi Thaosen, Assistant Professor, Department of Anthropology, Gauhati University, Guwahati, Assam.
E-mail: huthaosen@gmail.com

Dr. Merry Baruah Bora, Assistant Professor (Sr) Dept. of English, Cotton College, Guwahati.

Minakshi Duarah, Assistant Professor, Eastern Karbi Anglong College.
E-mail: minakshiduarah3101@gmail.com

Prasanta Gogoi, Assistant Professor, Eastern Karbi Anglong College.

Rabindranath Jana, Sociological Research Unit, Indian Statistical Institute, Kolkata.
E-mail: rabindranathjana65@gmail.com

Anil Kumar Choudhuri, Sociological Research Unit, Indian Statistical Institute, Giridih.

Lilu Rani Hasnu, Ph. D. Research Scholar, Department of Anthropology, Gauhati University, Guwahati, Assam.
E-mail: rani85hasnu@gmail.com

Jushna Beypi, RGNF, Ph.D. Research Scholar, Department of Anthropology, Assam University, Diphu Campus.

Bandita Teronpi, Research Scholar, Department of Political Science, AUDC.
E-mail: bteronpi@yahoo.com

Joyshree Bora, Ph.D. Research Scholar, Department of Anthropology, Assam University, Diphu Campus, Diphu, Assam-782462.
E-mail: joyshreeb55@gmail.com

Prerna R. Lepcha, Ph.D. Scholar, Department of Education, Visvabharati Santiniketan.
E-mail: prerna_lepcha@yahoo.com

Kunal Choudhury, Research Scholar, Department of Anthropology, Gauhati University, Guwahati, Assam.
E-mail: choudhury09kunal@gmail.com

Mon Mayur Bora, M.Phil, Department of Anthropology, Assam University, Diphu Campus, Assam-782462.
E-mail: mon.mayur23@gmail.com,

Bipasha Rosy Lakra, Assistant Professor, Department of Political Science, Gargi College, University of Delhi, Delhi.

Dr. Natalie Jo-Anne Diengdoh, Folklorist & Media Professional, Shillong.
E-mail: natalie.diengdoh@gmail.com

M. Elonbeni Ngullie, Ph.D. Research Scholar, Department of Sociology, Dibrugarh University, Dibrugarh, Assam.
E-mail: elonbeni@gmail.com

Papiya Bose, Research Scholar, Department of Anthropology, Gauhati University, Guwahati, Assam.
E-mail: papiyabose05@gmail.com

Yaisna Rajkumari, Stella Maris College, Chennai.
E-mail: haze.lilly14@gmail.com

Nabajit Das, Assistant Professor, Department of Economics, G.K.B. College, Tipkai, Kokrajhar, Assam.
Email: Id-dnabajit@gmail.com

Y. Monojit Singha, Research Scholar, Department of Political Science, Assam University, Silchar.
E-mail: ymonojit@gmail.com

Nirupoma Kardong, Research Scholar, Department of Folklore Research, Gauhati University, Guwahati, Assam.
E-mail: nirupomakardong@gmail.com

Bamonkiri Ronpi, Ph.D. Research Scholar, Department of Anthropology, Assam University, Diphu Campus, Assam-782462.
E-mail: bamonkirie@gmail.com

Rengmini Tokbipi, M.Phil. Research Scholar, Department of Anthropology, Assam University, Diphu Campus, Assam-782462.
E-mail: rengminitokbipi@yahoo.com

Introduction

The present volume is an academic outcome of selected research papers presented in the ICSSR sponsored two days National seminar on "Indigenous Ethnography, Emic Perspective and National Cultural Heritage: Focusing North East India", held on 6th-7th January, 2016, in the Department of Anthropology, Assam University, Diphu Campus, in collaboration with Bharatiya Itihas Sankalan Samiti, Assam.

Being the editor, we are extremely grateful to ICSSR and Assam University Silchar for their financial support. We are extremely obliged to the Honourable Vice-Chancellor of Assam University, Silchar; to the Honourable Pro-Vice-Chancellor of Assam University, Diphu Campus, Head of the Department of Anthropology, Assam University, Diphu Campus. We are grateful to the renowned resource persons, to the faculty members and research scholars of different Universities of India for their kind presence and academic discussion during the seminar.

Indian civilization is comprised of two distinctive but inter-related cultural traditions, one is formal, written, literate and reflected few, while the other is informal, oral, illiterate and un-reflected many. The Great traditional parts primarily include Sanskrit Vedic Hindu literature and are being cultivated in different schools and temples in different places. These places are often visited by the rural people and they observe the cultural practices. Little traditions are those practices which are performed by their own means among the village communities, which works itself out and keep itself going in the lives of unlettered village communities.

The societal dimensions of these two traditions are the great community and little community. These two traditions are not mutually exclusive but are interdependent—"two currents of thought and action, distinguishable yet, flowing into and out of each other".

North East India is very rich in its multiethnic and multicultural diversity, with nearly 300 distinct indigenous communities (of which 125 are recognized as Scheduled Tribes). The daily livelihoods of the indigenous groups are closely related with their surrounding environment and the indigenous culture is nourished in the lap of nature. Their cultural heritage, traits and elements are not merely for the individuals rather it is for the entire community as a whole. However, with the changing dimension of time and influence of globalization, a number of social and cultural changes can be noticed among the indigenous communities and their cultural heritage is facing a major challenge, which is ultimately creating an identity crisis for them. On the other hand, as their cultural practices, social norms, values and customs are oral in tradition, these are remaining undocumented.

In this context, to understand about the traditional aboriginal culture, contemporary period demands an in-depth analytical research from the emic perspective to write the ethnography of indigenous communities to properly document their identity and culture. The conglomeration of intellectuals in this endeavour will enrich the knowledge to know about the heritage of Indian civilization through ethnographic analysis, which in turn will try to build the co-relation between central and marginal traditions to frame the holistic national integrity in multiethnic and multicultural India.

In the context, to understand the traditional aboriginal culture, contemporary period demands an in-depth analytical research from the emic perspective to write the ethnography of indigenous communities to properly document their identity and culture. Through this seminar on "Indigenous Ethnography, Emic Perspective and National Cultural Heritage: Focusing North East India", we have tried to find out the similarities in between different cultural traditions, rather not to explore the wide gap of differences existing among them, as well as to find out the relevance of such traditions in the greater dimension of Indian civilization as a whole.

Dr. Somenath Bhattacharjee and
Dr. Anup Kumar Dey
(Editors)

SECTION-I
Theoretical and Methodological Framework

1
Do Not Measure Our Head Only—Try to Measure Our Heart

Buddhadeb Chaudhuri

Introduction

It was around 50 years back when I was a research student in the Department of Anthropology, University of Calcutta, a seminar was organized in Calcutta on North East India and mainly focusing on the tribal situation and I still remember what one participant said, "Do not measure our heads only, try to measure our heart also." What he wanted to communicate was very clear. Are the non-tribals really aware about the needs, requirements and socio-cultural traditions and problems of the tribal regions in general and North East in particular? Because of various socio-political reasons, economic condition and development, the region was passing through a very difficult time. Has the situation changed or improved dramatically? About 25 years back we conducted a study on the health situation of mother and child sponsored by UNICEF and noted the alarming health condition in many places of this region.

The indigenous peoples have rich tradition, wisdom and knowledge related to health but facing various problems due to dominant development models, deforestation and commercial afforestation. Again, socio-cultural dimensions of health, is it myth or reality? Often the tribals are held responsible for not accepting western medicine because of superstitious beliefs and practices.

But it is often not examined whether the western medicine is available and access to health facilities is very limited or not in these areas.

The health situation in most of the countries in this region is really critical. Despite our entire technological breakthrough, we still live in a world where a fifth of the developing world's population goes hungry every night, a quarter lacks access to even a basic necessity like safe drinking water and a third lives in a state of abject poverty--at such a margin of human existence that words simply fail to describe it. More than a billion people in developing countries still lack safe drinking water. In developing countries, the major causes of death are infections and parasitic-diseases, which kill seventeen million people annually, including 6.5 million from acute respiratory infection, 4.5 million from diarrhoeal diseases and 3.5 million from tuberculosis. Most of these deaths are linked with poor nutrition and an unsafe environment, particularly polluted water, which contributes to the nearly one billion cases of diarrhoea a year. In both developing and industrial countries, the threats to health security are usually greater for the poorest people in the rural areas and the indigenous people. The disparities between the rich and the poor are similar for access to health services: in the developed countries there is 1 doctor for 400 persons whereas in the developing countries, it is 1: 7000. Spending on health programmes is also very different and it is quite low in the developing countries; for example it is only $7 per individual per year in Bangladesh. The situation is not much better in many other developing countries. Considering this alarming situation, out of the seven important targets put forward for human development in the Agenda for Social Summit, four were related to health. They are as follows:

1. Primary health care for all with special stress on the immunization of children.
2. Severe malnutrition to be eliminated and moderate malnutrition rates to be halved.
3. Family planning services for all willing couples.
4. Safe drinking water and sanitation for all.

Let me start narrating some health indicators and very related factor like education in the context of India.

Table 1.1: Sex-ratio in Selected States

States	*Sex-ratio*		*Child Sex-ratio*	
	2001	2011	2001	2011
India	933	943	927	919
Kerala	1058	1084	960	964
Mizoram	935	976	964	970
Bihar	919	931	942	935
M.P.	919	931	932	918
Rajasthan	921	928	909	888
U.P.	898	912	916	902
Chhattisgarh	989	991	969	975
West Bengal	934	950	960	956

Note: Lowest Sex Ratio in 2011-618 (Daman Diu), Lowest Child Sex Ratio in 2011 – 834 (Haryana).

Apart from high maternal mortality, the sex ratio is also an area of serious concern. Though there is marginal improvement, the situation is not very encouraging. Apart from Kerala, which has the highest sex ratio (and also highest literacy), the sex ratio is above 975 in the tribal dominated states of North East and Chhattisgarh (1991). But the area of main concern is the decline of child sex ratio even in the last Census year. Lack of proper care in the context of a girl child has been reported in many studies and even UNICEF has produced documentary to create awareness of people. The son preference in many communities has created the problem more complex. Lack of proper health facility and safe drinking water are the major health problems in many places resulting mortality particularly child mortality. As the survival is uncertain, it leads to more frequent pregnancies affecting the health of women.

Table 1.2: Literacy in Selected States

States	*2001*			*2011*		
	Male	*Female*	*Total*	*Male*	*Female*	*Total*
Kerala	94.24	87.72	90.86	96.11	92.07	94.00
Bihar	59.68	33.12	47.00	71.20	51.50	61.80
M.P.	76.06	50.29	63.74	78.73	59.24	69.32
Rajasthan	75.70	43.85	60.41	79.19	52.12	66.11
U.P.	68.82	42.22	56.27	77.28	57.18	67.68
Mizoram	90.72	86.75	88.80	93.35	89.27	91.33
Chhattisgarh	77.38	51.85	64.66	80.27	60.24	70.28
West Bengal	77.02	59.61	68.64	81.69	70.54	76.26

To understand health and health related problems in a proper perspective, it is very important to consider the socio-cultural issues, economic dimensions and environmental aspects. This is more relevant in the context of tribal people particularly living in the rural areas.

The National Health Policy formulated in 1983 and 2002 have yielded results but in several areas, the outcome has not been as expected. Government initiatives in the public health sector have recorded some noteworthy successes over time. Smallpox and Guinea Worm disease have been eradicated from the country; Polio is on the verge of being eradicated; Leprosy and Kala Azar can be expected to be eliminated in the near future. There has been a substantial drop in the Total Fertility Rate (TFR) and Infant Mortality Rate (IMR). The success of the initiatives taken in the public health field is reflected in the progressive improvement of many demographic indicators over time.

Table 1.3: Achievements through the Years—1951-2000

Indicator	*1951*	*1981*	*2000*
Demographic Changes			
Life Expectancy	36.7	54	64.6

Out of the communicable diseases which have persisted over time, the incidence of Malaria staged resurgence in the 1980s before stabilising at a fairly high prevalence level during the 1990s. Over the years, an increasing level of insecticide-resistance has developed in the malarial vectors in many parts of the country. In respect of TB, the public health scenario has not shown any significant decline in the pool of infection amongst the community, and there has been a distressing trend in the increase of drug resistance to the type of infection prevailing in the country. A new and extremely virulent communicable disease–HIV/AIDS—has emerged on the health scene since the declaration of the NHP-1983. As there is no existing therapeutic cure or vaccine for this infection, the disease constitutes a serious threat, not merely to public health but to economic development in the country. The common water-borne infections—Gastroenteritis, Cholera, and some forms of Hepatitis—continue to contribute to a high level of morbidity in the population, even though the mortality rate may have been somewhat moderated.

The statistics bring out the wide differences between the attainment of health goals in the better-performing States as compared to the low-performing States. It is clear that national averages of health indices hide wide disparities in public health facilities and health standards in different parts of the country. Given a situation in which national averages in respect of most indices are themselves at unacceptably low levels, the wide inter-State disparity implies that, for vulnerable sections of society in several States, access to public health services is nominal and health standards are grossly inadequate. Despite a thrust in the NHP-1983 and 2002 for making good the unmet needs of public health services by establishing more public health institutions at a decentralized level, a large gap in facilities still persists.

National Rural Health Mission (NRHM) under the Ministry of Health and Family Welfare (MoHFW), Government of India has brought out a document (2008) entitled "India Guaranteeing Quality Primary Health Care for All: An Agenda for Action". The public health challenges have been identified state-wise and the key challenges are as shown in Table 1.4.

Table 1.4: Health Problems in Different States

Indicator	*States with high incidence / low performance*
Infant Mortality	M.P., U.P., Orissa, Rajasthan, Chhattisgarh, Bihar, Assam
Maternal Mortality	Assam, Bihar, Madhya Pradesh, Orissa, Rajasthan, Uttar Pradesh
High expenditure in Government hospitals	Bihar, Haryana, Punjab, Rajasthan, Uttar Pradesh, Assam, Karnataka, Orissa
High TB cases/suspect cases	Jharkhand, Bihar, Gujarat, Uttar Pradesh, West Bengal, Assam, Andhra Pradesh, Tamil Nadu
High TFR	Madhya Pradesh, Uttar Pradesh, Bihar, Jharkhand, Chhattisgarh, Rajasthan
Full Immunization	Rajasthan, Uttar Pradesh, Madhya Pradesh, Bihar, Jharkhand
Diabetes	Kerala, Tamil Nadu, Tripura, Goa, West Bengal, Delhi
Asthma	West Bengal, Kerala, Mizoram, Sikkim, Tripura
Malaria	Assam, Maharashtra, Karnataka, West Bengal, Orissa, Rajasthan, Uttar Pradesh, Gujarat, Chhattisgarh, Jharkhand, Madhya Pradesh, Arunachal Pradesh, Meghalaya
Tobacco & Alcohol	Rajasthan, Chhattisgarh, Madhya Pradesh, Bihar, Jharkhand, Orissa, West Bengal, Mizoram, Meghalaya, Tripura, Nagaland, Assam, Arunachal Pradesh, Sikkim, Andhra Pradesh, Goa, Kerala, Tamil Nadu, Punjab

Access to, and benefits from, the public health system have been very uneven between the better-endowed and the more vulnerable sections of society. This is particularly true for women, children and the socially disadvantaged sections of society. The facts given in Table 1.5 highlight the handicap suffered in the health sector on account of socio-economic inequality.

Table 1.5: Variations in Health Status among Socio-economic Groups

Indicator	*Infant Mortality/1000*	*Under 5 Mortality/1000*	*% Children Underweight*
India	70	94.9	47
Social Inequity			
Scheduled Castes	83	119.3	53.5
Scheduled Tribes	84.2	126.6	55.9
Other Disadvantaged	76	103.1	47.3
Others	61.8	82.6	41.1

There is one factor common among all tribal communities except the North East, it is the educational backwardness. The tribals form the bulk of the illiterate population in India and the close link between education and health is all well-known. It has also been noted that child mortality, under 5 child mortality are the highest among the tribals. It has also been noted that among the tribals there is high incidence of communicable diseases including—

(a) vector-borne malaria, dengue,
(b) water-borne diarrhoea and hepatitis, and
(c) Air-borne pneumonia, measles, T.B.

Incidentally, all these diseases are due to poverty, malnutrition and certain environmental factors like poor sanitation and unsafe drinking water. Now there is a growing trend to give more emphasis on non-communicable diseases than on communicable diseases which affect a much larger segment of the population, primarily the disadvantaged people and this can be reduced, if not eliminated, if certain efforts are made without much financial commitment.

Crucial Issues and Myths

A number of myths have been systematically created against the non-western systems in general and indigenous systems in particular. It is essential to demolish them to evolve a proper health policy in the developing countries, particularly for the indigenous people and the poor.

1. Quite often it is said that the rural people, particularly the tribals, are all superstitious. Thus if the rural people worship a deity for cure, it is automatically assumed that they are superstitious and would not accept the so-called modern health practices. But when the same thing is done in the cities of India, it becomes tradition and when it is done in the Churches of Europe, it is labelled as convention. The question of rationality cannot be judged or examined in isolation, without examining the eco-system, the health facilities available and the economic condition. Again, the mere presence of a health centre does not necessarily mean that people would depend on it, if proper and adequate facilities are not available in it or if the people are not convinced about its efficiency. In fact, bulk of the social scientists, who have studied health culture of the rural population in India or in South Asia, have been overenthusiastic in discussing superstitious health beliefs and practices and have not paid adequate attention to the forces which have been instrumental in causing decay and degeneration of their health culture.

2. The traditional method of treatment does not mean that something counter to development is suggested. The point is that there may be many positive aspects in a traditional system, which should be encouraged and propagated. In fact, the need is to provide all the alternatives and not to depend on only one system.

3. The argument often put forward in favour of the introduction of the western system (and of the replacement of the traditional) is that tribal and similar traditional approaches do not have an answer to many diseases. This is an undeniable fact but does not necessarily reflect the limitation of the traditional system. Apart from the fact of the non-availability of many herbs, one should add that many of these diseases were formerly unknown. Naturally, the question of any traditional system having a remedy for them does not arise. In fact, for the same reason, western medicine also does not have remedies for many diseases.

Documentation and Challenges

Knowledge and documentation of traditional medicine, including the tribal medicine, is urgently needed. It is important for the modern system to begin with the base existing in the rural-tribal society and build on it, rather than replace it. In order to achieve this, information about traditional medicinal practices should be documented before they are forgotten. A study of the indigenous methods of treatment may help to identify new methods of treatment of various diseases with certain modifications. In fact, a number of ethno-botanical studies have helped in identifying a number of medicinal plants used by the tribals to treat different types of diseases. Many of them may be very useful to treat diseases and it is urgently necessary to document them and try them after proper scientific experiment. This has been observed in the few studies that have been made on tribal medicine, especially in terms of efficiency, which is very encouraging. This, however, needs to be further substantiated by sustained research. It may be said that the achievement of traditional/tribal medicine is quite revealing. However, to utilize the research findings for further development and application for benefiting the vast majority of the rural poor, particularly the tribals who are living in areas which have very little or no modern medical facilities, needs an integrated and multidisciplinary research and follow-up dissemination efforts.

Documentation should be made but at the same time one has to be aware of the risks involved and the use of commercial interest can put it to. Hence, it should be done with certain reservations. Cases are not lacking when, after the publication of research reports on traditional medicinal plants used by the rural people, particularly the tribals, many such plants were collected in bulk by outside big industries for commercial use for profit. As a result, they are no more available to the traditional medicine-men to whom they are so essential for treatment. As a result, the rural people, including the tribals, are deprived of their traditional system without the modern system becoming accessible to them.

Forest, Food, Nutrition and Medicine

Women are mainly responsible for providing food and nutrition to family members. Due to deforestation and commercial afforestation, traditional food items and herbal medicines are no longer available. Water has become polluted and small fishes in the paddy fields, which used to provide nutrition to poorer families, are no longer available due to use of insecticides and pesticides.

Women are mainly responsible for the collection of fuel, fodder and food from the forest. Deforestation and commercial afforestation have affected this practice. In some of our studied areas we have seen how women are having eye problem due to use of leaves of commercial plants as fuel. Again proper western medicines are often not available and they have lost their traditional health culture. This has created life very difficult.

The relation of treatment and nutrition with forests among tribal communities is quite obvious. The traditional herbal treatment is people's knowledge and an oral tradition. In many cases, many persons in the concerned community have the knowledge and in some cases, a few selected persons, the traditional medicinemen, are more knowledgeable. But in any case, people depend on nature, particularly on forests for these medicinal plants. Thus, deforestation and commercial afforestation of mono-plant forest may seriously affect the availability of these medicinal plants. Even the nutrition may be similarly affected. Thus, access to forest resources can affect treatment and nutrition.

Need for an Alternative

The prevailing health and medical system, the western system, has unfortunately failed to meet the need of the world's majority. The failure of the Alma Ata Declaration in fulfilling its objectives of achieving Health for All by the year 2000 gives more urgency to looking for an alternative. In most countries, a very frightening policy change is being maneuvered by agencies like the World Bank and International Monetary Fund to give less and less emphasis to the social and welfare sectors and higher emphasis to the economic and infrastructure sectors. As such the financial allocation for health is going down in most Asian countries. The implication of such a trend in countries where health insurance is unaffordable to the majority is unimaginable. Based on current trends in health care financing and the failure of the Alma Ata Declaration to take a grip of the situation, the condition of the poor, particularly the rural poor and indigenous people, has become more critical and difficult.

Generally, when we talk or think about science, we refer to the western or industrial society. In the context of scientific development, we prefer to discuss more about the so-called modern scientific innovations assuming that science is only there in those societies and quite often implying that scientific rigour or interest is absent in other societies. The role of science is to help mankind to meet the various demands exploiting the natural resources in the best possible way without adversely affecting the environment. Thus, in the given socio-economic and historical context, the knowledge of making fire revolutionised human society. People have developed their own science and technologies based on the demands of the concerned societies, but quite often these are ignored. What I want to impress here is that we need to look at indigenous science and technology, particularly when an existing body of knowledge is available. Perhaps it is better to develop it instead of replacing it in the name of scientific development and modernization. A number of social anthropologists are now deeply involved in studying the traditional wisdom and knowledge of the people, particularly the tribals.

References

Banerjee, D. 1986. *Social Science and Health Service Development in India.* New Delhi, Lok Paksh.

Carstrairs, G.M. 1955. "Medicine and faith in Rural Rajasthan", In: *Health, Culture and Community,* ed. by B.D. Paul, pp. 55-58. New York: Russel Sage Foundation.

Chaudhuri, Buddhadeb. 1979. Cultural Dimensions of Health: A Study on West Bengal Villages' 1st International Congress on Traditional Asian Medicine, Canberra, Australia.

Chaudhuri, Buddhadeb. 1986. *Tribal Health: Socio-cultural Dimensions.* New Delhi, Inter-India Publications.

Chaudhuri, Buddhadeb. 1986. "Social and Cultural Aspects of Health." *Journal of Social and Economic Studies,* 379-388.

Chaudhuri, Buddhadeb. 1989. "Social Science, Health and Culture: The Tribal Situation", *Social Action.* 39(3): 243-253.

Chaudhuri, Buddhadeb. 1990a. "The Case of Tribal Medicine." In: *The*

Philosophy of Science, ed. by J.V. Narlikar and others, pp. 124-126. Shimla: Indian Institute of Advanced Study.

Chaudhuri, Buddhadeb. 1990. *Cultural and Environmental Dimensions on Health*. New Delhi, Inter-India Publication.

Chaudhuri, Buddhadeb. 1993. "Health, Culture and Environment: The Tribal Situation in India." In: *Continuity and Change in Tribal Society*. ed. by Mrinal Miri, pp. 76-78. Shimla: Indian Institute of Advanced Study.

Chaudhuri, Buddhadeb. 2003. *Forest, Health and Development: The Tribal Situation*. New Delhi, Inter-India Publication.

Lewis, Oscar 1958. *Village Life in Northern India*. New York, Random House.

Jain, S.K. 1968. *Medicinal Plants*. New Delhi, National Book Trust.

Joseph, A.N.T. 1992. Ethnozoology of Reptiles in Relation to Health care among Tribals in Madhya Pradesh. In: *National Development and Tribal Deprivation*. ed by Walter Fernandes, pp. 65-67. New Delhi: Indian Social Institute.

Marriott Mckim. 1955. "Western Medicine in a Village of Northern India." In: *Health, Culture and Community*, ed. by B.D. Paul, New York: Russel Sage.

Population Foundation in India. 2010. *Population, Health and Social Development*, PFI, New Delhi.

Roy Burman, B.K. 1982. *Report of the Committee on Forest and Tribals*, Government of India, New Delhi.

Roy Burman, B.K. 1990. "Development Hazards to Health in Tribal India." In *Cultural and Environmental Dimensions on Health*, (Ed.) Buddhadeb Chaudhuri. Inter-India Publications, New Dehli.

Roy Chandreyee. 2009. Forest and Tribals: Right to Access Over Natural Resources, Ph.D Thesis, Human Rights, Calcutta University.

Valunjkar, T.N. and H.R. Chaturvedi, 1967. "Religion and Illness in Hindu Society", *Journal of the M.S. University of Baroda*, 15 & 16(2): 45-52.

2
An Exploration of the Sacred Complex Vasisthasrama of Assam

Birinchi Kumar Medhi and Kunal Choudhury

[I]

Assam is situated in the tropical latitudes 24.3° N and 28.0° N and latitudes 89.5° E and 96.1° E. Among all the states of North East India, Assam is the most populous state. The Vasisthasrama, popularly known as the Vasistha, is an immensely revered temple located in Guwahati, the capital city of Assam. "Assam is an ancient land and it has a thought-provoking history. In the epic period the land was referred to as Pragjyotishpura (the land of eastern light) and in the *Purana* and *Tantra* periods it acquired the name Kamrupa (where the god Kamadeva regains his physique). The name Assam is an anglicized formation of the Sanskrit term '*asama*', which means 'unparallel' or 'peerless' (Medhi, 2008: 91). Assam is a place of temples and shrines. Guwahati being the capital of the state for prolonged period, and because of this place is booned by picturesque beauty with Brahmaputra and other rivers, serpent like green hillocks and mesmerizing plain areas, a good number of temples and shrines are established here. The Vasisthasrama (hermitage of Vasistha), is a renowned temple situated at a distance of about 11 kms in the southern direction from the centre of Guwahati city. According to the *Kalika Purana* due to the penance of sage (*rishi)* Vasistha divine river Ganga came as three rivulets, viz., the Sandhya, the Lalita and the Kanta, to the Sandhyachala hillock of Guwahati, and the confluence of these three rivulets is known as the Vasistha Ganga. The Ahom king Rajeswar Singha had constructed a temple nearby this water source during AD 1751-1769. In the temple wall there is an inscription on stone of the time of the Ahom king Rajeswar Singha, which was inscribed in 1686 *saka*. Inside the temple there is a pair of foot marks and the Hindus believe that these are the footprints of the great *rishi* Vasistha (Neog, 2008: 263).

It should be noted here that amidst the overwhelming majority of the Siva temples only a few religious centres devoted to the other gods and goddesses are located in Guwahati. The principal deity of the Vasisthasrama is also lord Siva known as Golokeswara Siva ('Golok' means 'Vaikuntha', a place in heaven, the abode of lord Vishnu) and *'iswara'* means 'authority', that means authority of Goloka. 'The name Siva is unknown to *veda*, but Rudra, another name of the deity, and almost equally common, occurs in the *veda* both singular and plural, and from these the great deity Siva and his manifestation, the Rudra, have been developed. In the *Yajur-veda* there is a long prayer called *Satarudriya* which is addressed to him and appeals to him under a great variety of epithets....In *Upanishadas* his character is further developed. In *Ramayana*, Siva is a great god, but the references to him have more of the idea of a personal god than a supreme divinity. The *Mahabharata* also gives Vishnu and Krishna the highest honour upon the whole. But it has many passages in which Siva occupies the supreme place, and receives the homage and worship of Vishnu and Krishna (Dowson, 1987: 296-297).

Shiva, the dissolver and reproducer, is the third deity of the Hindu triad, the other two are Brahma, the creator, and Vishnu, the preserver. Lord Shiva is generally imagined as garbing by a tiger skin, body is smeared with ashes, bearer of divine river Ganga (*Gangadhara*), having matted hair (*Jatadhara*), wearing in neck a garland of human skull (*Kapalmali*) and a serpent with conspicuous hood (*Phanidhara*), moon crested (*Chandrasekhara*), blue-throated (*Nilakantha*), three eyed (*Trilochana, Trinayana, Tryambaka*) and so on, and having a trident (*trishula*) called *pinaka* and a *dambaru*, a kind of musical instrument, in his hands. He is habituated to consume regularly thorn apple fruit (*dhatura*) and *bhang* (*Canabis Sativa* L.). Like other Hindu gods and goddesses Siva also have a good number of names and epithets, some of which are: *Aghora* (the terrible), *Bhairava* (the terrible destroyer), *Chandradhara* (middle of his forehead is surmounted with a creseant of moon), *Dhurjati* (loaded with matted hair), *Digambara* (the naked one), *Girisha* (mountain lord), *Hara* (the seizer), *Ishana* (the ruler), *Mahadeva* (the great god), *Mahakala* (the great time), Mahesha (the great god), *Mahayogi* (the great ascetic), Maheswara (the great god), *Mrityunjaya* (vanquisher of death), *Panchanana* (five faced), *Pashupati* (lord of animals), *Pinakpani* (who holds a *pinak*, i.e., a trident), *Rudra* (from the Sanskrit root *'rud'*, means 'to weep'), Sadasiva, Sambhu, Sankara and Siva (the auspicious), *Ugra* (fierce), and so on.

Like almost all the Hindu gods and goddess lord Siva does not live in heaven, but resides at the Kailasa hill. He also sometimes lives in the cremation ground along with the ghosts and imps (*bhuta*), for which he is known as Bhutanatha and Bhuteswara. Siva moves around riding on a milky white healthy bull known as Nandi. It is a paradox that he is the lord of the universe (Viswanatha), but lives on begging. In an Assamese folk song this character of Siva is depicted in a conspicuous manner:

> *'O Siva Bholanatha he*
> *Tomar shire jata*
> *Jagataka bar diya Apuni*
> *nangatha. '*

The broad meaning of the song is: O Siva Bholanatha, you have matted hair in your head, you offer boons to all, but you are naked.

[II]

In Assam Shiva is a immensely popular god and generally known as Bholanatha, Mahadeva, Sadasiva or Siva, but most popularly revered as Burha Gosai (the old god). In every locality of Assam one can observe the worshipping places carefully preserved for this omnipotent god, which are identified as Burha Gosair Than, the appeasing place of lord Siva. It is a known fact that Assam is an abode of a good number of tribal communities and most of these communities believe in a pristine tribal god, whose physical features and attributes are akin to those of the lord Siva. As for example, the Bathou of the Boro, Langa of the Rabha, Ublei of the Khasi, Burha, Balia Baba or the Pisadoma of the Deuri are some of the tribal gods resemble closely to the Hindu god Siva. The sanskritized tribal groups of Assam referred such traditional gods as Siva or Mahadeva. Overwhelming majority of the Siva temples of Assam prove the popularity of this god in this remote part of India. Till today the parents of Assam, both tribal and non-tribal, named their offsprings after the names of lord Siva like Bhairab, Bholanath, Chandrasekhar, Dhurjati, Gangadhar, Gaurisankar, Girindra, Girish, Harendra, Ishan, Mahadeb, Mahesh, Maheswar, Pinakpani, Sailendra, Sankar, Sasankasekhar, Sashadhar, Sashindra, Satish, Siva, Sibasish, et al.

In Hinduism destruction implies reproduction. Lord Siva is also *Kameswara,* the lord of carnal desire. This epithet clearly relates the deity with reproduction. Due to this character, Siva is generally not appeased in anthropomorphic form, but propitiated in his symbol *linga* (phallus), typical of reproduction. Sometimes, a *linga* is worshipped alone or with the combination of *yoni,* the female organ. It is pertinent to note here that in all the temples and shrines of lord Siva, the deity is worshipped with his consort Sati. In different births Sati acquired different names like Gauri, Parvati, Uma, *et al.,* and therefore, in the different Siva temples and shrines lord Siva is appeased with those forms of Sati. In all the Sakti temples also the goddess (Devi) is worshipped with her consort lord Siva. In Vasisthasrama lord Siva is worshipped with his consort Tara.

Shiva is principally propitiated with cow milk, the symbol of sperm or breast milk, wood apple fruit and leaf, which are also symbols of fertility cult. The Monday is believed to be the birthday of Siva, and therefore, auspicious to appease this god, and due to this connection lord Siva acquires the name *Somnatha* (authority of Monday). It is strongly believed by the Hindus that among all the gods lord Siva is the best husband, and therefore, the damsels worship this god particularly on Mondays observing some religious taboo to get good husbands and to acquire fortune. It is also believed that this god is very handsome, calm and quite in nature and could be satisfied easily, for which he acquires the name *Ashutosa.* The Hindus sincerely believe that this coy and amiable god only becomes terrible and turbulent through the vexatious deeds of somebody. His third eye is very destructive, which is located vertically in the middle of his forehead above the two eyes and generally remains close. Lord Siva's wrath is intensified through opening of the third eye, which sight could reduce anything to ashes in a splits of a second. In such furry he sometimes perform *tandava,* a kind of vigorous dance, and during that time the whole universe trembles in fear and agony.

[III]

The mythology says that Vasisthasrama is the hermitage (*ashrama*) of the sage Vasistha, where he meditates to erase a curse cast by the king Nimi. The sage establishes the hermitage in Sandhyachala and lives with his wife Arundhati there. The stone form of Arundhati is lying there in the eastern side of the *ashrama* at a distance. The Ahom king donated 857 *bighas* (1 acre= 3.025 *bigha*) of land to the Vasisthasrama. At present only eight *bighas* of land is with Vasisthasrama and the rest is illegally occupied by the people belonging to different communities including the citizens of Meghalaya, one of the neighbouring states of Assam.

'Polytheism is the pivotal feature of Hinduism. It is also a faith in unity in multiplicity. The faith originated in the initial stage of Hinduism in one of the primary scripture *Rig Veda,* where the concept of one god is conspicuous among innumerable gods and goddesses. In the *Rig Veda* it is described like this: "They called it Indra, Mitra, Varuna and Agni. And also heavenly beautiful Kirtiman. The real is one, though sages name it variously. Although polytheism and heathenism is conspicuous in the *Vedas,* the most dominant tendency of the scriptures is monoism, the realization of one in many. The philosophical evolution of Hinduism from polytheism through henotheism to monotheism also give rise to a number of sub-religions in Hinduism" (Medhi and Bhunya, 2015: 18).

In the course of evolution of Hinduism, Saivism also originated. The rigid worshippers of lord Siva are known as *Saiva,* who appease the god as the supreme being. In Assam, there is a strong flow of Saivism which is conspicuous by the good number of Siva temples situated in different parts of the state, "Saivism or the worship of Siva prevailed in Assam from remote period and it was the popular form of religion both among the aboriginals and Aryanized people. In an analysis of the name of sacred places given in the *Kalika Purana* clearly shows that the number of sacred places connected with Siva worship is larger than that of the places associated with Vishnu and Devi worship" (Barua, 1951: 165). A large number of people in Assam regarded Saivism as an acute expression of their inner feelings to adore some supernatural force controlling the whole universe. The worshippers of lord Siva gives him more than one thousand names. He is also imagined as a combination of male (*purusa*) and female (*prakriti*) and that form is known as *Ardhanariswara*.

In almost all the temples of Assam lord Siva is propitiated in phallus form. Monier Williams points out that "Siva is represented as less human and more mythical than that of the incarnated Vishnu. The character in which he is worshipped is that of an omnipotent god, taking the place of Brahma, the creator, granting new life to all created things, but only through death and disintegration. Hence he is not represented by the image of a man and by a mystic symbol, perhaps the best symbol of delegated creative power" (cited in Medhi and Talukdar, 2012: 13-15).

[IV]

It has been already stated that Vasisthasrama is situated in the Sandhyachala hillock in Guwahati, the only city of North East India. The hillock derives its name from two Sanskrit words: '*sandhi*', means 'joint' and '*achala*', means 'hill', that is 'joint of hills'. It is believed by the Hindus that sage Vasistha was the worshipper of Jogeswara Siva, Jogeswara means "the great aestic, in whom is centred the highest perfection of austere penance and abstract meditation, by which the most unlimited powers are attained, marvels and miracles are worked, the highest spiritual knowledge is acquired, and union, with the great spirit of the universe is eventually gained" (Dowson, 1987: 298). However, in the Vasisthasrama, the principal deity lord Siva is worshipped as Golokeswara Siva. The Vasisthasrama is integral to a good number of legends. According to one of them Vasistha has acute enmity with Viswamitra, a Kshatriya sage, and on one day Viswamitra killed all the sons of Vasistha. Then Vasistha moved from Gandhara to Kamrupa and built the hermitage at Sandhyachala and appeased Siva with great reverence. Lord Siva was pleased by the penance of the sage and blessed him with three streams from the heavenly Ganga River, and also offered the lives of his deceased sons.

According to the *Kalika Purana* (Neog, 2008: 263), Vasistha, the mind son (*manasa-putra*) of the creator god Brahma, had lost his body in the curse of the king Nimi. Vasistha was very angry and due to his wrath the king also lost his physique. Vasistha took shelter in Brahma, who advised him to propitiate lord Vishnu in the Sandhyachala of Kamrupa to regain his body. Vasistha came to the Sandhyachala following the suggestion of Brahma and started worshipping Vishnu there. In his acute reverence the Ganga river came down from heaven to Sandhyachala in the forms of three rivulets. The meeting place of these rivulets is known as Vasistha Ganga, where sage Vasistha used to take his bath regularly. Due to the great penance Vasistha obtained his body. Vasistha appeased lord Vishnu in Sandhyachala to fulfil his desire, but how the Siva temple originated there instead of the Vishnu temple, history is silent about that.

The Vasisthasrama is situated in such a place that the scenic beauty of which can fascinate easily any person. The low green hill with frequent curves makes this corner of Guwahati city an indescribable source of eye-pleasing beauty. This temple is located in a more or less plain area on the lower part of the Sandhyachala, which is principally divided into two parts—the *garbha-griha* (sanctum sanctorum) and the *nata-mandira* (the open hall). Inside the *garbha-griha* lord Siva and Vasistha are located together in a single stone, which is the principal object of revere in Vasisthasrama. In almost all the Siva temples of Assam lord Siva is propitiated in his phallus form. However, in Vasisthasrama and some other Siva temples and shrines of Assam the objects for appeasing the deity are some mythological remnants. It is believed that after the death of sage Vasistha he had mingled with lord Siva and took a stone form, which resembles a lying person. Along with the Siva-Vasistha stone goddess Tara is also worshipped in the *garbha-griha*, which is represented by a comparatively smaller stone. It is pertinent to note that Tara is one of the forms of goddess Durga, the wife and female energy (*Sakti*) of lord Siva. The *nata-mandira* is a spacious hall and an extension of the main temple where the devotees gather and the household rituals and community prayers are also arranged. Outside the *garbha-griha*, a phallic form of lord Siva is there. Ganesha, the son of Siva and the remover of obstacles, is worshipped along with *Devi Saraswati* (goddess of knowledge) in another temple situated at a shouting distance from the main temple within the sacred complex. In that temple there is a big stone where meticulously engraved figure of *Siddhidata* (who fulfils desires) Ganesha is conspicuous. In the same stone engraved figure of Saraswati is also present. At a short distance from the Ganesha temple there is a statue of sage Vasistha standing in open air. The devotees visit the Ganesha temple to appease the god, but no ritual integral to Ganesha and Saraswati is observed in the Vasisthasrama. There is a tiny Assam Type house within the temple complex known as *dharmasala* for sheltering the devotees of distant areas. Due to the lack of renovation at present devotees could not be kept in that abandoned house. Opposite to the *dharmasala,* in the other side of the main temple, there is another Assam Type house consists of three rooms, which is used as the living house of the priests. On the back side of the *garbha-griha* the Sandhya, the Lalita and the Kanta are flowing gently and at a distance their confluence make the Vasistha Ganga. Adjacent to the Vasisthasrama near the main gate, a few shops are there, which provide articles like clay lamps, incense sticks, flowers and leaves, etc., for propitiating the deity in the temple.

The Ahom King Rajeswar Singha had appointed two sets of persons, the *sevait* and the *paik,* for the maintenance of the temple. The *sevaits* were the Brahmana males coming from the Chamata village of Nalbari district, Assam, engaged in the priestly duties. Till today their decendants are engaged as priests in the Vasisthasrama. The *paiks* are the non- Brahmana male persons, who were entrusted to conduct non-priestly duties integral to the Vasisthasrama. The *paiks* mainly included the Mali (flower supplier), potter and goldsmith, who provided flowers and leaves, earthen wares and gold objects, respectively, required for appeasement of the deity. However, at present there are no *paik* in the Vasisthasrama, and necessary articles used in worshipping the deity are purchased from the market. There are fourteen priests in the temple now, who are referred to as *bar-deuri.* Two persons are appointed there on the basis of monthly salary to keep the temple clean and tidy.

There are two management commitees to look after the maintenance of the Vasisthasrama. One of the committee is known as The Management Committee of the Vasisthasrama Devalaya, constituted of eight members from the temple priests and the citizens of Assam headed by the Deputy Commissioner of Guwahati city. The other one is The Vasistha Ganga Seva Samity, constituted by the priests of the temple, which is popularly known as the Purohit Samaj. The Vasisthasrama is somehow maintaining its own existence and surviving only on the money (*arihana*) given by the devotees without any grant-in-aid from the government. Renovation is not done in the temple for a long time due to the dearth of money.

The principal deity in the Vasisthasrama with his consort is appeased through daily, annual and occasional rituals. The daily rituals (*nitya puja*) are performed for three times in a day—at morning, noon time and in the evening. In each morning the deity of the temple is ritually awakened and given ceremonial bath. After that the principal and the subordinate deities are appeased through Vedic norms. At that time the devotees are not allowed in the *grabha-griha*. At the noon time sacred food (*bhoga*) prepared by the *bar-deuris*, consists of rice, pulses and vegetable curry, is ritually offered to the deity. In the evening *sandhya arati*, i.e., the propitiation of the god through earthen lamps is performed.

The principal annual rituals (*batsarik puja*) of the Vasisthasrama are Surya Grahana (solar eclipse), Chandra Grahana (lunar eclipse), Sivaratri, literally 'the night of lord Siva', Ashokastami, Ambubachi and Makar Samkranti, which are observed in the temple in accordance to the Hindu almanac with pomp and gaiety. Makar Samkranti is observed in the month of *Puh* (15th December to 14th January), when a luxurious fair (*mela*) is held in the temple campus. The Sivaratri is another cherished ritual of the temple observed in the month of *Magh* (15th January to 14th February), when good number of devotees and tourists visit Vasisthasrama to observe the elaborate rituals. During the Sivaratri also a grand fair is arranged in the temple campus. In the rituals integral to the solar and lunar eclipses, observed in the temple good number of devotees take a dip in the Vasistha Ganga to wreath with the benediction of lord Siva. Along with these pristine rituals performed in the Vasisthasrama a new ritual is added principally percolated from the Hindi speaking Hindu communities of India. This ritual is commonly known as Bol Bom, literally 'utter the name of lord Siva', observed in the month of *Saon* (15th July to 14th August), and a colourful fair is held in the temple complex during the ritual which is known as Saoni Mela. During this time, the devotees carry holy water from the Vasistha Ganga and pour it on the Siva *linga* of the Sukreswara temple situated on the hillock

Hastachala on the southern bank of the mighty river Brahmaputra in Panbazar area of the Guwahati city. The occasional rituals of the Vasisthasrama principally include some of the crises rite of the Hindus like *Chudakarana*, i.e., tongturing of the male child for the first time, *Annaprasana*, first solid food giving ceremony to a child, *Upanayana*, i.e., sacred thread giving ceremony to a boy, *Vivah* (marriage), *Sraddha* (mortuary rite), etc.

In the Vasisthasrama, the Assamese women perform *nama*, i.e., singing of sacred songs as the ode to the lord Siva, particularly on the ritual day. Some of such songs are given below:

(a) *Ai mai ane dekha-suna nai*
Jatiya bhangura
Gale mundamala Dum
dum dambaru bajay.

The broad meaning of the song is: Mother, I have not seen or heard like this; he is with the matted hair, who consumes cannabis regularly, wearing a garland encircling the neck, is beating *dambaru* making dum-dum sound.

(b) *Bhang khai pagala holahe Mahadeu*
Aphu khai pagala hola
Kailasare para Gangak namai ani
Jatate lukuai thola.

Mahadeu, you are becoming mad by consuming cannabis and poppy; you brought (divine river) Ganga from the Kailasa and hid it in (your) matted hair.

[V]

Shaivism is one of the oldest belief systems in the world. The remnants as well as existing temples in Thailand, Laos, Champa (Vietnam), Indonesia, China, Korea, Japan, Central Asia and Tibet speak of the spread of the Shaivism in the far corners of the world, from its origin in India. In India the Shaiva tradition continues uninterruptedly. "The twelve Jyotirlingas situated at different centres from Kashmir to Rameswaram stand to prove its widespread existence. The names of the regions like Telegu region 1, Trissur 2 in Kerala come from names of Shiva, and Shiva temples exist in huge numbers in the map of India which also includes, Nepal, its form and traditions may though differ from region to region" (Sharma, 2015: 85).

From time immemorial there is a strong current of Saivism in Assam which is proved by the innumerable temples and shrines devoted to lord Siva scattered over the hills and plains of the state. Besides the Hindus, many of the sanskritized and animist tribal groups of Assam appease this popular deity through household and community rituals. The Assamese Sikhs made sacred offerings in the village Siva shrines to get their lost cows. In a good number of Assamese folk songs, the appearance, epithets and the virtues of lord Siva have been described in attractive manner. All the villages of Assam are heterogeneous and each of the village is adorned with one or more worshipping centres to adore this lovingly deity, sometimes who is more human than god. Large number of the people in Assam have practised the Saivism and Saktism, and due to the close relation of these two ways of worship, it is near to impossible to differentiate the Saiva and the Sakta in this remote part of India.

There are a good number of Siva temples in Guwahati distributed over both the banks of the Brahmaputra river. Most of these temples are mythologically integral to the different holy places of India and their mentions are conspicuous in the prime Hindu scriptures. The Vasisthasrama relates this north-east corner of India to the pristine religious canvas of the country. Although due to the flaccid economic condition at present the physical structure of the Vasisthasrama is not praiseworthy, yet this sacred complex attracts a good number of pilgrims and tourists from within and outside the state. Besides the tribals and non-tribals, the Vasisthasrama is the meeting place of different language groups of India and abroad, which has created a congenial environment contributing immensely towards peace, amity and acceleration of the country.

References

Barua, B.K. 1951. *A Cultural History of Assam*. Gauhati, Bina Library.

Dowson, John. 2003. *A Classical Dictionary of Hindu Mythology and Religion: Geography, History and Literature*. New Delhi, Rupa and Co.

Medhi, Birinchi K. 2008. "Concept of Jagannatha among the Assamese

Hindus", In: *R.N. Dash.* (ed.) *Jagannatha in Historical Perspectives,* pp. 90-102. Delhi: Pratibha Prakashan.

Medhi, Birinchi K. and Himarjyoti Talukdar. 2012-13. "Ethno-historical and Socio- cultural Dimensions of a Shiva Temple in a Riverine Island of Assam." *Bulletin of the Department of Anthropology,* Vol. XIV: 13-25.

Medhi, Birinchi K. and Monimugdha Bhuyan. 2015. "Advent of Vaishnavism in an Animistic Environ: The Case of the Deori's." *North Bengal Anthropologist, Journal of the Dept. of Anthropology,* Vol. 3: 17-26.

Neog, Maheswar. 2008. *Pavitra Assam.* Jorhat, Assam Sahitya Sabha.

Sharmah, Nirmala. 2015. Lord Siva Across the Northern Land. *The Journal of Vivekananda Kendra Institute of Culture,* Vol. VIII (2): 85-105.

3

Indigenous Communities of North East India and Prospects of Applied Anthropologists

Kh. Narendra Singh

Introduction

Applied anthropology is the application of anthropological data, perspectives, theories, and techniques to identify, assess, and solve contemporary social problems. In other words, it is the use of anthropological knowledge to address human real world problem. Applied anthropologists work for groups that promote, manage and assess programmes and policies aimed at influencing human behaviour and social conditions.

Radcliffe Brown was the first to use the term 'applied anthropology', in an article published in 1930. In the 1940s, most anthropologists focused on the application of their knowledge. According to Chamber, "applied anthropologists use the knowledge, skill and their discipline to help solve human problems and facilitate change" (1985: 8). Malinowski used "practicing anthropology", implies applied work outside of academia, though it has also been used synonymously with applied anthropology (Chambers 1985: 16).

Mair (1968) viewed applied anthropology as an extension of the ongoing research activities for the purposes of decision making. Whereas, anthropologists like Clifton (1970), Tax (1970), and Bastide (1973), considered it as an action-oriented application of anthropology.

Naik (1972) and Vidyarthi (1978) reported that majority of the researches classified as 'applied anthropology' envisaged the role as–consultant, advisor, coordinator and evaluator. Agrawal, Rao and Reddy (1985: 4) in their Yanadi Action Research Project found that dual roles of anthropologists i.e., as researcher and change agent within an *emic* perspective were complimentary and inseparable.

Since the 1980s, anthropologists working outside of research institutions at times have been called "practicing anthropologists". Applied or practicing anthropologists are almost never licensed or certified. They may, however, perform legally mandated studies, such as gender analyses or environmental impact assessments for governments or international agencies.

Today, most applied anthropologists use cross-cultural knowledge and anthropological methods for research and action around the world. Practicing anthropologists are engaged in the domains of health, education, communication and development and human services.

Applied Medical anthropologist unites biological and cultural anthropologists in the study of disease, health problems, health-care systems, and theories about illness in different cultures and ethnic groups. Medical anthropologists serve as cultural interpreters between local systems and Western medicine.

North East India is the homeland of a large number of ethnic groups with more than 200 distinct ethnic communities belonging to different linguistic groups and having varied socio-cultural traditions. The North East India is one of the most ethnically, linguistically and geographically diverse regions in India and Asia as well. The location of the region is strategically important as it has international borders with Bangladesh, Bhutan, China, Myanmar and Tibet. At present, North East India comprises of eight states viz., Arunachal Pradesh, Assam, Manipur, Meghalaya, Mizoram, Nagaland, Sikkim and Tripura having its distinct cultures and traditions. An important feature of the North East India is its heterogeneity and each state of the region has its unique culture and traditions. Among the famous dances of the region, the world famous Manipuri dance of Manipur, the Bihu dance of Assam are noteworthy. The prominent tribes of North East India are Bodo, Garo, Khasi, Jaintia, Mizo, Naga, Adi, Nyishi, Hmar, Karbi, Dimasa, Bhutia, Kuki, and Deori. Except the Khasis and

Jaintias of Meghalaya state that belong to follow the matriarchal society and their language is known as Mon-Khmer which belongs to the Austro-Asiatic family. The rest of the tribes of northeast India belong to Tibeto-Burman language family. Agriculture and farming are the major occupation of the tribes and shifting cultivation is also practiced by some tribes of the region.

The ethnic communities of the North Eastern region are undergoing through some challenging issues such as identity issues and conflicts, unemployment, youth unrest, problems in social development, poor health condition and transport and communication. Anthropologists with the holistic understanding of the tribal culture can address these issues and facilitate the development activity in an effective way in their development.

Objectives

The present chapter is an attempt to explore the application of Anthropological knowledge and practices to address and find ways to resolve issues of the indigenous communities of the North East India.

Methodology

The present study is based on secondary data. Relevant secondary literary sources in the form of books, journals and articles have been intensively studied in the preparation of this chapter.

Discussion

Diverse Culture of North East India

The North East India is considered as one of the most culturally diverse regions of the world and is the home of more than 200 tribes that captured the imaginations of anthropologists from all over the world. Almost every ethnic community of North East India can be considered as a repository of a distinctive body of knowledge, cultural traditions, social institutions and technologies, which have evolved over a long period of time. Because of its rich cultures, traditional technologies and enduring social institutions, the North East India had been a study ground for the colonial scholar-administrators, who documented and recorded each aspect of their culture. The cultural trends are reflected beautifully in their dance, costume, art, festivals and other community occasions. Agriculture and farming are the major occupations of the tribes. They also depend for their livelihood on weaving and rearing of woolly animals. Despite impressive social and economic changes, the ethnic communities still retain a great deal of the pristine elements of their age-old lifestyles.

Anthropology and Tribal Development in North East India

Anthropological studies play a fundamental role in the development process. It is imperative to study the background, ethnic profile, cultural norms, behaviour patterns, attitudes, beliefs and practices, before administering any intervention programme or development plan. Anthropologists have been trained and refined to have an eye to "redefining an issue"; that is, collecting data to reveal particularly problematic relationships, bureaucratic difficulties, or conditions harmful to local populations, to provide critical evaluation, and call public attention to issues that have national or global impact.

The issue of tribal development is extremely expansive with much social, economic, political and geographical diversity. Some of the pressing tribal development issues include education, lack of infrastructure, poverty, extremist movements, literacy, health, tribal identity movements, unemployment, displacement, and so on. Therefore in the presence of such issues and problems, the concept of development needs a detailed and careful analysis. Development in North East India must be treated with the utmost urgency and an all-round approach.

Roy Burman had opined that: "there are four phases in the foci of tribal development planning in India. In the first phase, the emphasis was on providing immediate relief to the general mass of population, who were denied amenities of life during the colonial rule and at the same time to build up the productive infrastructure for the future growth. In the second phase, the emphasis was on resource mobilization and provision of social service infrastructure in the countryside. In the third phase, the emphasis on educational level shifted to reduction of disparity and growth with justice. Fourth phase emphasizes programmes for meeting the basic needs of the population and poverty alleviation had been stepped up. The advantage of the tribal development of the first phase was mainly taken by the non-tribals living in tribal areas who were having more contact with those who have administrative power" (1989b: 5-6).

Sharma (1989: 27-33) has argued that the question of tribal development has not yet received concerted attention that it deserves, both in planning circles and in tribal studies. The real challenge of tribal development is to modernize the tribal economics and to integrate them with the larger national economy without at the same time disrupting their ecological existence, their socio-cultural systems and their traditions of socio-economic equity and innocence. Non Governmental Organizations (NGOs) came into the development scene, during the late 1960s and 1970s in India (Sen, 1999: 337-338). New dimensions in development approaches pave the way to the idea of *participatory development* in the 1970s and 1980s. Then *participation* gets prominence in development, in terms of practice and policy. It had two reasons, first was that the benefits of centrally planned development strategies had failed to reach the poor. The emphasis of development programmes on large-scale, and heavy industry in the 1950s and early 1960s had little impact on the predominantly agricultural population, while green revolution technologies favoured regions with irrigation, and infrastructure (Bernstein, 1992: 56-57 and Ghosh and Bharadwaj, 1992: 155-156). It produced a class of rich modernized farmers, an increase in income disparities between regions, and people, and increased marginalization of the rural poor. A second reason for the attention to *participation* was that alternate *top-down* planning.

Anthropology and Employment Problems

North East India has large number of young population and unemployment is a serious concern. Rapid growth of the economy is an essential requirement for achieving a steady increase in employment and incomes for large numbers of population of the region. There is a need to place a greater emphasis on promoting the growth of the industrial sector in the region. Social development is also facing some problems which are making the path critical to inclusive growth. Some of the problems in social sector are: ethnic issues; low level and slow growth in public expenditures particularly on health.

Poverty is predominantly a rural phenomenon with close to 90 per cent of the population being rural. Rural poverty is more than twice that of urban poverty. Urban poverty in Assam is much lower than all-India urban poverty whereas rural poverty is at a similar level as all-India. Whereas urban poverty decreased steadily rural poverty showed fluctuations with very little decrease over the years. The population growth in the region also implied that there has hardly been any reduction in the absolute number of the poor over the years.

The main reasons for poor performance in terms of rural poverty are the continuously declining real wages of non-skilled agricultural labour and increasing unemployment among the youth. Growth of the rural economy is therefore the key to poverty reduction in Assam. Incidence of rural poverty is the highest among agricultural labour and least among self-employed in non-agriculture. The vocational training centers introduced by the Government and NGOs needs to be functional to all tribal areas and enrollment fee to such training centres should be free or with minimum cost. Advance courses with adequate infrastructure needs to be developed for organizing such centres.

Conclusion

The strategy for tribal development needs to be associated mainly with agriculture and allied activities. Action anthropologists are to play a very specific role in the process of development of the tribal youths. The role of anthropology should be to clearly recognize that the rights to determining the final goals of development are with the people—the civil society at large and anthropologists in particular will facilitate the process. Unless we recognize, and are willing to change, that development is not just categorizing to communities/societies, and development is basically antagonistic in nature. Anthropologists should sincerely believe that it should be to strengthen *reversal tribal development strategies* since the tribal development so far is mechanical, ineffectual, and vague.

Action needs to be taken to increase the effectiveness of service delivery; to encourage decentralization for better accountability and governance; to improve quality of public service provision through innovative means; and to transfer expenditure authority to local bodies that are directly responsible and accountable to the local people.

There is an urgent need for research studies on tribal youths of the state as well as the region so that corrective measures may be taken for sustainable development. There is a tremendous need to empower local communities, hamlets and pockets of population with options to explore and select from, so that there can be 'informed choice'. Anthropologists with the *holistic* understanding of the tribal culture can address tribal issues and facilitate the development activity in an effective way in their development. Applying anthropological knowledge and data in development programmes and bringing theoretical strategy into action is the prime focus of applied anthropologists and is also the need of the hour for the progress of civilisation, for justice, peace and harmony and for the oneness of society. There is an urgent need to work for groups that promote, manage and assess programmes and policies aimed at influencing human behaviour and social conditions. Applied anthropology, therefore tries to make positive contributions to public life and serves needs for the communities and organizations.

References

Bhagabati, A.C. 1992. "Tribal Transformation in Assam and North-East India: An Appraisal of Emerging Ideological Dimensions." In B. Chaudhury (Ed.), *Tribal Transformation in India.* Vol. III, Inter-India Publication, New Delhi,.

Baba, Marietta L. and Carole E. Hill (Eds.). 1997. *The Global Practice of Anthropology.* Williamsburg, VA, Studies in Third World Societies.

Chambers, Erve. 1985. *Applied Anthropology: A Practical Guide.* Englewood Cliffs. NJ, Prentice-Hall Inc.

Das, S.T. 1993. *Tribal Development and Socio-Cultural Matrix.* Delhi, Kanishka Publishers Distributers.

Dubey, A. 2000. *Hunger and Poverty in North Eastern States, Implications for Food Security.* Paper presented at the National Seminar on Food Security in India, CESS Hyderabad, March 25-27.

Dube, S.C. 1977. *Tribal Heritage of India,* Vol. I. New Delhi, Vikas Publishing House.

Foster, George M. 1969. *Applied Anthropology*. Boston, Little Brown and Company.

Census of India. 2011. *Provisional Population Totals*, Office of the Registrar General and Census Commissioner, Ministry of Home Affairs, New Delhi: Government of India.

Ghurye, G.S. 1963. *The Scheduled Tribes*. Bombay, Popular Prakashan.

NSSO. 2006. *Employment and Unemployment Situation in India, 2004-05*, 61st Round, Report No. 515, New Delhi: Government of India.

Podolefsky, Aaron and Peter J. Brown. 1997. *Applying Cultural Anthropology: An Introductory Reader*. Mountain View, CA, Mayfield Publishing.

Roy Burman, B.K. 1989b. "Tribal Development in Perspectives." In *Tribal Development: Past Effort and New Challenges*, J.P. Singh and N.N.Vyas (Eds.), Udaipur: Himanshu Publications.

Sen, S. 1992. *The Tribes of Mizoram*. Delhi, Gian Publishing House.

Sharma, S.L. 1989. "Tribal Development: Perspectives and Issues." In: *Tribal Development: Past Effort and New Challenges*, J.P. Singh and N.N.Vyas (Eds.), pp. 65-67. Udaipur: Himanshu Publications.

Singh, J.P. and N.N. Vyas (Eds.) 1989. *Tribal Development: Past Effort and New Challenges*. Udaipur, Himanshu Publications.

Van Willigen, John. 1991. *Anthropology in Use: A Source Book on Anthropological Practice*. Boulder, Westview Press.

Van Willigen, John. 1993. *Applied Anthropology: An Introduction*. Westport, CT, Bergin & Garvey.

Willigen, et al. (Eds.). 1989. *Making Our Research Useful: Case Studies in the Utilization of Anthropological Knowledge*. Boulder, Westview Press.

SECTION-II
Indigenous Ethnographies and Cultural Perspectives of Seven Sister-States

4
Natural Textile Dyeing with Indigenous Plant Materials and Methods
A Traditional Practice in Shyamgaon, Assam, India

Sangeeta Chakravarty and Rani Hazarika Kakaty

Introduction

The different Tai groups of people who migrated to Assam from South West China and North Myanmar in the historical past are the *Khamyangs, Khamtis, Phakes, Turungs, Aitons* and *Ahoms.* They were basically Buddhist of the Theravadas. Tai Khamyangs are popularly known as Shyams. They are originated from mongoloid population of mainland South East Asia. There are three villages of Shyam tribe population in Titabor subdivision of Jorhat district of Assam in North East India—*Betbari-Shyam Gaon, Na-Shyam Gaon,* and *Balijan-Shyam Gaon.* Our visit for case study was into Shyam Gaon-Betbari on 1st June 2013. Few women of the village have been running a weaving centre, to sustain their livelihoods and also with intention to preserve their culture and traditions. They make traditional dresses with handlooms, weaving different types of cloths used by Shyam tribe and Assamese communities. It was found that weavers are skilled in weaving; they create mesmerizing motifs and use attractive colour combinations. But they lack interest in traditional dyeing methods. They dye clothes only for their own use, for their lower garments which is mostly dark blue or black in colour, known as *mekhela* (a traditional wrap-around).

The new generation is not interested in learning or carrying on the tradition of dyeing with Rom, because the process is very laborious and lengthy. They also do not like the smell of the fermented leaves. And most importantly, nobody knows the importance of this Indigo dye yielding plant, since all the yarns available in the market are dyed with cheap synthetic dyes and are easy to get. Synthetic dyes have replaced the traditional dyeing process; therefore the culture is almost vanishing. They make clothes only if the customer demands as these take long time, laborious and therefore become costly also.

The visit to the Shyam Gaon and meeting the women of the unique village was a step towards understanding the process of dyeing with hands on practical, and also with the aim of documenting the traditional methods.

Natural Dye

Natural dyes are dyes or colorants derived from plants, animals, insects or minerals. Natural dyes are prepared from dye bearing plants, animals, minerals, or insect bases, utilizing the various properties of the substance. Most of the dyes are obtained from parts of plants—leaves, stem, barks, seeds, flowers, roots etc. Dyeing is an ancient art which predates written records. Primitive dyeing techniques included sticking plants to fabric or rubbing crushed pigments into cloth. The methods became more sophisticated with time and techniques using natural dyes from crushed fruits, berries and other plants, which were boiled into the fabric and gave light and water fastness. Some of the well-known ancient dyes include *Madder*, a red dye made from the roots of the *Rubia Tinctorum*, blue indigo from the leaves of *Indigofera tinctoria*, yellow from the stigmas of the saffron etc. In Assam, Indigo is obtained from *Strobilanthes cusia*, the local name of which is Rom.

Some of the parts of plants with examples of dye yielding plants, from which natural dyes are extracted are—

1. Flowers—*Sewaliphul* (Night Jasmine), *Gendha* (Marigold)
2. Leaves—*Jetuka pat* (Henna), *Nil* (Indigo), *Segun* (Teak Tree)
3. Barks—*Kothal* (Jack fruits), *Chandan* (Red Sandalwood)
4. Skins—*Dalim* (Pomegranate), *Piyaj* (Onion)
5. Roots—*Munjistha* (Madder), *Halodhi* (Turmeric)

6. Seeds—*Sendur* (Bixa).

Until the second half of 19th century, everywhere in the world, natural dyes were the prominent sources of colours for everyday textiles and were used as aesthetic value, symbolic power, and therapeutic functions.

Natural dyeing is practised in almost every part of the world from the early times, and the processes of which pass from generation to generation mostly orally. In Assam, dyeing culture was mostly practiced by the indigenous peoples ofAssam by *Garo, Karbi, Rabha, Mishing, Tai-phake, Tai-turung* communities etc. Assam is gifted with unlimited colours from nature, but all colours are not for dyeing textiles.

Vat Dyeing

The vat dyeing technique was used specially for dyeing Indigo. This gives deep blue colour on wool, silk, cotton etc. It exhibits good fastness against washing, crocking and sunlight. Dye bath are called vats. Wooden vats, earthen pots were used in the early days, which were partially buried in the ground to maintain the temperature, so that the vat was not disturbed.

Fresh leaves of Assam indigo can be used or directly applied for dyeing, but many other Indigo yielding plants, which are also used in other parts of the country or abroad, are normally powdered first. There are many plant sources which produce Indigo dye. Natural indigo is obtained from indigo bearing plants; the most significant one is *"Indigofera tinctoria"*.

One which is available in Assam is—

Local Name: Rom
Common Name: Assam Indigo
Botanical Name: *Strobilanthes Cusia*
Natural Dye: Blue dyestuff for textile
Part of plant: Leaves and stems.

This is one of the most ancient natural dyes used by human in textiles. Indigo is about 2-3 feet long plant, cultivated on normally wet and shadowed ground. The whole plant is used for extraction of dye and the extracted liquid form of dye is used directly for dyeing yarns or cloths. The plant is cut twice a year during July and October. Flowering of Rom starts from October to December. The flowers are purple in colour.

Mordant Dyeing

A mordant helps the dye to become permanently fixed to the fiber, in case of some dyes which do not bind strongly with textile fibers. In indigo dyeing with Rom, natural mordants are used in Shyam Gaon. A mordant blends the dye stuff to the fibers, with added benefits of increased light and water fastness. Mordant solutions are stored in a glass or plastic bottle during the dyeing process. Mordanted fibers can also be dried and stored for later use.

Case Study: Indigo Dyeing at *Shyam Gaon—Betbari*

Women of the village were interviewed in their homes. Mostly females in their middle age, 30 to 50 years, were engaged in making textiles, weaving special traditional dresses of various Assamese communities. They were asked about the dyeing process with Rom, from which Indigo colour is obtained. Indigo colour bearing plant is cultivated in each and every house of Shyam Gaon from ages. Most women of the village know how to dye with the fresh leaves of Rom. Their dyeing process is same in each house. Among them, 3 ladies demonstrated their dyeing processes, which were documented by observation, questioning, picture documentation and video-photographing. They can speak Assamese, and a bit Tai language. The leadwoman, who was first connected through telephone, is Hasna Shyam, 49 years old. She dyes few other colours (natural) from *Segon* (teak wood), Lac, apart from Rom. Hasna learnt to dyeing with Rom leaves from her mother, at the age of 9/ 10 years. Dyeing in Shyam Gaon is done only by the women. Rom is also used as medicinal plant. The women are skilled dyers and weavers with proper understanding of colour contrasts, material of fibers (mostly cotton and different varieties of local silks like– Eri, *Muga* and *Pat*).

Our main interest and aim was to know the process of dyeing with Rom and specially to see the plant and the process with our own eyes.

Demonstration of Natural Dyeing of Rom Plant

We observed indigo dyeing of Cotton and Eri yarn used for weaving *Mekhela,* a traditional wrap-around, at the workshop. They have not used any fixed measurement or proportions during the entire process and everything was done on the basis of their own assumptions, which they skillfully maintain.

Steps Used

1. At first, the yarns are cleaned with pond water, so that the starch is removed.
2. Then the whole plant of Indigo, leaves, stems and branches, everything was dipped in water collected from pond, in an aluminium vessel, covered and left untouched for 1 weak to 13 days (depending on the temperature), for fermentation. This was done prior to our visit.
3. In warm days during summer time, it only requires 2/3 days for fermentation. Fresh lime was mixed in the solution through stirring and fine mixing is to be ensured.
4. After the dye bath ferments and a pungent smell come, foam appears on the top of the liquid and the colour becomes pale bottle green. The Rom is ready for dyeing the yarns.
5. Little mustard oil was rubbed on the palm and mixed in the dye solution and within second the foam disappears.
6. The solution was kept undisturbed for 1 or 2 nights, so that the residue settles on the bottom of the vessel. The unwanted water from the top was poured and the residue which is left was used for dyeing the yarns. It can be stored for later use also.
7. Before dyeing, the residue was mixed with *Kharpani* (a mixer of water with wood ash of bamboo), *Medicine-pitha* (a local rice-beer cake), and *Thekera* (a local variety of orange).
8. When foam appears on the top, the solution is ready for dyeing. The yarns dipped into the solution and keep for half a day. Then the yarn was taken and again dipped with a wooden stick, so that the colour fixes or enters into the yarn.
9. Second day, same ingredients were again mixed, within

that solution, and the yarn was dipped in the solution for 2nd dip for 2 hours.

10. Repeat the 3rd dip for 1 hour and 4th dip for half an hour. If required, more residues are added for darker colour or darker shade of Indigo colour.
11. Then the yarn was taken outside the solution, the colour darkened as soon as it is exposed to sun and air. Colour of the yarn changed from Green to Blue.
12. Last step was to put the fabric dipped in a solution of fixer or mordant made from the bark of *Udal* tree (cut into small pieces and dipped in water for few days). The yarn was kept in that solution and then taken out for drying.

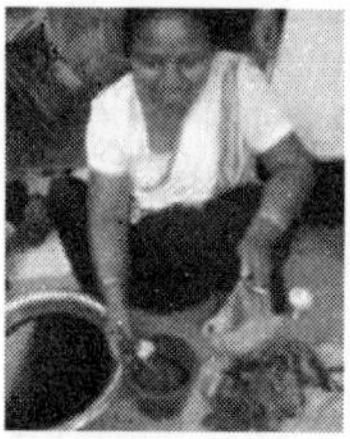

Hasna Shyam in the Dye Preparation Process

Old Lady from Village showing Rom Plants to the writer

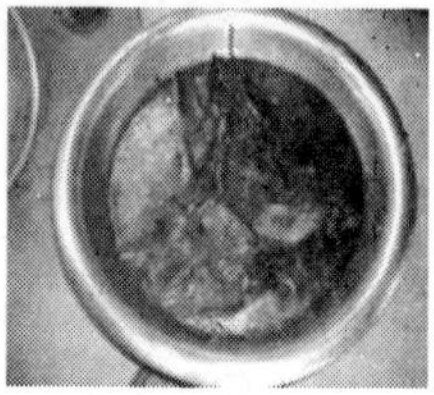

Fermented Rom Plant in dye bath

Few important notes as described during the whole process:

i. If the dye is not fermented for long enough, the colour will not be fast.
ii. Stir occasionally in between and check temperature of the dye bath. If the dye bath is too cold, the colour will not come and need to increase the temperature by adding more lime.
iii. In some places Rhubarb powder or yeast powder is added.
iv. A conventional proportion followed by them is–200 gm residues, 400 gm Wood ash water, 50 gm Rice beer cake, 2 pieces *Thekera*.

Advantages of Such Dyeing Process

- Eco-friendly and do not cause any harm to skin.

- Antiseptic, ethno-medical properties of many plants. Such dyed cloths are good for babies and allergic people.
- Relaxation therapy–it is believed that we absorb colour energy through our skin.
- Most dyes are easily available and are biodegradable.

Few Disadvantages as we Observed

- Very complex process.
- Colours are not accurate, exact shades are impossible to create, because of change of place, season, techniques, water or mordants etc.
- Difficult to get colour fastness, especially in cotton, therefore require a mordant.
- Natural dyeing practices are almost vanishing; very little documentations are available.

Originally an indigenous practice (by ethnic tribes), need to do documentation, preservation of the dye yielding plants and the practices before it gets vanished, still practice the process. Unfortunately, no such serious attempts have been made to document, preserve and to take advantage of this immense treasure of traditional knowledge of natural dye preparation confined to the indigenous people. It is the high time to document these treasures of indigenous knowledge systems. Otherwise we will lose this vital information on the utilization of natural resources around us. Indigenous knowledge systems and methods of traditional utilizations of bio-resources of the ethnic groups of the state need to be documented to rescue them from loosing forever. Commercialization of some of the natural dyes can be of successful venture to the rural population of the state through systematic and scientific approach with identification of resources; and formalizing the process of extraction, purifications, chemical structure. Social, academic and governmental promotion of use of natural dyes would contribute enhancing economy of those people. Systematic approaches with scientific inputs would help in conserving the important plant resources, and the indigenous knowledge base confined to the ethnic groups along with the associated process of extracting and processing for natural dyes.

Few Terms and Local Names etc.

Thekera—Local variety of Orange, very thick peel. (*Garcina* Sp)
Medicine-Pitha—A local cake used to make Rice Beer.
KharPani—Water mixed with wood ash of bamboo.
Pira—A wooden stool, very low, normally less than a foot height.
Udal Tree—Local tree in Shyamgaon.
Mekhela—A wrap-around like lower garments of women used in Assam.
Eri—Raw silk from Assam.

[**Acknowledgement:** We are thankful to the people of the Betbari Shyam Gaon, Titabor in Jorhat district of Assam, India.]

References

Ahmed, M.M. and P.K. Singh. 2008. *Plant-Lore with Reference to Muslim Folksong in Association with Human Perception of Plants in Agricultural and Horticultural Practices.* Notulae Botanicae Horti Agrobotanici, Academic Press.

Amy S. Frey. 2006. *Revival of Natural Dyes in Central Tibet.* Proceedings of International Symposium on Natural dyes, UNESCO, Hyderabad.

Karolia, Anjali and Baiahunlang Ladia. 2012. "Traditional textiles and costumes of Karbi and Biate tribes of Meghalaya." *Indian Journal of Traditional Knowledge,* 11(2): 309-316.

Diana K. and Susan S. Bean. 1994. *From the Land of the Thunder Dragon: Textile Arts of Bhutan.* New Delhi, Timeless Books.

Dominique, Cardon. 2007. *Natural Dyes—Sources, Traditions, Technology and Sciences.* New Delhi, Archetype Publication.

India, Flint. 2006. *Alternative (and safer) Mordants for Plant-based Dyes,* Proceedings of International Symposium on Natural Dyes, UNESCO, Hyderabad.

Priti, C. Nartiang. 2011. *Natural and Vegetables Dyes in Northeastern Part of India,* National Workshop and Seminar on Vegetable Dye and its application on textile, Silpa-Sadan, Visva-Bharati.

Ruby Ghuznavi. 2006. NEEL: The Magical Indigo of Bengal. *Proceedings of International Symposium on Natural dyes,* UNESCO, Hyderabad.

Shalini, Sahoo. 2006. *Ethical Dyeing and the Tribes of North East India. Proceedings of International Symposium on Natural Dyes,* UNESCO, Hyderabad, India.

Sonowal, Ripunjoy and Barua Indira. 2012. "Indigenous knowledge and Bioresource Utilization among the Tai-Khamyangs of Assam,

North East India." *International Research Journal of Biological Sciences,* 1(7): 38-43.

Sakthivel, V. 2011. Traditional Indigo Dyeing. *National Workshop and Seminar on Vegetable Dye and its Application on Textile,* Silpa-Sadan, Visva-Bharati.

5
Food and Dietary Habits
An Empirical Observation among the Deoris of Assam

Arifur Zaman and Nabanita Dey

Introduction

Food is an important element of each culture. Every human community has their own way of rejection and acceptance of food. Human beings depend on food for their survival and maintenance of life. Food is one of the intrinsic objects of culture complex in any society because different elements like custom, tradition, religious beliefs and practices, taboo and so forth are integrally related with it. As Levi-Strauss very rightly said that the art of cooking is a major aspect of the civilization of the society. In general, food, besides satisfying hunger and giving energy also enhances friendliness and social warmth. The traditional foods processed and prepared by the tribes of North East India are intimately bonded to their socio-cultural, ecological, spiritual life and health. The processing and preparation of ethnic foods not only describe the creativity and treasure of food heritage of tribes but also their incremental learning to sustain the life and ecosystem as a whole. Food habits are the ways in which individuals or group of persons, in relation to social and cultural pressures, choose, consume and make use of available products. The ethnographic study on food habits in cross-cultural perspectives has been carried out by pioneers and others like Smith (1925), Hutton (1969), Mills

(1980), Playfair (1998), Deori (2002), Gurdon (2002), Endle (2007), Saikia (2009), Zaman (2009) and so forth. In the present endeavour a humble attempt has been made to study the food habits of the Tengapania Deoris of five villages of Upper Assam.

The People

Assam is located between tropical latitude of 24.3°N and 28°N, and eastern longitudes of 89.5°E and 96.1°E. It is an abode of a good number of communities both tribal and non-tribal. The Deoris are one of the important Scheduled Tribes inhabiting the plains of Assam. The word 'Deori' is originated from the Sanskrit word *Deva Grihika,* meaning 'in charge of the temple or the priest'. Deori (2002: 33) mentioned that "the word 'Deori' literally means priest. The person who has a better knowledge about gods and goddesses and can appease them are known as Deoris." The original habitat of the Deoris were on the banks of the river Dibong, Tengapani and Patarsal, which were within the jurisdiction of Lohit district of Arunachal Pradesh and Dibrugarh district of Assam. Racially the Deoris are Mongoloid and Mongolian characteristics are still visible among them. Dalton (1872) writes about the Deoris that "An isolated colony on the river Dikrang in Lakhimpur calling themselves Deori Chutiya was found who had a peculiar language which they called Chutiya and they were styled Deoris." At present main concentration of the Deoris is found in the district of Lakhimpur, Sonitpur, Jorhat, Sivasagar, Dibrugarh, Dhemaji and in the Sadia region of Tinsukia District. The main occupation of the Deoris is agriculture and are also involved in governmental and non-governmental services, poultry, petty trade, etc. On the basis of places of origin, there are four divisions (*khel*) among the Deoris and each division is composed of number of lineages (*bamsa*). The Deoris, who were believed to reside near the bank of the river Dibang are known as *Dibangiya,* those near Tengapani and Barpani or Borgang are known as *Tengapania* and *Bargaya* respectively. Again the people who lived in Pat Sadia were named as *Patargaya.* The people of the five villages where the present study is carried on belongs to the Tengapania divisions who have seven sub-divisions or lineages (*tikas*) among themselves. These are– *Machiotika, Bikramiyatika, Phagimegeratika, Khutiotika, Sanabariatika, Phapariatika* and *Sakusarutika.* The Tengapania Deoris are the followers of Sakta cult, the worshippers of Sakti. They still retain their traditional beliefs and practices. Balia baba is their supreme god who is believed to be the parochial version of Lord Siva or son of Siva. Other than Balia Baba they also have other indigeneous gods and goddesses like Na-Konwar and Sat-Konwar who are considered as eldest and youngest son of Balia Baba, respectively, Lohit Devata also known as Bhaba Raja or Jala-Narayana, Burha Deo, Indra Devata, Ai Deo, et al. The overwhelming majority of the Deoris are rural inhabitants, and agriculture is their mainstay. Irrespective of caste and creed the Deoris are non-vegetarian, and use to take fish, egg, meat, etc., along with rice. Areca nut and betel vine leaves is taken by Deoris irrespective of age, sex, social status at any time. The utensils which they use for serving different items of food are also spectacularly different from those of other parts of India.

The Micro Field

The intended study is based on food habits of the Tengapania Deoris. Five villages inhabited by Tengapania Deoris in Demow Town of Sivasagar district, Assam, have been selected as the field of study. Sivasagar district formerly known as Sibsagar is one of the 27 districts of Assam state in north-eastern India. Situated in the eastern part of Assam, Sivasagar stands high and tall with its rich aesthetic appeal. The main communities living in the district are Ahoms, Tea-tribes, Sonowal Kacharis, Mishings and Deoris. There are also a few villages of Buddhist tribes like Khamyang and Turung. Sivasagar was the capital of the Ahom rulers for six centuries which ended with the arrival of British rulers in the 19th century.

In Nitaipukhuri area of Demow town there are five Tengapania Deori villages viz., Chamuguri Deori village with 50 household and a population of 294, Chingiyoni Deori village with 78 household and a population of 603, Borpather Deori village with 46 household and a population of 360, Kotiyori Deori village with 92 household and a population of 560 and Kokilamari Deori village with 202 household and a population of 1274 respectively. These villages are situated about 17 kms from Demow town of Sivasagar Distirct. All the above mentioned villages come under Bamrajabari post office and Nitai out-post. For the said research purpose sample will be taken from each village focusing the food habits of the members of the household.

Objective and Methodology

The present study has been carried out in five villages inhabited by Tengapania Deoris in Demow Town of Sivasagar District, Assam. The Tengapania Deoris are the sole inhabitants there. The study is exploratory in nature and realizing its importance in socio-cultural life of the people under study, certain standard anthropological methods is adopted for collection of authentic data in relation of their food habits. The primary data are collected with the help of methods like non-participant observation, household survey schedule, structured and unstructured interview, concrete case study method. The observation method is applied for gathering information regarding the involvement of womenfolk in their day to day activities, their role in economic life, availability, types and preparation of different food items. Interview method is applied to collect empirical information on the different customs and tradition in relation with kitchen, acceptance and observance of food restriction during the time of their crises period, preservation of their different food items. Case study method is used to evaluate the different ingredients used for preparation of food items, food in different ritual contexts, food and pollution, and the contemporary changes that have taken place in their food items. Again, the data gathered by one method will be cross-checked by another method as and when situation demands.

Result and Discussion

The relation of food with the society and culture is very significant. Human being depends on food for their survival and maintenance of food. Womenfolk usually cook food for their male counterparts and even take food after men. The parallel between food, age and gender is very conspicuous in the Deori society. Food plays an important role in cyclic, crisis and other rites and ceremonies. Kitchen plays a significant role in the socio-religious life of the people. Traditionally, the Deori kitchen is divided into two places. One is the fire place (*juihal*) and the other is the cooking house (*pak ghar*). In the fire place, the fire is kept burning and they take tea and snacks (*jalpan*) sitting beside it. In the evening they even drink rice beer (*suje*) along with some food items at that place. The elder male member of the family sits in the eastern direction of the fire place and the other members sit with him in a clockwise direction. This type of sitting arrangement shows respect to the elder member of the family. The second one is the *pak ghar* where cooking takes place and outsiders or members from different community are not allowed to enter. In the *pak ghar* there is a two layer platform which is made of bamboo, raised high up in the wall. The first layer is known as *gisong* in which they keep their food items such as various dried vegetable items and also fermented fish products like *hukoti*, etc., and the second layer is known as *lureng* in which they keep their utensils. The place where they cook is a raised platform known as *thipahi* and above it is the place where they burn fire to cook food and is known as *siyya*. The rice beer is also kept in one corner of the kitchen. The kitchen is considered as very sacred among the Deoris. The married womenfolk in every household never enter the kitchen without bathing. During menstruation period also they do not cook food for three days. The cooking pots are usually made of steel, brass, cast iron, etc. They use rice pot (*vator saru*), cooking pan (*kerahi*) and also kettle for their regular preparation of food. They mostly use circular dishes (*kahi*) which is made of steel and bell metal for eating of cooked rice along with vegetables and bowl (*bati*) is used for serving curry, rice beer, etc.

The granary is always placed in the front side of the main house and not towards the back. It is roofed with thatching grass and bamboo materials. Customarily the granary is made in the direction of east. In the granary every household stores their crops. The female are not allowed to enter the granary at the time of their menstruation period.

The Deoris have diverse food habits and agriculture is their mainstay. Boiled rice is their staple food. Along with rice they also consume green leafy vegetables, fish, meat, pork, etc., which is usually made by boiling, sometimes frying and roasting. They usually take two meals a day, i.e., lunch and dinner. Whereas in between they also drink tea with snacks like flat rice (*cira*), parched rice (*akhoi*), puffed rice (*muri*), and also various types of rice cakes (*pitha*) and in the evening they drink *suje* along with fish and other vegetable items. They mostly eat boiled food items. In the context of daily food items they prepare fish (*mas*) with elephant apple *(ow tenga)* or cherry tomato (*kon bilahi)* along with potato and *lopha saak* (a kind of green leaves). They also eat *aloo pitika, mas pitika, hukoti* along with cooked rice. They even take chicken curry which is made by using spices along with potato and colocasia leaves *(kosu sak)* and the same process is applied in case of pork curry. They further consume vegetables like cauliflower, cabbage, banana flower, pumpkin, bitter gourd, and some seasonal leafy vegetables. *Tamul pan* (betel nuts and betel vine leaves) is an integral part of Deori food which is taken at any time. They offer betel nut and betel vine leaf to entertain their guests as well convey respect to them. The utensil which they use to serve the same is made up of bell metal and is known as *bota*. This element reflects devotion, respect and friendship.

Another aspect of food and its consumption is related to religious and ceremonial functions. Their supreme deity is Balia Baba. They offer soaked moong (*mah*), banana (*kol*), jackfruit (*kothal*) and other available fruits to their deity in religious ceremony. They mostly worship in the month of *Magh* (January-February), Bohag (April-May), *Saon* (July-August), and in the 1st Wednesday of every month. There is a worshipping place (*than ghar*) in their village where sacrifices of fowls, pigs, etc., are made. The Tengapania Deoris celebrate a number of festivals including Bihu which is a major festival for the entire community. They mainly celebrate Magh Bihu and Bohag Bihu with lots of fun and prepare varieties of food items. Every household prepare special food items like *ghila pitha* (a kind of pan cake), *til pitha* (a small elongated cake wrapped with sesame and rice powder), *sandoh gura* (pulverized parched rice) and also *suje* (rice beer) which plays a very important role among the Deoris. For preparing *ghila pitha,* a kind of sticky rice (*bora saul*) is soaked for few minutes and is then grounded in *dheki* (pounder for husking paddy). After that they mix the grounded *bora saul* with *gur* (jaggery) and water. They then fry this mixture in oil in circular shape. For *til pitha* in one side they fry the *til* (sesame seeds) in a pan and mixed it with *gur*. On the other hand, they soak *bora saul* for few minutes and then grounded it in *dheki*. After that the grounded *bora saul* is placed in the pan in circular shape whereas the fried sesame is placed over it. The preparation of *sandoh gura* is simple. Firstly the rice is to be fried in a fry pan and is then grounded in *dheki*.

They further observe Saonor Bor Puja in the month of July/ August. They observe this *puja* when the paddy is grown and is ready to eat. They then prepare food items like *kesa pitha guri* (uncooked rice powder) along with sugar mixed with it. Lakshmi puja is observed yearly in every household in their granary in the month of *bohag*. The members of the family offer banana, *saulor pitha* (rice cake), *akhoi* (parched rice) in the granary with *tulokhi* (sweet basil leaves) to the goddess Lakshmi. In all these religious rituals *suje* plays an important role in Deori society. The members of the family offer it to the *bhakats* and other elderly person in a small bowl and take blessings from them. At first they sprinkle a drop of *suje* in the ground in the name of god and then they all drink it.

The Deoris also have special food in the occasions of birth, marriage and death. As soon as the child is born they provide honey in the mouth of the child for sweet voice of the child. The pregnant women also have certain food restrictions for the well-being of the child. Those are *khar* (alkali) as it causes miscarriage, sour food, spicy food, jackfruit as it makes the baby's skin rough, eggs with the concept that the newborn might be bald headed and also pork so that the intelligence of the child may not be dull. She also consciously avoids having food during the time of solar and lunar eclipses, which are considered as very inauspicious hours. Diet of a pregnant woman is considered to be of great importance because it also depends on the proper nutrition of the foetus inside mother's womb. After the birth of the child also the parturient mother is provided with some special food. In case of marriage, when a girl becomes of marriageable age then with due permission from her guardians, the bridegroom's guardians along with some elderly relatives or close friends visit the bride's house with a *sarai* (disc on stand) with a paired betel nut and leaf, a scaly fish and a pot full of rice beer (suje) to express their view that they want to choose the girl for their son. Death is also considered as one of the important rites of passage in Deori society. After the death of a person, a period of seven days is considered as polluted. They observe some custom regarding food, consumption of meat, fish, eggs, curries of an alkaline condiment (khar), etc., are tabooed during those days (Zaman, 2012).

They further have certain taboos regarding food consumption in their regular course of life. They do not intake meat of buffalo, fox, eagle and so forth. Snakes and other wild animals are also forbidden. Not only food consumption, they have restrictions regarding serving of food items. A woman never offers food to her husband's elder brother in hand or by touching him in any regard and they also never eat food together facing each other. However, the people belonging to Machiotika lineage do not eat goat as they consider it as the fictitive mythological member of their lineage.

Apart from these, the Deoris have some special method of preparation of preserved food. For preparing the fermented fish product which is known as *hukoti,* medium or small sized fishes are mostly used. The fishes are washed and scattered on a *borchaloni* (large bamboo sieve) and kept it above the fire place for some days. Later on these dry fishes are grounded in *dheki* to make it as powder. Grounding continues till it becomes a coarse paste. Then these paste fish is kept in *bahor sunga* (narrow cylinder made of bamboo). After filling, the mixer is covered with dry paddy straw or even covers the mouth of *bahor sunga* air tight with fine ashes to prevent it from bacteria. This covered *bahor sunga* is placed above the gisong. After 2-3 months, the prepared *hukoti* is ready for consumption. Preparation of *hukoti* is usually done in monsoon and post-monsoon months when the small sized fishes are available in plenty. It is often made by the womenfolk in the month of September to November.

Consumption of *suje* (rice beer) is a common practice among the Deoris. It is not only a popular drink but it is also considered as very pure and sacred. *Suje* is preparerd by the female members of the community. Preparation of *suje* consists of two parts, i.e. preparation of the *pitha* and *suje* brewing. For the *mod pitha* they require *bora saul* (sticky rice), *dala* (a round bamboo utensil), *saloni* (bamboo sieve), *dheki,* and various plant species. Each of the plants leaves, roots, bulb, barks that will be used are cleaned and kept in a *saloni* to dry for about 2 hours. Almost 3 kg a saul is soaked in water for 2 hours. After that this soaked rice is mixed with the dry plant parts and grounded in the *dheki.* The grouded powder is taken out and spread in a *saloni* and the coarse part is given in the *dheki* again for grinding. This process continues until a fine powder is obtained. Now this powder is put in a *soriya* (an aluminium container) and mixed with water to obtain a sticky paste. They make round ball of cake with this sticky paste and keep in a *dola.*

It is then kept in *gisong* for drying. This baking procedure of *mod pitha* continues until the *mod pitha* becomes hard and is ready for use in *suje brewing*. For *suje brewing* 3-5 kg of rice is mixed with water and is cooked in a *kerahi*. It is stirred by the *heta* (spatula) while cooking to avoid burning of the *saul*. Now the cooked rice is put in a *dola* and 2-3 *mod pitha* is mixed with the cooked rice smoothly and then *biholongoni paat* is spread over the mixture and then it is covered by banana leaves. This mixture is then poured in a *koloh* (an earthen pot) and the mouth which was closed by *biholongoni* and banana leaves is wrapped tightly with a piece of cloth and stored it for fermentation. Nowadays they keep this mixture in a big plastic bucket also. Sometimes two days are enough for fermentation in summer whereas in winter more than a week is required. It is then poured in a *sakoni* for filtration and the filtrate is ready for consumption.

In most of the religious ceremonies of the Deoris like Bohag Bihu, Magh Bihu, Saonor Borpuja, suje is an essential food item. However in some ceremonies like Aai Sabha, Lakhimi Puja consumption of suje is not mandatory. Apart from these ceremonies, in each life cycle ritual i.e. birth, marriage and death suje is compulsory.

Food habits of every people irrespective of their caste, creed, is unique to its own which differ in respect of their social environment in which they are inevitable part. Levi-Strauss argued that human being consider food not only for fulfillment of energy and nutrients just like other animals, rather their society has decreed regarding acceptance and rejection of food and kinds that should be eaten and on what occasions. (cited by Leech: 1970).

Ecology and environment also has an impact on food habit of human society. The Deoris are very rich in flora and fauna and it is observed that most of the food items they consume are locally available. Due to the climatic condition much spice is not used rather sour dishes (*tenga*) are preferred in preparation of dishes and influence of indigenous caste population and other tribal food is also conspicuous in their diet. However, the Deori food is a mixture of different indigenous styles with some degree of external influences. In recent years winds of change has percolated in Deori society and culture, resulting changes in the food habit of indigenous people. Due to the progress and development in transport and communication system, educational system, as well as influences of modernization and industrialization people now reside in different places, due to which dietary habits of other society has an immense impact on Deori diet. Deoris have a rich traditional food habit which represents the socio-cultural aspect the society. However, as a matter of fact, in spite of the numerous traditional dishes in a Deori society, it is often noticed that some new food items are made up by the people, and the reason is due to modernization and influence of the neighbouring communities. In course of time, it is seen that some of their food items are getting extinct from the society which might affect the identity of the community. Though lots of changes have taken place in the food habits of the Deori people, still indigenous items like *bhat, sak, hukoti, suje* and so forth are considered as very suitable items of food among the Deoris of Upper Assam.

References

Deori, P. 2011. *Deori Sanskritir Itihaas*. Dhemaji, Kiran Publication.

Deori, S. 2002. *Religious Practices of the Deoris*. Guwahati, Bina Library.

Endle, Rev. Sidney. 2007. *The Kacharis*. Guwahati, Bina Library.

Gurdon, Major P.R.T. 2002. *The Khasis*. Delhi, Low Price Publication.

Hutton, J.H. 1969. *The Angami Naga*. Bombay, Oxford University Press.

Mills, J.P. 1980. *The Rengma Naga*. Gauhati, Spectrum Publications.

Playfair, A. 1998. *The Garo*. Guwahati, Spectrum Publications.

Saikia, S.K. 2009. *Food Habits in Assam: Land and People*. New Delhi, Thomson Press Ltd.

Smith, W. Carlson. 1925. *The Ao Naga Tribes of Assam*. London, Macmillan.

Zaman, A. 2009. Dimensions of the Assamese food. *Bulletin of the Department of Anthropology*, Dibrugarh University, Vol. 37: 91-98.

Zaman, A. 2012. "Aspects of Death and Disposal Among the Tengapania Deoris of Assam." In: K. Jose SVD, Gautam K. Bera, Brinchi K. Medhi and R.P. Athparia (Eds.), *Concept of God and Religion*. pp. 263-274. New Delhi: Abhijeet Publications.

6
Symbolic Interpretation of *Cowrie* Shell among the Dimasa Tribe of Karbi Anglong, Assam

Lilu Rani Hasnu and Dwipen Bezbaruah

Introduction

Anthropologists explore the symbolic meanings of an object and action which is attached to different cultural behaviour through its own observation and techniques (Rosman *et al.* 1995). One of the symbolic object Cowrie shell was a main accumulation in Maldive Island in Indian Ocean which was traded in early times to Southeast Asia and beyond. It is clear from the earlier research that the Cowrie shells means to valuable object (Campbell, 2003). It is interesting to know that far beyond the sea shore in different parts of the world the two types of Cowrie shells—'*Cypraea moneta*' and '*Cyparea annulus*' plays a significant role as a symbol of wealth, medium of exchange and religious accessory since time immemorial (James, 2012). Towards the 19th century these marine Cowrie shells were traded from Indian Ocean by some traders to the tribes of North East India having its monetary as well as symbolic functional value (Campbell, 2003). It is evident from the archaeological research that the Dimasa tribe of Assam uses Cowrie shell as a significant value (Chowdhury, 1991). The Dimasa tribe of Assam mostly colonized in homogenous character in two hill districts of Dima Hasao and Karbi Anglong. The Dimasa society is patrilineal in nature and follows the rule of descent respectively. Every Dimasa people observe the rites and rituals in their socio-religious life under the guidance of village priest *'Hoja'*. Moerover, the whole Dimasa population is the believer of 12 religious areas or territorial jurisdiction called *'Daikho'* in which the God and Goddesses reside in that particular *'Daikho'* to protect them and control their destiny (Bordoloi, 1984).

Aim of the Study

The present chapter makes an attempt to interpret the symbolic meanings of Marine Cowrie shells in foretelling future by the priest among the Dimasa tribe in their ritualistic way of life. The main aim of the investigation is to analyze the necessity of a Cowrie in *'Sama naiba'* ritual with a view to portray the changing attribute in contemporary situation.

Methods Applied

The research undertaken is based on primary data as well as secondary data to query on significance of Cowrie shells in depth. The investigation was undertaken to gather data from the Ekorani

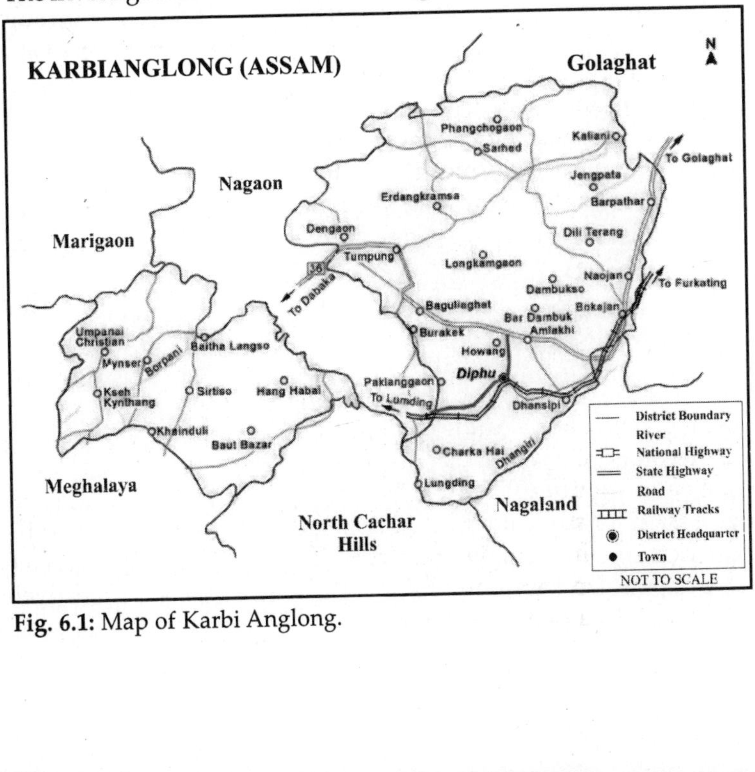

Fig. 6.1: Map of Karbi Anglong.

village, Manja sub-division of Karbi Anglong district of Assam which was carried out in 2013-2015. The Ekorani village is dominated by Dimasa tribe. To gather data on symbolic meanings an observation method was applied to observe the rituals and Cowrie bead. On the other hand, an interview method was also used to collect data on significance of Cowrie shells from the aged person and priest of the village.

Cowrie Shell as Bead

As Cowrie shell *'Khauthi'* is a marine object with a size of 1 cm. In Dimasa community, *'Khauthi'* is valued as a very precious object and belief to be God of ocean or sea. It has a deep significance as beads especially for babies and are used to make amulet *'Jingsdu'* in which one or three Cowrie shells are stringed with black cotton thread along with three circular and one rectangular shaped black colour glass beads. And this amulet is tied around the waist of a baby in belief as a symbol to eradicate the evil eye or evil spirit *'Sagain Madai'*. According to religious belief among Dimasa tribe when the evil eye tries to harm or attack the baby, they return back by looking the Cowrie shell tied around the waist of a baby that there is a God of Ocean.

Cowrie Shells in *'Shama Naiba'* Ritual

Every Dimasa household depends on *'Shama naiba'* ritual, which is a religious practice performed by a priest known as *'Hoja'*. To perform this religious practice only male gender could be a priest who is known to be sacred. Among the Dimasa, any social problem related to family or community is first of all suggest to perform these ritual *'Shama naiba'*. Ritual *'Shama naiba'* is of two types—*'Shama naiba'* through stem of a plant and another *'Shama naiba'* through Cowries *'Khauthi'*. The ritual is practiced to foretell the future of any cause of the malevolent problem, illness of health or any problems related to social life. With the prediction of the problem, the priest *'Hoja'* also suggest the solution which might be any rituals including sacrifices or offering prayer to God *'Sibrae'* to eradicate the problems. The ritual *'Shama naiba'* through *'Khauthi'* is performed by the priest *'Hoja'* early in the morning in an empty stomach facing towards the direction of sunrise. Most of the rituals among the Dimasa community are foretold by the priest 'Hoja' through ritual *'Shama naiba'*. The material needed to perform *'Shama naiba'* ritual is sacred Machete *'Sheng'*, 4 cowrie shells *'Khauthi'*, a basil leaf 'Tulsi' to spread the holy water.

To perform the *'Shama naiba'* ritual firstly, the plot or place where the ritual would conduct has to be made sacred by marking an imaginary line then it is made sacred through cleaning the particular soil with water. This selected place is made sacred through spraying holy water with basil leaf *'Tulsi'* around the place within an imaginary line. Then the sacred Machete is erected in the middle towards the sun rise in which the 4 cowries were repeatedly thrown in that sacred place through uttering prayer by the priest *'Hoja'* with that imaginary line to foretell or predict the problem of the person. The priest *'Hoja'* with his divine power offering prayer to God *'Sibrae'* would predict or foretell the future and cause of the problem.

Analyses 1. If a baby is not healthy and suffering from fever for days, after being medical consult then the family member of a baby prefer their village priest to see the cause of the problem through *'Shama naiba'* ritual.

Analyses 2. Among the Dimasa tribe, if each member of the family had a high tempered or quarrelling with each other they depend on *'Shama naiba'* ritual to find out the cause and solution. And if a person lost their property like animals, fowl, jewelry, cloth etc. then they prefer to consult with the priest through this ritual.

Analyses 3. A *'Phara khoba'* ritual is the outcome of *'Shama naiba'* ritual. In astrological term if the one of the planet *'Naksatra'* is not good the person might face a failure in success then this *'Phara khoba'* ritual is performed by the victim of the problem to regain success in life. In this ritual, a cowrie shells plays a symbolic behaviour as a medium of exchange. This ritual is of three types—*Phara mashni* (7 cowries), *Phara masugu* (9 cowries), *Phara majra* (15 cowries). It is belief among Dimasa that the bad fortune of a person can be exchanged with cowrie shells to the God of Planet *'Naksatra'* in order to return the good fortune back to their body. Here, the Cowries symbolize precious object of God of Ocean as a medium of exchange.

Conclusion

It is obvious from the above that Cowrie shells *'Khauthi'* are associated with sacred object in ritualistic life of the Dimasa people. From the historical evidence it is clear that the Cowrie shells *'Khauthi'* were traded since time immemorial. But it is noteworthy to mention that society is always changing in nature i.e., in religious and socio-cultural aspects and it is important to note that use of Cowrie shells *'Khauthi'* is gradually in declining. With the progress of civilization and modern outlook, the Dimasa tribe less depend on traditional religious practices which have not only waned but also affect age old traditions. Now, if they suffer any social problem they depend on the Hindu temple priest and medical treatment and also among the Dimasa people the use of *'Khauthi'* as amulet is noticeable only in rural context.

Male Priest performing *'Shama naiba'* ritual

Cowrie shell *'Khauthi'* as amulet *'Jingsdu'*

Different varieties of Cowrie shells *'Khauthi'*

References

Bordoloi, B.N. 1984. *The Dimasa Kacharis of Assam.* Assam, The Director, Tribal Research Institute.

Chowdhury, R.D. 1991. "On Three Hoards of Cowries from Assam." In: *Archaeology of North-Eastern India XVII.* ed. by J.P. Singh *et al.*, pp. 228-231. New Delhi: Vikas Publishing house.

Campbell, C.B. 2003. "Heirloom Beads of the Naga and Kachin." *Beads: Journal of the Society of Bead Researchers.* 20: 15-21.

Rosman, A. and P.G. Rubel. 1995. *The Tapestry of Culture, An Introduction to Cultural Anthropology,* Fifth Edition. Barnard College, Columbia University.

7
Cultural Heritage of the Khasi Community of North East India

Bhola Nath Ghosh

Introduction

From among the numerous races which inhabit the North-Eastern corner of India, we find the matriarchal system of society present only in two tribes—the Khasis and Garos. They live close to each other, the Garos are the extreme western and the Khasis just east to them in the same range of hills which forms the southern boundary of the Brahmaputra valley. But the two tribes are distinct from one another. They differ in many of their laws and customs.

The distinction between the matriarchal and patriarchal societies starts from descent. We speak of the descent as patriarchal when a child belongs to the social group of his father and as a matriarchal when he belongs to the social group of his mother.

Therefore, heritage can be observed of a community through the social structure, inheritance, religion, culture, festivals, customs, rituals and marriage.

Most of the states in India are patrilineal but in Meghalaya it is matrilineal. The Khasis is one of the tribes living in Meghalaya State of North East India. This tribe draws much attention of the Sociologists especially Social Scientists, because this tribe practices matrilineal system characterized in terms of marriage, inheritance and residential status after marriage. It is commonly believed that the status of women in matrilineal society is higher compared to that of patrilineal society. This can be seen in terms of empowerment and other roles played by the women. However, it may not imply that the women are more empowered than men in Meghalaya. The Khasi society of Meghalaya is such a society, commonly known as matrilineal where female folks determine authority, title, inheritance, and residence after marriage and succession. So, it is presumed that the right of the society is already established and they do not require any special effort for their rights. But the question is whether they are aware about the social, economic and other issues as compared to the awareness of male.

Therefore, a question may arise whether in Khasi Tribe, the status of empowerment of women is ascribed or prescribed by the society. In Meghalaya the female, normally inherit the property and holds the keys to social and economic activities.

If we ask a question: who is a Khasi? The answer is not easy, as in the present situation, it is a difficult task to identify in the true and pure Khasi traits of culture. Material culture seems to be rapidly changing and the institution; the homes and so on can rarely be identified as pure Khasi.

Any person can claim or identify himself as a Khasi if he or she fulfils any one of the following conditions:

1. That he or she believes that his or her forefathers were the Hynniewtrep Hynniiewskum (seven huts-seven clans), the first inhabitants of these hills, who resided in the house of God.
2. That he or she is born of Khasi parents.
3. That at least his or her mother is a Khasi.
4. That should a Khasi (man) marry a non-Khasi woman, his wife and their offspring become Khasis if she agrees to obey, follow and adopt all the traditional norms, religion, customs and rituals performed by the Khasi. As the Khasi is a matrilineal society, a non-Khasi mother has to become a Khasi by performing certain rights; religious sanctions have to be obtained for the new title of the clan through rituals.

   Khasi society evolved with the adoption of the concept of *ka kheim-kur, khein-kha, tip-kur-tip-kha.*

The acceptance of the above kinship structures as the source gives the race its unique characteristic from time immemorial to the present day and endows the Khasi man and woman with distinct identities and well-defined roles in their society.

There are certain principles, precepts and tenets which clearly define the duties and responsibilities expected of a Khasi man and a Khasi woman.

From among the numerous ethnic groups which inhabit the North-Eastern corner of India we find the matriarchal system of society present only in two tribes—the Khasis and the Garos. They live close to each other, the Garos at the extreme western end and the Khasis just east to them in the same range of hills which forms the southern boundary of the Brahmaputra valley. But the two tribes are distinct from one another. They do not speak the same language and differ in many of their laws and customs. The Khasis belong to the earliest bands of immigrants and it has been very difficult to trace their origin. Linguistically, the Garos belong to the Bodo group and are closely related to the Kacharis, Rabhas, Mwech and other tribes with a patriarchal form of society, who settled in Assam Valley. It has been said that the Garos during the course of their wandering towards Gauhati were enslaved by the Assamese, but released by a Khasi Prince, who settled them in the neighbourhood of Boko. The place was infested with tigers and demons and the Garos being afraid of complete extinction moved away from this place and ultimately settled in the place where they now inhabit.

It might have been possible, therefore, that the Garos copied the matriarchal system from the Khasis. The institutional laws as we find is more potent and active amongst the Khasis profoundly influencing their social and political life.

Difference between Patriarchal and Matriarchal Societies

The distinction between the matriarchal and patriarchal societies starts from descent. We speak of the descent as patriarchal when a child belongs to the social group of his father and as matriarchal when he/she belongs to the social group of his/her mother. The Khasis say "Khein Jaid na ka Kynthei'. Descending from a common ancestress are said to belong to the same "Kur", i.e., clan. All others who do not belong to the same clan are known as "Kha." Indeed "Tip Kur Tip Kha", i.e., to know those who belong to the same can and those who do not belong is the fundamental feature of Khasi life. It is the basis of their social structure, and governs every walk of life, their religion, belief and all social laws and customs.

Area of Study

The present study is conducted among the Khasi tribe of Meghalaya. The two villages wherein the research study has been conducted are Ringkesh and Kyton-u-mon situated under the Khasi Hill district of Nawlyngknang block.

The capital of Meghalaya, Shillong lies on the eastern part of the state. Between the two villages chosen, Ringkesh lies near to Shillong and Kyton-u-mon is few kilometers away from the capital. Both the villages are poor in nature.

Methodology of the Study and Data

Process of matrilinity of the Khasi society here has been studied through primary survey in two villages from East Khasi Hills District of Meghalaya. These villages are Ringkseh and Kynton-u-mon under Mawlyngknang block. The villages are chosen purposively on consideration of conveniences, such as access and communication, security, expenditure involved in survey etc. However most of the features of the rural Meghalaya have much in common in the aforesaid selected villages.

There are 257 households (119+138) in all in those selected villages. The ratio of male and female-headed families in the selected villages was found to be 1.6: 1 in Meghalaya. Though the society of Meghalaya is commonly known as matrilineal, more than two third of the families are run by males and only around 1/3rd are headed by females. Then question naturally arises whether the society of Meghalaya is gradually approaching towards patrilineal or the dominance of female still has been prevailing in the same manner and the change has been just for the convenience without any major change in balance of gender distribution in any respect. We have stratified the families according to the characteristics of sex of family head, caste, occupation, education etc. and finally chosen 95 households; 37 out of 175 male-headed households and 58 from 82 female-headed households. Data have been collected, from the finally chosen households, on different aspects like family size, sex, education, caste, occupation, income and expenditure, mode of expenditure and also on their attitude/opinion towards social, political, cultural aspects i.e. on social, cultural, economical, political, religious and psychological aspects of the heads as well as other members of the families. From that information we tried to understand the process of empowerment by analysing the data. The study is mainly descriptive and exploratory.

Basic Characteristics of Sample Households

From the Table 7.1 we observe that out of 37 male-headed households about 68 per cent of the heads are in the below 50 age group and over 43 per cent are in the below 40 age group. Whereas among the female-headed households about 36 per cent of the heads are in the below 50 and around 20 per cent are in the age group of 20 to 40. On the other hand, around 22 per cent of male heads are in the above 50 age group and about 64 per cent of the female heads are in the similar age group.

Table 7.1: Age-wise Sex Composition of the Sample Households

Sex of Head	*20-30*	*31-40*	*41-50*	*51-60*	*61-70*	*>70*	*Total*
Male	4 (10.8)	12 (32.4)	9 (24.3)	6 (16.2)	4 (10.8)	2 (5.4)	37
Female	3 (5.2)	9 (15.5)	9 (15.5)	14 (24.1)	17 (29.3)	6 (10.3)	58
Total	7 (7.37)	21 (22.11)	18 (18.95)	20 (21.05)	21 (22.11)	8 (8.42)	95

Source: Field Survey. Significance level of the Chi-square test: 0.0031.[1] Results of the Chi-square test to see if sex and age are independent: The sig. value is .003 (one sided). This was found after converting the table into a 2×2 contingency table as follows.

Sex of Head/Age	*20-50*	*51 or more*
Male	25	12
Female	21	37

Note: Figures in the parentheses represent percentage to total of the respective sex.

Table 7.2 reveals that among male-headed households the percentage of families with family size 5 or less is almost same as that of family size more than 5, whereas among female-headed households the percentage of families with family size less than 6 (about 60 per cent) is much higher than the percentage of families having size 6 or more (around 40 per cent). Almost at every educational level especially in the illiterate category, female heads are having a tendency to keep family size lower than the male heads.

Table 7.2: Distribution of Families by Family Size across Different Educational Categories of the Head of the Household

Sex of Head	*Education*	*1-5*	*6-10*	*> 10*	*Total*
	Illiterate	1	6	0	7 (18.9)
Male Headed	< M.P.	9	7	2	18 (48.7)
	> M.P.	7	5	0	12 (32.4)
	Sub-Total	17	18	2	37 (100)
	Illiterate	12	6	0	18 (31.0)
	< M.P.	18	12	1	31 (53.5)
Female Headed	> M.P.	5	4	0	9 (15.5)
	Sub-Total	35	22	1	58 (100)
	Grand Total	52	40	2	95

Source: Field Survey, Significance level of the Chi-square test taking '1-5' and '6 or more' as the categories of family size and '<MP' and '≥ MP' as the categories of education level.
Sex of head Vs. Family size: 0.122, Sex of head Vs. Educational level: 0.047 and Family size Vs. Educational level: 0.501.

Table 7.3: Distribution of Households According to Marital Status of the Head

Sex of Head	*Unmarried*	*Widow*	*Divorced/ Separated*	*Married Once*	*Married more than once*	*Total*
Male	3 (8.1)	2 (5.4)	-	27 (73.0)	5 (13.5)	37 (100.00)
Female	1 (1.7)	18 (31.3)	11 (19.0)	26 (44.8)	2 (3.4)	58 (100.00)

Note: Figures in the parentheses represent percentage to total of the respective sex.
Source: Field Survey, Significance level of the Chi-square test: 0.006.

From Table 7.3 it is observed that about 50 per cent of the female heads are due to automatic choice as they are either widow, divorced or separated and hence there is no chance of male to be head. Around 48 per cent of female heads are married and barely 2 per cent are unmarried. But in case of male heads, around 86 per cent are married (once or more than once) and about 8 per cent are unmarried.

Table 7.4: Distribution of Household by Earning Status of the Head of Families of Different Age-Group

	Age	Dependent	Earner
Male	20-40	1 (6.2)	15 (93.8)
	41-60	1 (66.7)	14 (93.3)
	> 60	1 (16.7)	5 (83.3)
	Sub-Total	3 (8.1)	34 (91.9)
Female	20-40	4 (33.3)	8 (66.7)
	41-60	2 (8.7)	21 (91.3)
	> 60	6 (26.0)	17 (74.0)
	Sub-Total	12 (20.7)	46 (79.3)
	Grand Total	15 (15.79)	80 (84.21)

Source: Field Survey, Note: Figures in the parentheses represent percentage to total of the respective sex.
Significance level of the Chi-square test (Sex of Head Vs. Dependent/Earner): 0.085

If we look at the case of inheritance of property the traditional custom is to inherit ancestral assets primarily to the females especially the youngest daughter of the family. However the other daughters of the family also get the share of the ancestral property informally but not equal with that of youngest one and the settlement is done with the consent of the daughters' maternal uncle. The data reveals that about relatively very less male heads (about 35 per cent) have received share of ancestral property i.e., about 65 per cent of male heads do not inherit any property. The male heads who inherited property are either with no sisters or received through will from parents.

Table 7.5: Distribution of Heads according to the Inheritance of Ancestral Property

Sex	Property Inherited	Not Inherited
Male Head	13 (35.14)	24 (64.86)
Female Head	29 (50.00)	29 (50.00)

Note: Figures in the parentheses represents percentage to total.
Source: Field survey, Significance level of the Chi-square test: 0.113.

Table 7.6 shows that monthly average per capita family income in case of female-headed households is much lower than that of male-headed household. Also average per capita expenditure on food, education, travel and other purposes (entertainment, drink, dress etc) are comparatively higher in case of male-headed household than that of female-headed household. Only in case of health care and electricity female-headed household spends more than a male-headed household. But the coefficient of variation in income and expenditures across families are much higher in case female-headed household than that of male-headed household. This is because many of female heads are either widow, deserted or separated with small children and hence have very poor income to spend. This indicates the disadvantageous condition of the rural females in spite of being known as matrilineal society.

The youngest daughter known as the "Khadduh" inherits the ancestral house and property and the other sisters especially after marriage are given only a share sufficient to maintain them. The youngest daughter is not, however, the full heir but in most cases she is only the custodian of the family property. The actual management is in the hands of her eldest maternal uncle or brothers and ancestral property cannot be sold without the knowledge and consent of the uncles and brothers.

Table 7.6: Percentage of Family under Below Poverty Line across the Sex of Heads

Sex of the Head	*BPL*	*APL*
Male	3 (8.1)	34 (91.9)
Female	14 (24.1)	44 (75.9)
Total	17 (17.9)	78 (82.1)

Note: Figures in the parentheses represents percentage to total.
Source: Field survey, Significance level of the Chi-square test: 0.040.

From Table 7.6 we observe that incidence of poverty is relatively more in case of female-headed household than that of male-headed household. Also the occupational status of the heads, which yields people some position in the family and society, is shown in the Table 7.6.

Table 7.7: Occupational Pattern of the Heads across Sexes and Education

Sex	*Educational Qualification*	*Cultivator*	*Agri-Labourer*	*Govt. Service*	*Pvt. Service*	*Business*	*House wife*	*Old Age*	*Other*
Male	Illiterate	0	4	0	2	0	0	1	0
	< Madhyamic	4	7	1	3	2	0	0	1
	> Madhyamic	0	2	6	1	2	0	0	1
	Sub-total	4 (10.8)	13 (35.1)	7 (18.9)	6 (16.2)	4 (10.8)	0 (00)	1 (2.7)	2 (5.4)
Female	Illiterate	1	7	0	0	2	2	4	2
	< Madhyamic	2	6	1	2	8	3	4	5
	> Madhyamic	0	0	4	1	3	0	0	1
	Sub-total	3 (5.2)	13 (22.4)	5 (8.6)	3 (5.2)	13 (22.4)	5 (8.6)	8 (13.8)	7 (12.1)

Source: Same as Table 7.1, Significance level of the Chi-square test of Sex of Head Vs. Occupation (with categories 'Cultivator or Agri. Labourer' and 'Others'): 0.054.

From the Table 7. 7 it is clear that because of lower educational background female heads are comparatively less in government and private services but they are more in business (here actually petty businesses). Earlier women were also predominant in agriculture. Bur now-a-days men are increasingly participating in agriculture as cultivator or agricultural labourer. On the whole, females are relatively in lower level occupation than their counterpart men in our study area. In the society if women can work and participate in different social and entertaining activities freely their position improves than if they cannot. In the backward traditional societies, normally women do not become even member of any such social organisation. In rural areas of Meghalaya also we find very few women especially the well-educated one are member of similar organisation compared to men as shown in Table 7.8.

Table 7.8: Sex-wise Distribution of Head according to Membership of Club, Community Centre, Social Organisation or NGO

Sex	*Member*	*Non-Member*	*Total*
Male	12 (32.43)	25 (67.57)	37 (100)
Female	2 (3.45)	56 (96.55)	58 (100)

Source: Same as Table 7.1, Significance level of the Chi-square test: 0.000.

Though most of the females are not the member of different social organisations or clubs, they can move alone freely and join any party, function or ceremony and mostly without the permission of senior or male members. The tendency is more for the more and more educated females and also with the increase in age (Table 7.9 and 7.10). Therefore education makes the female to think independently and act without any fear even in the villages of Meghalaya.

Table 7.9: Education-wise Distribution of Female Heads according to Participation in Meeting/Function/Fete etc. outside the Village

Education	*Participation in Social Meeting, Social Gathering, Function etc*			*Total*
	Alone	*With men/women of the same or other family*	*Others*	
Illiterate	7 (94.4)	(5.6)	(0.0)	18 (100)
< Madhyamic	3 (74.2)	(19.4)	(6.5)	31 (100)
> Madhyamic	9 (100)	0	0	9 (100)
Total	9 (84.5)	(12.1)	(3.4)	8 (100)

Source: Same as Table 7.1, Significance level of the Chi-square test Education Vs. Participation (Alone and not alone): 0.193.

Table 7.10: Age-wise Distribution of Female Heads Visit nearest Town With/Without the Permission of Men

Age	*Yes*	*No*	*Total*
20-40	15 (83.3)	3 (16.7)	18
41-60	28 (90.3)	3 (9.7)	31
> 60	8 (89.0)	1 (11.0)	9

Source: Same as Table 7.1, Significance level of the Chi-square test: 0.373.

Political Status

Though females in Meghalaya are much aware about their rights and position in the society, but there are hardly any woman actively participating in politics. Even the society does not allow women to participate in political decision-making. Till now any woman Headman of a *Dorbar* is hardly found. Also they do not participate much into political discourses. Only recently women are allowed on a very limited scale to participate in *Dorbar* meeting. Though women in Khasi society are relatively free, still there are discriminations (social and psychological) as explained above, yet the women do not seem to be much interested in politics. Actually, most of the rural women think even reservation of seat for the females in the local bodies or *Dorbar* is not beneficial to them. The opinion of both male and female heads in this regard is presented in Table 7.11. Even some of the females do not bother about whether their name is in the electoral role or not. Of course most of the females exercise their franchise in the election and that percentage increases with the rise in educational level of the rural females as is observed from Tables 7.11 and 7.12.

Table 7.11: Sex-wise Distribution of Heads according to the Opinion about Reservation of Seats for Members in the Local Bodies (Gram Panchayat/ Dorbar)

Sex	*Very Bad*	*Bad*	*Not so Bad*	*Good*	*Very Good*	*No Idea*	*Total*
Male	22 (59.5)	4 (10.8)	5 (13.5)	1 (2.7)	0 (0)	5 (13.5)	37
Female	35 (60.3)	11 (19.0)	2 (3.4)	2 (3.4)	0 (0)	8 (13.8)	58

Source: Field survey.

Note: Figures in the parentheses represents percentage to total. Significance level of the Chi-square test of Sex of Head Vs. Opinion (Bad or not bad): 0.223.

Table 7.12: Education and Sex-wise Distribution of Households according to Inclusion and Exclusion of Head in the Voting List and Exercising Voting Right

Sex of Head	*Educational Qualification*	*Name included in the Voting List*		*Exercise Voting Power*	
		Yes	*No*	*Yes*	*No*
Male	Illiterate	5	2	5	2
	< Madhyamic	16	2	16	2
	> Madhyamic	11	1	11	1
	Sub-total	32	5	32	5
Female	Illiterate	14	4	14	4
	< Madhyamic	29	2	29	2
	> Madhyamic	8	1	8	1
	Sub-total	51	7	51	7

Source: Field survey, Significance level of the Chi-square test of Sex of head Vs. Vote: 0.536.

Observation

Development of the Law on Property

The fundamental precepts have largely influenced the customary laws of the Khasis on the use, application, transfer and alienation of property and wealth among Khasis.

Analysing from both angles of ascription *vis-à-vis* achievement of women in Khasi matriliny we found that:

(i) The rule of matrilineal descent is intact without any structural change,
(ii) domestic decision of women is restrictive, male members have an upper hand,
(iii) Religious authority within indigenous faith or having changed to other religion, women enjoys no authority,
(iv) Inheritance and management of ancestral property is restrictive to women. While self-acquired property is subjected to the earner's authority,
(v) Traditionally political belief does not permit women as active participants while they are in position of authority in rational legal institutions, and
(vi) Matriliny and gender (both male and female) restricts the role and authority of both. The restrictive structure to build within the matrilineal framework is gearing towards a gender debate in the society at large.

In the political and administrative sphere, women do not have any right. Disputes are settled primarily in the villages by the village councils composed of a Sirdar and four or five headmen elected by only the male members of the village. If there is dissatisfaction the dispute is then tried by a council of a 'Raid', an area comprising of different villages. The members of the council are elected from certain clans. Ultimately the dispute is tried by the Siem and his Myntris. The Siem is the head of the State. It may be noted that women are not only debarred from being members of these councils but do not even have the right to elect the members. The office of the Siem cannot also be held by a woman, but descent is always through the female line. And yet, when it comes to giving women a role in politics, Meghalaya seems to be reluctant.

Although Khasis are religiously following the matrilineal society, in the upper of civil administration as well as in the 60-member Meghalaya assembly, participation of women is very less. At the time of data collection there were only three women legislators — **Debora C. Marak, Maysalin War** and **Rosan Warjri.** None of the stalwarts of Meghalaya politics have an answer to this.

Conclusion

This contentious issue has come into the public domain when a section of Khasi intellectuals, led by Mr Michael Syiem, Convener of Maitshaprang Movement, asserted that Khasi men were not engaging themselves much in economic activities because of the matrilineal nature of the society.

More than fifty per cent of the women surveyed said that they were not interested in electoral politics. Almost all villagers said "Basically, women think that politics is not their cup of tea". Although society in Meghalaya is theoretically matriarchal, in practice men have all the economic power and therefore men have the ability to control politics. Since women do not have economic power, they lack confidence to step into politics. Even now, the village councils or *dorbars* do not have women in decision-making positions. Another factor that prevents women from coming forward and demanding political space is that they are not groomed to take part in public discourses as a matter of tradition. It is observed that no bank provides any financial assistance to any male Khasi entrepreneur because they cannot pledge any immovable property. This is a major practical problem which our society wants to gloss over.

Only a few Khasi people are interested to change the laws in terms of property inherence. But change of inheritance law means change of social structure, which majority of Khasis do not like. A similar attempt to change the law was made by the Khasi Students Union (KSU) in the eighties but it was given up as the traditional Khasi society did not show enthusiastic response. The society is divided on the issue as those seeking change had been finding it difficult to come out of the shadow of tradition.

The results of household survey made during 2009-2010 reveal that the women still enjoy the accession to inheritance, and control over the resources. However, the situation is changing very fast. Though the role of Khasi women seems to have been prescribed, but most of the activities of women are becoming ascribed. Though Meghalaya is known as the matrilineal society, now many of the families are headed by the males. The tendency is increasing with the increasing involvement of male in the socio-economic activities, expansion of education, emergence of nuclear families etc.

However in the family there is no discrimination among the

male and female child. This is partly because of the economic independence of the females and their customary laws, which is still dominant in the rural areas.

Though traditionally the women (especially the youngest one) are supposed to inherit ancestral property, men also inherit property under different circumstances.

Though earlier females used to dominate in the field of various economic activities now-a-days males also are involved in different activities. Relatively more females are illiterate than males. Data reveal that, now the high collar jobs are mostly occupied by the males and the income of the female-headed households are relatively less and associated with significant inter-family variation. Also incidence of poverty is more in case of female-headed household. Yet the female better manage the family and give more emphasis on the human development indicators like education, health etc.

We apparently observe that some changes among the people of this community and now the women are no longer the sole inheritor of their ancestral property. Now men are also controlling the property. To some extent through the major economic and non-economic activities are guided by the decision of their counterparts.

At present, however private ownership of property has acquired greater importance over the old ideas of joint ownership and the desire to live in harmony amongst all members of the clan seems to have yielded slowly to the notion of economic domination through the ownership of private property. It is therefore likely that the law especially with regard to property will gradually change.

It is observed empirically that the Khasi community in its traditional arrangement, neither male nor female has absolute authority. Both enjoy their restricted roles. Therefore at present, the Khasi matriliny is in the transition phase and its future is still not properly defined.

Note

1. Only the significance value of Fisher's exact (one sided) test is reported here. If the value is less than 0.05 then the two variables are not independent, i.e., they are related. The same procedure is taken in all other tables.

References

Altekar, A. 1973. *The Position of Women in Hindu Civilization*. New Delhi, Motilal Banarasi Das.

De, U. 2011. *Gender Deprivation and Empowerment of Women: An Indian Perspective*. GmbH & Co. KG, Dudweiler Landstr, 99,66123, Saarbrucken: Lap Lambert Academic Publishing.

De, U. 2004. *Issues on Empowerment of Women*. New Delhi, Mohit Publications.

Ghosh, B.N. 2015. *Gramin Netritva O Unnayan*. (Bengali), Kolkata: 37A, College Street.

Ghosh, B.N. March, 2010. Empowerment of Women: A Study in Tripura & Meghalaya. *South Asian Anthropologist*, Vol. 10. No.1: 11-28. (Clarify)

Ghosh, B.N. 2015. *Empowerment of Women in North East in India*. New Delhi, Concept Publishing Company (P) Ltd.

Ghosh, B.N. 2008. "Problems of tribal Identity in North-Eastern Region." In: R. &. Karmakar, *Contemporary Social Problems in India*, Vol.-I, pp. 125-132. Kolkata: Readers Service.

Ghosh, B.N. 2015. *Process of Empowerment of Women in North-East India*. New Delhi, Concept Publishing Company Pvt. Ltd.

Ghosh, B.N. 2006. *Process of Empowerment of Women in Rural Areas: Case Studies in Two North Eastern States*. Kolkata: Indian Statistical Institute.

Ghosh, B.N. 2008. *Women Governance in Tripura*. New Delhi, Concept Publishing Company.

Ghosh, B.N. 2008. *Women's Speak*. New Delhi, Mittal Publications.

Ghosh, B.N. 2003. *Human Development Report*. UNDP, Geneva.

Ghosh, B.N. 1997. *Human Development Report*. UNDP, Geneva.

Majumder, V. 1989, December-16. Reservation of Seats of Women. *Economic and Political Weekly*, pp. 16-26.

Mitra, A. 1979. *Status of Women: Household and Non-Household Economic Activity*. New Delhi: ICSSR Programme of Women's Studies.

Pal, M.B. 2009. *Gender and Discrimination, Health Nutritional Status and Role of Women in India*. New Delhi, Oxford University Press.

Pal, M.P. 2012. *Gender Issues & Empowerment of Women*. New York, Nova Science Publishers Inc.

Patel, V. 1994. Women & Structural Adjustment Programme in India. *Social Scientist*, pp. 10-12.

Ray, B. 1999. *From Independence Towards Freedom: Indian Women since 1947*. New Delhi, Oxford University Press.

8
Alien Factors in the Traditional Marriage among the Hmar Tribe of Assam

Arindita Goswami

Introduction

Every culture known to mankind is unique in the sense that each possesses its own distinctive set of cultural patterns that speak volumes of its customs and tradition. The different material and non-material elements of culture be it economy, religious belief and practices, ceremonies, festivals, food habits, dress pattern, art and craft, etc. occupy a significant position in the life of an individual as these are the hallmarks that identify him or her to be a member of a particular society. Among the numerous aspects of culture marriage holds a pivotal space in terms of its universality and variability that forms an important area of interest for anthropologists worldwide. What makes marriage so fascinating is the adornment of this custom with a variety of ceremonies, solemn ritualistic acts and a host of other performances that vary from society to society. Moreover, marriage is regarded to be the foundation of family which is the basic unit of human society. In fact, marriage and family are complimentary to each other. In the common parlance marriage is the formal union between a man and a woman. From the anthropological perspective there are a wide range of definitions covering marriage in all its forms and features. But, it is difficult to have a universally applicable definition of marriage because of the existence of rare forms of marriage found in certain communities around the globe that render such definitions invalid. Nevertheless, a good number of stalwart anthropologists as well as sociologists have attempted to define marriage by indicating the universal core functions of the institution which basically deals with the control of or rights over activities related to mating and the legitimation of children. Westermarck in his monumental work *The History of Human Marriage* (1922) attempted to provide an explanation on marriage as: "Marriage is generally used as a term for a social institution... Marriage always implies the right to sexual intercourse: society holds such intercourse allowable in the case of husband and wife... At the same time, marriage is something more than a regulated sexual relation... It is the husband's duty...to support his wife and children... That the functions of the husband and father in the family are not merely of the sexual and procreative kind, but involve the duty of protecting the wife and children, is testified by an array of facts relating to peoples in all quarters of the world and in all stages of civilization. ...As for the origin of the institution of marriage, I consider it probable that it has developed out of primeval habit."

Various marriage practices have existed throughout the world. A wide range of differences is observed in the societies all around in respect of the forms of marriage, selection of spouse, post-marital residential pattern, ritual and symbolic acts and the like. In the case of North East India as well a vivid diversity is observed in the system of marriage among the different ethnic groups inhabiting the region. North East India comprising of the states of Arunachal Pradesh, Assam, Manipur, Meghalaya, Mizoram, Nagaland, and Tripura presents a rich cultural mosaic with the distribution of a myriad population of tribal and non-tribal communities of various ethnic affiliations having different social structures and cultural heritages. Surrounded by the foreign territories of Bhutan, Tibet-China, Myanmar and Bangladesh on the north-south and the east and connected to the Indian mainland in the west by a narrow land passage through the state of Sikkim which was recently added and separated from the original group of seven North Eastern states, the region is the homeland of a large number of tribal groups belonging to different racial and linguistic stocks, many of which migrated to the region at different historical times. Das (1970) mentions of the different streams of Mongoloid people who came from the north and east of the region at different periods. These groups settled in different habitats forming separate entities and are presently referred to as tribes which as opined by Marak (2012) number over 300 individual communities presenting diverse social customs and as per 2011 Census Report of India account for 27 per cent of the North East's total population of 45.5 million. In this context, it is pertinent to note that among most of the tribal communities of this region great importance is attached to the clan affiliations of the persons who are going to enter into matrimonial alliance which is considered before the formal negotiation process is started. Again, as in other non-tribal societies where dowry is a common feature, the tribals in this region attach great considerations on the payment of bride price which has got wide variations across different groups. Also, tribe endogamy and clan exogamy is the common rule found among the tribal communities of this region, although exceptions cannot be ruled out.

Change in any culture is inevitable with the degree and agents of change varying from society to society. Throughout history humans have replaced or changed customary behaviours and attitudes as their needs have changed and hence every cultural pattern is susceptible to change. To quote Malinowski (1945: 1),

> "Culture change can be said to be the process by which the existing orders of a society, that is its social, spiritual and material civilization is transformed from one type to another".

Religion being an inseparable element of human culture plays a conspicuous role in maintaining the stability or affecting changes in the culture concerned. According to Kallenberg (1995), conversion is the emergence of a new mode of life occasioned by a self-involving participation in the shared life, language, and paradigm of the believing community. Religious conversion is an important social phenomenon taking place from the past and is still a reality now which implies the adoption of a new religion that differs from the convert's previous religion. Such shift in religious beliefs can bring about minor or major changes in the total lifeways of the converted group depending on the degree of change and new elements accommodated in the forms, rituals, ceremonies and the core philosophy of the original religion. In the realm of human social life marriage as an institution has an integral connection with the other elements of the society and from the anthropological holistic viewpoint it can be aptly said that an alteration in the religious faith of that particular society is definitely bound to cast an impact in its marriage system where certain new traits get accommodated while certain others are retained according to necessity and importance.

The Hmars

The Hmar is a distinct group of people having an entity with their own language and culture. The Hmars belong to the Lushai-Kuki-Chin group of people of the Tibeto-Burman linguistic family. They may be said to be a part of the Mizo group of tribes inhabiting the North Eastern region of India, especially domiciled in the states of Mizoram, Manipur, Assam, Tripura and Meghalaya (Bapui, 2008: 253). They are regarded as one of the Scheduled Hill Tribes of India. In Assam they are mainly found in the hill district of Dima Hasao (previously known as North Cachar Hills district), while some Hmar populations are also present in Cachar district and the hill district of Karbi Anglong.

The Hmars do not have any written historical records of their past. Origin and history of the Hmars can only be traced with the help of their oral traditions. Folksongs regarding their original homeland reveal that they migrated to India from Chinlung or Sinlung, in the Sichuan province of south-west Central China. Traditionally, the Hmars were animists but now all of them have embraced Christianity. They have a patriarchal society. They have several clans and sub-clans which are exogamous, but now exogamy is not strictly followed by them. Cross-cousin marriage is always preferred. Monogamy is the prevailing rule, although there was no bar to polygamy before. They have the system of bride-price. Traditionally they are shifting cultivators but now wet cultivation is also practised by them. The bachelors' dormitory of the Hmars is known as *zawlbuk* or *buonzawl* which was once a very important institution in their society as it used to play instrumental roles in shaping the life of a young Hmar man (Bapui, 2011: 91). The Hmar women are expert weavers and the menfolk are adept in making wooden, bamboo and cane articles of day-to-day use.

Aims and Objectives

This chapter intends to look into the changes that have been brought about in the traditional system of marriage among the Hmar tribe of Assam in the wake of the adoption of Christianity—an alien religion by the study population.

Materials and Methods

The present study is based on empirical data collected from two Hmar dominated villages of Dima Hasao district (formerly North Cachar Hills) of Assam which shelters a good number of tribal communities like the Dimasas, Kukis, Baites, Zeme and Rongmei Nagas, Hrangkhols, etc. Established in 1870, the village Retzawl is inhabited by the Hmars with a total population of 1,220 distributed in 170 households. The other village is Muolhoi, established in 1949 consisting of 4,892 individuals distributed in 823 households and is the biggest Hmar village in the entire state of Assam. The former village is entirely a rural area located at a distance of 19.5 kms. from Haflong town, the district headquarter while the latter is located within the Haflong town and is regarded as an urbanized village. In both the villages, a good number of Nepali people are also found to reside either permanently or on a temporary basis as tenants. Marriages between the Hmars and Nepalis have also been found in the study areas. The literacy rate in Retzawl is 90.10 per cent while that in Muolhoi is 98 per cent. The former village is mostly an agricultural one (68.85% agriculturalists) while the people in the latter village engage mostly in non-agricultural economic pursuits.

For the purpose of collecting empirical data standard anthropological methods have been used like non-participant observation, structured and unstructured interview, case study and genealogical methods. In-depth interviews with selective informants involving both individual and group discussions have been conducted as well. Secondary data has been collected from numerous published books, research journals, and unpublished documents.

Findings

The empirical data have revealed certain interesting facts regarding the Hmar marriage system which has undergone profound changes particularly due to their acceptance of Christianity. It is to be mentioned that among the Hmars in Dima Hasao district the first native evangelical preacher was Rev. Kama who was the paternal uncle of Rev. H. Thiek, a Church minister and a retired school headmaster of Muolhoi village. The researcher's personal interview with Rev. H. Thiek and Dr. Rev. L.S. Khawbung another Church minister and Director of Mobile Theological School, Synod, Haflong, brought to light the fact that Rev. Kama's father was Rev. Thiek's grandfather's elder brother. As Rev. Kama had no son and only daughters so he had adopted Rev. Thiek as his son. According to the above mentioned sources:

Kama Thiek Buhril was baptized in 1918 in Sartuinek, Manipur. He was a *thiempu* (traditional priest) who thought that sacrificial worship was not enough for obtaining salvation. He had a great desire to spread the Gospel of Christ among the Hmars in Assam and so with this zeal in mind he landed first in Hnachangzawl, a Hmar village in Dima Hasao and then settled in another neighbouring village called Vongzawl. Both these villages are located at a distance of about 55–60 kms. from Haflong town in the interior ranges of the Barail mountain. As he had a great knowledge on customary law he was accepted by the locals though after much hesitation and resistance. Though he was not educated himself but he could read and write in his mother-tongue and by that time the Roman script was already introduced among the Hmars. He opened Sunday school and started preaching about Christ from village to village. He was also a selfless worker among the orphans. In 1930 in the Synod meeting at Jatinga, Kama was made a member of the Sunday School Committee. In 1934 he was ordained as an evangelist at Harangajao village which was inhabited by Khasis then. Again in 1939 the missionaries ordained him as a Pastor in the church at Gobolchera, a Khasi village. Rev. Kama breathed his last on 26th December, 1972 in Vongzawl at the age of 102 years.

Since then the seeds of Christianity got sown among the Hmars of Dima Hasao district of Assam with the untiring efforts of Rev. Kama and his followers in the later days. The first church in

Retzawl and Muolhoi is the Presbyterian Church of India (P.C.I.) established in the year 1930 and 1949 respectively.

The system of marriage among the Hmars has undergone radical changes after their conversion. Much of the old ritual practices have now been replaced by new ones but certain important ones have been retained with modification. Generally from previous times marriage by negotiation and service are the preferred forms of marriage but marriage by choice is not uncommon while marriage by elopement is strictly dealt with by the imposition of fines and punishment. Previously marriages were conducted with the active involvement of the family members only but now the Church and the Church Ministers play an important role in the ceremony. The patriarchal Hmars follow clan exogamy though at times it is not strictly adhered to. The maternal uncle's daughter or a marriageable girl from that same clan is usually the preferred choice which prompts the sealing of bond between a man and his maternal uncle or *pu*. Previously polygamy was practised but now monogamy is the prevailing rule as the former is not supported by the church organizations. The maternal grandfather till now plays a decisive role who has the right to solemnize the marriage of his grandchild and takes the role of a father even if the parents are against it.

Traditional Marriage Rituals

In the previous times in marriage by negotiation, go-betweens called *palai* including the groom's side consisting of one of the son-in-laws and two other responsible adults of the clan along with a married lady would go to the selected bride's house for giving a formal notice of the invitation. Customarily a pot of *zu* or the locally brewed rice-beer would be carried along which would be sipped during conversation. Irrespective of the approval or disapproval of the girl's family a second visit would be made by the *palai* in which they used to bring *thirdam*, a hand-made iron hoe or axe and a girl's loin cloth called *puondam* the acceptance of which by the girl's father denoted the marriage agreement. The bride-price called *manlebul* and several other subsidiary prices in terms of *siel* or bison at the rate of Rs. 40 or Rs. 30 would be fixed on the second visit itself.

On the day of marriage when the groom's party would arrive,

the bride's father would arrange a grand feast. A big pig would be cut length-wise into two symmetrical halves, the head being excluded and the tail being added to the side that would be offered to the girl. The part offered to the groom's side would be cooked and eaten by the go-betweens immediately on arrival of the bride to the groom's house. The remaining half of the pig would be cooked and served into two equal parts in a big plate called *bongthleng* made of teak wood (*Gmelina arborea*). Each halves would again be divided into three smaller parts which would then be consumed together by go-betweens from both the groom and bride's side. This special pork preparation for the go-betweens is called *satuokthlang* which symbolizes the cementing of bond between both the families. Further, the go-betweens were to solve any dispute that might arise between the couple in future. There is no dowry system in the Hmar society but the bride receives certain goods from her father like personal belongings and apparels as clothes, baskets, necklaces, beads, country loom (loin loom), gin, spinning wheel, tools for field-work and many more amongst which *puonri* is a must which is a special cotton rug measuring six to eight feet made by females in the bride's family and given to her with the blessings of having many healthy children. In all the ceremonies related to marriage drinking of *zu* was a common feature.

Christian Marriage Rituals

In course of the researcher's interview with several Church Ministers, elderly as well as young couples it has come to light that even after conversion certain traditional norms are strictly adhered to by the people till today. Marriages are now solemnized in the church preferably in that church of which the groom is a member and a marriage certificate is issued to the couple after the wedding by the church concerned. The system of visit by the go-betweens from the groom's family to the girl's place is still prevalent but the carrying and drinking of *zu* has been replaced by the use of black tea. They carry teapot and other ingredients of tea and on reaching the girl's house the groom's brother-in-law takes to brewing of tea for all. The giving of *thirdam, puondam* and *puonri* is still practised by each Hmar. But, now-a-days mostly in the urban areas as there is dearth of experts for weaving of *puonri* so normal cotton quilt is used in lieu of it. The paying of *siel* or Rs. 40 as bride-price has been replaced by an amount ranging from Rs. 100 to Rs. 800 and sometimes above because of the scarcity of *siel* and the fact that the old rates are regarded as degrading the honour of the girl. Also a new system of putting up a notice in the respective churches of both the bride and groom regarding their marriage details around fifteen days ahead of the wedding is practised. Anybody who is against the marriage can tear the notice secretly but in such cases valid cause has to be presented in front of the church members or else the offender is fined.

The day before marriage the send-off ceremony takes place in the girl's father's home which is a formal way of bidding farewell to the to-be bride. The groom and his family's presence are optional. A prayer is conducted by the Church Minister (Pastor, Elder or Father) in presence of family members, relatives, friends and other guests who offer gifts as token of love and blessing to the to-be bride. After feasting in some cases the bride leaves for the groom's home if it is located in a different village or stays back in her father's home itself if the groom is also from the same place. The following day marriage is solemnized in the church where the Pastor conducts prayer and the couple takes vows and exchange wedding rings. On the same day or sometimes the next day, according to convenience a feast is organized in the groom's place. In many cases when the bride reaches the groom's home his mother called *nu* ties a turban called *hmarluokhum* on his forehead and spreads a specially woven shawl called *thangsuopuon* over the newly wedded couple and offers them boiled flesh of goat limb wrapped in banana leaf to eat. The belief attached to this particular customary practice is that the eating of goat flesh will render the bond of the newly married couple to be strong and durable capable of facing the adversities of life.

Previously in case of elopement the amount of bride-price was increased and additional heavy fines in the form of cattle were imposed on the boy's family. Also it was difficult to carry out negotiations. Now-a-days in case of elopement, the church plays a decisive role. The membership of both the run-away couple is temporarily suspended for six months during which they cannot take part in any church activities like preaching, attending service, Sunday school, etc. But repeated request from both the families as well as application for re-membership can bring down the period of punishment to three or four months after which they can participate in church activities like before. Also in case of elopement mostly on the request of the couple's parents a symbolic ceremony is allowed to take place in the outer verandah of the church in presence of the Pastor and only the immediate family members with as little publicity as possible. This is known as the second law of marriage or *danhnina*. In the first law of marriage applicable in case of marriage by negotiation, the ceremony takes place normally inside the church and is called *dankhatna*. Inter-tribe and inter-community marriages are found now-a-days among the Hmars. In the case of one of the spouse being a non-Christian he or she has to convert into Christianity before the marriage. Instances of marriages between Hmar and Nepalese have been found in the study areas where the Nepali males have adopted Hmar name, title and way of life.

Conclusion

The foregoing discussion points out certain vital issues concerning the acceptance of Christianity by the Hmars of Assam and its impact on their traditional marriage system. The Hmars are observing their customary practices which have been surviving since time immemorial. Marriage is held in high significance in the Hmar society. Though the entire population has embraced Christianity which has brought in certain new elements that are totally Christian in nature like solemnizing of marriages in church, wearing of wedding gowns and formal suits, exchanging of wedding rings, feasting with cakes and other bakery products, replacement of *zu* with tea and the like but the traditional marriage system has retained much of the pristine traits which point to the fact that the structure of the system is in the concrete state. The present marriage system of the Hmars is an admixture of two cultural elements which shows the syncretistic co-existence of the Christian as well Hmar way of life.

References

Bapui, V.T. 2011. *Oral Traditions of the Hmars,* 1st edition. Guwahati, Assam Institute of Research for Tribals and Scheduled Castes.

Das, B.M. 1970. *Anthropometry of the Tribal Groups of Assam, India*. Florida, Field Research Project.

Kallenberg, Brad J. 1995. "Conversion converted: A post-modern formulation of the doctrine of conversion." *The Evangelical Quarterly*, 67(4): 362.

Malinowski, Bronislaw. 1945. *The Dynamics of Culture Change, An Inquiry into the Race Relations in Africa*. New Haven: Yale University Press.

Marak, Q. 2012. "Culture change and continuity among the tribal communities in North East India: An overview." *Journal of Indian Anthropological Society*. 47 (2): 153-166.

Westermarck, Edward. 1992. *The History of Human Marriage*. Vol. I. New York, The Allerton Book Company.

9
Popular Myths, Legends and Folktales of the Dimasas

Humi Thaosen

Concept of Myths, Legends and Folktales

Quoting Simpson and Roud (2000: 254), myths are "stories about divine beings, generally arranged in a coherent system; they are revered as true and sacred; they are endorsed by rulers and priests; and closely linked to religion. Once this link is broken, and the actors in the story are not regarded as gods but as human heroes, giants or fairies, it is no longer a myth but a folktale. When the central actor is divine but the story is trivial....the result is religious legend, not myth."

According to Bascom (1981: 98), "myths are prose narratives which, in the society in which they are told, are considered to be truthful accounts of what happened in the remote past." Therefore, one can relate myths to those stories based on traditions, which are believed to be true to those who tell and hear it. The deep meaning behind a myth enables it to survive for a really long period of time.

It can be said that myths are the solutions given by men, to problems of origin in the past, which later came to be solved by science through inductive reasoning. In the words of Lalruanga (1984: PhD Thesis) "...myths speak about the creation of man, of animal, of the world, why a certain animal has its characteristics, why and how certain natural phenomena occurred, and how rituals and ceremonies originated. They are accepted on faith and taught to be believed."

Legends have been distinguished from myths by Delehaye (1907) in his words, "legends, on the other hand, has of necessity, some historical or topographical connection. It refers imaginary events to some real personage, or it localizes romantic stories in some definite spot." According to Bascom (1981: 98) "legends are prose narratives which, like myths, are regarded as true by the narrator and his audiences, but they are set in a period considered less remote, when the world was much as it is today." They tell of migrations and deeds of past heroes as well as local tales of buried treasures, ghosts and fairies etc. Though they are believed in as facts and may contain a certain element of historical truth, they cannot be treated as accurate accounts of historical events. The ideas can be faulty in its extreme form but appears as the nearest to the right way of looking at the matter. Thus, one can say that legends are generally used as a source to provide historical information about a particular culture or civilization.

Again, folktales are tales or fables, passed on from one generation to another, generally whose authors are unknown. They "are prose narratives which are regarded as fiction" (Bascom, 1981: 97). There may be many versions of the same folktale, which may also sometimes be regarded as partial truth, in course of time of their passage. Unlike myths and legends, folktales can be regarded as timeless and placeless and may be set in any time and at any place. Folktales usually recount the adventures of animal and human characteristics and can be categorized in many ways, such as, human tales, animal tales, trickster tales, jokes and humorous tales and moral tales etc. The important characteristic of folktale is the traditional nature of the material. It is handed down from the father to the son or from one person to another as it is remembered from generation to generation by word of mouth. In the folktales of many communities, they have conventional opening and closing formula, such as 'once upon a time...' and '...lived happily ever after.'

It is actually difficult to classify myths, legends and folktales into separate categories owing to the fact that they often overlap over one another. Earlier, it was taught that myths were stories devised to explain or to accompany rituals, but although the evidence suggests that the theory does not account for the origin of all myths, whose genesis remains a matter of speculation. In the last century, it was popular to think of myths as no more than naive attempts to explain the existence of natural phenomenon (Savill, 1977).

However, the three can be differentiated in the following manner: Three Forms of Prose Narratives (Lalruanga, 1984)

Form	*Belief*	*Time*	*Place*	*Attitude*	*Principal Characters*
Myth	Fact	Remote past	Different world: other or earlier	Sacred	Non-human
Legend	Fact	Recent past	World of today	Secular or sacred	Human
Folktale	Fiction	Anytime	Any place	Secular	Human or non-human

The Dimasas

The Dimasas are regarded as one of the autochthonous communities who have settled at the northeastern region of India. They are mainly distributed in Dima Hasao, Karbi Anglong, Cachar, Nagaon and Hojai districts of Assam, and Dimapur area of Nagaland. They follow their own pristine religion in altars called '*daikho*' and do not have any idol worship. Gods worshipped in '*daikhos*' have been termed 'area gods' by Damda (1978), owing to the fact that these *daikhos* are located in twelve different areas of jurisdiction of the ancestor gods. Therefore, there are twelve *daikhos* in total. The Dimasas propitiate a number of benevolent gods and goddesses; they also believe in malevolent gods or evil spirits who have to be appeased in order to prevent themselves from falling under their wrath of harm. The Dimasas had their ancient capitals at Dimapur, Maibang and Khaspur each of which still bears a host of archaeological ruins, proving of the rich architectural and royal grandeur of this group of people.

Objectives

The main objective of the chapter is to find out the myths, legends and folktales, based on popular personalities and deities, which bear important meaning and significance in the Dimasa society.

Methodology

Data for this chapter has been primarily collected by interview method from a few Dimasa resource persons, during the time period of May 2013 to September 2014, as well as by observation method, and by analysis of some secondary sources in the form of books. As most of the Dimasa oral narratives lack proper documentation, it was necessary to have a face-to-face conversation with the resource persons, who were mostly elderly persons, so that the required data on the pristine myths, legends and folktales could be properly collected. Mention may be made of the key informants: Mr. Sushindra Naiding (82) from Haflong, Mr. Lobam Kemprai (51) from Longma, Mr. Joinasaron Bathari (69) from Haflong et al.

Findings and Discussion

The Dimasas have a rich amalgamation of ancient myths, legends, folktales, ballads and fables, which speak boldly of their culture, traditions and the royal legacy they bear since the time of their glorious rulers. In this chapter, as already mentioned, attempt has been made to highlight some of the popular myths, legends and folktales mainly regarding the high persons, Gods and Goddesses, kings and queens, and common personalities. Although the three prose narratives—myths, legends and folktales are used ambiguously, yet based on the theory, they are discussed as follows:

1. *Arikhidima*

This story narrates the origin of the Dimasas; it is believed that at the beginning of the creation of the earth, an island in the sea was under the jurisdiction of one Bangla Raja who lived with his consort named Arikhidima, a divine bird. The latter wanted to create human beings in the world, therefore, after a divine conception, along with her husband, they searched for the suitable place and settled at a beautiful one, at the confluence of two rivers, namely, Dilaobra and Sangibra. Here, Arikhidima laid seven eggs, of which the first six hatched and were named as Sibarai, Du Raja, Naikhu Raja, Wa Raja, Gunyung Braiyung and Hamiadao respectively. They became the six Gods of the Dimasas who are also known as their ancestors. However, the seventh egg did not hatch leading to the youngest God Hamiadao to forcefully break it open and eventually outlet a plethora of evil spirits. These evil spirits are considered to be the main reasons behind all the disharmony, sickness, diseases, natural calamities and mishaps. Sibarai, the eldest son is regarded as all-in-all by the Dimasas as He is believed to guard them from the wrath and harmful works of the evil spirits.

2. *Dishru/Disrik*

There is a very popular legend among the Dimasas, regarding a princess named Dishru. A mighty Dimasa king had long wanted a son, as it was prophesized that if a son was born to him, his kingdom would flourish and if it was a daughter, then, it would bring a downfall to the kingdom. After ordering his queen and ministers to see to the proper birth if it were a son and to kill if a daughter would be born, the king left for a battle in another land for thirteen years. Alas, a daughter was born, and that being a very beautiful one, so much so that the queen and the ministers had no will to kill her. Therefore, the daughter was secretly brought up in the absence of the king. She was named Dishru; she grew up to become an even more beautiful maiden. On the return of the king after thirteen years, he happened to see Dishru and instantly fell for her beauty, without having the least clue that she was none other than his own daughter. The king declared that he would marry Dishru, which shocked the queen and the ministers. The queen was left with no other option but to tell him the truth about Dishru. This came as an utter shock as disgrace to the king. As he was lamenting over the blunder he committed, Dishru left the kingdom to some other place, far away from such a huge shame. The king realized his mistake and sent his ministers to go, look for Dishru and bring her back to the kingdom as the princess, as he is utterly guilty for his blunder. However, the ministers had some other intentions—they knew that if they brought back Dishru, she would be made the heir to the kingdom, which went against their desires to grab the power of the empire. Therefore, they went to search for Dishru, but on finding her, they conveyed her the wrong message saying that the king has ordered her to chose any of the two conditions: first, to return back to the kingdom and marry the king, or secondly, to never return back to the kingdom or keep any ties, again. Hearing this, the already saddened Dishru, was completely disheartened and promised never to return back to the kingdom.

On her way, Dishru met a few Dimasa men and as she lost track of her path, she asked them the way. However, much to her dismay, they didn't show her the path. Further ahead, she met a few Manipuri people, who showed her the path very promptly. Immediately, Dishru cursed upon the Dimasa people, that owing to her disgrace because of her beauty, let the all the beauty go away from the Dimasa girls to the Manipuri girls. This curse is still believed to be true among the Dimasa people.

3. *Snemduri*

A very known tragic legend or rather a fable, goes about a beloved sister of seven strong brothers. The name of the girl is Snemduri and she was one lovely girl, who knew the art of weaving beautiful clothes with expertise. As her brothers were very protective, they would never leave her alone. There was a giant demon, who would always seek for an opportunity, with the help of his witch sister, to capture Snemduri, as he wanted to marry her.

One day, Snemduri's brothers decided to go out to the forest to get the raw materials of her weaving loom. As she would be alone in the hut, the brothers locked her behind seven strong gates inside the hut and carefully asked her not to open the gates for anybody other than them. The demon and his sister had however been eavesdropping all this time and heard all the conversation of Snemduri and her brothers. The witch sister called out Snemduri's name aloud in the voice of one of her brothers to which the innocent girl thought to be really her brother. She immediately opened the gates and the demon entered inside shutting down all the seven gates. Finally, when the seven brothers arrived and called out for Snemduri, there was no response. They couldn't open the gates either and thought that their beloved sister died. In this depression, all the seven brothers committed suicide by making a big dump with what they had collected from the forest, setting it on fire and jumping into it.

Meanwhile, the demon was enthralled at the death of the seven brothers, before he could do any harm to Snemduri, she asked him to fetch some water from a river with a leaky bamboo pot.

The demon agreed and while he went to collect the water, Snemduri dressed herself with the best of the lot, put the husker in her position with another of her dress, jumped into the fire in the courtyard and met her death.

4. Hidimba

There is a legend by which the Dimasas are traced of their origin from the *Mahabharat* figure, Ghatotkach. During the exile of the Pandava brothers in a forest, the Pandava prince Bhim came across a demoness named Hidimba and her demon brother Hidimb. As the sister-brother duo try to make Bhim fall into their trap, instead Hidimba ends up falling in love with the prince and asks him to marry her. After a thorough consent from Kunti, the mother of the Pandavas, Bhim and Hidimba are married and Ghatotkach is born to them, who has a short yet major role to play in the *Mahabharat* battle. The Dimasa are said to be the descendants of Ghatotkach. In fact, many believe that the word 'Dimasa' has been derived from the name 'Hidimba' or 'Hirimba'.

5. Phanthao Raja

According to this legend, there was a lady who had six sons. The lady would prepare food and curry from her own kitchen garden, for her sons and herself. One day, when she plucked vegetables, there was some excreta of a python deposited on the vegetable. The lady had no other option but to cook it along with the excreta. After cooking and serving the food, the sons were amazed at the great taste of the curry and thought that the meat of the python would be more delicious. Therefore, the six brothers went out to look for the python. On the way, they met an old lady who adviced them to fetch water in a bamboo basket called '*dikhang*', the success of which would enable them to find and kill the snake. The brothers followed her instructions but failed.

Meanwhile, when the mother of the six brothers was plucking a brinjal from her garden, one of its thorns cut her finger and she conceived a son. Therefore, she named him Phanthao Raja, as '*phanthao*' in Dimasa means brinjal. Phanthao Raja grew up hearing about his six brothers' expedition for the python; he too decided to look for the python and kill it. Despite, the already anxious mother, Phanthao Raja left in search of his brothers and to kill the python. He again came across the same old lady who gave him the same task of collecting water from the bamboo basket. Witty as he was, Phanthao Raja succeeded in doing the said task and therefore met the snake which was a huge and long one. He killed the python and out of its stomach came out his six brothers, all unconscious. They woke up and seeing the dead snake, claimed that they had killed it and had been asleep all the time.

The six brothers did not listen when Phanthao Raja informed them that he was their youngest brother who had saved them from the snake, by killing it and setting them free. Instead, they took away the whole flesh of the python and refused to give any share to Phanthao Raja. This enraged the youngest brother and he cursed all of them saying that they all shall turn into reptiles like lizard and chameleon. This immediately came true, followed by the short demise of their mother, out of depression and dismay.

6. *Asampha*

The humorous tales of Asampha are very popular among the Dimasas. Asampha is the name of a foolish Dimasa man, who causes a lot of chaos and problem due to his foolishness. One of the popular tale goes as follows: Asampha's wife just bore a baby and the mother-son duo were laying on the bed under blankets. Asampha could not recognize his own baby and was scared to even go near him, despite his wife's constant convincing. He was sitting on top of the wooden log supporting the hut, immediately above the bed, staring at his own baby. Finally, when he was convinced, he jumped down directly from the wooden log to the bed over the newborn baby, with a heavy thud, killing the poor baby. This led to a great hue and cry all over the village and the wife of Asampha screamed out in agony. The villagers blamed Asampha for his foolishness and carelessness. They were very sorry for the wife for having been cursed with the fate of having as foolish a man, as her husband.

The Dimasas generally bury the corpse of a baby instead of cremating it. So, as supposed to, Asampha rolled his dead baby inside a mat and carrying it over his shoulders, started on his way to the place of burying. Foolish as he was, he unknowingly slipped off his own baby from the mat, on the way. After burying the mat alone, he returned back home. On the way, he came across the corpse of a baby, which was none other than his own. He stopped and looking over the baby's corpse, proudly exclaimed, 'It is not just mine, but also other man's babies who die.' Saying this, he laughed out loudly and returned home happily.

Even at present, when any person acts foolishly, he is mockingly called 'Asampha' by the Dimasa people.

7. Amaluh-Dimaluh and Longlabdao

The story of Amaluh-Dimaluh and Longlabdao is based on love and treachery, as well as reflects the significance of the forty male and forty-two female clans in the Dimasa society. Longlabdao belonged to the royal Hasnusa clan and was well-known for his valour in climbing hills and sloppy terrains. As a child, he was very fond of two girls namely Amaluh and Dimaluh, who grew up to be witches with extraordinary powers. The childhood affection between Longlabdao and the two witches grew into youthful love; however, since the witches were outside the forty male and forty-two female clans, marriage was not possible between them; also Longlabdao's mother was in hunt of a suitable bride from a respectable clan.

Sensing the situation, the witch sisters planned to trap Longlabdao; they lured him to accompany them to a deep forest, asked him to climb a champa tree and pluck flowers for their hair. Trapped in their sweet words, Longlabdao with all his sincerity did as asked. However, as he was plucking the flowers, the witches charmed the tree to gradually eat up Longlabdao's body. Having realized it, Longlabdao appealed them to inform his parents about the whole matter. The sisters agreed and called his parents, who, thereafter, came with a host of men to pray to the witches. The men began cutting the tree but it was too late; by the time it was done, everything of Longlabdao's body had already been devoured by the tree, except his tuft of hair.

One of the sisters, Amaluh, disappeared in fear of punishment, while the body of Dimaluh was found dead below the tree. The later had committed suicide, as she was truly in love with Longlabdao.

8. *Johaya*

According to legend, Johaya was a young and handsome man who lived in the village Delom Bathari, near Gunjung of Dima Hasao. Johaya had a special skill with playing drums, catching fishes and singing. Therefore, he was sought after the most in his village. However, he had to leave his village for another far-off village named Bosora due to the newly introduced conscription policy of the British. His life at Bosora was however worse—he was infested by mosquitoes and leeches, and also bore a harsh climate. He could never return back to his original village. The story of Johaya is narrated in the form of a ballad with a tinge of sadness.

9. *Harifa and Dumaidi*

The story of Harifa is another legend based on love between two individuals. Harifa was a young trader of a place called Lamsakhang of Karbi Anglong district. He had come to Dima Hasao district (then, North Cachar Hills), through the river Diyung, in order to sell his commodities at the market. As he rowed his boat upstream, he saw a young girl named Dumaidi on the banks of the river, who fell in love with Harifa, by seeing his charm. Dumaidi followed and asked him to marry her. She took him home, for the consent of her family. However, Harifa was humiliated and insulted by all her seven brothers and ageing mother. Therefore, he left for his land; but as he was rowing his boat downstream, Dumaidi stopped him and pleaded to take her with him. Initially, Harifa declined her proposal; but finally, he agreed, took her along, and lived happily together.

Thus, having narrated the nine popular myths, legends and folktales, most of which are transmitted to the next generation through oral narratives in the form of ballads, there are few implications which each one of them generate–either in social, religious, economic, historical and other aspects of the Dimasa society; two are highlighted as follows:

1. The story of Arikhidima, the divine bird, narrates about her hatching of seven eggs, of which the first six are propitiated as the benevolent ancestor gods in the traditional religious institutions called *daikho* as well as

the appeasement of malevolent gods who are regarded to be emerged from the seventh egg. The twelve *daikhos* has these very benevolent ancestor gods propitiated along with a host of many others. Thus, Arikhidima's story not only talks of the origin of man on earth, but also about the religious life of the Dimasa people.

2. The story of Dishru can be said to be the most popular one, owing to its unusual and tragic series of events. The father wanting to marry his own daughter, though unknowingly is something unheard of; moreover, her meeting the other tribes of the region, her curse and so on, generates a period-based plot during the Dimasa rule and contemporary Ahom, Manipuri and Naga rulers. A few theatre groups have been conducting plays on Dishru and earning huge laurels for spreading this legend to the world. A recent one was staged at Srimanta Sankardev Kalakshetra on 27th December, 2015.

Conclusion

Among many tales and folk beliefs of the Dimasas, the above discussed ones show the more popular ones. These are myths or legends, which are 'believed to be true' as they are narrated to ascertain their significance in the Dimasa culture and tradition. Some other personalities like Demalu (Demalik), Sengya Sambhudhan Phonglo and others are regarded more of historically important as freedom fighters and cultural heroes, rather than mere legends and myths.

A few things can be pointed out in this regard:

1. The myths and legends of the Dimasas enable to ascertain the kind of socio-religious significance that they bear in the society, as well as define their origin.
2. It is difficult to place each of these popular Dimasa folk narratives under one particular category, as myths, legends and folktales overlap each other.
3. There are slight differences in the same narratives, given by different people of the Dimasa community, which becomes difficult to ascertain the amount of authenticity

from the first source of narration passed down since the ancient times.

4. There are rarely any books written on the rich Dimasa narratives on folktales, ballads, myths and legends.
5. It is the need of the hour to collect and record as many folk narratives as possible of the Dimasa community and be preserved in writing.

References

Barua, Nagendra Nath. 1980. *Dimasa Society and Their Folk Songs:* N.N. Barua, Guwahati.

Bascom, W.R. 1981. *The Forms of Folklore: Prose Narratives, Contributions to Folkloristics.* Meerut, Archana Publications.

Chakraborty, Minakshi. 2000. "Traditional Culture and Folklore in Dimasa Society." In: *Tradition and Folklore in North East India.* Chapter 23, pp. 165-173. Delhi: Uppal Publishing House.

Hilaly, Sarah. 2006. "Defense of the cult of the wasr Goddess in the Formation of the Dimasa state." Ed by Sristidhar Dutta and Byomkesh Tripathi In: *Martial Tradition of North East India,* Chapter 18, pp. 211-219. Kolkata: MAKAIAS concept.

Lalruanga. 1984. A Study of Mizo Folk and Literature. Ph.D. Thesis submitted to Department of Folklore. Aizawl College, Mizoram.

Mukherjee, Rila. 2011. *Pelagic Passageways: The Northern Bay of Bengal Before Colonialism.* Delhi, Primus Books.

Muthukumaraswamy, M.D. 2006. *Folklore as Discourse.* Chennai, National Folk Centre Support Centre.

Savil, Sheila. 1977. *Pears Encyclopedia of Myths and Legends—Western and Northern Europe, Central and Southern Africa.* Londopn, Pelham Books Ltd.

10

Ethnicity, Certain Issues of It: With Special Reference to Karbi Anglong District of Assam

Minakshi Duarah and Prasanta Gogoi

Introduction

Ethnicity can be defined as a group of people who have distinct cultural traditions and distinguish themselves from most other people of the same society. It is a shared cultural heritage among the people of the group. It is used by people to identify themselves common to the people of same group but to differentiate from the other people of the same society. It differentiates people of the same group from other people of different groups in terms of race, kinship, language, culture, customs and religion. Ethnic issues are emotional and may take violent turn at any time. Extreme ethnicity divides a society into probably hostile and political families based on their ethnicity. Under ethnicity people believe themselves to be different from other ethnic groups in terms of race, language, culture, customs, etc. which leads to ethnocentrism, the assumption of the innate superiority of one's own culture and society which ultimately leads to ethnic conflict.

Ethnic group is a group of people, large or small, belonging to a particular race with their own common culture and tradition different from common culture of the country. The sociologists define an ethnic group as a cultural group of people based on race, language, territory, religion, customs, and beliefs who share common physical and/or social, cultural characteristics.

Karbi Anglong, being the largest district of Assam, is the habitation of principal tribal community the Karbis, with their own ethnic identity including other tribal communities like Dimasas, Bodos, Kukis, Tiwas, Garos, Rengmas, Kacharis, Adivasis, Man-Tai speaking, Khasi Tribe, Chakmas and non-tribal people. The Karbis belong to the Mongoloid group racially and linguistically belong to the Tibeto-Burman group. Although at present the Karbis inhabitate in Karbi Anglong District but they are also living in different districts of Assam like Dima-Hasao, Kamrup, Morigaon, Nagaon, Golaghat, Karimganj, Lakhimpur and Sonitpur districts. The Karbis along with other Tibeto-Burman language speaking people entered Assam from Central Asia. Culturally the Karbis are very rich and unique with their traditional dresses, ornaments, dances, music and folklores. They have their rich heritages, ritual traditions, customs, cultures, beliefs, language and legends etc. Like other tribes, the Karbis celebrate many festivals. The major festivals observed by the Karbis are Chomangkan, Rongker, Cho-jun, Hacha-Kekan, Chokkeroi etc.

Objectives

The objectives of the study are as follows:

1. To examine the causes of emergence of ethnicity among the Karbis of Karbi Anglong district of Assam.
2. To give a bird's eye view of the ethnic conflicts of the district.
3. To study the consequences of the ethnic conflicts.

Methodology

The study is analytical in nature. Data used in the study are collected from different sources like Journals, Newspapers, Books, Magazines, Records of police station, Research papers etc.

Ethnicity among the Karbis

Although ethnicity is a uniting force within a particular ethnic group, it often creates misunderstanding, and even in some cases leads to conflicting situations between and among different groups in a society which is ethnically diverse in nature. Although Karbis is the major ethnic group of Karbi Anglong, the district is the habitation of diverse ethnic groups for which ethnicity is very sensitive in the district. The major causes of growing ethnicity among the Karbis are as follows:

1. Fear of losing identity.
2. Feeling of deprivation and discrimination.
3. Growing number of educated unemployed.
4. Influx of outsiders
   a. Inter-district, b. Inter-state, c. Suspected illegal migrants from Bangladesh.
5. Encroachment of tribal traditional cultivable land by outsiders.
6. Mal-interpretation of leaders for political gain.
7. Large-scale underdevelopment.

Fear of Losing Identity

Fear of losing identity is a genuine and common problem of all the indigenous ethnic groups of N.E. India. In spite of having rich socio-cultural traditions people of different ethnic groups of North-East (particularly the small groups) have been suffering from the fear of losing identity because of uncontrolled influx of outsiders to their locality. They are even in the fear of losing their political hold in their locality. The Karbis are also not exception in this regard. Though the Karbis have political safeguard, socio-culturally they are also feeling discomfort and consequently they are becoming more ethnic.

Feeling of Deprivation

Feeling of deprivation is another major cause of ethnocentric developments among the Karbis. Many of the educated Karbis believe that they have been deprived and discriminated. The feeling of discrimination and distrust of Karbis towards the Government of Assam and its office bearers is fueled by the activities of many inefficient as well as corrupted administrative officers and other officers. Role of opportunity seekers are also to be mentioned in this regard.

Growing Number of Educated Unemployed

Growing number of educated unemployed is another cause of growing ethnicity among the Karbis. Because of increasing number of educated youth among the Karbis and lack of sufficient scope to be absorbed many have to remain unemployed. In the appointments made in the district both Karbis and Non-Karbis are getting appointments. On political ground also many appointments are made in the district. Money also play crucial role in this regard. The educated Karbi youth who have neither political backing nor money to bribe are deprived from the jobs. Some of the youth of Karbis feel that because of the presence of the non-Karbis they are not getting the job which leads to ethnocentric feelings.

Influx of Outsiders

Uncontrolled less and continuous influx of migrants to the district is another major factor contributing to the growth of the feeling of insecurity among the Karbis. The influx of outsiders to the district can be divided into four major forms as:

a. Inter-district
b. Inter-state
c. Immigrants from Nepal
d. Suspected immigrants from Bangladesh.

Many people from the other districts of Assam entered into the district for service or other purposes and some of them settled in the district permanently in some pockets of the district. Besides, some of the Assamese speaking people as well as other indigenous tribes have been living in the district even before creation of Karbi Anglong.

People from the overpopulated states of Bihar etc. of the country have entered into the district in a large scale and settled permanently occupying huge pockets of the district and started engagement in agricultural as well as business activities.

Silent immigration of Nepalis into the district is another serious matter of concern. Although most of them belong to ex-army families of Indian army, many of them have entered the district in search of free grazing land for their cattle.

The most serious immigration to the district is the immigration of suspected Bangladeshis. Number of Hindu Bangladeshis entered into the district at the time of war of independence of Bangladesh which is even still going on. Large scale immigration of suspected Muslim Bangladeshis is visible at the Assam-Nagaland border areas as well as border areas of Nagaon district.

All kinds of influx of outsiders into the district have created cloud of doubt among the Karbis regarding their identity in their homeland because the percentage of Karbi people is declining day by day.

Encroachment of the tribal traditional cultivable lands, by outsiders is another major cause of growing ethnicity in Karbi Anglong. Considering free areas many of the 'Jhum' areas of the tribal people are occupied by the outsiders. Besides, taking advantage of illiteracy many outsiders have taken the lands of tribal people in lease in return of small amount. At the time of election, many of the political leaders use ethnic identity for their political gain. For this they even don't hesitate to create misunderstanding among different groups of people of the same society.

Large-scale underdevelopment is another cause of dissatisfaction of Karbi people. In spite of receiving large amount of money for developmental activities the district is backward.

Ethnic Conflict in Karbi Anglong District

Ethnic conflict is a conflicting relationship between one ethnic group and the larger pluralistic society. It may be a conflict among two or more ethnic groups. It is a great challenge to the democratic setup of North-East India, consisting of Assam, Arunachal Pradesh, Meghalaya, Manipur, Mizoram, Nagaland and Tripura (Excluding Sikkim). Though ethnic conflict of the region, like the Naga conflict, originated from the British period, which became more acute only after independence, more particularly from 1960 onwards. At present, the ethnic conflict is visible in all the states of North East India, more particularly in Assam, Manipur, Nagaland and Tripura. Out of the entire districts of Assam, ethnic conflict is more acute in Karbi Anglong, formerly known as Mikir Hill district.

The two hill districts of Assam, Karbi Anglong and North Cachar Hills districts have been demanding an autonomous statehood since 1970 for the achievement of rapid socio-economic and political development. The two hill districts did not join in Meghalaya at the time of its formation because of the promise offered by the Government of Assam to provide greater autonomy and due to the fear of dominance by Christianized tribals.

The Karbi Anglong Autonomous State Demand Committee (KAASDCom.) constituted by political and non-political parties, inspired by Assam movement and supported by the youth organization like Autonomous State Demand Committee (ASDC), Karbi Students Association (KSA), All Dimasa Student Union (ADSU) demanded autonomous state under 244 (A) of the Indian Constitution. In spite of getting Autonomous Council under 6th Schedule of the constitution the ASDC and other youth and students organizations have been continuing their demand. Joint Action Committee for Autonomous State (JACAS) constituted by number of socio-political organizations of the district has been launching a democratic movement for the creation of an autonomous state in the district.

The district has been experiencing different internal conflicts as mentioned below:

Karbi-Kuki Conflict

Karbi-Kuki conflict continued from October 2003 to March 2004 between militant Karbi and Kuki tribal groups in Karbi Anglong district. The Kukis in the district are mainly scattered in Sinhason Hill based on ginger cultivation producing high quality of ginger every year. As a result of imposition of 'Gunda tax', abduction of Kuki ginger cultivators and imposition of economic blockade on ginger cultivation and marketing by Karbi outfit group United People Democratic Solidarity (UPDS), which was the main profession of the Kukis, the Kukis hired Manipur based Kuki extremists and formed Kuki Revolutionary Army (KRA) to protect their economic interest. Besides majority of Kuki population in Sinhason with their increased number and capture of unutilized land by the Kukis in the hill worried the Karbis. Moreover, the demand of Regional Council by the Kukis under Article 244 (B) of Indian Constitution is another cause of Karbi- Kuki conflict of the district. As retaliation of the killing of four Kuki students at Manja and throwing of a child to the fire by unidentified extremists, the Kukis abducted 12 Karbi villagers and the conflict outburst. In the conflict total 102 numbers of innocent Karbis and Kukis were killed and thousand of houses were burnt down.

Karbi-Khasi Conflict

In 2004 the ethnic conflict between the Karbis and the Khasis started in West Karbi Anglong for the frontier clash between Assam and Meghalaya. It resulted the killing of 10 persons and burning of more than 100 houses.

Bihari-Adivasi Conflict

The ethnic conflict between the Bihari and the Adivasi started on 18th July of 2005 at Ganapad village of Bokolia. Five persons were killed in the conflict and 88 houses were burnt down.

Karbi-Dimasa Conflict

Karbi-Dimasa conflict started on 27th December, 2005 because of the conflict between UPDS and Dima Halam Dauga (DHD). The demand of UPDS for withdrawal of DHD's designated camp stationed at Dhansiri as well as demand for 'Dimaraji' by the DHD including a large portion of Karbi Anglong district caused cold conflict between them. In September 26, 2005 as a result of the abduction and killing of 3 Auto-rickshaw drivers in Karbi village Rongkimi by unidentified Karbi extremists, 5 Karbis were killed by suspected Dimasa extremists on 2nd October, 2005 as a retaliation at Hemrai Terang village and the Karbi-Dimasa conflict was sparked off which continued for more than one month and resulted in brutal killing of at least 200 lives and burning of more than thousand houses.

The Nepalis and the Biharis are also targeted by the Karbi extremists from time to time as an effort of ethnic cleansing. On 8th August, 2007, 8 Hindivasis were killed by Karbi Longri North Cachar Liberation Front (KLNLF) in Aam Pahar. On 10th August, 2007, KLNLF killed 13 Biharis at Rong Terang village at Dolamora. On 11th August also another 3 Hindivasis were killed at Rongbongghat.

Adivasi (Ex-Tea tribe) ethnicity is also active in the district which is developed to ethnocentrism under the conscious effort of All Adivasi Students Association (AASA) and Adivasi outfit organisation All Adivasi National Liberation Army (AANLA). The goal of AANLA is to protect the tribal culture of Adivasi and is demanding the scheduled tribal status and rehabilitation of the displaced members of the community.

Karbi-Rengma Conflict

Karbi-Rengma conflict continued from December 2013 to January 2014 due to violent clashes between the ethnic insurgent Karbi People's Liberation Tigers (KPLT) and the Rengma Naga Hills Protection Force (RNHPF). The KPLT has been demanding the Hemprek Kanthim (self-ruled homeland) for the Karbi people. The RNHPF was formed in 2012 to protect the Rengma Nagas from the attack of KPLT and is demanding the creation of a regional council for the Rengma Nagas of Karbi Anglong. The main cause of the clashes between the two is attempts made by the KPLT to establish its control over traditional Rengma Naga areas. Ethnic clashes between the Karbis and the Rengma Nagas have led the death of 20 people; more than 3,000 people took shelter in relief camps.

Consequences of the Ethnic Conflict

Though the ethnic conflict has strengthened the unity of the concerned ethnic group, it has affected negatively on social system, economic system, educational environment and political scenario of Karbi Anglong. Many people lost their lives; thousand of houses were burnt down, looted. Huge amount of money have been diverted from the development activities to rehabilitate the ethnic conflict victims. The conflict has disrupted the normal life of the people. A general feeling of fear and mistrust has emerged among the people. In spite of being the largest district of Assam, Karbi Anglong is economically backward and it has few roadways, schools, hospitals, lack of adequate drinking water facilities, electricity facilities although the district has autonomy and huge amount of fund is provided by both Central and State Government per year for its development. People belong to remote hilly areas (for instance, Singhason hill) are still living in the primitive stage of development. Vast majority of people are engaged in old traditional practices of Jhum cultivation. In spite of having mineral resources like limestone, petroleum, forest resources like wild animals, valuable trees, the district is economically not advance because of lack of goodwill of the administration, terrorism, ethnic conflict, lack of consciousness among the general people etc.

Ethnic conflict has negative consequences on economy of the district. Multinational companies are not interested to invest in it because of its tense situation of frequent insurgency. The conflicts have created adverse environment for the native entrepreneurs also. The native entrepreneurs are also not encouraged to invest their money in the district in any productive activity because of demand of money by different extremist groups. Peace and co-operation, the pre-conditions for sound economic growth has been deteriorating in Karbi Anglong.

The outfits of different ethnic groups have attracted the attention of new generation towards terrorist activities and easy money neglecting the work culture. Infrastructural constructions have been delayed because of it. Most part of the district is yet to be connected by roadways for which the farmers can't get sufficient markets for their products and have to depend on middlemen.

Often bandhs called upon by different ethnic groups have adversely affected all-round development of the district. At the time of Karbi-Kuki conflict, huge amount of gingers and some other agricultural products were damaged.

In spite of having good prospects, tourism is not transformed into industry due to terrorism created by outfit of different groups. The tourists both foreign and native hesitate to visit the district.

Though the Central and State Govt. has provided huge amount of money for development of the district, the Karbi Anglong Autonomous Council has its own income sources like forest, land revenue etc., the district is still backward. Lion share of the developmental funds are appropriated by the dishonest bureaucrats, politicians, officials etc. The practical condition is that the corrupted persons have to pay a large sum of money to different militant groups in return of 'license' for more indulgence in corruption. All the facilities are consumed by the emerging (Creamy Layer) of the tribal groups; rich are becoming richer without change in economic condition of the poor tribal people.

The Government of India has undertaken different steps like Special Area Development Programme, Tribal Sub-Plans, Block Level Planning etc. for attaining integrated rural development and to create employment opportunities which (The Tribal Sub-Plan) seems to be in the conceptual level in Assam. It is not effective in Assam as the same scheme is implemented in different areas without considering local as well as ethnic group based problems.

Suggestions

Certain measures as mentioned below can be considered to solve ethnic conflicts:

- The Government should generate job opportunities and different self-employment programmes to educated, interested tribal youths. It will prohibit them from joining the extremist groups as well as reduce ethnic hatred.
- Entrepreneurship development is a very effective measure in this regard. It will attract the new generation to the work culture to earn money honestly instead of easy money.
- Spread of democratic values through education is a long termed but very effective measure to reduce ethnic conflicts. Tolerance, peaceful co-existence, mutual respect to the socio-cultural traditions of each other can easily reduce ethnic problems to a great extent.
- The govt. should not consider the ethnic extremism as mere law and order problem but should take initiative for political negotiation with the underground groups. It should take utmost steps for the rehabilitation of the extremists who are coming out to the main stream through proper training and financial assistance.
- When the situation of conflict arises, Government should take immediate and effective measures to control the situation so that it can't be spread.
- Steps should be taken to build confidence among the various conflicting ethnic groups, though it is a slow and long term process. Cultural tours, social works etc. help to establish mutual confidence among different groups which finally minimizes ethnic conflict. Both concerned

authority, social workers, non-governmental organizations can play active role in this regard.

- The newspapers, media should create trustworthiness among the people of different ethnic groups. They can create conducive environment for peaceful living.
- There must be proper manpower planning in the district to create educated, trained, healthy and conscious generation which will contribute to the economic development of the country as well as will help to reduce the extreme ethnicity.
- Law and order should be strictly maintained.

Conclusion

Karbi Anglong is a mini version of Assam where numbers of ethnic groups live. So, the probability of ethnic conflict is always acute here. But recently tense of ethnic conflict is decreasing to a great extent in the district which is a very positive indication. Leaders of the extremist groups are coming back to the main stream with their caders. The educated conscious section of the ethnic groups, intellectuals of the district, the Autonomous Council and the State Government can play important role to minimize the ethnic conflicts and the suggestions cited above can also be considered in this regard.

References

Baruah, Santi Saya [Eds.]. 2012. Extremism and Mass Violation of Human Rights in India with Special Reference to North-East India. Bokakhat: JDSG College.

Choudhury, Lutfar. 2014. "Ethnic Identity Question and the Autonomy Movement in Karbi Anglong." *The Ecoh* 2(3): 207-216.

Goswami, Namrata. 2006. *Terror in the Assam Hills*. Institute for Defense Studies and Analyses.

Kumar, B.B. [Eds.]. 2006. *Problems of Ethnicity in the North-East India*. Delhi, Astha Bharati.

Kumar, Praveen. 2004. "Strategic Analysis: Karbi-Kuki Clashes in Assam." *Institute for Defense Studies and Analyses*. 28(2).

Rahman, M.J. 2007. "Karbi Anglong: Theatre of violence." *Institute of Peace and Conflict Studies*.

11
Significance of *HOR* in the Cultural Tradition of the Karbis in Karbi Anglong, Assam

Bandita Teronpi

Introduction

The Karbis are one of the earliest settlers in the North East according to scholar. They speak a branch of the Tibeto-Burman languages and the majority of them live in the hilly region of Karbi Anglong in central Assam. They are the most numerous of all hill population in the present Assam who are also found scattered in various parts of the state and neighbouring states in the North East. Karbis who live in the plains of Guwahati, Sonapur and Morigaon in Assam and in the Ri-Bhoi areas of Meghalaya speak a dialect of the language which however has over 80 per cent of lexical similarities. The hill Karbis enjoy an autonomous administrative arrangement under the Sixth Schedule of the Indian Constitution which empowers them self-rule, though restricted in many ways. They had three (3) well-defined traditional kingdoms which still exist today in much reduced form and status. These traditional kings however continue to preside over the religious, cultural, judicial, and administrative functions governing the majority of the Karbis and their daily lives. Village chiefs, clan representatives and wise elders administer a Karbi village. Karbis have been traditionally known to be an 'industrious' farming community who cultivate paddy alongside varieties of other tubers, vegetables etc. Karbi women are excellent weavers who produce a range of intricate textile motifs which command high market values of today. Karbi social system is organized around five major clans with large number of corresponding sub-clans. Intermarriage within the same clan is forbidden.

They have a living oral tradition and folklore rich with varieties of creation myths and legends. According to a myth, Karbis trace their origin from the eggs of bats.

Review of Literature

The purpose of the literature review is to get an idea, an entry path to reach into the in-depth of the study. A perspective to the study is that it might have a direct or closely related conceptual design that would help to prepare a framework to the said theme. Though in many writings, it has been found that traditional drinks is very prevalent food items of the ethnic tribes of the North East and Assam, yet the difference is on which each tribe becomes unique is the ways of preparations and the beliefs in the culture. In an article, *'Biotechnology in Tradition–A process technology of alcoholic beverages practiced by different tribes of Arunachal Pradesh, North East India'* by methodology followed by Arunachalees for traditional fermented beverages have similarities with that of methods applied by tribes of states like Assam, Darjeeling Hills and Sikkim. Some myths are also associated with preparations of beverages like it is believed that certain members of the family have special ability to prepare the beverages and touching by anyone other than them spoil the whole preparation hence in almost all houses, there are special rooms exclusively for the preparation of drinks. In this room, no other persons are allowed to enter while process is in progress except those involved or permitted. Thereby, contamination by unwanted micro-organisms is controlled.

Another Article by a group of scholars on *'Jou: The traditional drink of the Bodo tribe of Assam and the North East'*, establishes that Amao is a potential source of yeast a medium used for fermenting cooked rice and preparing different kinds of *jao*. It has a large bearing on the social-cultural and personal lives of the Bodos of Kokrajar district of Assam and North East India. Plants species used in the preparation of *Amao* in present days is limited in comparison to older days and hence in-depth study or investigation of such technique would reveal the lost knowledge of those plants.

Yet another article is on *Hor, the traditional alcoholic beverage of Karbi tribe in Assam* by Robindra Teron, gives us the idea in the preparation of the yeast used while making alcohol, *thap,* the procedure of the distillation of the *Hor*. The paper gives the idea on the science of *Hor* along with the scientific nomenclature, but it does not give the idea of how this culture or the traditional knowledge came into the society or the creation story of it. How the knowledge of *Hor* began.

Materials and Methods

The area of study for the present work is the entire Karbi population of Karbi Anglong. As it was impossible to carry out other methods of data collection so sampling is done by purposive sampling. The purposive sampling is carried out in the rural areas in the two sub-divisions along with the headquarter of Karbi Anglong. Elderly men and women were exclusively selected for the study. The study was conducted to achieve the objective to study and to document the creation story of the *Hor*—the traditional drink of the Karbis of Karbi Anglong. The methods of data collection are both primary and secondary. Primary Data is collected by participatory method of structured and unstructured Interview and schedule. The questions included the history of the drink, the folklores of how it was created and the importance of the drink in the community, the method and the components used, the age group using mode of consumption, etc. The folklores of the Karbis are known through the various songs sung by the elders. The elderly people of the rural areas were requested to share their knowledge on the creation story of how *Hor* became a part and parcel in the community. The womenfolk were requested to share the process of preparation. The Secondary Data is collected from local published and unpublished articles and materials in local language.

Result and Discussion

Hor, its folklore and importance

Hor is a general term for all alcoholic beverages. *Hor Alang* is rice-beer which is generally used in religious rituals and varieties of social customs. According to Teron, *Hor Alang* is 'produced by fermentation of cooked rice with locally prepared yeast culture called *Thap…'* and is an 'integral part of the socio-cultural life of the Karbis.' This statement outlines the importance of *Hor* in the overall Karbi religious, social, and cultural milieu.

The importance of *Hor* can also be outlined by the fact that there are versions of the ritual songs about which talk about the origin of *Thap*, a yeast culture. The origin of *Thap* is actually the origin of *Hor*. According to a version of the myth of origin, a pair of birds, '*Kong*' and '*Ching*' gave up their lives to offer their '*angthin*' (livers) as per a divine wish. Women prepared '*thap*' by mixing the '*angthin*' with cooked rice as instructed divinely and made the first brew called '*Hor Alang*'. The following stanza from '*Thap Keplang*' (origin of *Thap*) is sung at rituals –

Do Ridem sar kangthim
Ridem Sar Kangthim the complete one Si bang kimlin rongloring
(So they led construction village loring)
Ridem sarkangthim si (Ridem
Sarkangrhim)
Mekar pen dolin (Village members with live)
La Kongchingpi angthin This Kongching-great heart Pen
thamra
pen
kujing
(With thamra bark for fermentation)
Bang tok pamolangjin
(They pounded nicely)
Si eri Ve-Domhin
(Thus our mothers Ve and Dom) Bang runrun atiprin (pen)
(They each house?)
Eri ser beleng
(Our mother gold bamboo winnowing tray) Si bang nangplang thap
ahim (ta) (Thus they came to being thap cake)
Bang pap langso mehin (They caused to become nice) Anonam etbin?
(Si run run atiprin pen) Ra'i nangnapkling? (So each house)
Si jo-thom bang nangpleng (Thus nights-three they came to pass)
Si alangbok doikling
(So water bubbles sparkling)
Si eri Ve-Domdhin
(Thus our mothers Ve and Dom)

Thapso pinkhailin
(Thap-sweet caused to become) Si bang sertharlim mehin (ta) (So theygold mat nice)
No nangkronglin (Ear sew at one end) Si linlanso vekling (So dangling hung)
Long porma angnim (Get porma [rice] aroma)
Si thapso ingtanghin
(Thus thap [fermented cake] matured)
Si urti kangdukhin (So earth tender)
Eri vedomhin
(Our mothers Ve and Dom)
Kathi angthipkling
(Kathi [earliest known variety of rice/deified] purest)
Bang tun ru pinchongcheng (They cooked caused to be first one)
Si bang thapso mehin (Thus they fermented cake well)
Pen ra'i mo langjin (ti) (And ? later sweet)
Dok nempru angnim (Sweet aromatic flavor) Hing aHor longcheng....
(Cooked brew obtained first...)

The above passage describes how *thap* first originated in a village called *'Rong Loring'* when the chief was *Ridem*, the complete one. The full version of the song describes how village women who went down to a beautiful hill stream to get water when the 'Father of the Universe' was observing from above. His two children, *Kong* and *Ching*, in the guise of birds came down flying and were circling above the hill stream. They flew over the *Loring* village. They flew over upstream and downstream where they gave their lives away. The women brought *Kong* and *Ching* and brought to the notice of elderly *Kave* and *Kadom*. They soaked the rice of *Dimro* and made it soft. They pounded the soft rice to powder and made rice-cakes. They mixed the dried *Kong-Ching* 'heart' with the rice. They fermented the cake with the heart of *'Kongching'* to make *'thâp'*.

When *'Thap Keplang'* is performed in rituals, both religious rituals and customary occasions, the origin myths of Rice or *'Sok Keplang'* and *'Bong'* or Bottlegourd are also recited. *Thap* is prepared from rice, the main ingredient from which *Hor* is prepared. The alcoholic beverage after distillation is then stored in *'bong'* bottlegourd with which it is offered to the Karbi deities or guests in old days. It is, therefore, customary for ritually performing the origin myths together.

How much importance the Karbis attach to *Hor* can be understood by the existence of these interesting folklores. There is another version of the origin of *Hor,* or *thap* described in the form of song. According to this version, *thap* was made from bird dropping as wished by Karbi divinity. *Hor* therefore is a divine gift in Karbi tradition.

Karbi worship can be complete. Actually, *Hor arak* as the distilled variety of alcohol so widely used in worships came to be used much later, according to oral tradition. *Hor Alang* or rice-beer was the standard item of oblation in older days which was also used in other important social customs such as *Adam Asar,* the Karbi traditional wedding ceremony.

In *Adam Asar,* wife givers are offered *Horlang* (*Hor alang*) in *bongkrok* (bottlegourd shell/Lagenaria Siceraria standl.) which is filled with *Horlang*. In such a formal occasion, the origin of *bong* is performed by a singer. A portion of the song is cited below –

Si chu urti kangdukjong So then earth tender
Si murong rongthirklong And Murong village strongly built
Murong athak-jong
Murong above-just
Si muring la asong
Thus Muring this group
Bang murong athakjong
They Murong above just
Chiphong patijong Village lie (stay)
Si murong rong asong
Thus Murong village group (or people) Junsok paberrong
Drink-raise (water) below Si murong rong-asong So Murong villagers
Bang ju chingvai lembom
They consult-discussed again and again Sumphi
pen sumphong
Sumphi and Sumphong Jerpo bang kethom
Friends they three
Ai li junsok paberrong
All we drink-raise downstream
Muring la asong
Muring this group/villagers Bang itangrem thu: ong
They looked down too much Mar'ik nangjojong
Clothes-soiled washed

Suva nangjojong Impurities washed Si tangrem thu'ong
So despised us too much Ronmai nangjibon Confront if need be
Pu bang sumphi pen sumphong Thus they Sumphi and Sumhong Tam achong kangton
Copper shields spared/prepared Tam anok kangton
Copper swords stored
Si bang ni-me sojitjong So they day good fixed
Si museng pen mulong
Thus Museng and Mulong (names of villages?) Si lolonang dei ron
So leave for battle
Pu sumphi pen sumphong Said Sumphi and Sumphong Moti bang-kethom Brothers' they-three
A-hakli-mar-jong Sisters all
Pen jengki chehopon
From clothes took out Si jengki tortomlomg So clothes covered with
Sipong pavenbong Turban caused to be cleaned Si chengtin avambong
Thus tucked waist
Si bangtam achong chepon
Thus they copper shields carried
Tam anok venvon
Copper swords shining
Si bang jerpobangkethom (le)
Thus they friends they three Bang chelo chom pa chom
They leave in uniform motion
Seng ui'ui pong pong Hearts blowing hot and cold Si la eri velidom
So this our mothersVe (kave)
Ka (dom) Aseng munthijom
Minds thinking deeply Murong rong angbong Murong village middle
Bang Harlongbi asong
They Harlongbi (name of person) group
Velongbi asong
Velongbi group Non klemji jeng chedon
Now will work thread bridging Pinchongji nim-rokom Will create traditions...

The origin story goes back to a period 'when the earth was young'. The story evolves from two warring villages called *Murong* and *Muring*. The two villages quarrel over use of river water which brings to the verge of a confrontation. *Murong* prepares to attack *Muring* with shields and swords. Two elderly women *Kave* and *Kadom* intervene and try to dissuade the youth to attend a wedding ceremony in the house of *Harlongbi* and *Velongbi*. Wisdom prevails finally as the warring parties abandon their weapons to take part in the wedding. In the wedding ordinary bottles of *Nongnong* (*Thungbergia grandflora* Roxb.) were used as alcohol container. Father of the Universe was saddened to see how pitiable it was for the Karbis because they did not have a proper bottle for ritual and social ceremonies. The father of the Universe then prayed with his divine colleagues and asked his two sons *Mon* and *Jon* to be dropped on the earth, in the middle of *Murong*. The elderly *Velibom* and *Velidom* picked them up and carried them on their backs as grandsons. They took them to the venue where wedding ceremony was in progress. Chief *Harbamon* was also excited and narrated how a dream revealed to him about the divine gift. The bottle gourds he dreamt were so similar with the ones now brought to the ceremony by the elderly women. It was how the Karbis obtained proper '*bong*' (bottle gourd) for ritual propitiation of *Pothe* (Great Father) and *Pithe* (Great Mother) and for offering to invited guests.

Hor—Beyond Culture

There is no society in the world which is immune to alcohol. Among the many many substances which humans 'have learnt to ingest in order to get special bodily sensations', alcohol is considered 'culturally the most important by far.' Scholars have argued that 'It was anciently the most wide-spread in use, the most widely valued as a ritual and societal artifact, the most deeply embedded in diverse cultures.' They also observed that 'Tribal people of all the major parts of the world knew alcoholic drinks.'

In one of the earliest observations during the colonial period, an American Baptist missionary, Rev. J. Rae, who visited the Karbi inhabited areas, bordering Sibsagar and Noagong, sometime between January to December 1836, had this account –

> "The Mikirs are very much addicted to the use of fermented liquors; everything it seems being regulated according to the liquor they get to drink; all ceremonies

of whatever nature, marriages, burials, etc. must have this indispensible beverage."

Rev. Rae, perhaps the first European to have ever set foot in the 'Mikir Country' had several such mentions of 'mad' addiction among the Karbis who otherwise 'did not indicate poverty…their women and children covered with silver bangles and earrings…some had brass, mixed with silver; and every village seemed to have an abundance of fowls, pigs, and sometimes goats.' This picture of drunkenness as portrayed by the missionary among the Karbis is a stark reminder of the reality which existed nearly two centuries ago, and unfortunately it still does.

Horlang was offered to guests, relatives and strangers in Karbi households as respect. The drink used to be a food item when members, young and old, would consume it together over a lunch or dinner without any taboo. The drink is consumed in community religious gatherings or festivals. There is a practice in many Karbi regions when a newborn's mouth would be smeared with a sprinkling of the drink to welcome the baby. Similarly, it is a must to offer a drink to a dead person at funeral ceremonies. This religious-cultural practice of offering *Hor* to the dead echoes similar tradition among northern Nigeria's Koyfer people who believe that 'a man's way to god is with a beer in hand', as mentioned by Mandelbaum.

But the cultural context of the use of *Hor* seems to end there as wholesale drunkenness has also caused a huge socio-economic problem in the society. As a result, the traditionally used *Horlang* or rice-beer has been replaced by *Hor,* the distilled variant, known as *arak* which is more lethal and poses a greater health risk. The use of *Hor acho* or concentrated alcohol has been known to Karbis as cure for dysentery, pharyngitis and cholera as mentioned by Teron. Besides this, the medicinal use of *Hor* among the Karbis seems to be extremely limited. What is notable is the brewing of alcohol in which is becoming a 'home-based industry' for many rural households, mainly engaged by women who have kept alive the traditional skills of alcoholic fermentation.

Conclusion

Hor is a common drink of the Karbis. However, religious, social, and cultural statuses determine if one deserves to be offered a bottle of *Hor* as a mark of respect. But the *Hor* is shared and consumed by all. Any one, irrespective of gender bias, may be honoured with *Hor* depending on the occasion. *Hor* is therefore a socially, culturally and religiously approved drink among the Karbis. But it was *Horlang* or rice-beer which was the common drink in older times. The switch over to *Hor* or the distilled variety may have been of much later occurrence according to existing folklore. Rice-beer, which according to current research, is found to possess a number of nutritional and therapeutic values. The anti-oxidant properties in rice beer may be beneficial in fighting many diseases. Researchers claim that 'antioxidant activity in the rice beer is most likely caused by the presence of phenolic acids, polyphenols and flavonoids from various indigenous herbs used in the preparation of the starter culture cake. These compounds are known to inhibit the oxidative mechanism that are responsible for many disorders and diseases in humans such as infections, diabetes, arthritis, cardiovascular diseases, cancer, Alzheimer's disease, AIDS and so on.' Researchers therefore claim that rice-beer 'has all the potential to become a value-added beverage.' Therefore, the consumption of *Hor* which accounts for considerable economic drain and health risks, there is reason to be optimistic about the benefits of *Horlang* if proper supervision and marketing can be ensured in the days to come.

References

Mandelbaum, David G. 1965. "Alcohol and Culture." *Current Anthropology*. Vol. 6, No. 3.

Teron, D.S. 2011. *Karbi Studies-Vol. 1.* Guwahati, Assam Book Hive, North East Printers.

Teron, R. 2006. "Hor, the traditional alcoholic beverage of Karbi Tribe in Assam." *Natural Product Radiance,* Vol. 5(5): 377-381.

Times of India, Jan 26, 2015 *NE's* rice beer has therapeutic value.

http://timesofindia.indiatimes.com/city/guwahati/NEs-rice-beer-has-therapeutic- value/articleshow/46014461.cms, accessed on December 7, 2015.

12

Reflecting on the Constitutional Dynamics of Real Versus Virtual Affirmative Action: Scheduling the *Adivasis* in Assam

Bipasha Rosy Lakra

Introduction[1]

Adivasis in classic representations or popular historiography by colonial ethnographers or anthropologists opened up new vistas for defining the cultural and identity prospects during colonial times which did serve as a mosaic of discourse of *adivasis* as the indigenous people. Later colonial administrators got engaged with the people and their land while contending with the indigenous knowledge and belief system. An observation by James Bodley that, 'revisionists assault on the "noble savage" and the wilderness idea come at the historical moment when the global culture's unsustainable cultural imperative of perpetual capital accumulation is reducing the earth's stocks...' highlights a void created amongst the idea of tribe in India.[2] However, Colonial epistemology also drew conclusions from Brahmanical notions of caste and the idea of race. Therefore, Victorian anthropology during these times was dominated by ideas of socio-cultural evolution that gained ground in the ethnography of Colonial administrators, dismantling appropriate meanings of 'caste' and 'tribe'. Moving away from the commonplace question of dominant non-tribal groups of India from the plains assimilating or integrating the tribal people, this study examines the case of a powerful tribal group suppressing another, i.e. Bodo tribe of Assam and settler *adivasis* from Central India. The present study takes up an unusual case of conflict between the local Bodo tribes of Assam and the Santhals, Uraons, Mundas and so on of Central India who migrated to Assam and other parts of the North-East since the nineteenth century as labour in the tea plantation industry. The major contention is the denial of Scheduled Tribe status to the *adivasis* in Assam; those migrated from Jharkhand, and Central Indian Tribal belt, for plantation purposes. Significantly and more ironic is that, the same racial tribal groups have maintained ST status in all states where they have migrated to or are original inhabitants, except Assam.

The *adivasi* migrants, in large numbers, living there for over a century have made the place their home. They reclaimed virgin land from forest not only for the tea plantation industry, but also for themselves, creating clusters of villages. This way they have nurtured and cultivated their tribal culture of the homeland. Today they form a distinct cultural group in the ethnic mosaic of Assam and claim, like their brethren in central India, that they are *adivasis* or original inhabitants of India like other tribes. The local tribes of Assam, especially Bodos, deny them this status, though it is conceded that they are also tribals, but as migrants they lose that status. That is why they label them disparagingly as 'tea tribes'. The major concern of the Bodo tribe regarding granting ST status to the *adivasis* would be a decline of various opportunities provided to them under the Constitutional provisions of being Scheduled Tribe in Kokrajhar and Udalgiri districts, where the study would be situated.

This phenomenon of ethnic conflict is often seen in tribal-majority regions, especially in the North-East. This has given rise to inter-tribal conflict, of which a commonly known example is the Naga-Kuki clash. However, the clash between *adivasi*-Bodo and other tribe has created the basis of exclusion of the suppressed group, which can be envisaged in binary terms: majority-minority, 'sons of the soil'-immigrants, local-outsiders, tribal-non-tribal, hills-plains, inter-tribal, or intra-tribal.

Given the strategic and sensitive border areas, low level of development, immense cultural diversity, and participatory democratic processes, social exclusion has resulted in perceptions of marginalization, deprivation, and identity losses, all adding to the strong basis of brands of autonomy seeking movements in the garb of regionalism, sub-nationalism, and ethnic politics, most often verging on extremism.

It is argued that settled *adivasi* community's anxiety for preservation of culture and language, often appearing as 'narcissist self-awareness', and their demand of autonomy, cannot be seen unilaterally as dysfunctional for a healthy civil society. Their aspirations should be seen rather as prerequisites for distributive justice, which no nation-state can neglect. 'Consciousness of kind' has long been an attribute of human groups, be it tribal or national communities. This 'consciousness' arising out of sharing a common habitat and culture—including language and social traditions—gives the tribe or a nation the resources for developing a common identity so essential for unified action as a group. It is a reference to consciousness, found expression in the assertion for self-identity, which is maintained and innate to them. Identity redefinition of the tribes on a wider scale and its assertion may be viewed as part of the overall process of social change and modernization of various groups of tribes in North East India. The study situates the case in a manner that puts forth certain basic questions to the provisions of the supreme law of the land—the Constitution under the scanner of development.

Questions

The centrality of the chapter lies in the research questions. The questions raised in the research chapter are as follows:

(1) How does the state make policies and accommodate certain binaries such as majority-minority, *adivasi*-tribes, local-migrant within its multi-cultural polity.

(2) How does one analyze and examine the concept and internal contestations of the term 'indigenous' and 'tribe' as articulated during colonial times and post-Independence.

Methodology

Research method employed in the chapter is that of secondary sources majorly owing to its theoretical rationale. Primary and secondary literary sources have been casted in the research chapter.

Primary literatures such as District Gazetteers, Supreme Court judgements, Government of India documents on classification of Scheduled Tribes in India are used.

Secondary literature such as newspaper articles, research articles, edited books, monologues, review articles are simultaneously referred to.

Brief History of Migration and Transplantation of Tribes

The study would analyze and study the quest for identity, claim of rights and development opportunities of the *adivasis* in a multi-cultural society of Assam. It critically analyses further the failure of the government to provide the provisions of Sixth Schedule and Scheduled Tribe status to the 'tea tribes' (a common terminology for the *adivasis* in North East).

The quest has developed into a militant phase particularly after the persecution by Bodos who were bent on being the only Scheduled Tribe in the Bodo Territorial Autonomous District (BTAD). The self-reliance and the dynamism of the *adivasis* born out of long struggle with nature are bound to shrink if the aspect of social solidarity, the self-maintenance and self-regulatory moves caused by the 'ethos' of the people are not taken into consideration. This in turn would worsen the condition between exploited and exploiter that took a sustained exploitation in addition to inherent underdevelopment. This lack in political lacunae, from where the question of identity and identity conflict is borne out of the cultural society, seems to disturb the parity between the *adivasis* and non-*adivasis* in Assam.

The context of political recognitions and its repercussions across ethnic lines is adopted and present in contested histories. The issues of cultural diversity are studied and theorized in various forms. Certain studies also entail distinctive normative and institutional structures. As one begins to delve with the particular communities involved in the conflicts, it is important to highlight their status and role in such ethnic complexities. The present situation dates back to their history of forced migration as tea plantation labourers. They were transplanted from areas such as the Chhotanagpur belt of now Jharkhand, Chhattisgarh, Madhya Pradesh and Odisha. However, the context of Permanent Settlement of 1793[3] meant to make tax collection easier in the

Calcutta Presidency, depended on individual land ownership and landlordism. The British Raj turned the *thikadars* and *jotedars* into *zamindars,* whom the local kings had appointed as tax collectors. Post the land laws, most of the tribes were denied their customary rights for their sustenance. Besides this they were ignorant of the land taxes, therefore leading to their smooth exploitation. The Permanent Settlement Act sparked the process of marginalization of *adivasi* communities that depended more on community property resources wherein land and forests belonged to an entire village. However, most tribes in Central India followed a form of individual ownership known as *khuntkatti,*[4] linked to the right of the descendants of the founder in a village to cultivate land in it, but even among them forests were community owned.

Permanent Settlement Act had serious repercussions on the community property resources as practiced by migrated tribes in Assam. It dislocated and eroded their cultural identity, weakened economic security leading to their impoverishment in a new land. The British Raj enacted the Assam Land Act, 1834 followed by the Wasteland Grant Rules, 1838 in the North East[5] for easy and quick availability of land for establishing huge tracts of tea estates. It was believed that the deprivation of livelihood of the tribes—North Eastern and central Indian—were a good choice for such labour. Owing to their alienation in their own land, tribes such as Ahom, Koch and Bodo[6] did not agree to work as tea plantation labourers. Also the Chinese bought by the Britishers could not match to the work conditions in the industry. Thus, the tribes from Central India were compelled to migrate, being cheapest source of indentured labour and ideal to work in the tea plantations as well as the factories. A considerable population from Bihar too, migrated for better wage payments in the industry. Therefore, most of the *adivasis* either migrated to the plantations forcibly, or to evade economic downswing due to droughts. In the latter context they worked in eastern and North Eastern India for about 6 months also known as *Chhau Masiya,* and then returned to their state for cultivation leaving their fields fallow for half a year.

Tea Plantation Labour and Framing of Identity—'Native versus Outsider'

The study envisages a critical notion of difference attached to *adivasi* dwellers in Assam. While most of the *adivasi* populations residing in Assam are tea plantation labourers, yet their settlements differ. A particular section of tribes reside in *bastis* and the other in tea garden colonies. Common to the two are their thought of 'self-image' and 'identity'. Therefore in a plantation regime, the notions of 'self' and 'identity' are interdependent.

The 'tea tribes' are a majority in lower Assam comprising of Kamrup and Goalpara regions. The *adivasis* form the majority in lower Assam while the other division is scantily occupied by the same community. While the *adivasis* in lower division of Assam speak Jharkhandi languages and are not fluent in *Akhomiya* languages, the population in upper Assam speak *Akhomiya,* but also speak Sadri—a common language used by the different tribes in Central India. Moreover, the tea garden management has made efforts to isolate the *adivasi* communities, considering them as 'outsiders'. Thus, their regimented work culture adds to their sense of dependence on the tea garden making their exploitation more intense and severe, owing to the fact that they have not been guaranteed Constitutional rights and supported politically.

While understanding and analyzing the context of guaranteeing Constitutional Rights *vis-à-vis* the concept of Human Rights issues that re-emerge in a single problematique, one has to remember the rigidity of their political status that has been static since Independence. Therefore, identity assertion and claim for certain Fundamental Rights raises and projects basic Constitutional questions in the work and policy formulation of the Indian Union. It brings forth a problem of the historically marginalized population and in a region where there has been an age old traditional conflicts between various ethnic communities and lines. Besides this, the *adivasi versus* the tribal conflict is a messy contention. The *Bodos* engaged in farming as opposed to *adivasis* who are mostly tea plantation labourers seem better in terms of self-assurance of their identity and as a being in their state. The *adivasis,* having lost their 'community property resources' and being more dependent on the tea management and plantation work have been robbed of their claim for indigenous identity of their own. However, the present political movements mobilized by few elite and educated *adivasi* people and stirred by *adivasi* students Union has been a blessing in disguise for the *adivasi* population. The educated and students union along with certain non-governmental organizations have managed to voice their concern on behalf of the remaining *adivasi* population, acting as their interpreters. Such *adivasi* mobilizations are opposed by the Bodos and the Assamese locals. One such incident witnessed some violence in a peaceful march in Kokrajhar district in the year 2007. As North East has witnessed certain ethnic tensions and conflicts, but there has been difference of reason for these. Pre-colonial tensions were based more on tribal principles and customary obligations, wherein the recent conflicts are guided by individual as well as common interests, not necessarily having inherent tribal connotations. The study faces certain challenges, in terms of already existing ethnic tensions in North East which could redefine the thought of Constitutional legislation.

An *Adivasi*—A Beastly Man?—An Anthropological Discussion

How do historians, anthropologists, sociologists and social scientists understand and interpret the meaning of the term '*adivasi*', 'tribe' and 'indigenous' people/community *vis-à-vis* the caste-centred hierarchical Indian society? In context of North East and Assam what is the common thread that differentiates 'tribe' from an '*adivasi*'? What should be the point of reference to examine and connect the histories of 'tribes'—both constructed as well as non-fabricated of North East and Central India?

A fresh attempt to review the above questions one needs to engage with certain historical and sociological dimensions while dealing with the concept of 'tribe', '*adivasi*' and an array of such terms associated with or its construction. However, one has to move beyond the paradigmatic study of Claude Levi Strauss' study of the *savage mind* or Verrier Elwin-G.S Ghurye's assertion of *isolationist* and *assimilationist* tendencies of the tribes to relate to it in contemporary times. The centrality of the term *adivasi* as an analytical term in humanities and social sciences subjects to constructions and contestations in cultural and political academic scholarships in its representations. The concept of *adivasi* is often associated with being 'indigenous' or disrupts/recognized with a 'tribal identity' appearing in Indian academic and activist writings. While both the terms—'Adivasi' and 'tribe' have a bearing on each other, however there is no singular trajectory to order them. Given the heterogeneous meaning of 'tribe' and 'Adivasi' in academic representations, one might categorize them into separate subjectivities.

The term *adivasi* is a Hindi term literally meaning—'original inhabitants' in a given geographical area.[7] The term has various connotations in terms of their relationships and wide ranging topographies and habitations. As noted by S. Bosu Mullick[8], the term was first used in a political context in the Jharkhand region of eastern India, with the formation of *Adivasi Mahasabha* (the Great Council of Adivasis) in 1938. Nationalists and non-tribal activists mobilized the term in 1940s, however, the debates on tribes were confined to aboriginals.[9]

However, the sociology of the term would not follow any suitable chronology due to the use of the term in a given tribe pertaining to Central India. The term is now translated as 'Indigenous Tribal People', and some refer this as 'First nations' those supporting the Cascadian Independence movement, to resonate with the inclusive agenda of International indigenous movement, which highlights and links indigenous autochthony to political, cultural and social aspect of the state as well as the globalised world.

The term 'Adivasi' being an old idea yet being defined and implemented in newer ways is articulated and in political and representational tensions within the fold of nation-state. However, these tensions are being re-read and produced in a manner so as to cater to the wide ranging academic and activist's contexts. Racial difference and multiculturism, which seems to underscore the idea of 'Adivasi' and its association with ethnicity, previously gained its legitimacy through ethnographic representations of India's 'aboriginal tribes and castes' and official responses to anti-colonial movements led by, and including these communities.[10] Tribal societies gained visibility in subaltern studies and exponents of radical historiography and indigenous studies have since interpreted these assertions as identity seeking movements and asserted that these movements enhance their articulation of defining 'Adivasi consciousness'. Memories and oral narratives pooled in opportunities to fashion political foundations as *Adivasi,* and bring colonial and post-colonial phases of ideological coordinate into action.

Adivasis in the 'Empire's Garden'

Adivasis constituted a major element in tea labour plantations of Assam. Advent of seventeenth century witnessed tea production as staple to the European commerce and trade. Under the impression that the British Raj would fare well in tea production in Assam, compelled them to introduce indigenous tea forests similar to Chinese model of production. They were convinced that Chinese skill and labour would be essential to transform the Assam forests into tea gardens. Therefore to cater to a large scale industrial production of tea, British white men needed a vast pool of cheap, docile, and labour that would be easily available. They relied on the assistance of the colonial state and other expertise from the imperial plantation enterprises. In the wake of 1830s, sub-continental labourers were recruited to the sugar plantations in Caribbean and Mauritius as replacements for African Slaves.[11,12]

The recruits also referred to as 'coolies' were tribes from Central and Eastern India. Anthropologist, Kaushik Ghosh describes the nineteenth-century phenomenon of the British conquest of Bengal's "wild frontier", the Chotanagpur-Santal hill territory, physically and economically dislocated its habitants. Fiery clashes between the Britishers and *adivasis* and rebellions pre-occupied the *adivasi* heartland in 1831-33—Kol rebellion, followed by the Santal rebellion of 1855-56. They were suppressed in a harsh manner while the momentum that was gained by *adivasis* soon lost its vigour. Colonial policy-makers as well as the White rulers had determined to "pacify" the Central Indian region and the *dikus*[13] such as the money-lenders; traders and landlords assisted them fulfilling their endeavours.

These groups were popular as recruits to work on mines, roads, and plantations. These recruits were also referred to as 'coolies' or 'hill coolies'. One of the major elements that got attached these coolies were their primitive traits of obedience and physical toil. In the early nineteenth century Brian Hodgson classified the tribal inhabitants of Chotanagpur and Assam as Turanian aboriginals belonging to the Tamulian race. By 1860s, ethnographic manuals separated the two groups in terms to match their status as colonial labourers. Bengal's lieutenant governer George Campbell modified Hodgson's scheme to reflect on inherent difference between the two communities. Campbell distinguished between two groups of aboriginals: Kolarian people of Chotanagpur and Kacharis of northeast frontier.[14]

Campbell argued that Kolarians were far superior to their fellow aboriginals—the Kacharis as tea plantation labourers, employing tenets of race science. He praised the Chotanagpur labourers as simple and industrious people unlike others who succumbed to the onslaught of modern civilization. The Kolarians steadily multiplied and provided for congenial labour required for various works. He expresses:

Partly on account of their tractable disposition and freedom from all caste and food prejudices, and more especially, I think, because of that want of attachment to the soil which distinguishes the Aboriginal from the Arian.[15] Campbell in his seminal work—*Ethnology of India*—worked finely on the different characteristics of Kolarians and Kacharis. The reality of Kolarians being brought to Assam for tea plantations and had plantations as their sole source of living, whereas the Kacharis peasants often had some land and hence had control over their labour. This trait of withstanding alien land and people was transformed by Campbell as racialised distinctions between Kolarians and Kacharis.

Kacharis and Chotanagpur Kolarians became tea's archetypal coolies. "Coolie" as a term originated from the term "Kuli", a Tamil word was used to denote low-level workers in the Indian Ocean labour market. However colonial ethnographers prescribed the term "Dhangar" to Kolarians, generically referred to aboriginal labourers in Calcutta. Therefore it gained a specific racial sense. In 1883, the influential Anglo-Indian lexicon Hobson-Jobson defined Dhangar as "the name by which members of various tribes of Chutia Nagpur [sic] are generally known when they go out to distant lands to seek employment as labourers (coolies)".[16]

Hence, Dhangar was the term associated with the Chotanagpur tribals which was absorbed as their identity. Their migratory existence lured the British colonial authorities to pave way in their heartland to exploit such opportunities for expanding their production processes. Steamers, roads and later railways carried women, men and children to the jungles of Upper Assam which was viewed as the "end of the world" and an unknown wilderness by the Kolarians.[17] They were compelled to migrate as there were scant opportunities and choice, as the British policies caused immense political and socio-economic dislocation. Forced commercialization by the British Raj, natural calamities and loss of livelihood forced the people to work in distant places. The famine of 1873-74 in North Bihar caused fresh spate of migration to Assam.[18] From the 1860s onwards, the British authority was looking forward to establish a legal establishment for coolie plantation labourers. An earlier problem of labour recruitment was reported as wrong policies. Earlier tea labouring groups such as the Chinese, Assamese and Kacharis were regarded as "lazy", "aggressive" or addicted to opium in contrast to the Kolarians who proved favourable to work under harsh conditions and environment but it also required submission to the British Raj, which neither the Chinese nor the original inhabitants of Assam were willing to do. Therefore, the colonial state passed a law such as the Native Labourers Act (1863) to facilitate the recruitment and control of Assam's migrant workforce.[19]

By the end of nineteenth century, Chotanagpur coolies were placed highest among Assam coolies, also known as "Class I junglies" in the planters. They were ranked the highest due to their physical resilience, labouring abilities and resistance to disease. A special correspondent of the *Times* reported on the tea coolie:

> The labourer has been withdrawn from the fierce battle of the millions amid the storm and stress of varying seasons into the constant shadow of prosperity and peace. For him and his like alone among the poor of India the problem of life is solved.[20]

The study puts forth the demand for Scheduled Tribe status to erstwhile 'Coolies' or 'Dhangars', or as popularly known as "tea tribes". Common to the study is the thought of 'self-image' and 'identity'. Therefore in a plantation regime, the notions of 'self' and 'identity' are interdependent. The phenomenal processing of self-image and identity is in proportion to the British Raj's ethos and sentiments they attached to the *adivasis*. Perhaps it mutated with the innate hatred of the host Assamese locals. This however culminated in newer forms of conflicts mostly referred to the ethnic clashes. Therefore, it is not a new phenomenon for an ethnic clash to persist, but a clash between two tribes for basic Constitutional privileges and guarantees is a reminder and questions the base of India being a modern liberal democracy.

Movements of populations belonging to different race, ethnicities and linguistic groups from one place to the other are an ongoing process within India over a century. Thus, a group or groups which are indigenous in respect to the country may not be indigenous to a particular region or state. Likewise, any community being indigenous and having specific Rights in a particular region and the same community being denied its Rights in some other region has found ground on its claims for development and Rights, which poses pertinent questions on the debates of affirmative action. This gains importance in the whole discourse of recognition due to specific realities of social marginalization of the tribes in India. Virginius Xaxa asserts that if one has to take into account the history of the *adivasis* in the Indian sub-continent—such as Oraons, Santhals and Khariyas, then it would date before the advent of certain tribes in North East itself. Tribes such as Oraon, Santhal, Ho, Khariya could be racially and historically different in Central India, but their geographical proximity, bound by culture and conventions define them under a singular idea—'Adivasi'.

Amidst these arguments, it is interesting to note that *adivasis*—especially Oraon, Munda, Khariya and Ho tribes who have a Scheduled Tribe status in Central India have not attained a similar status in Assam where they were coaxed and cajoled to migrate and work in the tea plantations of Assam. However, a basic question arises in this light is—whose problem is it anyway? Who should one hold responsible for such Constitutional and Human Rights ignominious debacle? The recognition as Scheduled Tribe forms the basic provisions for the *adivasis* in the Constitution.[21]

These provisions were aimed at undoing certain past wrongs by providing the legal basis for what is termed as *affirmative action*. In the infamous Nandabai Judgment of 2011 in Maharashtra,[22] the Supreme Court of India states:

> "Thus the generally accepted view now is that the original inhabitants of India were not the Dravidians but the pre-Dravidians Munda aborigines whose descendants presently live in parts of Chotanagpur (Jharkhand), Chhattisgarh, Orissa, West Bengal, etc., the Todas of the Nilgiris in Tamil Nadu, the tribals in the Andaman Islands, the *Adivasis* in various parts of India (especially in the forests and hills) e.g. Gonds, Santhals, Bhils, etc."[23]

A similar argument posed by Member of Parliament and an ardent advocate of *adivasis*, Jaipal Singh Munda is of fundamental nature to the study and engagement of due respect, Rights and privileges to the tribal community. The Constituent Assembly debates called on for righting old wrongs, meaningful engagement with what it means and signifies to be an *adivasi*, lack of legal and political autonomy and the Fifth or the Sixth Schedule too have not been able to resolve innate and deep-seated problems. This could also be called an extension of colonial oppression in a post-colonial modern empire. A brief speech of Jaipal Munda in the Constiruent Assembly brings to light the intricacies of forging ahead an argument for *adivasis*, their upliftment and respect for them as beings as opposed to '*junglies*':

> Mr. Chairman, Sir, I rise to speak on behalf of millions of unknown hordes—yet very important—of unrecognized warriors of freedom, the original people of India who have variously been known as backward tribes, primitive tribes, criminal tribes and everything else, Sir, I am proud to be a *Jungli*, that is the name by which we are known in my part of the country. Living as we do in the jungles, we know what it means to support this Resolution. . . . The whole history of my people is one of continuous exploitation and dispossession by the non-aboriginals of India punctuated by rebellions and disorder, and yet I take Pandit Jawahar Lal Nehru at his word. I take you all at your word that now we are going to start a new chapter, a new chapter of Independent India where there is equality of opportunity, where no one would be neglected...[24]

It is only by dealing justly, and not by a proclamation of empty words, that we will be able to shape a constitution which will mean real freedom.

The question that is of central importance here is: (1) how does one identify the autochthony of a particular tribe in relation to a territory, (2) and how does the government define such blurred boundaries of defining and scheduling the tribes in India. People living in a particular territory believe that they belong to a particular community and weave a strong sense of attachment to that region. There is an indication of recognition that they imply to themselves that they have prior rights as opposed to migrants. This is however evident when threatened by the incoming of other ethnic communities. It gains a negative impression when the opposing communities vie for political/legal rights or autonomy. In such a discourse, time plays a pivotal role to define the legitimacy of claims and rights. There have been numerous migrations in any given region that no "*jati*' exclaims Beteille[25], can make genuine grounds for making claim to be original inhabitants. This gains importance in the whole discourse of recognition due to specific realities of social marginalization of the tribes in India.

Conclusion

Identification of indigenous people and its recognition was a past problem for the government. New forms of problems have risen pertaining to recognition and fair amount of politics involved in it. Whether those associated with a given territory are indigenous to the territory is always contested. However, a pertinent question arises is the question that—'who then is the son of the soil?' Seemingly there could be no proper conclusion to it but the idea of Scheduled Tribe could be resolved with the positive intervention of the state and its mechanics.

Communities tend to promote self-patronage for their own interest. Further, the term 'Adivasi' is indeed expanded cutting across different tribes speaking different languages or dialects with distinct traditions. It is important to note that how is the category 'tribe' perceived by different sections of people. For the administrative, legal practitioners and academicians it would be as it is listed in the Constitution of India. However, for tribes and *adivasis*, it would be a sense of belonging to a particular tradition, custom and community, irrespective of their geographical placements.

Representation of history could be addressed to recover the sites of *adivasi* articulation, even if these sites emerged before the emergence of international indigenous peoples' discourse. It would be critical awareness and engagement of these representational practices that would elaborate the meaning of recognition and politics of belonging. However, the study opens new vistas of studying such communities, nonetheless notwithstanding any criticisms it showcases certain complexities attached to the emergence of post-modern phenomena in India. By chalking out the colonial and post-colonial frameworks of indigeneity, it would be easy to discern the path of *adivasi* studies in the academic scholarship.

Notes

1. The term 'tribe' has been used interchangeably with 'adivasi-s' to highlight the nature of Scheduling as per the Constitution of India.
2. James Bodley, "Revisionism in Ecological Anthropology", *Current Anthropology*, Aug-Oct, 1997.
3. Schverin, Detlef.1987. "The control of land and labour in Chhotanagpur, 1853-1948", in Dietmar Rothermund and D.C. Wadhwa (eds). *Zamindars, Mines and Peasants: Studies in the History of an Indian Coalfield and its Rural Hinterland*. New Delhi: Manohar Publications, pp. 21-68.
4. Sarkar, M.C. 1993. "Customary Rights in Land and Forest of the Tribals of Chhotanagpur-Santal-Pargana region," in Mrinal Miri (ed), pp. 97-108.
5. Goswami, Priyam.1999. *Assam in the Nineteenth Century: Industrialization and Colonial Penetration*. Guwahati and Delhi: Spectrum Publications.
6. *Ibid.*
7. Xaxa, V. (1999) "Tribes as indigenous people of India", *Economic and Political Weekly*, 34(51): 3589-95.
8. Bosu Mullick, S. (2003) "Introduction", in R.D. Munda and S. Bosu Mullick (eds.), *The Jharkhand Movement: Indigenous People's Struggle for Autonomy in India*, Copenhagen: International Work Group for Indigenous Affairs, iv-xvii.
9. Hardiman, D. (1987). *The Coming of the Devi: Adivasi Assertion in Western India*, New Delhi: Oxford University Press.
10. Xaxa, V. (1999) "Tribes as indigenous people of India", *Economic and Political Weekly*, 34(51): 3589-95.

    Bates, C. (1995). "Lost innocents and the loss of Innocence: Interpreting Adivasi Movements in South Asia", in R.H. Barnes, A. Gray and B. Kingsbury (eds) *Indigenous Peoples of Asia*, Ann Arbor: Association for Asian Studies, 103- 99.
11. Carter, Marina. (1995). *Servants, Sirdars and Settlers: Indians in Mauritius*. Delhi: Oxford University Press, 1995.
12. Tinker, Hugh. *A new System of slavery: The export of Indian Labour Overseas, 1830-1920*. London: Institute of Race Relations, 1974.

13. Diku, a Santali term meaning an 'outsider' amongst *adivasis* in Central India. The adivasis hated the Dikus for their exploitative character. They were seen as alien in their land.
14. Campbell, George. "The Ethnology of India". *Journal of the Asiatic Society of Bengal*, 30, no. 2 (1865).
15. *Ibid.*
16. Burnell, Arthur Coke, and Henry Yule. *Hobson-Jobson: A Glossary of Colloquial Anglo-Indian Words and Phrases*. London: Murray, 1883.
17. Assam Labour Enquiry Committee, "Remarks by Rev. W. Wuesti, German Lutheran Mission, Govindpur, Ranchi District."
18. Mackenzie, Alexander. *History of the Relations of the Government with the Hill Tribes of the North-East Frontier of Bengal*. Cambridge University Press, October 2013, Cambridge.
19. Meer, Y.S. *Documents of Indentured Labour: Natal, 1851-1917*. Durban: Institute of Black Research, 1980.
20. Cotton, H.J. *Indian and Home Memories*. London: Unwin,1911.
21. See the Indian Constitution, Articles 15(4)-(5), 16(4), 16(4A), 17, 46, 244(A), 330, 332, 335, 338(A), 339, Schedule V, Schedule VI.
22. Kailas & Ors v State of Maharashtra, [2011] 1 SCR 94 (India).
23. CRIMINAL APPEAL NO............ 11 .... /2011 (Arising out of Special Leave Petition (Crl) No. 10367 of 2010); Kailas & Others. Appellant(s) vs. State of Maharashtra TR. Respondent (s) Taluka P.S., paragraph-26.
24. Constituent Assembly Debates, note 49, vol 1 (19 December 1946) at 143-45 (Jaipal Singh). Chaired by Dr. Rajendra Prasad.
25. Beteille, A. (1998), "The Idea of Indigenous People", *Current Anthropology*, 39(2).

References

Akhup, A. 2015. *Identities and their Struggles in North East*. Kolkata, Adivaani.

Banerjee, M. 1993. *An Historical Outline of Pre-British Chotanagpur: From Earliest Times to 1765*. Ranchi, Educational Publications.

Banerjee, R. 2014. "Actualising Adivasi Self-Rule—The Only Panacea." *Yojana*. 22-25.

Bara, J. 2006. *Ordeals and Voices of the Indigenous Tribal People of India*. Guwahati, Indian Confederation of Indigenous and Tribal Peoples, North-East Zone.

Ch. Zama, M. 2013. *Emerging Literatures from North-East India: The Dynamics of Culture, Society and Identity*. New Delhi, Sage Publications.

Chhetri, H.B. 2005. *Adivasis and the Culture of Assam*. Kolkata, Ansh Publishing House.

Daniel J.Rycroft, S.D. 2011. *The Politics of Belonging in India.* London, Routledge Publications.

Das Gupta, S. 2012. *Narratives from the Margins: Aspects of Adivasi History in India.* New Delhi, Primus Books.

Debates, C.A. (Thursday, the 19th December 1946). CONSTITUENT ASSEMBLY OF INDIA-Volume I. New Delhi, Government of India.

India, S.C. 2011. *CRIMINAL APPEAL NO.11/2011 Arising out of Special Leave Petition (Crl) No. 10367 of 2010).* Supreme Court of India, New Delhi.

Jayal, N.G. 2013. *Citizenship and its Discontents: An Indian History.* New Delhi, Permanent Black.

Leuva, K. 1963. *The Asur: A study of Primitive Iron-Smelters.* New Delhi, Bharatiya Adimjati Sevak Sangh.

Pulloppillil, T. 1999. *Identity of Adivasis in Assam.* New Delhi, Indian Publishers Distributors.

Sharma, J. 2012. *Empire's Garden: Assam and the Making of India.* New Delhi, Permanent Black.

Sharma, K.R. 2008. *Agony of Plantation Workers in North-East India.* New Delhi, Kalpaz Publications.

Singh, Bhupinder. 1984. *The Saora Highlander: Leadership and Development.* Bombay, Somaiya Publication Private Limited.

Srivastava, V.K. 2013. *Tribes in India: Concepts, Institutions and Practices.* New Delhi, Serilas Publications.

T.B. Subba, 2003. *The Anthropology of North-East India.* New Delhi, Orient Longman Private Limited.

Xaxa, V. 2014. "Constitutional Provisions, Laws and Tribes." *Yojana.* 4-7.

13
KA SIAT BISEI (Archery): Mighty Stick and String of the Khasi

Natalie Jo-Anne Diengdoh

Introduction

Throughout the world scenes of archers with bows and arrows are common right from prehistoric to modern times though a precise indication of its invention is blur. Reflections of the importance of the bow and arrow register in numerous written and oral histories, artistic representations, literature and folklore. Early archaeological evidence is equally ambiguous because archery equipment consists of perishable materials, often little or none of it appears in the archaeological record except for arrow points. Small projectile points found at Old World Upper Palaeolithic sites may be the earliest evidence of bow-and-arrow technology (Clark, 1963: 59–61; Hong, 1992: 9), but their function is indefinite; they could have served as tips for either arrows or darts (McEwen et al. 1991: 76).

A prominent feature among the Khasi culture since ancient times is the invention of *U Khnam* (arrow) and *Ka Ryntieh* (bow), which is used in times of war, as a sport called *Ka Siat Bisei* (Archery) and in recent times as entertainment called *Teer*.

Objectives and Methodology

The chapter has the prime objective to reveal the cultural aspects and tradition of archery as prevalent among the Khasis. It has been prepared by consulting different secondary data sources. Primary data has also been collected to informal discussion and experiences through emic views are also shared.

Findings and Discussions

- *Ka ryntieh*–The Khasi bow is made of bamboo about 5 feet in height. The bamboo bowstring is called *"U spit, u shken and u siej-lieh."*[1]
- "A Bow is a curved bamboo which is joined at the ends by a string. It shoots aerodynamic projectiles called arrows. When the string is drawn back and then released the potential energy of the flexed stick is transformed into the velocity of the arrow."[2]
- *U Khnam* (arrow) is a slender bodied bamboo with a pointed head and feathers at the end."Khasi bows wielded by experts carry up to 200 yards. The average range may be said however to be 150 to 180 yards."[3] The *khnam* (arrow) are of two kinds *kipliang* (barbed headed) used for hunting and *sop* (plain headed) for *ka siatbisei* (archery).

"A Bow and arrow are interdependent on each other whether in hunting, war or in the sport of archery. *Ka ryntieh ïawbei* (ancestress's bow) and *u khnam suidnia* (maternal uncle's arrow) of a clan are protection and support to society at large."[4] Folk recount of *Ka Siat Bisei* (Archery) as a sport reminds us of *Ka Mei Ka Hukum* (Mother *Hukum)* who appeared before *U Mangring* in the form of a motherbearing a child on her back. She instructed *U Mangring* to design and make *U Khnam* (arrow) and *Ka Ryntieh* (bow). Overjoyed by the new sport the siblings *Batiton* and *Shynna* sons of *U Mangring and Ka Shinam* engaged in the sport of *ka siatbisei* (archery). With the advancement of time the sport gained popularity and people across the hills and dales would frequent the area to catch a glimpse of the brothers striking a target or two. Concerned with a good win gradually confusion crept in and as a solution *Ka Shinam* made *ling-dieng* (wooden plate) to be used as target to derive an articulate win. However, since the arrows had no identifiable difference, argument over the number of arrows that hit the target cropped up numerous times. Seeing this *U Mangring* marked *Batition*'s arrows with lime paste on the head and *Shynna*'s arrows with lime paste on the tail-end, which later came to be known as *U thohkhlieh* (head smeared) and *U thohtrai* (tail smeared). Once again *Ka Hukum* appeared before *U Mangring and Ka Shinam* and taught them how to smear bee wax mixed with herbs on the arrows to differentiate between the two sets. Till date the two coloured arrows namely *U namsaw* (red arrow) and *U namïong* (black arrow) are used, the red chosen by *Batiton* and the black by *Shynna,* identification of which is retained till the present day to identify the arrows of two opposing teams or individual archers.

Due to jealousy that sprung from the cordial relationship among the brothers *Kajang*'a neighbour of the village, broke the target (plate) and once again *KaHukum* appeared and designed a target called *U Mangkaliang* (cube made of bamboo sliver) which is used till the present day.

Mention must be made that *U Khnam* (arrow) and *Ka Ryntieh* (bow) have found expression in most ritual performances of the Khasi. It is observed that in the ritual performance of *Ka Jer Ka Thoh* (naming ceremony) of the Khasi, *Ka Ryntieh Ïawbei* (ancestress's bow) and *u khnam suidnia* (maternal uncle's arrow) are essential items for the sacred performance as they are considered as protection and support to the clan and society at large. "*Lai tylliki khnam ba la loit ïa u sop (ladadeiia u shynrang)*–It is only a *khunshynrang* (son) who bears the weight of a *ryntieh* (bow) and *laitylliki khnam* (three arrows) in *Ka Jer Ka Thoh* (naming ceremony). The three arrows used should be *ba la loit ïa u sop* (without the sharp iron at the tip), since its use at the ceremony is symbolic. The first arrow is to *ïada ïa lade* (self-defense) and protect *ka ïing ka sem* (home), the second to defend the *kur* (clan) and the third arrow is to safeguard *ka shnong ka thaw* (locality), *hima, shynshar khaddar* (territorial jurisdiction) of the *Hima* (state) or village. In times of war he is the protector, when disgrace is brought unto his *kur* (clan) he is the defender as a *kñi* (maternal uncle). Once he is sanctified with the three arrows he is also a *nongdwai* (performer/preacher) for he is empowered with the three arrows. The bow and arrow therefore is reckoned as a person's life time companion. Its presence in *Ka Jer Ka Thoh* is very important since it is associated with the child's responsibilities in life."[5]

Ka Siat Bisei (Archery) when associated with decrypt of dreams is called *Thoh-tim* or *Teer* which could translate into a rich windfall or heartbreak. *Teer,* a game of chance is the first form of gambling to be given official recognition in Shillong by the state government in 1982. Practiced since the 50s *Teer* is to a large extent associated with an understanding of numbers and numerology. Every element that features in a dream when recalled has significant figurative representation and decrypted in tabulation of numbers as a Khasi man is number 6 while a woman is represented by the number 5. The number 4 signifies blood, 7 is for a non-Khasi and animals, 9 for death, elders/ancestors and elephants, 3 for teeth, 8 for money, vehicle and water. These numbers when arranged appear in a rhythmic pattern as dreams of an accident as a cause of death of a Khasi male is 47 or 74 (as accident is bloodshed). Successful combination of numbers may quiver to a rich downpour.

Ka Siat Bisei (Archery) as the traditional sport of *UHynniewtrep* (seven huts) is also known as *Ka Rong Biria U Khasi,* believed to be as old as the Hills and a companion of man. Justice being the spirit of the game in the essence of *Ka Mei Ka Hukum* (Mother Hukum) or Creator the Mother Decree manifests in observation of the truth, dignity and righteousness. The might of renowned archer PhrunKharumnuid of Umphrup (Smit) about 15.8 km from Shillong is relived annually at *madan ïa sit, Hima Khyrim* (archer's ground of Khyrim State) at Smit. *KaRong Biria* in memory of PhrunKharumnuid is an annual rendezvous of archers from across the hills and dales of *U Hynniew Trep* (seven huts). Enthusiastic archers from Khadarshnong, Diengsong, Swer, Laitkroh, Nongjrong, Mawjrong, Mawrah, Mawkynling, Mawlai, Pynthor, Lumshyiap, Nongmynsong, Lumsohphoh, Upper Shillong, Mawpdang, Smit, Umphruh, Thangsning, Umtngew, Umpling, Laitkroh and Laitryngew were present at the 4th Bah PhrunKharumnuid Memorial Archery Competition, organized by the Regional Sports, Arts and Cultural Academy, held at MadanïasitSmit on the 23rd of January 2016.

With the passage of time *Ka Siat Bisei* (Archery) has evolved with tremendous folkloric expressions in terms of *Ka Shad Khasi* (Khasi dance) where male dancers drape *ka ryngkaprupashadien ha kaba la siehlaitylliki khnam rupa* (silver quiver with three silver arrows) around their shoulders, the lore of the dramatic separation of U SajarNangli, a General of Syiem (King) of Hima Sutnga in Jaintia Hills and MarkuhaiñSyiem in 1520 A.D. U. SajarNangli and 280 *Kur* (clans) dug the famed Thadlaskein Lake near Jowai with the tips of the arrows to celebrate the exodus. Another tale that depicts a lamentable scene is the tragic death of U SierLapalang on the slopes of Shillong Peak. The wail and cry of U SierLapalang's mother now translated into a dirge titled "*U SierLapalang*" still penetrates into the hearts of many a listener.

Notes

1. Gurdon, P.R.T. 2010 (Reprint). *The Khasis*, p. 24.
2. Diengdoh, Natalie. 2015. *Ka Jer Ka Thoh (naming ceremony) of the Khasi*, p. 28.
3. Gurdon, P.R.T. 2010 (Reprint). *The Khasis*, p. 56.
4. Diengdoh, Natalie. 2015. *Ka Jer Ka Thoh (naming ceremony) of the Khasi*, p. 28.
5. *Ibid.*, pp. 28-29.

References

Clark, J.G.D. 1963. "Neolithic bows from Somerset", England, and the prehistory of archery in northwestern Europe. *Proceedings of the Prehistoric Society*. 29: 50–98.

Greyson, Charles E. 2007. *Traditional Archery from Six Continents*, The Charles E. Grayson Collection. Columbia and London, University of Missouri Press.

Hong, Y. 1992. *Weapons in Ancient China*. New York, Science Press.

Kharmawphlang, Desmond L. 2006. "Poetry, Lore and Language. The Khasi Phawar Tradition", pp 26-30. In: *Folklore as Discourse*. ed by M.D. Muthukumaraswamy, Chennai: National Folklore Support Centre.

14
Culture and Tradition of the Naga Tribes of Nagaland

M. Elonbeni Ngullie

Introduction

The Nagas lived a life centred around agriculture and headhunting and the various rites and rituals connected to the two activities. The Naga people belong to the Mongoloid ethnic group. While dealing with the culture and history of the Naga people of the North East India one has to be conscious of the limitation because of their diverse social customs, tradition and belief practices, dialects etc.

The nineteenth century constituted a significant landmark in the history and culture of the tribal people of North East India. It witnesses a transition from tradition to modernity. It was also a period of social transformation and Cultural Revolution, like all other primitive oriental races the tribal people of North East India too came under the impact of colonial rule.

The impact of education and modernization on Lotha Naga society during the period under review does not only signify spectacular progress, gradual development incredible changes in the socio-economic, religious, educational and cultural fields, eradication of some evil practices such as head hunting, slavery, human sacrifices etc. Primarily based on superstitious beliefs, and unscientific understanding but also denotes the gradual decline in tribal art, craft and other creative impulses, disappearance of traditional administration, customary law and justice, social customs and tradition, abandonment of art and wood carving, destruction of indigenous industry, extinction of the popular social, and political institution. The alien culture dominated the indigenous culture which being detrimental to their tender sentiments greatly jeopardized their interest reflected in the age-old tradition system.

Objectives of the Study

1. To make a documentation of the oral history and traditional customary practice of the Lotha Naga tribe of Nagaland.
2. To study the Lotha Naga from tradition to modernity in the light of social mobility and change.
3. To examine the factors responsible for bringing change.

The specific hypothetical assumption for the present study is as follows:

1. To study the rich cultures and tradition of the Lotha Naga tribes of Nagaland.
2. Modernity and Christianity had a great impact on the culture and traditions of the Lotha Nagas.

Methodology

Research methodology is partly descriptive and partly casual. For this study, data and information has been collected with the help of direct interviews, unpublished manuscripts, literatures and magazines.

Naga Life and Culture

It is very difficult to give a general account of many tribes, covered by the word Naga. For there are both similarity and differences among different tribes, Like the Lotha shawls are also of several pattern and indicates the number of several gennas performed by the warriors. The ordinary shawl of the Lothas is known as Sudam, a white cloth with broad dark with blue horizontal strips, which is worn by boys and men who had performed no social "gennas".

The Phangrhup shawl can be worn by a man who had performed social genna. There is no cloths assigned to be worn after performing second social genna. The southern Lothas wear a cloth 'etasu' after performing the third social genna. Finally, a man who has completed a series of social genna by dragging a stone wear handsome cloth, which is called 'eshụmsu'.

The skirt of an unmarried girl is a plain blue one. On marriage, she wears a pretty skirt called *Loroesu*, dark blue with big squares of narrow white and redlines giving a sort of tartan effect. When her husband has dragged stone, she may change over to a skirt called Lungpensu.

Headhunting

Inter-village wars, culminating in the taking of enemy's heads were part of the everyday life among the Lotha Nagas in particular and the Naga society in general. Head-hunting was a practiced which organized out of beliefs that the soul-matters, on which all life depended, was stored in the head of the human being. So whatever a person was beheaded and his head taken to another village. The soul-matters inside the several head was also transferred to that village, the recipient village it was believed would gain in prosperity, its population would increase, cattle would multiply, and the crops would be luxuriant.

It would seem that the entire philosophy of the Lotha Naga life revolved around the practices of headhunting. It was not only the causes and effect of war, it was also the inscription for the Lotha Naga works of art. Most of the traditional Naga carving and patterns of textile have head-hunting as their motif. The village drum could not be beaten unless a head had been taken and placed on it.

The warriors who hunted a head were entitled to wear a special kinds of dress and ornaments, a person who did not have a single head to his credit had difficulty in getting a bride and become an object of ridicule with the girls. Women and children were not spared in head-hunting. In fact, women's head were considered a more prized trophy for a variety of reason. As the women were always given the maximum protection by the village folk, taken a women's head means penetrating deep into the adversary's rank with all its risk. Another reason was probably to reduce the population of an enemy by killing their womenfolk, and yet another reason could be the desire for women's hair which was useful for ornamental purposes.

The practice of headhunting which was of fundamental cultural and religious importance had completely disappeared. Young men hunt and killed it only to return in triumph and get ready for marriage. In curving the human figures emphasis is laid on the head by the artists.

The second important source of inspiration is the need for decorating the morung for the purpose of prestige and magic. The morung is the center of the male social life among the Lothas, it is a dormitory for the young unmarried men. Morung are guard – houses, recreational clubs, and center of education and have an important ceremonial purpose. Morung may vary in functions and size varies from tribe to tribe. There is no single pattern of architecture for the building. Morung pillars are adorned and carved in high relief and large and life size with human beings, tigers, elephants, hornbills mithuns etc.

Art and Craft

In the traditional Indian concept there is no clear-cut distinction between art and crafts. The Sanskrit term *Shilpa* includes both because it was felt by the ancient that art and craft are governed by the originality of expression and aesthetic consciousness. The art and craft of the Lotha Naga are inseperable for they are mostly associated despite their utilitarian aspects, with socio-religious rituals and ceremonies. Pottery is not a widely practiced craft in Nagaland. Revolving wheel is not used and the Lotha Naga tribal women have their own unique method of making pottery with hands. Usually the techniques vary according to the tribes and the geographical areas they inhabited. The most peculiar feature of the Lotha Naga pottery is that the design and motifs have been inspired by the design of the textiles.

Wood Carving

Wanchos, Konyaks and Phom tribes are some of the finest wood-carvers in the entire frontier areas. Wood carving finds expression mainly under three heads, firstly with head hunting, secondly with the decoration of the morungs or men's communal houses, and thirdly, the funerary images erected or other important person.

Ideas and Beliefs

The once unshakable faith of the Lotha Naga in their customary ways of life and approach to religion, the horizon that recedes as we approach it seems to be fast giving place to the new ideas. The tribesmen did not seem to have developed any mysterious relationship with any plant, animals or any other natural object. In other words, their religion was non-totemistic, unlike some of the Red Indians tribes which during the course of their long history acquired extremely intimate spiritual and mystic attachment with some plants or animals. Nagas have no idols and do not believe in image worship. The Ao's attach some importance to certain stones but they do it with the idea of worshipping them. The stones are supposed to be the abodes of certain spirits and it is to be appeasing the spirit and to offer sacrifices to the spirit to be kind to them that the stones are worshipped. The Lotha Naga religion and way of life is linked more heavenly bodies like the sun and the moon rather than the gods and goddesses that are merely figments of the imagination. The earth and the sky have greater significance in the traditional days. They had fear for supernatural power. The deities, it was felt, keep an eye on them and therefore, come to know the moments a man commits a crime, kills a person, steals or deprives some of the rightful property. Therefore, the villagers are afraid of doing something which is contrary to the customary belief or local practice. There are deities who control the earth, heaven and the land of the dead souls.

The supernatural forces managing the earth is held in greatest respect. And since this god can send any epidemic, storm, lightening, wind, etc., the whole village worship the deity periodically. Offering in the forms of cattle, pigs, fowls, eggs, and beer are offered during the worship. The religion of the tribesmen is neither a deep-rooted philosophy nor does it demand any spiritual or mystic participation by the followers. Human needs, biological functions, the fear of the unknown and darkness and many other feelings of wants and desires to a very great extent determine their religion which is not independent of magic, sorcery and ghosts. The Lotha do not think of religion, magic, sorcery and ghost separately, one independent of the other. For the Aos, the sun is the deity which can straightway affect the health of their cattle and crops. Therefore they go out to appease this force of nature by various ritualistic ceremonies involving great offering of mithuns, pigs, fowls, and eggs. Many other tribes hold the sun in high esteem. The Angamis believe the moon and the sun to be husband and wife. Their interpretation is very simple. The moon, they feel, is like a man who is not scared of moving about in the darkness while the sun remains hidden at night.

Generally, all tribes give a special status to the sun and the moon and it is only the interpretation that varies. Science being remote from the tribal life, the force of nature are the only benefactors. The sun, moon, earth-wind and water control their life.

Geena is often observed after every religious ceremony. It imposes upon an individual a number of restrictions. Thus, a person observing geena is not supposed to stir out of the house or village for a number of days. He is not supposed to talk to strangers. After religious ceremonies, the person is likely to be attacked by evil spirits and so he must keep chaste and to do this he had to refrain from eating meat and abstain from sexual intercourse with his wife. Geena is also observed in some cases unusual incident like fire, or earthquake took place or when someone dies under unnatural circumstances. As a result of this, the entire village would not go out or work for a number of days.

In case a person falls sick, many taboos are observed. Sickness is the doing of a spirit and the only way to relieve a person of suffering is to appease the spirit concerned by making appropriate sacrifices. It is believed by the Nagas that there are certain people amongst them who are capable of contacting the spirits. Such diviners, right from their childhood, exhibits such and are kept as understudies to the old masters of this art. Generally, they get trained and when they grow up, they are capable of falling in a trance. Many other items that can construed as instruments of magic are used to contact the spirit. These ceremonies which are probably one of the most ritualistic affairs of Lotha life gets into full swing when incantations are chanted. A lot of other sentences of magical significance are also uttered. The tribesmen feel that there exist certain spirits which are sympathetic to these religio-magical authorities. And on being invoked by them, these spirits pass into their bodies and they stay temporarily till the trance last.

Soothsayers are the men who have within them some divine powers to retrieve a man from the claws of an annoyed spirit. All these functions involving psychological conditions of a man are special jobs and thus the philosophers and the doctors. They are the mediator between spirits and ghosts and the powerless human beings. And they control the supernatural by appeasement and appeal.

All those phenomena that occur either due to nature's creations or due to man's own efforts are attributed to the powers of the supernatural as no explanations based on scientific principles are sought. The brave and hardy Naga is a firm believer in superstitions. A dream can be a serious affair. There are some that are taken to be the forerunner of good luck. Many dreams convey that some bad luck is about to befall. There are certain dreams that are still more serious and one that conveys an impending enemy attack has to be announced to the entire village. A dream would thus bring the whole village on guard and the villagers would start hectic preparations. It is not surprising that in some of the cases, the tribal dreams had proved true but there is no doubt that the majority of them proved otherwise.

Probably the effects of the dreams are more psychological than magical. It is said that when the body is asleep the spirit leaves the body and establishes contact with other spirits. Thus they know of the events to come in advance. The village priest presides over all the village functions and conducts all the ceremonies. The villagers work for him in his fields voluntarily and show him great respect.

In this way, the village priest and the soothsayers, along with several other functionaries, guide the tribesmen along the established code of conduct. By appealing to and appeasing the supernatural, by interpreting the dreams, and by helping the people to sustain their faith in religio-magical thought-system, they regulate the life of the great Naga community.

Religion

Before the introduction of Christianity in 1870s, the Lotha Nagas were animists. They used to believe in different malevolent and benevolent spirits and used to propitiate the spirit to cure the illness and ward off untoward happenings. This they used to do by offering rice, rice-beer, meat etc. to the spirits. Of course they had the idea of a Supreme One and considered him aloof from the worldly affairs. They believe in soul and thought that the dead men go to the particular place and stayed there without any reference to heaven or hell. There was no connection of sin or virtue or bad or a good place for the soul to repair after death. These beliefs and practices are still found among the non-Christians and even among the Christians in interior villages where the Christian philosophy had not yet taken deep root.

Christianity came to Nagaland little before the British administration entered here. Christianity was already in Assam, since 1836. Before the British came to Naga Hills, and the people of the border areas came in contact in Assam. The earliest case of Christian conversion occurred in 1851 when some Aos got converted in Sibsagar. Probably they were staying there and got themselves converted. Later after two decades some people of Molung village of Ao areas themselves got converted in December 1872 in the village itself and that is the beginning of Christianity in this soil. Among the Lothas, the first Christian was W.E. Whitter. He started his work in 1885 in Vankhousung about five kilometers from Wokha town. And gradually the religion spread among the Lothas. Though Whitter did not found much favour with the people, the work was accomplished by subsequent preachers.

Ao being the pioneer in Christianity and education. They started preaching the religion among other tribes. Not only the Ao Baptist Christian Association organized the Christian activity among others but it was also that organization which brought out *Bible* in other tribal languages also.

Things continued like this for many years and all this time it was the foreign Missionaries who were at the head of all these activities. During the year of transfer of power to India, or Independence of India and thereafter, the Nagas were demanding separation from India. It was believed that the foreign Christian Missionaries had a strong hand in making the Nagas this claim. And therefore from early 1950s, the visas of foreign missionaries were not renewed so gradually in the place. After their departure the responsibilities of the Christian Mission work had developed to the Nagas themselves.

One of the principles of American Mission is this that one of the sacred duty of a Christian is to preach it. Because of this, it is being practiced by many people at present. The overwhelming majority of Christians in Nagaland belonged to the denomination of American Baptist Mission, though later there have come other denominations also such as Roman Catholic Assembly of God, Penticostal, etc. The Roman Catholic of late, have made a sound footing, and they have started many schools, almost one to every administrative centers.

After becoming Christian, the people have given up some of their old beliefs and practices but since traditions die hard some of them still persist or have modified to suit Christian philosophy. One of them is the belief in spirit. Though in the villages still the belief in the spirits continues, the educated Christians called it *Satan*. Another is personification in the animals, or wraith. It is believed that some people can take it in the forms of tiger will get injured or killed as the case may be. This belief is common among the Christians too, apart from these, there is a magic cure of illness. In some villages are found medicinemen and women who claim to cure illness of a person by drawing out pebbles, piece of ponds chewed leaves, etc. from the body of the sick person without leaving any mark where it came from. Apparently this is a magic cure and the entire villages believed in it.

Rituals, Feasts and Related Art Forms

An integral part of the social system in the life of the Lotha Naga used to be a remarkable institution called Feast of Merits. There were a series of celebrations the exact nature of which differed from group to group and marked in all groups the growth of a man's wealth and its consequent rise in status. The series was strictly prescribed and everyman try to proceed as far in its as his means permitted, for on the feasts he had given his social status depended. Each step cost more than the preceding one, though none was obligatory.

A man could carry out as many as he can afford. The ceremonies required the killing large number of cattle and pigs for feasting the village community and sometimes friends from neighbouring villages. An essential part of every ritual feast was this sacrifice of animals. A mithun was sacrificed at the final. The sacrificed animals according to the custom of some tribes such as Northern Sangtams were dragged through the village and then killed by an old man of the clan in front of the feaster's house, while tied to the forked wooden post called "genna post", set up in memory of the feast. He dispatched them with a spear.

The sacrifice fire was lit at the spot from embers of a specific fire previously kindled inside, the feaster's house for brewing rice-beer. In some tribes, the ceremonies included the pulling of a stone and its erecting it in memory of the feast.

Among the Angamis, Maos and Marams, the final ceremony was preceded by sacrifice of mithuns and also by pulling of its stone and its erection in front of the house of the giver of the feast, or in some conspicuous places near one of the path of the field. In the areas inhabited by these tribes may be seen dotted all over the villages and its outskirts great number of monoliths some of inconsiderable size, others occasionally so massive as to make the observer wonder at the labour which must have been necessarily to haul them up to the village and erect them where they stand even today. These monoliths were erected to commemorate the final ceremony performed by the individual at which they feasted the whole community.

Various types of monuments to commemorate the feast were erected usually near the giver's house. Some tribes set up stone, other raised Y-shaped wooden posts to which the sacrificial animals were tied and killed during the ceremony.

Events of Social Change

There are certain eventful factors which has been responsible for bringing social changes among the Lotha society:

1. Advent of the missionary to Nagaland and bringing education to Lotha society in particular and Naga people in general.
2. Carving Naga Hills as part of Assam for bringing effective administration control and thus paving the way for the incoming of all official and intermixing with the native people.
3. Rapid growth of education at primary, secondary, college and university level and few professional education solved many problems and created new gaps as well modernization in Naga society needs to be looked into the background of

the physical features of the state, and historical events. Ensuing discussion confirm the role of education in bringing modernization in the Naga society. Modernization stands for discriminate selection between what is worthy and what is unsuitable in the particular situation.

Education as an Agent of Modernization

As modernization emphasizes new way of thinking, it can be achieved only by improving and extending education. In fact, experts are of the opinion that "one sure way to modernize is to spread education to produced, educated and skilled citizens and train and adequate and competent intellegentsia"(Anand 1980). In this ways, Lothas too are moving to the world of knowledge visualized by Spinoza in the seventeen century. "The more the mind knows, the better it understand its force and the order of its nature, the more it understand its force or strength, the better it will be able to direct itself and lay down rules for itself and more it understand the order of nature".

Education plays an important role in modernization and transformation of the Lotha Naga society. With the introduction of modern education, it has accelerated the process of development in all spheres of life. Education had impacted the Naga society like physical, social, economic, moral and their religious outlook.

Impact of Urbanization, Transport and Communication

Cultivation and especially Jhum cultivation is the mainly practiced since time immemorial. Both men and women participate in the Jhum culture right from the time of clearance of the jungle and burning till the paddy is finally stored in the granary. There is no significant division of labour between man and woman as everyone works according to his or her capacity. However, it is to be noted that, no self-respecting Naga man will ever assign hard work, such as carrying of heavy loads, etc. to a woman. In the traditional Lotha society men and women contributed, equally towards the economics of the family. It could be said that women contributed even more because while she could work equally with the men in the field, she also had to do work at home in which men did not help, household duties are the responsibilities of the women.

In addition to this many womenfolk are engaged in selling the agricultural and farm products in the market such as vegetables, fruits, cottage industries products like handicrafts, shawls etc. Many women are involved in running shops. The contribution of women in the service sectors i.e. government service until the attainment of government service was very negligible. However, with the introduction of modern education, growth of towns and cities, communication facilities women had access to employment opportunities and women are seen holding high ranking government offices. Educated women today are more into the profession of teaching, besides their home service. There are qualified female doctors, lawyers, nurses and state and central Administrative civil service officers.

They have begun to realize a new identity that they can hold any position which are not assigned in the traditional customs, convention nor by rights, by virtue of their own merit through competitive examinations. Women's entry into professional employment outside the home has opened a new chapter and therefore represents a radical change in the status of women in Naga society in general and women in particular. In modern economic business venture and small scale cottage-industry productions are successfully carried out more by women.

Impact of Science and Technological Development

The discoveries of sciences and technology have led to the greatest revolution in human history. Impact of science and technology has made considerable contribution to social mobility and social change among the Nagas in general and women in particular. The introduction of power driven machines and vehicles and adoption of sophisticated means of communication has brought about considerable change in the society. With fast growing urban towns, new classes have came into being and new ideologies have also been born. Impact of science and technology has affected in the sphere of family, marriage, social and economic, and political institutions. The first and foremost impact has resulted in the progressive decline of well-felling among the community life.

The values have undergone with drastic transformation. Changes in value also resulted in disorganization of family life. Marriage is no more an affair between families but also on individuals concern and selection. The status of women has considerably become higher and higher and they enjoy relative economic independence and their outlook on life has changed. Impact of science and technology is another important factor of social and occupational change that determines individual to climb up social ladder in the society.

The relation between various people are no longer based on tradition but are guided by the calculus of self-interest, materialism, individualism, impersonality, specialization etc., are the result of technological changes. In urban life the technological advance has produced decline in the community feeling, over-valuation of time, decline in social control, and decline in moral standards.

At present, weaving, domestic handicrafts and agricultural tools are produced with slightly improved technology. With the introduction of the cottage industries Training and Production Centers in several places, handloom and knitting machines are also introduced where training is imparted to local women. The D.R.D.A. Department assists by giving stipends for providing training to women who are interested to learn sewing, knitting and handlooms and for the class 10 passed students they also assist students in training like typing. The industry department also assists students to learn stenography for the class 12 passed and above. Blacksmithy, carpentry, woodcarving and pottery making are encouraged. Now a number of saw mills and stone crushers are being established in the area in which many women were employed as a labour (Singh 1987).

In agriculture production too, the use of organic economic friendly manures and fertilizers was also introduced by the agricultural department of the government and the response from the people has been encouraging. Thus, the impact of science and technology has been felt in the life of the Lotha Nagas in all walks of life from household activities to agricultural and industrial production. The process of change in traditional technology to modern technology is a fast changing process in the area due to development in education and related and inevitable and socio-economic development (Thongs, 1997).

Social change is the change in established patterns of social relations, or change in social values, or change in structure and subsystems operating in society. Social change may be partial or total, though mostly it is partial. Just as change in the examination systems is partial change in the educational system, similarly enacting a law which prescribes punishment for refusing entry to untouchables in Hindu temples, or a law which legally permits divorce in the society, or a law which does not permit marriage below the specific age, might be called partial changes in a society.

Social development is the process of planned institutional change to bring about better adjustment between human needs and aspiration on the one hand and social policies and programmes on the other. It is translating economic progress into better living conditions for people in society. A traditional society is one in which: (1) The status of a person is determined by birth, that is individual do not strive for social mobility, (2) individual behaviour is governed by custom and ways of behaviour of people vary only slightly from generation to generation, (3) Social organization is based on hierarchy, (4) individual identifies with primary groups and kinships relations predominate in interaction, (5) individual is given more importance in social relations than his position, (6) people are conservative, (7) economics is simple and economic productivity above subsistence is relatively low, and (8) mythical thought predominates in society.

Contrary to this, a transitional or a modern society is one in which: (i) individual's status in society is determined by his own potentialities and capabilities; (ii) a person's behaviour is governed more by law than by custom; (iii) social structure is based on equality; (iv) secondary relation predominates over primary relations, individual identify with different kind of groups as different situations require and may complete for higher rank in each context; (v) individual position in society is achieved and it is given more importance in social relations; (vi) people are innovative; (vii) economics is based on complex technology; and (viii) rational thought predominates in society (Ogburn 1976).

Conclusion

Today with the fast changing of the Naga society to adoption of western culture, the young generation should come forward to take necessary measures in preserving their valuable culture. The government too should give more importance to preserve the rich cultural heritage of the Nagas, so as to attract more foreign tourists in order to maintain an economical equilibrium between the rural and urban people.

The Lotha Naga society has been changing rapidly accumulating numerous factors starting down from the family to the clan and onward to their village and tribe. Through the intervention of British legislation, advent of Christian Missionary, attainment of statehood, the society has been moving towards the process of modernization.

References

Ao, Bendangyabang. 1998. *History of Christianity in Nagaland, A Source material*, Shalom Ministry, Bangalore.

Ao, A. Lanu. 1981. *Naga Culture Attires and Musical Instruments.* New Delhi, Concept Publishing Company.

Anand, V.K. 1967. *Nagaland in Transition.* New Delhi, Associated Publishing House.

Anderson, Neils. 1964. *Our Industrial urban Civilization.* Delhi, Asian Publishing House.

Desai, Neera and Krishnaraj, M. 1990. *Women and Society in India.* Delhi, Ajanta Publication.

Fischer, S. Claude. 1975. *The Effect of Urban Life on Traditional Values Social Forces.* Cambridge, Harvard University Press.

Ganguli, Milada. 1984. *A Pilgrimages to the Nagas.* New Delhi, Oxford and IBH Publishing Company.

Homan, Borgohain and Pratipta, Borgohain. 2011. *Scrolls of Strife: the Endless History of the Naga.* New Delhi India, Rupa Publications.

Hutton, J.H. 1969. *The Angami Naga.* London, Oxford University Press.

Kumar, B.B. 1993. *Modernization in Naga Society.* New Delhi, Omson Publications.

Kiranshankar, Maitra. 1991. *Nagaland Darling of the North-East.* New Delhi India, Mittal Publications.

Mozhui, Zanao, 2004. *The Impact of Christianity on Naga People.* Dimapur, New Screen Printer.

Murry, Ezamo. 2003. *The Introduction and the Growth of Christianity in Kyong (Lotha) area of Nagaland.* Jorhat, Assam Printing Work.

Ogburn, W.F. 1976. *Studies in Indian Culture.* Bombay, Asian Publishing House.

Reddy, T. Babi. 1998. *Rural-Urban Migration.* New Delhi, Reliance Publishing House.

Singh, K.S. 1972. *People of India Nagaland,* Volume xxxiv. Calcutta, Naveen Kishore Seagull.

Singh, K.S. and Sen, Sepra. 1986. *Tribes of Nagaland*. New Delhi, Mittal Publications.

Singh, Yogendra. 1977. *Social Stratification and Change in India*. Delhi, Manohar.

Thong, Joseph S. 1997. *Head-Hunters Culture: Historic Culture of Nagas*. Kohima, Nei-u Printing Press.

15

Indigenous Beliefs and Practices of the Khasis of Meghalaya

An Anthropological Study

Papiya Bose

Introduction

Khasi belief system is based on the relationship between man and God and this relationship is governed by two factors, namely, *Ka Nia* and *Ka Jutang* (reason and covenant). The principal reason being that man is a creature of God. Man belongs to God during his lifetime as well as after he leave this world. His permanent habitation is with God. The covenant on the other hand is that as long as man is alive in this world he should abide by and execute the command (*hukum*) of God by earning righteousness—and on God's part the covenant is that God shall take care of man (1981: 34-38). As is understood, "the Khasi religion was found on this covenant and the three basic tenets that formed the hearth stones of this religion were:

- **Ban Kamai ia ka hok:** It means to earn and multiply in righteousness by one's own toil and efforts.
- **Ka tip briew tip Blei:** It is the acquiring of self-consciousness, self-realization of one's own capacity and capability, a self-regulation in habits, in relation to the civil understanding and behaviour with other human beings.
- **Ka tip kur tip Kha:** It is to know and respect the matrilineal and patrilineal relationships, based on the matrilineal

system of society. Each clan or *Kur* following the matrilineal lineage can be traced to the first progenitress of the clan known as *Ka Iawbei*" (2011: 9).

The People

The Khasis are one of the major Scheduled Tribes of Meghalaya. Their main concentration is in the East and West Khasi Hills districts of Meghalaya. They are matrilineal tribe and belong to Mon-Khmer speaking population. Broadly, the term Khasi includes Amwis and the Lyngams. It also includes Bhois, Wars and Khynriams. Khasis have a matrilineal system of family structure and therefore, their system of inheritance is also matrilineal. Agriculture is the primary occupation of the Khasis. They practice wet rice cultivation as well as shifting or *jhum* cultivation. The Khasis believe in one supreme God called *U BLEI NONGTHAW* whom they consider to be the creator of all life and beings. The Khasis also believe in the existence of deities—benevolent and malevolent. They worship these spirits and other natural objects like sacred groves, hills and other peaks, forests, rivers.

Methodology

The study is primarily based on the data collected from Umniuh-Tmar village in Meghalaya. The village is situated in East Khasi Hills District, Meghalaya. It is 78 km away from Shillong, the capital of the state. It is located in the southern part of the district bordering with Bangladesh Border. Data for the present study was collected during the month of October, 2013. Informed consent was taken from the respondents prior to collection of data. Observation, interview and case study methods were mainly followed. Though English was the primary language of interaction, help of interpreters was taken to understand the Khasi conversations for the successful completion of the study undertaken. Besides this, help of secondary sources were also sought for authentic information required for the study.

Nature Worship and Environment Conservation

According to the Khasi beliefs God is omnipresent and manifests through different creations of nature and exists in the surrounding environment. That is why there is no particular place of worship in the village for the Khasi community. They respect and worship each and every object of nature like stream, river, tree, and animals. They always seek permission before using anything from nature. Moreover, they believe that in different parts of the Khasi hills some deities live in a specific area, mostly forests termed as sacred groves. Therefore, they restrict their activities in those areas and prohibit others from entering or exploiting the forest resources and worship at a regular interval. These kinds of areas are called 'Sacred Groves'.

The state of Meghalaya is full of biodiversity. It is the land of people calling themselves the *Hynniewtrep*—the seven huts. Ri *Hynniewtrep* consists of West Khasi Hills, East Khasi Hills, Ri Bhoi and the Jaintia Hills districts of East Meghalaya. Nature has showered her immense blessings in the form of rich collection of orchids, herbs and plant. Like many countries throughout the world like Asia, Africa, Europe and America, India has a long history of nature worship, and the practice continues even today especially through the veneration of sacred groves in different parts of the country. Sacred Groves are well-documented from North-East Himalayan region, Western Ghats, Eastern Ghats, Coastal region, Central Indian Plateau and Western desert. These groves are specific forest areas imbued with powers beyond those of humans. Untouched and undisturbed by human hands for comparatively many long years and preserved over a long course of many generations, they are a home to the flora and fauna of varied types in their natural state. Some of the richest groves of India are located at the Khasi and Jaintia Hills of Meghalaya.

The retention of rich flora is ascribed to 'Sacred Groves' which has been a remarkable feature in Khasi culture. The concept of sacred grove to a large extent is responsible for the protection of forests from destructive hands of wood cutter. These sacred groves contain beautiful timber tress of various kinds, rare orchids (2006: 5). Sacred forests and groves are a rich and precious heritage of the Khasis.

In Meghalaya, sacred groves occur in the form of a primeval forest patches forming a contrast to the surrounding grasslands and generally rimmed by a dense growth of Khasi oak trees. About seventy nine sacred groves are found spreading throughout the length and breadth of Meghalaya. They are called, in the Khasi language, *ki Law kyntang* or *Law lyngdoh* and have been preserved here since time immemorial. The largest and the most prominent of all are situated at *Mawphlang village*, which is about 25 kms south-west of the state capital, Shillong. The *Iang-Blah* clans are entrusted to perform rites and rituals for the welfare of the people. The former Director of the Botanical Survey of India, Eastern circle T.M. Hynniewta, has commented that the sacred groves in the Khasi Hills typify the eco-system conservation comparable with UNESCO's (MAB) Biosphere Reserve Programme. The Mawphlang sacred grove has amazing life form and it is an island of Biodiversity. The grove can serve as a gene bank to the eco- system and is a living natural laboratory. The grove can also generate ecosystem and environmental education. It is rimmed by a dense growth of *Castanopsis kurzil* trees, as if performing a protective hedge. There are also very ancient and large *Rhododendron arborea*, shrubs called *symplocos chinesis, Mohonia Pycnophylla, Lyonia ovalifolia, Agapeted* and flowers and herbs like *Gentiana quadrifaria, Swertia* to name a few. The Taxus baccata trees here have medicinal properties that are said to cure cancer and other diseases (2011: 20-21). According to the Khasi traditional belief, the sacred groves are held sacred due to the presence of *U Ryngkew U Basa,* the tutelary deity who is believed to act as a guardian and protector of the village or group of villages. It is a general belief that everything within the periphery of these groves is under the protection of the reigning deity. No one dares to enter or pass through them without sanctioning him to do so. Even the woods, shrubs, mosses, ferns and orchids are not allowed to touch or pluck either for medicinal purpose or ornamentation for fear that the deity might consequently react badly against the perpetrators. The Khasi people held very high esteem to these groves and never dare to toy with any practice relating to the institution of rites towards appeasing the deity. The belief goes that if anybody cuts a plant stem or plucks its leaves or flowers, the wrath of the deity would befall the person. Some other important sacred groves are located in Sohra in the vicinity of the krem Pubon Caves, on the slopes of Syntu Ksiar Valley of Jowai, in Nongkrem Village (2011: 21). Sacred groves are important not only for their spiritual value but they are invaluable treasures of great ecological and biological value too. Large undisturbed groves provide water conservation one of the most well-documented ecological service. They are important for their soil and water conservation activities which are beneficial for the local people in terms of less soil erosion, supply of water in lean season (Ray et al., 2010). Being undisturbed and kept in their virgin state, they are, undoubtedly, the storehouse of large number of rare and endangered herbs and medicinal plants. Tough and solid timbers of various kinds are housed in them besides rare orchids, ferns, mosses. These sacred groves are generally located in a strategic watersheds thereby maintains the ecological balance of the area. Thus, besides the religious tenor to the traditional beliefs they not only preserve their age old practices but also they strongly believe and play a great role in the environment conservation. The Seng Khasis make only prayer before cutting trees as they believe in the existence of God in nature itself. Therefore, before cleaning the land by cutting of trees they pray to the residing spirits to leave the place and move elsewhere. After cutting and drying of the forest the eldest member of the family goes to the field with three stones in hand and throw them in different directions which symbolises formal notification to the living deities to leave the forest so that people can set fire on it. Before sowing seed they utter prayer to the Mother Earth (*Mei Rymen*) to feed the land as well as for a good harvest. After the harvest is over, some portion of it is offered to the Mother and some to the animals living out there.

Role of Water in the Socio-religious Life of the Khasis

Water is one of the essential elements for survival of life on earth. According to the Khasi belief, water is one of the children of *Ka Mei Ramew*, the Mother Earth and *U Basa*, the progenitor. The Khasi word for water is *'Um'* and is often used for sacred purpose. The Khasis believe it has some healing power and are used in religious rites and rituals such as the birth of a child, naming ceremony, marriage, rituals performed for the dead and so on. During Nongkrem dance, water is used in various rituals collected from the sacred grove of Shillong peak. The water of *Um Iew* river is used for cleaning the drums and other musical instruments. This water is also used to cure people of diseases specially suffering from the Thlen sickness (people become yellowish, weak). *U Thlen* is a demonic snake deity that feeds upon human blood.

The people of Hynniewtrep not only regard water as sacred and holy but also try to preserve water and keep it clean. In Ri War, a small rivulet known as *Umsait sabon,* people perform an annual ceremony for propitiating the village deity and also create an awareness to keep the rivulet clean and pure. It is a popular practice to seek protection in the name of the deity of the rivers and hills (*Lei lum lei wah*).

The role of *U Lum Sohpetbneng Peak* in the life of the Khasis is very much important. It is believed that the Hynniewtrep set foot on earth atop *U Lum Sohpetbneng Peak,* the corporal Golden vine was then cut off and the Divine showered blessings upon the Hynniewtrep. *U Lum Sohpetbneng Peak* stands as testimony of Creation and the covenant made between the creator and the Hynniewtrep. People go on a pilgrimage to the sacred *U Lum Sohpetbneng Peak* on the first Sunday of February. On this occasion, the devotees observe rites and rituals and receive sanctified waters along with a few grains of rice. Thus, through the folklores and religious beliefs people have learnt to value the environment.

Dreams and Their Interpretation

By certain degree of analysis, the Khasi established that man's life constitutes of three composite entities each of which contributes in the making of a man. They exist within the sphere of human body but their location and form aren't easily identified, since they are formless. As radical entities attached to human, they function together in the performance of man's business in this world. Obstructing to the proper functioning of anyone of these will directly affect the man and his very inherent nature. Man's plans will be thwarted and, of course, he'll be doomed for his whole life.

(A) Soul (*U mynsiem*): It is the sole property of the creator. God is the owner of this; and, so when man dies, this will surely return to him. Soul generates all the energy in the functioning of human body systems. Parting of the soul means full stop. And obviously, life's journey ends.

(B) Luck (*Ka Bok ka Nusib*): It is the steering wheel to direct man to act, to reach his targeted goal in life. The other side of luck is talent. It is an identifiable part of it which is seen in the act of every talented person. A luckless fellow is a person who is off-track and hence never succeed and get the favour of winning how hard he tries and often he changes his course.

(C) Shade or Spirit (*Ka Rngiew*): It is the second self of God residing within man. God before parting man, in the covenant, indorsed his authority in the form of "a spirit" (ka rngiew) which will accompany him then and forever. Shade as the second self of God helps man to live well and to prosper in life. It acts as a propelling force in man's action. When the Khasi finds that something goes wrong in life, he presumes that there is anything wrong with the shade.

To set it right again, the Khasi has to perform a ritual styled *'Ka Pyneh Rngiew'*. When the man dies, the soul will fly to the owner; the luck will get lost here; but the shade as an endorsement will go nowhere. It will stay here in this earth. The Khasi built a certain home called *'U Mawbah'* (*sepulchre*) for all the spirits of the same clan to live and rest together under the care of the ancestral mother, *the progenitric*. A grand ceremony is observed and *puja* is performed at the time of taking the spirits to the *'Mawbah'* (clan Sepulchre). One very interesting thing about the shade's role is that it could predict of the impending danger and the eventful moments in the days to come. And here comes the "DREAM" which is a message given by the shade to the dreamer.

The Khasi never underestimate any 'dream' especially when it means much to self and family. Once had, the interpretation is there and then made, and as early as possible. Interpretation of dreams, in the Khasi, is based on the meaning of the objects and the events as seen, happening in the state of illusion. Teeth are vital in the eating process. If someone is dreaming that his teeth breaks—it is thus interpreted that he (dreamer) or any member of his immediate family is in the danger of losing one's life since loss in the eating process means loss of life. Similarly, if someone had a fall in his dream, it is said that the person will fail in his undertaking. If someone have a dream night time about his/her ancestor or his dead relative, then this indicates that they are directly talking to them. If the ancestor takes his/her descendants away with them it means some bad omen (manifestation) will happen to them in the near future. The Khasis believe that if in dreams their ancestor comes and beat them, it implies that some punishment is coming in the near future and in order to avoid it they need to change themselves and their behaviours.

Bad dreams with urgent message have to be dealt with without delay. The Khasi seeks the diviner in case of a nightmarish dream to have it interpreted by him as revealed in the augury. Having read the meaning of the dream, the rest depends on the demand of the situation, to let go unnoticed or to seek the intervention from the God for help protection. If a living person wearing fully white dress is seen moving away from his/her family to their own way it is interpreted in the way that he/she may die in the near future. For this the village people offer *puja* to please the ancestors so that they do not take away that respective person.

Dreams and their interpretations also made their impact on the economic aspect in the life of the people. If a person has a dream that his garden is full of harvest or having plenty availability of production, then in real world in the near future the said person will enjoy good income or good harvest. In dream if the dead ancestor gives his/her living descendants gold or silver then it is believed that the family will become rich in the near future.

Concept of Health, Disease and Treatment

Along with the modern concepts of disease there exist some primitive concepts regarding the occurrence of some health problems which is very much related to religion. According to the Khasi belief, each family possess their own clan protector (*Jingphan*). The name of the protector may vary from family to family depending on the surname of the family. If one member of a family or group receive emotional or physical assault from a member of another family or group then the earlier person may ask his/her protector to look upon the matter and as a result of which the latter person may suffer from some disease sometimes lead to fatal. In another case, if two persons are closely linked to each other, the protector of one person met also get attached with the another person as a result of which the latter may fall ill. There is also another concept among the Khasis of this village that if the protector is not pleased at a regular interval of time then it becomes angry and diseases fall on the family. For this, the *Nongknia* breaks egg and through divination examines whether the protector is happy or not and if not then why. The ritual is performed only among the kins having same surname. Here the maternal uncle plays an important role. The prayer is done for the satisfaction of the *Jinhphan* for its blessings and for the protection of the family thereby.

Taboos in Khasi Society

Taboo is a Polynesian term. It means prohibited. It derived from the Polynesian term "Tabu" meaning forbidden. Thus, taboo is a prohibition. It refers to an exceptionally powerful prohibiting norm violation of which by individual usually attracts strong sanction from the community. All societies have taboos of some forms or another that restricts the behaviour of the members.

To the Khasi, the word taboo i.e. *"sang"* in Khasi meaning applies to the act of sacrilege the sanctity of a sacred place, or idea, or objects having moral values with religious undertone. It is an offence committed or acted against religious sanction thereby provoking the wrath of deity and god. Entering into the sacred grove without official permission is a taboo which is accountable to the action of the community and the deity (*U Ryngkew U Basa*) as well. In the Khasi belief, the most serious offence or taboo is the incestuous cohabitation or the marriage between members of the same clan, since this is obviously the breach the contract of the covenant between man and god.

It is also said a taboo, in the past, if a woman re-marry within three years after the death of her husband. Had she already committed before the stipulated time, she should, in a formal manner, erect "U Maw klim" (Literally, stone erected for adultery to acknowledge one's betrayal); otherwise, her progeny would simply earn the sobriquet *"Ki khun ki ksiew klim"* (issues born of adulterous relationship). During pregnancy, a woman is prohibited from entering into restricted places, crossing any river. The husband of a pregnant woman is barred from carrying coffin and attends any funeral ceremony. If he does so, it is believed that the baby will get affected. During this time killing of snake is also forbidden. If accidentally or intentionally it is said that the tongue of the baby will remain outside forever. The father also is not allowed to work with any sharp object in the fear of affecting the eyes or appearing spots on the face of the baby. After birth, till the cutting the navel cord, the neighbours of that particular house should not involve in any kind of construction work and abstain from doing heavy works or carrying heavy loads like agricultural objects in front of the house.

Cosmic Body

There are some beliefs and practices regarding to movement of the cosmic bodies in the Khasi society. The elders and experts can predict many things about future from the location, colour and size of the cosmic bodies like sun, moon and stars. If the new moon is looking red in colour, then it indicates of rainfall in the very near future. In the new moon day when many stars are seen on one side of the moon, it is believed that accidental death may take place in the village. But if there are two stars pointed at both sides of the moon, it is the prediction of the arrival of a male baby in the village having bright future. During lunar eclipse when the moon is covered fully, people believe that some famine may happen in the village in the coming months. During solar eclipse, pregnant are prohibited to come out of the house with the fear that if the mother sees the sun, the baby will be physically handicapped or have abnormal body formation. Because they believe that the power of sun and its energy is totally disturbed and diverted to the eclipse. No proper energy or radiation can be obtained from the mother sun.

Changes in the Khasi Religion

Major contributory causes in the downsizing of the Khasi religion are many but the first and foremost cause is the impact of the western thought as propagated by the Welsh Missionary during the British regime. The Khasis are known to be upright, simple and god fearing-people. And, these were the very natures of the Khasis that the English took advantage to infuse their own belief and religious thought, which later on, under tendency of attachment, it really did take root in the Khasis and their family. The first interaction of the people of the Khasi and Jaintia Hills with the British was through the treaty of friendship made with Ram Singh, the Raja of Jaintia, entailing the military support to the East India Company who were apprehending a Burmese attack (Talukdar 2004: 29). The Khasi society with strong cohesive order and integrated social structure was bound to be affected by the presence of alien rulers, Christian missionaries, opening of new communication links and cultural contacts with the neighbouring Hindu and Muslim communities. Along with the abandoning of prechanged religious beliefs the practice of deposit of bones in the family or clan *mawbah* and erection of memorial stones were also discontinued (2006: 73-74). In the present day the concepts of *U Blei*, the *Iawbei*, the *Thawlang* and *Suidnia* are more or less forgotten especially by the Christian Khasis for whom Jesus and the Christian Saints have taken over these functions (2004: 19). The growth of urban centres and their attraction for job opportunities and the money economy is definitely another major factor for the change. The major reasons behind the changes are enumerated below:

(1) The Advent of the Welsh Missionary

The impact of the Welsh Missionary on the rift in the Khasi religious and cultural life cannot be exaggerated. Rev. Thomas Jones of Welsh Calvinistic Methodists Foreign Mission Society (WCMFMS) sets his maiden foot here on the 22-06-1841 at Nongsawli in Sohra (Cherrapunjee), one of the then Khasi states. This is the epicentre from where his missionary work traversed many neighbouring areas. It was in 1871 that 500 persons were converted (2011: 83). The Christian missionary offered the converts assurance both of eternal life after death and present peace of mind amid everyday trouble. Jones also invented Khasi alphabets. It is said that this was one of his subterfuge to get his missionary work more effective since by knowing the alphabets the Khasis would also know *Bible* reading, which would near them to God's words. This was really very effective. Most Khasi took pleasure in reading and eventually adopt Christianity.

"*Ka Kot Kitab Nyngkong* (First Khasi reader)" is the first book written in Khasi language. Later, "*Ka Kot Tikir*', was published as translated version of 'Mother's gift' or 'Rhodd Mam' in Khasi language.

(2) Rites and Rituals

The Khasi religion is ritualistic in nature. And whereas in other religions, ritual practices are overtly explained even to the common masses; in Khasi religion, rites and rituals are reserved to those only who have extra-ordinary powers in undertaking these tasks i.e., divination, egg-breaking, sacrifice etc. Those who are engaged in difficulties they have to get an aid from "*U Nongkhan Nong knia*" (diviner-cum-sacrificer) who are too few and far between here with us, especially in these new generations. Even in these days, when the light had penetrated into every household and in every corner of the land, yet there is still no record about these things. Stagnancy and sanctity, both being the terms in the Khasi blood regarding religious practices, undoubtedly contribute in the major outflow of Khasi believers to adopt other religions in the state.

(3) *Inherent Nature of the Khasi Religion*

In its very nature, Khasi religion doesn't practice conversion as do the other religions coming from beyond the seas. Likewise, it has also shown too much relaxation to others to propagate their religions. The Khasi elders were increasingly becoming aware of the fact that the younger generation was not serious about their traditional religion and culture. One of the reasons of the fast acceptance of new belief system was the emphasis of missionaries on the common features of the traditional religion with Christianity. The early converts probably treated the Christian God as more or less equivalent to their *U Blei.* Rev. Fr S. Sngi Lyngdoh was of the opinion that the Khasi religion was a 'waiting religion' (*ka NiamKaba ap Jingong*) and Christianity has brought about completion. Fr Sngi called this type of Catholicism *Ka Niam-Khasi-Pura ba ia Khie La Sam* i.e. pure Khasi religion but in full growth (2004: 92, 97). Thus people absorbed Christianity by asserting their traditional belief within the faith.

(4) *Inter-marriages*

Inter-marriage is another contributory cause in the change in the Khasi religion; and, as it is seen, most Khasis abandoned their traditional religion and associated with the religion of their spouses. Khasi religion, in this sense, is too loose to make its people realize themselves of having any religion. The Khasi thought they are independent; and so whenever a bond is created through marital relationship, they are readily attracted towards other religions.

(5) Lack of Funding Pattern

One of the major causes is the lack of funds. People could see the changing scenario in the human development and yet when seen fail to keep pace with the cycle of change, the changing life-pattern which is in synchronization with the need and requirement of the people. Poor people need aid and support, no hand was heard to stretch over to the needy for charity as done by the other religious organisation. The Khasi still stick with their religious aphorism *"Ka mai ia ka hok"* (to earn righteousness) which is in today's world less instrumental. Today's people want to grow materially as well as spiritually. The Khasi religion fails to supply nutrients for this and hence most of its people change their course leaving their own.

(6) Lack of Proper Facilities

From the educational point of view, it is seen that most students who had high aim in life had to seek admission in institutions, and as they were forced to get the favour of the management which often belong to other religion. It is evident that the followers of Christianity are provided with much better facilities like education, health and care etc. by the missions which attract the traditional people and eventually lead to the conversion. The missionaries set up several schools at Sohra and gradually in other parts of the land. Education changed the outlook of the society and developed their economic status. Particularly, the urban-dwellers switched over to white collar jobs which made their life comfortable enough and influenced the rural people to embrace that lifestyle along with other beliefs abandoning their own.

Changing Scenario and Revivalism in the Khasi Religion

Apart from the above mentioned causes that led to change in the traditional religion of the Khasis, there was a wave of resisting change and reinforcement of indigenous elements in the society.

On 23rd November, 1899, the SENG KHASI ORGANIZATION was established in order to resist the missionary activity, convey the traditional culture and revival of the religious rites and rituals of the traditional system. The organization served as an inspirational epitome. It made an attempt to acquaint the young generation with the traditional dances, music through various platforms like *Shad-Suk-Mynsiem* (dance of peaceful heart), *Seng Pyni* (Sunday school), started in 1976 for children to fraternize with those of their own tradition. The organization inspired the growth of many such socio-religious organizations like *SEIN RAIJ, SEIN KYNTU NIAM TRE, and SENG KHIH LANG* etc. Seng Kut Snem is the annual commemoration day of the Seng Khasi Institution which has evolved as the custodian of the spiritual, cultural and social heritage of the Hynniewtrep people, in preserving the wisdom of the ancients while seeking modern knowledge, and charting new directions for a better future. The Commemoration Day, November 23, has now been declared a State Holiday under the Negiotiable Instruments Act, 1881 (2011: 85).

The Christian Khasis do feel for the retention of their culture which they say is an essential feature of their entity. Most Christians feel that they were Khasis by birth and blood and kept the *Kur-Kha* relationship, they were totally Khasis (2004: 125). Though the joint family system is breaking down but the unity of each clan or *Kur* is reflected in many clan organizations called *'Seng Kur'*. People have understood the need to preserve, protect and promote indigenous interests. Nature plays a big role in the religious life of Khasis. Religion has not been a barrier to their pristine thoughts, practices and their love and respect for 'Mother Nature'. An urge is seen to re-discover their own root by believing in the ancient wisdom of—Love oneself and respect others—*Leid Ialade Burom Ia Kiwei.*

References

Bordoloi, B.N. 1991. *Tribes of Assam Part-III*. Guwahati, Assam Institute of Research for Tribals and Scheduled Castes.

Gurdon, P.R.T. 1863. *The Khasis*. New Delhi, Akansha Publishing House.

Karsten, L. 1935. *The Origin of Religion*. Edinburg, The Edinburg Press.

Khongkliam, S.S. 2012. *Religion of The Khasi*. Guwahati, DVS Publishers.

Malhotra, J.D. 2001. *Cultural and Ecological Dimensions of Sacred Groves in India Report. Indian National Science.* New Delhi and Bhopal, Indira Gandhi Rashtriya Manav Sangrahalaya.

Mawrie, H.O. 1981. *The Khasi Milieu.* New Delhi, Concept Publishing Company Pvt. Ltd.

Ray, et al. 2010. *Sacred Grove: Nature Conservation, Tradition of the Ancient World.* Bangalore, Centre For Ecological Sciences, Indian Institute of Science.

Rizvi, S.H.M. and Shibani Roy. 2006. *Khasi Tribe of Meghalaya.* Delhi, B.R. Publishing Corporation.

Saiwan, S.S. 2011. *Golden Vine of Ri Hynniewtrep: The Khasi Heritage.* Guwahati, Vivekananda Kendra Institute of Culture.

Singh, K.S. 1994. *People of India—Meghalaya.* Calcutta, Seagull Books, Published on behalf of ASI.

16

Assertion and Accommodation of Ethnic Identities in Assam

Y. Monojit Singha

Introduction

Contemporary ethnicity is the result of intensive interaction between ethnic groupings and not the result of complete separatism or isolation as the indigenous people did in post-colonial period. The colonial power, in fact, acts as 'glue' in sticking together some diverse groups within the framework of new, artificially established, centralized states. When the colonial powers withdrew, each group began to regain their original position under the new state system (Cohen, 1996: 83). Furthermore, bitter clashes broke out over new strategic positions of power mostly in the field of employment, taxation, funds for development, education, political positions and so on which starts since independence under the new state system. As a result of this intensified struggle, many tribal groups mobilized their forces and searched for ways in which they could organize themselves politically so as to conduct their struggle more effectively. In each of tribal mobilization in Assam, the groups either engaged themselves on resurgence of old culture and language or uniting small vulnerable groups on visible ethnic lines. Ethnicity is a straightforward concept. It can incorporate several forms of collective identities, including linguistic, religious, caste, and regional forms. Cohen (1985) argues that ethnicity should be regarded as a type of political resources for competing interest groups. In order to achieve the resources, elites mobilize the small groups by organizing[1] and manipulating different sets of symbols (mainly linguistic and religious).

This chapter is an attempt to analyse movements of diverse ethnic groups belonging to both tribal and non-tribal communities in the state of Assam as well as it also attempts to understand sources of such tensions. Examining the role of the state in asserting and confronting such tensions between the competing groups becomes another objective of the chapter.

Ethnic assertion, revivalism, and quest for a separate space are the major postulates around which identity struggle revolves. Most resistant and resurgent idioms are centred on the issue of language, which is linked with ethnic identity and its inhabitation. Again, this can be linked to the reorganization of states on the basis of language[2] in India since independence. States were carved out around the identity of major Indian languages and most of the states in India are identified with one or the other language.[3] Thus, policies related to language once used as an instrument of nation-building, institutionalize ethnic diversity, politicize linguistic divisions and render them permanent. The most powerful impact is that of multiple official languages. It is to say that such a policy institutionalizes and legitimizes linguistic conflict and thus maintains and perpetuates it. For instance, conflict over the making of Assamese or Bengali as the official language in Assam,[4] this brings in identity politics in the picture which dominates contemporary socio-political discourse in North East India.

Identity Politics and Ethnic Issues in North East India

It has been argued that issues relating to identity politics emerged most vividly in the twentieth century as a product of collapse of the modern grand narratives, rather than any novelty of diversity in our age (Engin and Patricia Wood, 1999: 57-58). It mostly relates to changing economic and political conditions. The manner in which modern nation-states try to construct common national identities creates a congenial environment for identity politics. Thus, through the process of nation-building, they (the majority) try to construct national identities, which lead to assimilation rather than accommodation of diverse socio-cultural identities into mainstream politics.

The homogenization of Indian national identity after independence marked the beginning of identity politics. The working of the Indian state reveals how the elements of Hindu identity, the most powerful and pervasive, received the widest favour and support from government agencies and institutions in the name of promotion of Indian cultural identity, whereas, other cultural identities (minority identities) were either marginalized or pushed towards the periphery of mainstream politics. This situation generated a congenial environment for politics of identity in India.

During the colonial period, the colonial masters initiated a process of recasting Indian social identities. In the same way, after independence, Indian leaders tried to recast them. However, in case of the former, such recasting occurred within largely autonomous cultural settings and colonial initiatives were by and large successful in creating political categories out of local identifications and affiliations. For the latter, the process of recasting social identities through the misconceived process of nation-building has proven counter-productive (Baljit, 2006). As a result, a number of anti-state forces can be seen in many states in post-independence period viz., Punjab, South Indian states and North Eastern states including Assam, among others. This initiative against the homogenization of mainstream culture rooted in the provisions of the constitution where promotion of minority identities and cultures is protected. In response to this reaction, the reorganization of states on the basis of language was a major step towards accommodating different identities (linguistic). Even after reorganization and creation of many new states, expressions of multi-layered identities such as "minorities within minority" took the form of native, even secessionist movements. Such politics of identity has given rise to new regional movements, parties and forces (Basu 1992).

Though the process of identity construction (nation-building) had started much before independence, the materialization and political involvement could be seen only after India's inception as an independent nation-state. Quite similar to the task of nation-building with special attention to incorporation of minority cultures, languages and religions, the Indian state guaranteed cultural, religious and linguistic freedoms by incorporating provisions in the Fundamental Rights and the Directive Principles of State Policy. India's practice of affirmative action or reservations for the underprivileged communities has contributed to both a growing sense of participation and empowerment (Muralidharan, 2004). However, the politics of reservation has also resulted in the process of formation and sharpening of identities in the public domain (Baljit, 2006).

In the late 1980s and early 1990s, the politics of identity had become more pervasive and eventually replaced the politics of ideas which had hitherto dominated Indian political space. The Indian brand of secularism and Hindi as a language were used as a mechanism to construct national identity but this was contested from many parts of the country; mainly, South India (Mahajan, 2005). Though the idea of imposing the national identities to the periphery regions were first contested by the south Indians, the two most significant political movements that brought identity and ethnicity to the forefront were in Assam and Punjab in the 1980s as also mentioned above. A separatist movement in the border region of Kashmir and the rise of the pan-Indian *Hindutva* identity also followed soon after (Surinder, 2001).

The "Assam problem" (Baruah, 1999) relates to the movement against illegal migrants. This was reflected first by the United Liberation Front of Assam (ULFA) which later clashed violently with the state. Initially, the tension in Assam was focused around two interrelated issues, the influx of Bengali speaking immigrants and the inability of the centre to accommodate the regional patriotism of native speakers within the state. The recent clashes between Bodo-Muslims and Bodo-Hindi speakers are the direct result of influx of foreigner problem. Baruah (1999) contends that the Indian state failed to resolve the Assam problem after the largely non-implemented Peace Accord of 1985 because it had conceptualized the conflict mainly as a "law and order" or "military problem". In contrast, he offers another way to conceptualize the conflict by applying the theoretical lens of "contentious politics" (Doug *et al.*, 1996). According to this view, the emergence of violent protest should not necessarily be seen as illegitimate but rather as the outgrowth of political demands that have not been resolved through non-violent means. Baruah (1999) argues that a lasting solution to the Assam problem will inevitably have to involve the acceptance of Assamese regional patriotism as being a legitimate political construction. Moreover, it will mean abandonment of the rigid idea of "pan-India", which views the unity of India as being un-debatable.

According to the estimate made by Singh (1996), North East India has 382 culturally and regionally distinct communities of various sizes at various stages of development. The leaders of such communities have begun to identify the values and interests which appeared to be universal to their respective communities. The articulation of such interest has led to much tension because such interests of a community invariably come in conflict with interests of other communities. The movements of various communities either asserting a new identity or preserving and protecting their ethnic identity from assimilation are the most significant aspects of the contemporary socio-political realities of North East India. The movements launched by the Assamese, the Bengalis, the Nagas, the Kukis, the Khasis, the Garo, the Mizos, the Bodos, the Karbis, the Kok Boroks and the Bishnupriya among others are significant. Many smaller groups with somewhat blurred cultural markers are now also beginning to assert their identities, some of which are even busily intervening in separate identities. At times, such assertions emerged as a result of political strategy for national and state-level elections. For instance, the Assamiya-Bengali in Assam and the Bodo-Non Bodo conflicts in the Bodo inhabited areas have a close relationship with the politics of domination and autonomy.

The movements mentioned above emerged as a result of resistance adopted by the smaller linguistic and cultural groups by initiating autonomy movements against the assimilating approach of the majority community. Besides, policies like "co-operative federalism" and "cultural federalism", which promised to protect cultural and linguistic minorities, also encouraged smaller groups to promote ethnic mobilization. For instance, the Naga-Kuki conflict and Kuki-Paite clashes in Manipur; Bodo-Non Bodo conflict in Bodo dominated areas of Assam, anti-Chakma movements in Arunachal Pradesh; anti-outsider movements in Meghalaya; Tripuri Tribal-Bengali settlers conflict in Tripura are the major issues being faced by the Indian North Eastern states (Priyadarshini, 2006).

Though, it is often difficult to trace the origins of ethnic conflicts, especially those occurring amongst various tribal communities (and also between the Hill People and the Plains

People) in the North Eastern states, it can be argued that the destruction of the peaceful co-existence that had historically existed between these groups started well before Independence and geared up in the post-Independence era particularly in the last three-four decades. Perhaps, this is because the British colonial administration and ethnic categorization has continued to have important ramifications in the post-Independence ethnic relationships in the region, highlighting certain unique features of ethnic conflict and identity assertions. Group rights are claimed not simply on the basis of their being a distinct ethnic community with common social practices and cultural traditions including a common language (Smith, 1986). Identities have also been constructed on the basis of some vague shared goals such as "freedom from mistreatment" by the larger community or "safeguarding common interests" *vis-à-vis* other groups and these have been contributed to the foundation of a "nation."[5] This departs from the traditional conception of a "nation" as a population that simply shares a common culture, language, and ethnicity and that shows strong historical continuity.[6] However, this has been partially effective. Smaller groups have been oriented towards and mobilized to pursue these goals. In the case of the Naga identity formation in Manipur, one particular method is of projecting a common enemy to consolidate otherwise scattered groups, thereby forging a new common identity based on anti-Meetei sentiments. The propagation of this political standpoint is encouraged by referring to the past which Bhagat (2003) spells as "ill doings of the (Hinduized) Meeteis to the Hill tribes." In the case of Assam, issues are not exactly comparable to that of the Nagas and the Kukis in Manipur. In Assam, ethnic mobilizations are mostly connected with demands for autonomy, ethnic participation in political affairs of the state by sharing administrative institutions, more specifically getting the ST status and inclusion in the Sixth Schedule of the Constitution of India. Any attempt to manage emerging ethnic tensions in Assam requires a clear understanding of historical and demographic background of the erstwhile Assam.

The idea of a nation-province for the ethnic Assamese[7] is basically an unrealizable goal within the present political boundary of Assam, primarily due to the fact that these two boundaries, viz., ethnic and political, do not coincide. Besides, the ethnic boundary of Assam not only includes the ethnic Assamese but also the Dimasas of North Cachar Hills, the Karbis of Karbi Anglong, the Bengalis of Barak valley, the Bodos, the Koches, the Miris, the Chutias, the Kacharis, the Deoris, the Rabhas, the Lalungs, the Morans, the Meeteis, the Bishnupriyas, Tea tribes and other indigenous populations (Hussain, 1993). Thus, historically evolved geographic and demographic structures in Assam are not in conformity with the claim of making Assam a nation-province for the ethnic Assamese. While members of a multi-ethnic state like Assam have multiple identities, i.e., one can simultaneously be a Bodo, an Assamese and a Christian, adoption of a singular identity and an attempt to magnify it only leads to inter-group conflicts and identity disintegration. Identity politics in Assam has many facets rooted in the remote as well as the recent social history of the state which needs to accommodate on the basis of social justice.

Managing Ethnic Conflict and State Response

In the case of Assam, those who did not want to be identified as Assamese slowly developed an aspiration to separate and hence, have started the struggle for separate identities, resisting cultural assimilation or forced erasure of ethnic affiliations by the majority groups. This involves two-way politicization of the elements of ethnicity and the role of the state along with the elements of deprivation and domination. The dominant group possesses a tendency to perceive all group aspirations and demands as a threat to national unity or secessionist tendency without going into their merits or demerits. One may refer to the methods of "accommodationist management", because such mechanism was used by the centre for political bargaining, which implies a substantial sharing of power and resources with people at regional and sub-regional levels. It prevents ethnic consciousness from switching to intense and destructive to national unity and democratic process. However, smaller groups always fear for the situation of identity crisis on the eve of forced assimilation in the name of accommodation and integration (Pranami, 2007).

The rise of desire for self-expression and separate identities from those of the dominant groups in Assam is also fueled by the policy of recognition and separate representation on ethnic lines.

The state policy of recognition of traditional institutions and identities; and representation of the ethnic groups in the decision-making bodies can nourish stronger sentiments and emotions of ethnicity among other groups (Pranami, 2007). Hence, recognition of cultural values that characterize "identity" of a community is an important element and an essential component of democracy. The importance of recognition is now universally recognized in one form or another. Besides, recent studies pointed out that economic, educational and employment facilities, along with the discriminatory policies of the centre[8] and political aspirations of the ethnic group leaders fuelled the intensity of the emergence of identity movement. As for instance, with the approval of Bodo Accord, small groups like Tiwa, Rabha, Mishing, Deori, Thengal Kachari, Sonowal Kachari, etc. started demands for more autonomy and rights.

The recent state responses to accommodate ethnic mobilization of smaller groups have been enumerated in Table 16.1 which Mahajan (2005) quoted as *multi-level federalism*.

Table 16.1: Institutional Arrangement for Ethnic Minorities in Assam

Sl. No.	*Institutional Framework*	*Status*
1	Karbi Anglong Autonomous Council	Sixth Schedule
2	Dima Hasao District Autonomous Council	--do--
3	Bodoland Territorial Council (BTC)	--do--

Source: Ministry of Development of North Eastern Region, Government of India.

Table 16.2: Institutional Arrangement to Ethnic Movements in Assam

Sl. No.	*Institutional Framework*	*Status*
1	Tiwa Autonomous Council at Marigaon	Legislative Act
2	Rabha Autonomous Council at Goalpara	--do--
3	Mishing Autonomous Council at Dhemaji	--do--
4	Deori Autonomous Council at Lakhimpur	--do--
5	Thengal Kachari Autonomous Council at Titabor	--do--
6	Sonowal Kachari Autonomous Council at Dibrugarh	--do--

Source: Department of Welfare of Plain Tribes and Backward Classes, Government of Assam, 2014.

Table 16.3: Institutions for Non-Tribal Ethnic Communities in Assam

Sl. No.	*Institutional Framework*	*Status*
1	Tai Ahoms Development Council	Legislative Act
2	Muttoks Development Council	--do--
3	Morans Development Council	--do--
4.	Koch-Rajbangshis Development Council	--do--
5	Chutiyas Development Council	--do--
6	Gorkhas Development Council	--do--
7	Adivasis Development Council	--do--
8	Sema Development Council	--do--
9	Tangsha Development Council	--do--
10	Mon Tai Linguistic (Tai Fakey, Tai Khamiang, Tai Khamiang, Tai Turung, Tai Khamti, Tai Aiton	--do--
11	Bishnupriya Manipuri Development Council	--do--
12	Manipuri Development Council	--do--
13	Mech Kachari Development Council	--do--
14	General Caste Development Council	--do--
15	Maimal Development Council	--do--
16	Saraniya Kachari Development Council	--do--
17	Moriya Development Council	--do--
18	Nath-Jogi Development Council	--do--

Source: Department of Welfare of Plain Tribes and Backward Classes, Government of Assam, 2014.

Table 16.1 shows the three autonomous councils, namely—the *Karbi Anglong Autonomous Council*, the *Dima Hasao District Autonomous Council*, and the *Bodoland Territorial Council* (BTC) set up in order to bring the tribal people into mainstream national politics and also for their welfare. Moreover, it brought in more and more people into the political process, giving them opportunities to participate actively and debate the issues that concerned them immediately (Mahajan, 2005).

A number of provisions were also incorporated in the Constitution to incorporate linguistic and cultural diversity. For instance, Article 244(2) of the Constitution of India provides for a Sixth Schedule for bringing about development of tribes of the North East only because it was assumed that these tribes have some special problems of their own. The idea behind the Sixth Schedule was to provide the tribal people with a simple administrative system of their own, so that they could safeguard their customs and traditions; and, to provide them maximum autonomy within the framework of the state in the management of their affairs (Jayanta, 2011).

Currently, there are ten Autonomous Councils, functioning in four states of North East India. Among them, three are working in present-day Assam. After working for more than six decades, the tribal problems have not been resolved and are continuing, sometimes taking dangerous forms. Perhaps, in Assam, ethnic conflict will continue as long as the various communities do not have the rights and resources necessary to affirm their cultures and secure their survival (Gosselink, 1994). With respect to failure of the present-day system to assure this, Jayanta (2011) condemns basically to the manipulation of the Autonomous Councils from the top of an extremely centralized power structure, which artificially impresses the formation, expansion or dissolution of different types of autonomous structures and depends on the wishes of the upper-most layers of the power hierarchy. The present need of the hour depends on the protection of their rights within the scope of the constitution and makes secure for financial freedom to some extent for regular running the scheduled areas.

Apart from the autonomous councils mandated in the Sixth Schedule, six other statutory autonomous councils were constituted in Assam after prolonged agitations by smaller ethnic communities, as illustrated in Table 16.2. Territorializing the autonomous council always poses tensions among the ethnic groups competing for the possession of central positions in the autonomous areas. Instead of difference-blind universalism, differentiated citizenship develops the sense of collective belongingness and equal respect for the "other". At the same time, a number of rights could be ensured and established, viz., special representation rights, multicultural rights, self-government or rights to self-determination, etc.[9] Thus, conflicts related to Bodo-Non Bodo, Karbi-Dimasa in Assam and Kuki-Naga in Manipur are the few examples which relate to politics of territorializing the autonomous councils.

On the other hand, de-territorializing autonomous councils will pave the way to constitute a number of other autonomous councils for the ethnic communities. The categories of all the above three tables differ in their institutional status, nature of autonomy and the laws that protect the autonomy. The first two tables, viz. Table 16.1 and Table 16.2 are of similar in nature which is protected by the Constitution of India under the Sixth Schedule and the latter is constituted by an act of the State Legislature of Assam.[10] Both types of councils are more or less similar in formation but differ in the measure of autonomy viz. absolute, relative and limited. The first two are meant for the tribes only and the third does not make any distinctions.

In another step to accommodate competing minorities, the Government of Assam has formed Non-territorial Development Councils for certain ethnic groups in 2010[11] and some others in 2013 respectively. The setting-up of these development councils for smaller ethnic communities was done to provide maximum participation by the people of various backward ethnic communities within the framework of the Constitution of India for social, economic, educational, ethnic and cultural advancement of the people belonging to those communities in the State.

Summing Up

Over the years, the special status has enabled vulnerable communities to survive and protect themselves from large-scale influx of "outsiders" (Baruah, 1989). For instance, due to non-existence of similar provisions for exclusion and protection for tribal communities in Tripura, their share in the total population has fallen enormously (Mahajan, 2005). Such mechanism protects the minorities or indigenous people from forced eraser of territorial right and culture as well as in the same time, in order to ensure that these communities are not entirely segregated from the Indian polity; separate representation was provided to members of Scheduled Tribes. Separate representation was intended to bring in the voice of these communities without undermining their cultural distinctiveness.

The homogenization of the Indian national identity in the post-Independence period has resulted in the emergence of identity politics in India. In the case of Assam, it can be seen from two main perspectives. First, a resistant step undertaken by militant revolutionaries against the state mechanism for homogenization of identity, and second, as a reaction of incentives provided in the name of distinct community or indigenous people. In both the cases, the state plays significant roles in the formation of concrete boundaries among the small communities in Assam.

Besides this, the most disturbing task before the political leaders lies in the growing illegal migrants from Bangladesh which becomes a factor for the political parties to compete for their votes and they promise to implement the Assam Accord and protect the rights of the indigenous people at the same time. Balancing the interest of both sides further deepens the conflict in the state, resulting in frequent bloodshed in recent decades. Thus, politicization of the elements of ethnicity and the role of the state, along with deprivation and domination of small communities in the hands of larger group becomes the source of tension in the state. Moreover, the tendency of the state as well as the projection of the dominant group to brand all the aspirations and demands of ethnic minority communities as anti-national or secessionist without going into the merits or demerits intensifies the potency of conflict in the state. Distribution and re-distribution of political institutions and economic benefits among the minorities or indigenous groups facilitated by the state policy create the expectations for further mobilization by other minorities which did not find place in any of the privileged categories mentioned in the above tables. For instance, the Khasis and Jaintias, the Rajbangshi or Dihans in south Assam are demanding either ST status or Development Council.

Notes

1. Ethnic organizations play a key role in monitoring and controlling information to their members, who will join them as long as they appear to deliver individual benefits.
2. The linguistic reorganization of regional boundaries has been a major instrument for protecting and nurturing linguistic diversity and the creation of linguistic identity based units, each with political rights to govern itself within a region. Its language became the official language of that state and the medium of instruction, public examination, communication and media networks. As a consequence, the regional majority language grew and flourished (Gurpreet Mahajan, 2000).
3. West Bengal is the homeland for the Bengalis, Maharashtra for the Marathas, Tamil Nadu for the Tamils, and Kerala for the Malayalees; and so on.
4. Assam is a multi-lingual state but in 1960, the Government of Assam declared Assamese as the sole official language. The people of Cachar launched a movement of protest against the language policy of the state and to put it down, the Assam Government opened fire on

Government opened fire on non-violent Satyagrahis on 19th May, 1961. As a result one girl and ten boys were killed. The Cachar Jilla Sangram Parishad and the Bhasa Andolan Samiti launched a non-violent movement demanding Bengali as the second official language of the state. "Three language" formula called "Shastri Formula" was evolved by Lal Bahadur Shastri by which "Assam Official Language Act" was amended so as to make Bengali the official language in Barak Valley. Fresh tension mounted in the valley as a SEBA circular (SEBA/AB/ Syllabus/11/85-86-1 dated 28.2.86) imposed Assamese language in the Valley.

5. The term "Nation" employed here is also synonymous with nationality or nationalism which is developed as a reaction against the domination by majority. It is mostly used by the people who organise movements to overthrow or prevent the action of the state authority or majority group. As for instance, Naga Nationalism, Meetei Nationalism.
6. If one conceptualizes the idea of a nation around the theory enunciated by scholars like Montserrat Guibernau, there is no problem when "shared goals" is made a foundational element of a nation. Nonetheless, when the so-called shared goals are imposed upon smaller ethnic communities who otherwise have a different cultural background, including language, and settle in non-contiguous areas with separate aspirations, many issues emerge. These issues are likely to be more complicated owing to the continuing movements for identity assertion, formation, and expansion led by select elites and leaders. See Montserrat Guibernau, "Anthony D. Smith on Nations and National Identity: A Critical Assessment", *Nations and Nationalism* 10(1/2): 125–41 (2004).
7. Assamese people do not include Bodo, Miri and Michings; they are believed to be the earliest known inhabitants of Assam. The Assamese identity is formed by people migrated from Central India in 13th and 14th century (P.C. Dutta and B.C. Pradhan, 2006).
8. Language policy and nation-building project, etc.
9. For more details see Krishna Sharma, Jayanta (2011) "An Alternative Formulation for Autonomous Councils in Assam", *Economic & Political Weekly*, August 27, 2011, Vol. XLVI, No 35.
10. The Indian Constitution also contains a safeguard that empowers the President of the Indian republic to appoint a special officer whose responsibility is "to investigate all matters relating to the safeguards provided for linguistic minorities." This enables the Central Government to intervene to prevent linguistic minorities from actual or potential discrimination. If these constitutional methods fail to resolve the problem, then Assam's legislature could consider other ways to grant greater privileges to linguistic minorities (Robert G. Gosselink, 1994).

11. Namely the Ahoms, Mataks, Morans, Koch-Rajbangshis, Chutiyas, Adivasis and Gorkhas, vide order no. TAD/BC/531/2010/136.

References

Basu, Sajal. 1992. *Regional Movements: Politics of Language, Ethnicity-Identity*, Manohar Publications, New Delhi.

Baruah, Sanjib. 1999. *India Against Itself: Assam and the Politics of Nationality*, Oxford University Press, New Delhi.

Bell, Daniel. 1975. *Ethnicity and Social Change*, In Ethnicity, N. Glazer and D.P. Moynihan, eds., pp. 141-174. Harvard University Press, Cambridge.

Bhagat, Oinam. 2003. "Patterns of Ethnic Conflict in the North-East: A Study of Manipur", *Economic and Political Weekly*, 38 (21): 2031–37.

Cohen, Abner. 1996. The Lesson of Ethnicity, In *Theories of Ethnicity: A Classical Reader*, Werner Sollors (ed), New York University Press, New York.

Cohen, Anthony, P. 1985. *The Symbolic Construction of Community*, Tavistock, London.

Hussain, Monirul. 1993. *The Assam Movement: Class, Ideology and Identity*, Manak Publications, Delhi.

Jodhka, S. Surinder, ed. 2001. *Communities and Identities: Contemporary Discourses on Culture and Politics in India*, Sage Publications, New Delhi.

Mahajan, Gurpreet. 1998. *Identities and Rights: Aspects of Liberal Democracy in India*, Oxford University Press, New Delhi.

Mahajan, Gurpreet. 2005. "Negotiating Cultural Diversities and Minorities Rights in India", In *Democracy, Conflict and Human Security: Further Readings (volume II)*, International Institute for Democracy and Electoral Assistance, Sweden.

Muralidharan, Sukumar. 2004. "Celebrating Cultural Diversity", *Frontline*, vol. 21 number 16 (July 31st to August 13th, 2004).

Pranami. 2007. Aspiration for an ethnic identity—Evolved or Created: A Question Asked in the Context of Assam, unpublished paper presented at the National Seminar on Ethnic Identity, Social Formation and Nation-Building with special reference to North East India, Dibrugarh University, Dibrugarh.

Priyadarshini, Susmita. 2006. "Ethnicity, Ethnic Conflict and Conflict Resolution in Northeast India." In *Ethnic Issues Secularism and Conflict Resolution in North East India*, Bimal J. Deb, eds. Concept Publishing Company, New Delhi.

Robert, G. Gosselink. 1994. "Minority Rights and Ethnic Conflict in Assam", *Third World Law Journal*, Boston College, India, Volume 14, Issue 1, Article 5.

Singh, Baljit. 2006. "Politics of Identities: Global, South Asian and Indian Perspective", *The Indian Journal of Political Science*, Vol. 67, No. 2 (April- June), pp. 205-220.

Singh, K.S. 1996. *People of Tripura*, Volume XLI, Anthropological Survey of India, Seagull Books, Calcutta.

Smith, Anthony D. 1986. *The Ethnic Origins of Nations*, Blackwell, Oxford.

Sharma, Krishna, Jayanta. 2011. "An Alternative Formulation for Autonomous Councils in Assam." *Economic & Political Weekly*, August 27, 2011 Vol. XLVI, No 35, pp. 23-25.

Engin F. Isin, Patricia K. Wood. 1999. *Citizenship and Identity*, Sage Publications, London.

McAdam, Doug, Tarrow, and Tilly, Charles. 1996. *To Map Contentious Politics, Mobilization*. 1: 17-34.

17

The Dormitory System of the Minyong of Arunachal Pradesh

Nirupoma Kardong

Introduction

The traditional institution dormitory, is one of the important social institutions found among the tribal people across the world. In India, such institution is found among the tribes of east, north-east, south-western and central India. Roy (1915) has reported the presence of dormitories, *jonkherpa* for boys and *palerpa* for girls, among the Oraons of Chota Nagpur. Guha (1964) has mentioned about *ghotul* of the Murias, *morung* of the Nagas and *moshup* of the Adis. Dormitories have some common features and they reflect various characteristics which are culture-specific. In North East India, a good number of tribes are reported to have dormitories, such as Garo, Karbi, Kuki, Naga, Tiwa, etc. Gurdon (1914) and Elwin (1991) have reported that the *Lynngam* of the Khasi Hills were having male dormitory which is not found among the other sections of the Khasis of Meghalaya.

Mill's (1926) following description of the tribes of North East India, Elwin (1959) examined elaborately the tribal people of Arunachal Pradesh and Nagaland. Haimendorf (1962) has reported the dormitory known as *Patang* among the Apatanis of Arunachal Pradesh. He mentions the function of youth dormitories as "an effective economic organization, a usual seminary for training young in their social and other duties and an institution for magico-religious observances". Lowie (1920) has depicted the important functions of youth organizations and age-grade systems of different tribal people. Haddon (1924) surveyed several tribes of India and described the functions of the dormitory as the central spot in the socials.

In Arunachal Pradesh, traditional institutions play an important role in the life of the Adi, Nocte, Wancho, etc. Among the Apatani, Khampti, Singpho, and Tangsa at present no dormitory has been found. Each tribe called in different term to similar institutions. Again the dormitory is called by different names by the different sub-tribes of the Adis. The Minyong call it *dere,* the Padam termed it *moshup,* the Milang and other allied sub-tribe called the institution as *ngaptek* and among the Bori and Ashing it is known as *bango.*

This chapter concentrates on the dormitories of the Minyongs focusing on the importance of dormitory, its certain rules and how it plays an key role for the balance and progress of the Minyongs society. The study is based on the field-work done in Rani, Oyan, Sile and Todang villages in the East Siang district of Siang valley of Arunachal Pradesh and various publications on the Minyong.

It was assumed that, rapid development, urbanization, education and various factors have played an influential role in changing the functioning of traditional dormitory in the state. The dormitories are consequently disappearing in the present day. scholars like Haimendorf (1982), Majumdar (1985) and Roy (1987) show that, the dormitories in North East India have been replaced by modern youth clubs and unions.

Arunachal Pradesh

Arunachal Pradesh was declared as Union Territory on January 20, 1972, and emerged as a full-fledged state from 1987 was earlier called as NEFA. Arunachal Pradesh is a hill state in the lap of the Great Himalayan mountain range. The whole state is covered with the eastern Himalayas and borders are Tibet and China on the north, Burma on east and Bhutan on the west and Assam in the south. The East Siang is situated between 27° 43° and 29° 20° north latitudes and 94° 42° and 95° 35° east latitudes. Home to indigenous peoples Arunachal Pradesh is the state where almost 110 sub-tribes and 26 major ethnic indigenous groups inhabit (People of India Survey, ASI, 1997). Being the home of different indigenous communities, Arunachal Pradesh is known to be one of the magnificent multilingual tribal areas of the world and make the area vivaciously vibrant in the realms of their different culture.

The Minyong

The Adi tribe of Arunachal Pradesh is divided into two sub-groups; Padam-Minyong group and Gallong group, which are in turn divided into various sub-tribes. They are concentrated over the Siang district and a part of the land between the Siang and the Yamne river of Arunachal Pradesh. The Adi tribe is known for their amiable and simple nature. The way they carry out the job of administering people, depict their democratic nature. Each community has a mother village and it comprises a number of villages. There is good number of sub-tribes under the Adi tribe and most of the sub-tribes have their distinct language and culture.

The Minyong is a sub-tribe of the Adi, who constitute the core of the study, inhabits the east Siang district. Borgohain (1995: 3) writes, "They are strong and courageous people mentioned in the history of British-Adi relation and known as one of the most progressive tribes having a great village solidarity". The Minyong belong to the Mongoloid stock. The Minyong language comes under the Tibeto-Burman branch of the Sino-Tibetan family. It is a patrilineal tribe and lives in pile houses constructed with bamboo, wood, palm leaves. They are agriculturalist and their day-to-day life is dependent on *jhum* cultivation. Beside *jhuming*, they also practice gathering, fishing, hunting and domestication of animal. Minyong girls are expert in weaving. Local disputes are generally solved by them through a social council (*kebang*) as per the customary rule in practices. Rice is their staple food and they consume home-made country liquor called *apong* (rice beer). Most of their rituals and festivals are integrally attached to cultivations.

Dormitory

Guha (1953: 83) opines, "There are two undying principles on which the institution (*dere*) is built, namely the creating of habit of discipline among the children in their formative stage of life and in developing a spirit of co-operation and collaboration so that the tribe can act as a unit, and fissiparous tendencies within the body politics of the tribe may have very little room for growth". Roy's (1966) comprehensive report on the Adis of Arunachal Pradesh establishes the vital roles played by youth dormitories. The dormitory is usually constructed in the centre of the village from where different approaches to it can be watched and guarded. Srivastava (1990: 111) writes, "The Minyongs society has mainly three types of dormitories—for the boys it is called *Dere* and for girls it is called *Rasheng* and *Retek* for the old person". Among the Minyongs dormitory is a house for the unmarried boys which are constructed by the villagers. The bachelor dormitory is a very important institution in the Minyong society. It is not only a training centre for all practical purposes but also the centre and upholder of cultural traits. Like some other tribes of North East India, the Minyong too have dormitory systems for young males, females and old man, called '*dere*', '*rasheng*' and '*retek*', respectively. These social institutions play an important role in developing the youth to responsible human beings by teaching them about discipline, co-operation, culture and customs.

According to Ved Prakash, "It is here that they are initiated into secrets and romances of life. The boys from different dormitory are permitted to visit *rasheng*; and the courtship often leads to happier alliance. A boy or girl is free to choose a partner for life" (cited in Srivastava, 1990). There are many different hearths (*merom*) in the dormitory according to clan-wise in some villages. Roy (1964: 195), "The village with huge populations has more than one hearth (*merom*). Each belong to a particular *merom* and sleeps in it". The dormitory provides a place to learn the art of living in an informal manner. They believe that this system develops the spirit of co-operation, mutual respect and adjustment and fellow-feeling among the children. The children of ten years and above can become members of the dormitory. Dormitory is used as a sleeping house by all young men from the age of 10 till they take wives to their homes. The dormitory is also used for holding different types of feasts, festivals and meetings, especially those of the Kebang.

It has been already stated that the Minyongs have a dormitory for girls called '*rasheng*'. It deserved to mention that *rasheng* means girls' dormitory. *Rasheng* is comparatively a small and is constructed in the corner of the village. It is in the *rasheng* that the girls choose their husband. A girl also learn weaving in *rasheng*. A girl retires from *rasheng* after she gets married and goes to live with her husband. A senior girl becomes the in charge of this house. During the day time it is generally vacant but at night spinning and weaving is carried out here. It is a small house comparing to boy's dormitory with only one square room with a fireplace in the centre, where the adolescent and unmarried girls of the village sleep in night and return to their respective houses early in the morning. *Retek* is another institution for old man found in the Minyong village. It is an individual dormitory made attached to the house. Here they do small works which require less time like making basket, fishing traps, bows and arrows, etc.

The Minyong celebrate their prime festivals, Solung and Dorung (the hunting festival), between the first week of September and January every year in the dormitory. In Dorung festival, the hunters stay over night in dormitory before going for hunting and make necessary arrangement. After returning from hunting the hunted animals were kept in the dormitory for whole night and next day all the hunters and the village elders gather in the dormitory and distribute the meat among themselves and the villagers. Solung is a harvest festival performed after the sowing of seeds and transplantation, to seek for future bumper crops. *Ponung* songs and dances are performed during the festival whole night in dormitory.

Culture of the Minyong and the Dormitory

Dormitories play an important role among the Minyong where certain rules are strictly observed. There is no formal initiation ceremony to admit the boys into the dormitory. A male can visit the dormitory of a female, although he is not allowed to stay overnight. At times, guardians will have to be around to guide the youngsters. In the *dere* and *rasheng,* the youngs are under the supervision of a senior and experienced boy and a girl, respectively, who maintain the discipline and are empowered to punish any defaulter. For girls, *rasheng* is the training institution for spinning, weaving, dancing, singing and discipline. Young boys from different dormitories come and join the girls in the *rasheng* at night and through this process they select their mates. In the Minyong society marriage succeed with the selection of a life partner by the boys and the girls during their stay in the *dere* and *rasheng*. During some festivals, girls are allowed to dance inside the dormitory of the boys. The *rasheng* is purely secular in nature and has no religious significance. The dormitory has its advisory board comprising the old and experienced people of the village. The board advise the young people on the matters of community life, hunting, fishing, etc. The old man and members of the village come to dormitory in day time together and gossip.

Festivals and Dances in the Dormitories

The fairs and festivals of the Minyong tribe reflect their rich culture and heritage. Their main festivals are Aran, Dorung, Etor and Solung. During those festivals songs and dances are performed, huge feasts are hosted, offering are made to different deities on various occasions all through the year. The Minyongs are very fond of dances. Generally they perform group dances. Popular dances among them are the *ponung, delong, yakjong* and *tapu* dance. The Minyongs celebrate a number of festivals, in particular Solung, in first week of September for five days and Dorung after harvesting in third week of January. The *ponung* dance is performed in group lead by a main singer (*miri*). The solung dance and song is called *ponung* and these *ponung* songs and dances are performed during the festival at night till morning for five days. It is a festival performed after the sowing of seeds and transplantation, to seek for future bumper crops.

The *Tapu* is a war dance, where the dancers dance vigorously to re-enact the actions of war, its glory in details and the triumphant cries of the warriors. The *Tapu* dance is also performed in the dormitory at night. These dances have led to certain forms of dancing which jointly narrate a story. The dancers are male, they wear traditional costumes like coat, war helmet, sword, etc. and it is performed for one night in *Dorung* festival after meal.

Roles of the Dormitory

The traditional socio-cultural, political, economic and religious life of the Minyong people is very much shaped by the code and conducts the dormitory. It is the centre of Minyong tradition and culture. The roles of the dormitories, which are present in the area till recent past, were very much important in the socio-cultural and economic life of the people. The origin of the dormitory among the Minyong is attached with several mythologies. The dormitories were used as the sleeping house by the youngsters of the village. Usually when a boy attained ten years of age, he can be a member of the dormitory till his marriage. The younger members have to obey the elders in the dormitory. The elders used to teach them the art of using bow and arrow, the skill of hunting and war fare. At night some elders narrate myths and folktales while other teach folk songs and dances. Dormitory is directly related to village protection, group work including hunting, fishing, and teaching of arts and crafts to the new generations. Thus, the younger people learn a major part of socio-cultural duties and obligations in the dormitories. The vital role of the dormitory was of the sexual life and the art of love making. It gives an opportunity to the young unmarried boys and girls for courtship prior to selecting a life partner. The guests and visitors are also entertained here and the trials of the village council (*kebang*) are held in dormitory.

Continuity and Change

The dormitory is still found in every Adi village like any other Minyong village in Arunachal Pradesh. The institution dormitory is still playing the crucial role in various aspects of the Minyong culture. It is maintained by the village people in every Minyong village. The village and community festivals, rituals, *kebang*, etc., are still held in the dormitory. In the celebration of the festivals, rituals, ceremonies and village council, the dormitory plays the most important role. However, due the transformation of the society from traditional to modern, some changes and innovations have come in the structure and function of the dormitory. The size of the dormitory is reduced and the hearth (*merom)* is decreased in the present day even though the village is a large one and the abode of a good number of clans.

There are various changes found in the dormitory from past. The building structure of dormitory is changed. The participation and gathering of the people in the dormitory are also decreasing in the present day. Earlier a dormitory was made of bamboo and wood and other local materials like thatch. Now it is made of concrete with brick, C.I. Sheet, and in small size. The *rasheng* (dormitory for unmarried girls) and *retak* (dormitory for old people) are almost disappeared in the present day in the Minyong people) are almost disappeared in the present day in the Minyong society. Still in every Minyong village dormitory are found with *merom* (hearth) and in the extreme left side of the dormitory the ordeal or oaths place called *bango* is built. The use of *bango* is very much important in village social council in proving one's innocence.

Conclusion

From the above discussion it is evident that both boys and girls dormitories provide lifeline of the Minyongs. These are the institutions through which socialization takes place and as a result people become aware of the various norms and values of their society. As the *dere* and *rasheng* of the Minyongs are the central institutions where the boys and girls receive practical training in traditional mode of life. It works as a centre of traditional knowledge like making bow and arrow, fish trap, etc., and transmission of such indigenous knowledge to the younger generation from the elder generation. The sharing of collective responsibilities for the tribe and the village are discussed in the dormitory, regarding the agriculture, religion, traditional polity, etc. Thus, dormitory plays a very crucial role in the Minyong society. However, like many other tribes of Arunachal Pradesh, the Minyongs are also passing through the process of transition. As a result of such vibrant and dominant traditional institution is at the crossroads. Undoubtedly, emergence of Christianity is one of the main factors but there are many other factors too like urbanization, education, etc., which have cumulatively remained responsible for such an emerging reality. On the issue of the relevance of dormitory, today there is no doubt, but it is however difficult to predict about their future.

References

Borgohain, H. 1995. *Handloom and Handicrafts of the Adis,* Itanagar, Directorate of Research, Government of Arunachal Pradesh.

Dutta, P.C. 1984. "Cultural and historical background of The Noctes of Arunachal Padesh," in *The Tribes of North East India,* S. Karotemprel (ed.), Calcutta, Firma KLM.

Elwin, V. 1959. *A Philosophy of NEFA,* Shillong, Directorate of Research, Government of Arunachal Pradesh.
Guha, B.S. 1964. *Moshup Abang,* Shillong, Directorate of Research, Government of Arunachal Pradesh.
Gurdon, P.R.T., 1914. *The Khasis,* London.
David Nutt. Haddon, A.C. 1924. *The Races of India,* Cambridge.
Haimendorf, C.F., 1962. *The Apatanis and their Neighbours,* London. Routledge and Kegan Paul.
Haimendorf, C.F. 1982. *Highlanders of Arunachal Pradesh,* New Delhi, Vikas Publishing House.
Lowie, R.H., 1920. *Primitive Society,* Liveright, NewYork.
Majumdar, D.N., 1985. "A Decaying Institution–Nokpante Gatos," in *The Tribes of India,* S. Karotemporal (ed.), Calcutta, Firma KLM.
Mibang, T., 1994. *Social change in Arunachal Pradesh,* New Delhi. Omson Publications.
Mills, J.P. 1926. *The Ao Nagas,* London, Macmillan and Co. Ltd.
Nair, P.T. 1985. *Tribes of Arunachal Pradesh,* Guwahati, Spectrum Publications.
Nyori, Tai. 1993. *History and Culture of Adis,* New Delhi, Omson Publications.
Roy, S. 1964. *Aspects of Padam Minyong Culture,* Shillong, Directorate of Research, Government of Arunachal Pradesh.
Sonowal, C.J. 1997. "Declining Youth Dormitory: A Case of Culture among the Adis of Arunachal Pradesh," in *Ecology, Culture, Development and Change,* K.C. Mahanta (ed), Special Issue, No. 6: 307-316.

SECTION-III
Ethnographies and Emerging Issues of Darjeeling Himalayan Region and Sikkim

18

Identity Struggle and Quest for Tribalization

A Case of 'Mangar' Population

Pinak Tarafdar

Introduction

A matured long standing debate on identity discourses initiates an inevitable query of proposition, whether the 'individual' or the 'group' would be considered or emphasised for necessary connotation. Although Human Rights activists argue vehemently for the former but identity with a group is legitimate substitution where ethnicity is not a silent phenomenon. Hence, ethnic identity is separate from one's personal identity whereas two may reciprocally influence each other and thus provide a sense of strength, competence and self-acceptance while negotiating complex environmental contingencies. Historical specific departure from any sort of conventional identity leads an inevitable struggle for re-establishing the same as proclaimed by the contextual situation.

At a point of time in India, the 'Hindu Social Structure' is conspicuously featured by the caste hierarchy on the basis of occupational involvement and the 'tribal' populations have been recognized as the separate entity outside the Hindu fold. 'Hindu Method of Tribal Absorption' has been recognized as the process for engulfing some of the tribal societies within the Hindu fold for accommodating them in a new survival strategies essentially required for that span of time. The events of westernization and subsequent independence have transformed the Indian social structure into a different dimension—evolving in such a way that demands re-identification of the ethnic groups in an entire rejuvenating paradigm.

Background of the Study

The concept of tribe and caste is little bit confusing in various aspects, specifically some marginalised caste groups are in transition of tribe to caste juncture. F.G. Bailey however, presented a more systematic international mode for considering the position of the tribe vis-a-vis caste as two ideal poles in a linear continuum. Later on the studies conducted by S.C. Sinha, H.N. Banerjee, Martin Orans and many more along with the epoch making work of N.K. Bose on 'The Hindu Method of Tribal Absorption' have enlightened as well as explored more aspects of tribe-caste continuum. The connotation could be revealed through their distinctive cultural practices exercised more often in life cycle associated rituals.

The 'Mangars'

The word Mangar is derived from the utterance *Mayur* which in Nepali means peacock. It is also believed that the actual pronunciation of the word is *Mongol*. The Mangars hold a link with Mongoloid stock which is well evident through their morphological features. Even their mother tongue *Mangrati* is plausibly affiliated with Tibeto-Burmese groups. The term Mangrati also might be derived from the place *Mangrat* situated in the southern part of Kathmandu—one of the places of their original habitation. Another place known as Mangar Zong in Sikkim-Darjeeling, Jalpaiguri and Alipurduar districts of North Bengal (northern part of West Bengal) and various parts of Assam and adjacent areas are either their initial habitation places or the settlement as a consequence of migration.

Central Asia is considered to be the actual place of the Mangars. They are believed to live in the regions of southern Kathmandu known as *Mangrat* which also gives literal meaning of the origin of their language known as *Mangrati*. However languages vary from the *Mangars* of the East and West which are known as *Purveli* and *Paschimi*. Affiliations with the king of Nepal have also been found in case of the Mangars who were mainly troops in his army. They have also been considered to live more than the five hundred years ago in a place called *Mangar Zong* in Sikkim. Mangar Zong (as *zong* means fort in Mangar) was the fort of a Mangar king which was located in the region of Yumthang in Sikkim.

Mangars have spread all along the hills of eastern Nepal as well as the Terai but afterward migrated and settled in the North-eastern regions in India. Mangars are now spread as far as the regions of Assam, the regions of Darjeeling, Kurseong, Kalimpong, Mirik, Chalsa, Sadarbazar, of West Bengal.

The Present Study

Keeping the spirit of micro-study in Anthropology, the present work has been conducted among the Managars of Sadarbazar, district-Alipurduar, West Bengal. The primary data have collected through intensive field studies among the Mangars population covering all of the families of Sadarbazar village. The field-work has been done on the basis of standard anthropological methods viz. census schedule, interviews, key informant interviews, case studies, and observation.

Onset of the Village

Construction of the Buxa-Fort might be one of the conspicuous pull factors for the migration which attracted a group of Mangar population to settle down in the area close to that site and the zone is already inhabited by the indigenous Drukpa people. Sadarbazar is the sole Mangar dominated village located in Buxa under the area of the Buxa-Duar Tiger Reserve the block of Kalchini with the main administration guided through Rajabhatkhawa.

The people of Sadarbazar believe to be the residents of the region inhabited by them since earlier times. But they also clear of the fact that earlier the village was known as *Satakha* and after entry of their forefathers into the area came to be known as *Mangar gau*. Although exact reasons to their migration still remain unknown but they also indicate that a large section of the population had earlier been employed as day labourers from the regions of Nepal at the time of the reconstruction of the Buxa Fort. The labour was a form of forced one and they were not paid enough.

Historical Background of the Village and the Community

It is already stated that Sadarbazar is the sole Mangar-dominated village and many stories has been accounted to the naming and origin of the village. The word Sadarbazar itself has meaning attributed to its very nomenclature. In the locally used language i.e. Nepali the word *Sadarbazar* can be broken into two halves, *Sadar* which means police while *bazaar* means market. Through this it becomes vividly clear that there used to be a market here and policemen also had a certain role in the area. This is just the outlying meaning. According to a former government surveyor and local shaman Laxman Thapa, Sadarbazar was not the original name of the village as it was actually a part of Bhutan. The ancient name of the village of Sadarbazar was *Satakha* and was predominantly dominated by the people of Bhutan.

Later, migration of the Mangars led to the settlement of the present population. This in turn led to widespread changes in the entire ethnic composition of the area and even the name of the village went on from being called 'Satakha' to 'Mangar gau' which is now presently called Sadarbazar.

At earlier times the village of Sadarbazar was a really flourishing one, there was a big *haat* or weekly market that used to be held at the last day of the week i.e. Sunday. Mostly everything desirable and required for the villagers had available at the *haat*. Even the Drukpas from far off places of Bhutan used to come to buy goods and even sold their products such as silk and even *churpi* or product made out of yak milk. They used to exchange ginger for other goods of luxury and even new types of clothes found and brought by the traders of Alipurduar to the *haat*. The main reason for the *haat* to be shifted to Santalabari can be accounted to the major thefts that had occurred in the zone.

Now coming to the issue of the word *Sadar* actually policemen were employed by the colonial regime of the British and even they were also responsible in maintaining order in the *haat*. Just a ten minute walk away from Sadarbazar is the Buxa Fort which was made by the British mainly for imprisoning freedom fighters who were a major threat along with notorious convict to the regime away from the mainstream population. The Mangars are considered to be *Matwale* as they require local fermented liquor called *jaad* made out of fermented rice in any formality be it religious or social.

Life Cycle Related Rituals (Birth)

In case of the Mangar Hindus rituals related to birth start early at the time of the pregnancy of the mother. The pregnant lady needs to face a kind of pollution period during which she is debarred from actively arranging any requirements of *puja* done at the house. Most specifically the lady is not allowed to participate in public festivals such as Sansari Puja and also private *puja* like that of the worship of the Kul Deuta. This pollution period is carried on until after the completion of the name giving ceremony of the baby. Pregnant ladies are also prevented from going under big trees as they would be followed by spirits of the forest. Tuesday as well as Saturday is believed to be highly dangerous for the health of both the pregnant lady as well as the baby inside her. This is mainly as the Mangar Hindus of Sadarbazar believe that it is specifically these days of the week that witches gain much power and may cast a spell on the lady or evil eye as the case may be.

Navran (Name-giving Ceremony)

Just like in many communities the name giving ceremony of the baby is one that is most significant and important for all the members of the family. Traditionally, the name giving ceremony of the Mangars is called *navran* and in earlier it was carried out in the presence of 12 chiefs of different clans known as 12 Mangrat. The 12 Mangrats seem to hold a significant place when it comes to the traditional practices of the Mangars. The Navran ceremony is not carried out at the day of birth of the child.

Even after the birth of the child, the mother faces and is subjected to a pollution period. She is now referred to as *sutkeri*. The period of being a *sutkeri* is considered to be the most delicate phase. Mangar women of Sadarbazar recount their experiences and say that at the time of delivering the baby they get immeasurable strength and protection through the family's *kul devta*. The phase of being a *sutkeri* is very delicate as the Mangars believe that the body of the lady experiences a near to death situation so she must be susceptible to the attacks of spirits of witches and the witches messengers called *chawdas* (a form of evil like creature mostly acting under the whims of the witch). The *sutkeri* is also advised not to keep her head exposed which should always remain covered by a cloth.

This is done to keep off evil as well as keeping her warm. Earlier conceptions and practices of being a *sutkeri* in the phase of pollution period involved taking bed rest for a period of twenty two days and most were even prevented from brushing of teeth as well. They were also barred from cooking meals and also not permitted to take entry into the kitchen. Locally fermented rice drink called *jaad* and also fermented drink made out of maize or millet known as *nigar* are the two conspicuous beverages significantly consumed by the pregnant mother during *sutkeri* partly as a traditional norms and partly with the known increase in milk yield that would help the growing infant.

The name giving ceremony or *navran* is very significant as it determines and sets a name for the infant imprinting a mark into the social ladder of the child. *Navran* is not carried out at the first day of birth of the child but in the community of Mangar Hindus it takes place from 3 to 5 days of birth. It is through this ceremony that the baby by having his personal name has an identity for himself in the society and among the community as a whole. So the entire *navran* ceremony is not only a private affair for the family but all the close-knit relatives as well as neighbours, known friends and family are cordially invited to partake in the ceremony. Even though everyone receives the invitation but the most important invitation is for the maternal uncle of the baby known as his *Mama*. The *mama* is invited a day before the ceremony in accordance to the traditional rules of the Mangar. The day of the ceremony starts with certain rites and rituals carried on as assigned the day earlier to the paternal uncle *mama* of the baby.

On the day of the *navran,* the maternal uncle or the *mama* at first purifies the site accounted for the *navran* to be held. The ceremony mostly takes place inside the House. The exact day and time for the start of the ceremony is looked upon by a Brahmin (priest) hired for the purpose. But traditionally in the earlier times the *wapa* was assigned the task of carrying forth the proceedings of the *navran* ceremony under the presence of the family, the entire community as well as the most important of all the 12 Mangrat chiefs.

Thereafter the ceremony begins and all members of the family gather on the parents of the baby sit crossed legs in front of the prayer fire known as *havan* done by the *Bawun bajey* as referred to the Brahmins. After much time and calculations, the alphabet for the name of the baby is revealed in front of all present.

Besides this even yarns of thread are also given to the infant. Along with these some may give other types according to their own wishes. These gifts are received by the mother who sits cross-legged with the baby in her lap. After all the guests visit the mother and child they are received by a grand feast that is prepared in the house. Before the commencement of the *navran* all members and also the paternal uncle *mama* had not taken meat and even garlic a day earlier. Celebrations are then made till late in the evening.

Bhaat Khwai

The rice feeding ceremony of the child is also a highly awaited one among the whole family. It is held after six months from the birth of the child. Earlier before the *bhaat khwai* the baby is fed exclusively mother's milk. Traditionally the period for *bhaat khwai* is six months for son and five months for daughter but nowadays differences on basis of gender is not followed and the ceremony is held after six months. The day for the ceremony is affixed by a *bawun bajey* (Brahmin Priest) and he looks upon the child's *janma kundali* in order to select a date and time that would be auspicious for the commencement of the ceremony. After the date is fixed all preparations are made and all relatives as well as friends and neighbours are invited for the celebration following the *bhaat khwai* of the infant.

The worship is held at the time fixed by the *bawun bajey* and after the completion of it a small ounce of rice mixed with ghee is kept in a *taba ko botuko* (small bowl made of brass); the mother of the baby is the one who feeds a bit of it to the infant.

Chewar

In case of the Mangar, the ritualistic hair cutting ceremony of the infant is known as *chewar.* This takes place usually a year after the birth of the infant. The ceremony is not a grand one rather a small occasion is held involving mostly the close-knit members of the family. *Mama,* the maternal uncle of the child is invited for doing the *mundan* of the child. A small worship is done before the commencement of the ceremony; the date and time of the *mundan* is ascribed by the *bawun bajey* (Brahmin Priest). After completion of the worship, the maternal uncle of the child is called for the proceedings of the ceremony. There is a small feast held for the family and items eaten are mostly vegetarian at noon followed by consumption of liquor and non-vegetarian items in the evening.

Life Cycle Related Rituals (Marriage)

The Mangar of Sadarbazar have specific notion and a long tradition of elaborate rituals that have been carried forth from the time of the *Tumthung* Mangars up to the present generation. Although influence of *Brahminical* Hindu rituals has led to slight alterations in the practices of marriage but the true essence of it remains unchanged. Endogamy is preferred but there is no strict taboo against exogamous marriages as well. The marriage among Mangars occurs in two ways:

- Marriage by negotiation or arrangement
- Marriage by elopement.

Marriage by Negotiation or Arrangement

This form of marriage occurs only when both the bride and groom belong to the same Mangar caste but different clans i.e. caste endogamy and clan exogamy is observed. This type of marriage can also occur between cross-cousins; in some instances the man is permitted to marry his maternal uncle's daughter but not that of his paternal uncle. Earlier the tradition was that the girl of the maternal uncle had to be sought first for the son of his sister. If the girl eloped with another then only the boy would seek other girls. But a lot of changes have been observed.

In case of this form of marriage, a messenger called *lami* goes to the girl's family to ask for her hand in the name of the boy. This is called *Mangani*. Here the background of the family is also asked and the boy and girl are met for one time. The representative of the boy then presents 1 *thegi (wooden jar)* of *curd, sweets, raksi* (country liquour), *betel leaf, flower, betel nut and a coin.* All these are kept in front of the girl's family while the proposal is made simultaneously. Here the clan of the girl and that also of the boy are made clear. It is up to the decision of the family and if they accept the relation then the items are accepted. This is done publicly in front of all the family members and relatives of the girl. Accepting the *thegi* is a form of assurance provided by the girl's family that the girl would not elope with another person. This ritual is called *thegi kaki,* if the family rejects the offer then the *thegi* is rejected.

These are the 12 Mangar *reet* which are taken where 12 items are asked by the bride's family comprising of:

- Male cock usually one in number
- 12 liters of local liquor called *rakshi* in mud vessel
- 12 kg meat of pig/goat/chicken
- 12 kg rice *alua/bagoda* carried in *thunchey* (bamboo basket for carrying items)
- 12 kg of solid unprepared portion of *hadia*
- 12 kori *Selroti* (1 kori=20 rotis)
- 12 coins of one rupee
- *Mawale bhale* (cock for maternal uncle of the bride) carried in *Perunga* (basket made of bamboo smaller than thunchey)
- Sidra (dry fish) any
- Turmeric, ginger filled in *perunga* respectively
- *Sinka* (small needle like stick made of bamboo) used mainly for making banana leaf plate known as *tapara.*
- *Dahi* (curd) kept in *Thegi* (wooden implement for storing curd/milk).

Traditionally, the girl used to wear *phariya, choli, hembari and gold ornaments comprising of ring called authi, bangles called chura and silver bangles on ankle.* Tilhari made of gold would also be worn but the practice has stopped among the Mangars of Sadarbazar and nowadays the bride comes by wearing a *sari* preferably red to symbolize marriage and the head is always kept covered either by the portion of the *sari* or a white cloth. The groom also instead of wearing the traditional attire known as *kaccha* is now found to wear three piece suit contrasting to the earlier practices.

The final step now requires conducting the ceremony which is on the day affixed by the *baun bajey* (Brahmin) as the Mangars of Sadarbazar comply with the Hindu form of religious practices in terms of marriage. Earlier the *wapa* who is the traditional priest of the Mangars used to perform this task but now due to their absence all rites are performed by the Brahmin. In certain families marriages had earlier been conducted by the maternal uncle as well so the variations are numerous. When the boy goes to the girl's house *naumati baja* are playd comprising of nine musical instruments. They are viz. *tempu, shehnai, jhyamta, doma, dholak, narsinha, manjura.* This is played in front of the boy's procession and mostly done by the *Damai* (a specific caste group) among the Nepali.

All the family members gather and everyone has a time of gaiety. The feasts are also prepared where all the relatives as well as villagers are invited. The groom is then introduced through a system called *chiley mata* where the *lokanti* goes to the house of the girl and salt tea is given to the groom and his friends. This is a form of joking relation which adds fun to the entire proceedings. After resting for a bit the ceremony begins through the occurrence of a *hom* (sacred fire) usually made outside the house, where, summoning of the God is done to bless the ceremony. In the middle of the ceremony both the bride and the groom have to make three rounds surrounding the *hom.* Here the girl is carried by her brother and even the groom is carried by another brother and three rounds are made. The groom then puts vermilion over the parting of girl's forehead and *potey mala* comprising of green beads and a *tilhari* made of gold is worn over her neck. The ceremony continues and here unlike other communities the *kanyadaan* (the daughter giving ritual) is done by the maternal uncle of the bride.

Everyone blesses them and the ceremony is then completed. A feast is held where everyone has a great time in celebrations for a great life of the newlyweds and the families associated with them. The completion of the marriage then accounts for washing of the feet of the bride by the maternal uncle.

Marriage by Elopement

Marriage by elopement is another form of marriage practiced among the Mangar. In fact I was lucky enough to witness certain proceedings of such a marriage as I had all been invited to attend the reception of a resident of Sadarbazar. Usually marriage by elopement occurs in the region when the boy and girl in a love affair and are of different castes and marry without any prior arrangements according to their own wishes; even being of the same caste and families agree with the marriage but sometimes the norms of the clans would not permit *Mangni beya* so mutual understanding is made between the families and the girl elopes with the boy.

Both the families are usually unaware in case of exogamous marriage where the girl is of another caste but in case of mutual understanding the families are aware. After bringing the girl home *sindoor potey* of the girl is usually done within 3 days at the groom's house itself. This is mainly done to ensure that the girl should not be taken away back by her family. Following this within 5 days of elopement, a group of persons known as *chor ko shor* comprising of 4 elderly members of the village along with the groom go to the bride's house to inform on her whereabouts. They also state that the girl is safe and also disseminate the news of the marriage.

The *chor ko shor* group does not go empty hand and take *a bottle of rakshi* (country liquour) *over which teetay pati (Artemesia vulgaris) is kept, some sweets are also offered while the information is being given.* All these items are offered by keeping them in a *kasa ko thaal* (brass plate) kept over a handkerchief as a sign of respect. At the ceremony except father and mother the maternal uncle is present and receives the ceremonial offerings in favour of the groom or may reject it. Once the ritual gifts are accepted the girl's family fixes the date for *dhog bhet* where the newlyweds are introduced to both the families.

The *dhog bhet* is done in the girl's family and acts as a means of socially introducing them within the wider circle of the relatives and kinsmen. At the ceremony a bottle of *rakshi,* sweets and flowers, betel leaf are placed in *kasa ko thaal* (brass plate) over a white handkerchief by the representative of the groom. Introduction is then made where both the bride as well as the groom is introduced by all the senior members up to the older members. This is done by respectfully touching the feet of the elders.

The members of the Mangar *Samaj* then create an authorization stating the legal sanction of the marriage which is now recognized by both the families as well as the society. At earlier times the 12 Mangars would look after such cases and further on 12 elderly Mangars of different *thars* (clan) would be invited to conduct the same. In case the girl is of a different caste then she makes a *maiti* within the community of Mangars. The *maiti* acts as her brother and she is given his clan name. Afterwards *chula chokhai* is done where the signature or approval of 12 elderly Mangars of different clans is required. The girl has to cook a meal where the 12 Mangars are invited and if any one stands on due course of the meal it is thought to have been disapproved. This form of ceremonial eating was practiced at the time of the elderly members of Sadarbazar but now the practice is replaced by official signature of the *Lafasang* which is the Mangar *Samaj* of Sadarbazar.

After *thar* the girl is also introduced to the *kul* (ancestral deities) of the family and is completely accepted as a Mangar Bride by both the family, socially as well as religiously after her introduction to the *kul*. Reception is done at the girl's house and *tika talo* where all members give blessings by putting *tika* (rice mixed with curd) is done. A grand feast is organized at the end of which the girl returns to the groom's house by being carried over by her brother outside.

Life Cycle Related Rituals (Death)

The Mangar of Sadarbazar confirm the traditional as well as the systems adopted through the adoption of Hinduism while performing rites and ceremonies related to the death of any individual. They believe death to be a part of the greater circle of life and take it as an event that ultimately unites all class and castes of people.

In case of death of a Mangar individual, a number of rituals are exerçised that require to be followed as sequentially as a social norm and belief. The body of the deceased is kept on the floor at a spot in the house by first smearing the region with *cow dung*. A *diyo batti* (a kind of lamp) is lighted near it along with incense sticks and one rupee coin is kept at the forehead. At this time family members refrain from all outdoor activities and moreover, mirrors and television sets are covered with cloth. Much noise is not permitted to be made. By this time people come to give last visit to the deceased by putting *khada* over it and condolence is given to the family. People from other castes are not allowed to touch the body and so are the children. The time for the body to be taken depends on the predictions affixed by the appointed Brahmin or *bawun bajey*.

The body is taken by keeping it over a structure made of *green bamboo* and at times coffin like structure is made. Before the body is taken people who form a part of going there have the responsibility of undressing the body and put it wrapped in a white cloth called *katro*. After the time is given the body now wrapped in *katro* is kept inside the coffin or over the bamboo structure. All the family members then take three rounds around the body and bid their last good bye. The leg of the body is kept at the direction of the place of burning. It is a very depressing sight and all the mourners find it emotionally weakening at this time. All the male members of the family as well as the relatives and villagers now go to take the body for cremation done by burning.

A Brahmin or *bawun bajey* is also appointed for the task. Females stay at the house and right before the body is taken out one of them smears the house with cow dung. The body is then lifted and the son is made to carry it from right arm and if the son is not present then the son-in-law or in his absence relative's son can take charge from the left side.

On reaching the site of cremation at Lal Bangla or Damanpur, the body is groomed by combing hair and washing face then its nail is cut by keeping it over the pile of woods. A handfull of rice is then kept over its mouth and the ritual is called *dharti kiney* as a reverence to the mother earth. The son then through the guidelines made by the *bahun bajey* makes three rounds of the body and then gives *daag batti* where coin is given in lip and camphor and milk is placed over it. After this the pile is lighted by the son. If the son is not present then any male relative could go for the entire process.

Later the son is made bald by a family member near the place of burial or even after returning home. In case of death of the mother the eyebrows of the son is also cut off. He is given white cloth called *katro* to wear and all accessories are prohibited for wearing until the funeral ceremony is over. A member who does not touch the body while taking it to the burning ground is assigned the task of taking *teetay pati* and making a small fire comprising of wood and *teetay pati* near or in front of the house while everyone returns back. They have to step this and pass it before entering the house for warding off spirits. All the people who participated in taking the body are called *Malami.*

At Sadarbazar most Hindu Mangars also practice putting *teetay pati* and water [comprising of black *til* (a kind of ingredients) and *gout* (cow's urine)] before entering house for the purpose of warding off spirits. The house where the person died is however considered impure i.e. *jutho lageko* for 12 days after which the funeral is done. The *Malami* must eat at the house of the dead where the female members cook *aloodum, puri,* and give a bit of ginger (to ward off spirits).

No one in the family eats any meal for the day and the son faces the period of pollution for 12 days. This is called *kuri basnu* and no one can touch him at this time. He is secluded from the family and a separate room is allotted where he cooks his own meal and observes strict discipline for ensuring the dead person would find his way easily to proceed in another world. They cannot talk and interact much with others. Even water has to be brought separately from the *dhobi khola* and he has to bath there each day. The food eaten by the son is simple comprising mainly of items such as rice, ghee, potato and fruits. *Diyo* (oil lamp) is burnt from the opposite side in the name of the deceased. The food eaten is on banana leaf kept inverted and always given in the opposite direction and needs to be finished at one serving only.

No one can stay near to the *kuri* as he is said to be subjected to be vulnerable to attack of the spirits. The pollution period continues for 12 days and on the 13th day the main funeral is done which is known as *kriya.* Here under the guidance of the *bawun bajey* worship is done for the purification of the house which is believed to be having the presence of the soul of deceased which would now go to its abode. After completion of the worship, the house is smeared with cow dung from outside to inside.

Preparations are made for giving food to all the relatives and villagers in the name of the deceased. At the same time the family members get purified by eating a bit of *gaut* (cow dung) and a small bit of salt, turmeric, sugar and oil. They are now purified and can go on with the regular chores.

At Sadarbazar usually on the 13th day after the main funeral a ceremony known as *chinta* is held at night for guiding the souls to a good path and knowing their whims. This is performed by a *jhankri* and starts at around 8:00 in the night. Here the deceased through the *jhankri* as a medium tell their grievances, conditions, at times tell about the items they desired and also whether they are at peace or demand certain things.

This is done in all Mangar houses of Sadarbazar and follows the eager participation of the villagers as well. At the end of the ceremony the *jhankri* also does protective acts such as putting sheet over young children and hitting with a bit of coal flares for keeping them safe against the wrath of spirits. Usually in such ceremonies sacrifices of cock is made in the name of the dead and the ceremony brings peace to the family on the issues that have to be dealt with.

The Mangar of Sadarbazar has lots of reverence to the workings of the *bawun bajey* as well as the *jhankri* in helping the deceased to attain a better state after passing away. The people believe that the balance of both the elements is necessary for helping the world of the dead as well as the mortals in balance. Pollution period of the son is a must and the customs practiced in a way highlights the patriarchal dominance in carrying out the rituals where the son is given first and outmost preference. The family does not celebrate any festival for a period of one year and the family members are prohibited from living in other places for the same period.

Conclusion

The life cycle rituals among the Mangars unfold a strong sense of supernatural connotation even in the initial phase of pregnancy as the movement of pregnant women also restrain with time and space. Pregnant ladies are also prevented from going under big trees as they would be followed by spirits of the forest. Tuesday and Saturday are believed to be highly unsafe for mother and baby inside the womb. The norms in the pollution period are mainly followed as observed among the mainstream Nepali Hindu population and the same is recongnised as *sutkeri*.

The exclusive traditional practices found among the Mangar is the consumption of locally fermented rice drink called *jaad* and also fermented drink made out of maize or millet known as *nigar*. Traditional knowledge of increasing milk quantity yields the recommended usages to the mother. Although in some of the cases Brahmin priests are called for *navran* (name giving ceremony) but the role and existence of Mangar priest *wapa* cannot be overruled. A different connotation has been revealed as the ceremony also unfolds the existence of ancestral spirit in abode of first name given to the new born.

Marriage by elopement and bride price makes the phenomena exclusive for Mangars that never been existed in the so-called upper caste Hindu segment. The conspicuous usages of *rakshi* (country liquour), cock, *teetay pati* (*Artemesia vulgaris*) and dry fish as the inevitable ingredients and beverage once more reveal the separate notion of rituals. Existence of cross-cousin marriage is not a usual phenomenon among the Hindu caste population (specifically in north India) but continuation of the same demands a different connotation.

As a part of syncretism most of the rituals related with death follow the tradition of Hindu Nepali culture with some blending features of Buddhism also. The usages of cow dung and urine, milk, rice, *ghee, khada* etc. show the mark of same legacy. But on 13th day an exclusive ceremony holds as *chinta*—a magico-religious performance occur to guide the soul for its future destination along with deciphering the whims of the same. Sacrifice of cock is also significant in this regard.

The present work is a tiny endeavour for exploring the indigenous cultural traits which could be depicted in the deepest layer of contingent paraphernalia of a particular community. Indeed the absorption and consequent blending were intensified in such a way which even blurred the basic distinction in the sway of the process. Hence more intensive and exploratory works are vehemently required for developing decisive knowledge on the issue—'quest for trabalization' among the 'Mangar'.

References

Bhasin, V. 1990. *Habit, Habitation and Health in the Himalayas*. Delhi, Kamal Raj Enterprises.

Bose, N.K. 1941. "The Hindu Method of Tribal Absorption." *Science and Culture*, 7.

Gennep, A.V. 1960. *The Rites of Passage: Anthropology & Ethnography*. USA, Redwood Burn Limited.

Northey, W.B. 2001. *The Gurkhas: Their Manner, Customs and Country*. New Delhi, Asian Educational Services.

Oestigard, T. 2000. *The Deceased's Life Cycle Rituals in Nepal: Present Cremation Burials for the Interpretations of the Past*. England, BAR International series 853, Biddles Ltd.

Pelto, P.J. and G.H. Pelto. 1978. *Anthropological Research, The Structure of Inquiry*. Cambridge, Cambridge University Press.

Srinivas, M.N. 1995. *India's Village*. Bombay, Asia Publishing House.

Tanka, K.C. 2004. *The Culture, Tourism Nature of Nepal*. Nepal, Folk Music Art Academy.

Tarafdar, P. 2007. Life cycle related Rituals and Health-care practices among the Santhals and Kora of Jhargram. *Bulletin of the Cultural Research Institute*. Backward Classes Welfare Department, Government of West Bengal. Vol. 23, No.1: 49-53.

Tylor, E.B. 1871. *Primitive Culture*. London, John Murray Albemarle Street.

19

Social Networks of Rural People for Understanding their Survival Strategy

Rabindranath Jana and Anil Kumar Choudhuri

Introduction

One of the survival strategies of the rural people such as marginal or small farmers, sharecroppers and landless labourers, is their potential and ability to get mobilized and act as a class in order to fulfil their needs or demands. On many issues, particularly the ones which are of collective interest or which require bargaining with those who have power and authority, mobilization as a class plays a key role as a matter of their strategy. Again, in course of their daily life, situations often arise when a need is faced by a household which it has to fulfil immediately even by taking help from others. In such circumstances they act individually as a household or a family. They interact with one another as neighbours, friends, kins, employers / employees, etc. Thus they gradually build up networks of regular interaction through these ties. We label these networks as social networks. These social networks work at household/family level and play an important role as a kind of strategy for survival of the rural people. Because one who belongs to such a social network can request others in the same network for help and support. Such flows of help and support operate, in an unnoticed manner, so to say, either directly, pair-wise, or through intermediaries in the network. Thus this process works beneath the surface, keeping a low profile, but steadily, to meet various urgent requirements of daily life and living that one cannot fulfil by one's own resources at hand. Social networks, in this sense, provide a strategy of resource mobilization individually from those with whom one has network connections. Keeping this in mind, the present chapter intends to apply social network analysis (SNA) approach for studying survival strategy of the rural people in Jharkhand and West Bengal and hope this study will be relevant to the policy-makers in the context of decentralization and devolution of planning not only at a particular state level but also at any regional/national level.

In literature one can trace discussions on social networks in various contexts. We cite a few: Homans (1950: 99-104); Moreno (1934, 1956); Moreno et al. (1960); Lazarsfeld and Menzel (1962: 422-440); Simmel's concepts of dyads and triads in Wolff (1964: 118-177); "The concept and use of social networks" by J.C. Mitchell (in Mitchell 1969 ed.: 1-50); endophily-homophily, internal differentiation of occupational groups, "coalitions" and social distance among them in Laumann and Pappi (1976); Berkowitz (1982); Burt and Minor (1983). Rao and Bandyopadhyay (1987) is an analysis of various measures of reciprocity in social networks. The findings show a marked variation in pattern of articulation of ties among the villagers in twenty-one villages studied in West Bengal. In most of the villages reciprocity is only moderate or even quite low. Social mobility, cohesion and inter-group integration in terms of social network has been discussed in Collins (1988: 412-448). Wellman and others (1991: 223-249) integrate individual, relational and network data. That the study of social network can be used to compare effectiveness of different systems of stratification, such as "caste" and "class" in India, in organising reciprocity has been shown in Chatterjee, Bandyopadhyay and Rao (1993: 15-22). For a comprehensive chronological review of the major streams of network studies one can see Wellman (1997).

The process of economic reforms was started in 1991 for taking India out of economic difficulty and speeding up the development process. It is now the second fastest growing economy and, according to PPP, 4th largest economy of the world. On the other hand, 20 per cent of the rural population lives only on Rs. 12 (1/4th of a dollar) a day. It is also well-known that the rural society in India is stratified by sharp economic inequality. During the last three decades socio-economic and administrative measures in West

Bengal (namely, implementation of land reforms, *Patta* distribution, minor irrigation schemes, Panchayats, Total Literacy Campaign, minimum wage rate, sharecropper registration, etc.) as well as market factors (such as opening of facilities for jobs and small business, mini-entrepreneurial opportunities, construction and improvement of road and transportation communication, etc.) have created noteworthy impact upon pattern of articulation of social relation in the villages (Bandyopadhyay and von Eschen, 1980). Specially noteworthy is the articulation of new power structure and rise of new centres of power from within the lower rung of the village society (Rao et al.1998; Bandyopadhyay 2003). In case of Jharkhand the striking feature is the absence of the above mentioned socio-economic and administrative measures. Under such conditions, the proposed study will investigate to what extent in the absence of officially induced socio-economic and administrative measures as above, only the mechanism of spontaneous social interaction can play an important role as a strategy for life and living of the rural poor. The study will also investigate the pattern of articulation of social relations and emergence of any new structure of power relations in the villages with respect to the basic characteristics of a social network which are relevant for the present study.

The situation is all the more aggravated since Jharkhand is, on the one hand, one of the most poverty-stricken regions in India, while, on the other hand, is sharply polarized by traditionally continuing caste-community based power structure which creates a strong barrier to decentralization and empowerment of the socio-economically weaker sections in the villages. Because of socio-economic and administrative measures implemented officially, West Bengal becomes a typical case whereas, left to traditionally continuing mechanism of market-based spontaneity, Jharkhand becomes an atypical example which may have been replicated in other states as well. In a way our findings from Jharkhand, in this sense, can be more representative in so far as the country as a whole is concerned. That adds to the importance of our study in Jharkhand. We next briefly recapitulate some relevant characteristics of a social network and then proceed to the subject matter of the present chapter.

Methodology

Terms and Concepts of Social Network

In most types of standard analysis including surveys, the object of investigation is a unit which may be an individual or a household, etc. Data like income and landholding are collected on each unit. However, this does not take into account the interaction between units. In SNA, the respondent is again an individual or a household but the object of study is which pairs of units interact and how. The analysis of such data calls for an entirely different type of methodology. A discussion of SNA in general may be found in Scott (1991), and Holland and Leinhardt (1979) and a discussion of reciprocity in social networks may be found in Rao and Bandyopadhyay (1987).

The present study denotes a social network as an articulation of ties of a social relationship among social units such as persons, families, households, etc. The ties are links between the individual and others in the network. The three elementary parameters of a social network are the *number of units* in it, the total *number of ties* in a network and the *number of reciprocal pairs of units* in it. The number of ties may be further disaggregated as the number of ties going out from a unit (*out-degree*) and the number of ties coming to a unit (*in-degree*). Incidentally, one may note that the total of out-degrees of all the units in a network and the total of all the in-degrees in it will be the same as the total number of ties. The numbers of units and the ties (including their directions) provide the basic data necessary to study a network in terms of social network theory. Using these social network data some sociologically useful measures can be derived as follows. *Reciprocity* is the number of pairs of households which are mutually tied up, standardised with respect to the range between the maximum and the minimum numbers of reciprocal pairs obtainable given the out-degrees of all the households as data (Rao and Bandyopadhyay 1987). It can be taken to be an indicator of *cohesion* among the households. Incidentally, in this case and subsequently, the household is our unit. Concentration of in-degrees provide a measure of *power* whereas out-degrees show the *extent of buffer* against vulnerability to risks, that is, the *potential* to mobilise social resources. As studied by Jana and Choudhuri (2013), few more parameters relevant for the present study are being described as follows. *Distance* is a measure of closeness (or separation as well) between a pair of households in a social network. It is the minimum number of steps (that is, links of the network) one has to take to reach the other. Distance can be measured in two ways, by considering the direction of a tie, or, not.

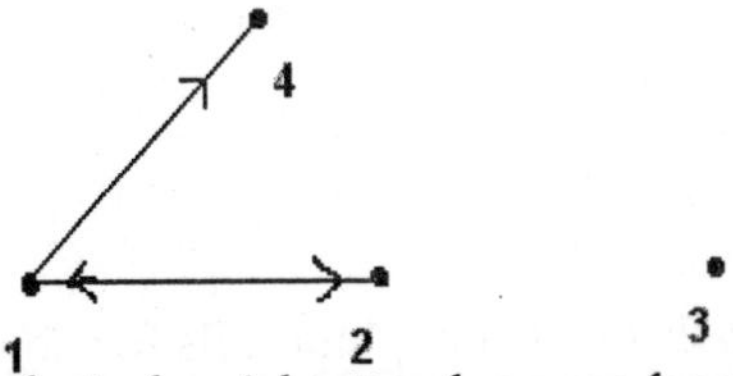

Fig. 19.1: A hypothetical social network among four units/actors.

Hence, Fig. 19.1 shows, distance from 1 to 4 is one and 2 to 4 is two. But from 4 to 1 or 4 to 2 as well as from 3 to 1 or 2 or 4 is infinity, since 1 and 2 are not reachable from 4 and 1, 2, 4 not from Ignoring direction, distance from 4 to 1 is one and 4 to 2 is two. *Reachability* is the proportion of ordered pairs of households (i, j) such that j is reachable from i in one or more steps out of all the pairs that can be formed given the total number of households. It indicates *connectedness* of households in a network. This, again, can be measured differently considering direction of a tie or not. For all practical purposes reachability in 2 or 3 steps is much more meaningful than, say, reachability through 5 or 6 intermediaries (Laumann and Pappi 1976: 104; Mitchell 1969: 14). Besides, it becomes possible to indicate degree of *hierarchisation* and *fragmentation* within the society.

With this introduction to social network theory, it is not intended to study all the aspects of the theory in this chapter, but only to investigate how this theory can be applied to capture the survival strategy of the rural poor by examining the pattern of articulation of ties among the social units within local communities such as villages, in the backyard of socio-economic conditions in the larger societal milieu.

Village Selection for the Study

Since the study is based on the rural poor of Jharkhand and Bengal, two villages, one from Jharkhand and another from West Bengal, have been considered for the study. The Jharkhand village is Mahacho (Thana No. 8G) in Ojhadih Gram Panchayat under Police Station and Block Bengabad; and the Bengal village is Raspur (J.L. No. 174) in Charicha Gram Panchayat under Police Station and Block Md. Bazar. These two villages were purposively selected for an earlier study in 2006 considering the fact that there had easy accessibility and scope of easy rapport building.

Data Collection and Analysis Level

All the households in each of the aforesaid two villages have been enumerated. A complete enumeration of each village was done because, otherwise, many of the parameters of social network cannot be analyzed from a sample (Knoke and Kuklinski 1988; Wasserman and Faust 1999; Jana 2005). In the study, both the quantitative and qualitative methods of obtaining data and analysis have been used. Structural data have been mostly collected by quantitative survey, interviewing respondents with questionnaires. This was supplemented by qualitative data collected from case studies, group discussions held in the villages, historical narratives told by locally knowledgeable "aged villagers" and so on. This part of investigation was focused to delineate villagers' perception and evaluation of a phenomenon. Similarly, in addition to conventional tools of analysis of quantitative survey data, methods of qualitative data analysis such as obtaining standardized entropy or index of qualitative variation were applied (Weisberg 1993).

1. Location and Other Facilities of the Villages

Briefly speaking, the study villages Mahacho and Raspur are un-irrigated rain-fed, mono-crop agricultural villages. The villages are far from wholesale markets and less urban exposure. As such, the villages are interior villages without much road and transport connection with any urban or market center. In this context, it is also noteworthy that although both agriculture and non-agriculture sectors provide sources of livelihood to the villagers in the selected villages, the latter is particularly the major source in all the villages (Table 19.1: Panel C). Our summary data regarding the villages also show the presence of different categories of Hindu castes and other communities in each village (Appendix B). A broad outline of locational characteristics and socio-economic composition of the villages are given in Panel-A, B & C of Table 19.1.

2. Social Stratification of the Villages

By Caste Community

The entire population in each village has been divided into two

Table 19.1: Panel A: Location of the villages

State	Village (alphabetic code).	Total house holds	Area in acres	Distance from District H.Q. (Km)		Distance from the nearest wholesale market (Km)	
				By road	Walking	By road	Walking
(1)	(2)	(3)	(4)	(5)	(6)	(7)	(8)
Jharkhand	Mahacho (Mc)	89	377	23	15	23	15
West Bengal	Raspur (Rp)	174	575	15	15	8	8

Panel B: Location of the Villages

Name of the village	Distance from (in Km.)												
	Police Station	R S*	Block Office	Bank	Bus route	CS.*	Post office	GP*	Hospital	P.H.C*	Collage	Primary School	High School
(1)	(2)	(3)	(4)	(5)	(6)	(7)	(8)	(9)	(10)	(11)	(12)	(13)	(14)
Mc	10	23	10	7	2	10	2.5	2	23	2.5	23	0	10
Rp	12	15	15	12	3	12	3	6	15	4	15	0	6

Panel C: Summary of Socio-economic Composition of Villages

Village alphabetic code	Principal sector of source of livelihood of a household (% in bracket)			Distribution of households by caste/community categories in each village (Exact number of castes/communities in a category within brackets)**							
	Agriculture	Non-griculture	Total	H1	H 2	H 3	ST	M	Total	% (H1+H 2)	% (H3+ST+ M)
(1)	(2)	(3)	(4)	(5)	(6)	(7)	(8)	(9)	(10)	(11)	(12)
Mc	50 (56.18)	39 (43.82)	89 (100.00)	00 (00)	28 (2)	51 (2)	00 (00)	10 (1)	89 (5)	31.46 (2)	68.54 (3)
Rp	101 (58.05)	73 (41.95)	174 (100.00)	1 (1)	44 (4)	56 (3)	64 (3)	9 (1)	174 (12)	25.86 (5)	74.14 (7)

* *RS= Railways Station, CS= Co-operative society, GP= Gram Panchayat, P.H.C.= Primary Health Centre*

** Traditionally followed ritual categories; Hindu high (H1), middle (H2), low castes including SC (H3), Tribal (ST) and Muslim (M).

categories, CCI and CCII according to broadly ascribed status based on the basis of caste-community ranking in the local social milieu.

On many instances it is conceptually more meaningful, as it is said, to see the "forest" rather than each "tree" by itself. In CC-I, there are Hindu High (H1) and Middle castes (H2). Incidentally, the Hindu Middle castes occupy most of the land in both Jharkhand and Bengal villages and they enjoy political and social power as well. Thus, they are no less "dominant" than the High-castes. Occupationally, they are engaged in cultivation, business and services. The only social difference between them concerns customs, which, however, are noticeably narrowing down. Our observations during the course of field study indicated that the economic condition of the Hindu High and Middle castes was, more or less, the same.

In the second category CCII, we include the remaining Hindu-Low (H3) (including Scheduled Castes), Scheduled Tribes and the Muslims. However, as and where found possible, the category H3 has been treated separately, because the people belonging to the castes in this category happen to be placed socially and culturally in the same line. Moreover, living condition, occupational pattern and distribution of land owned are similar. For their livelihood they often depend upon non-agricultural activities, mainly labour of various types.

On the whole, Panel-B of Table 19.2 summarizes that both villages are numerically more dominated by CCII (i.e., Hindu Low, SC and Muslim communities) than by CCI (i.e., Hindu High and Middle castes). If we consider H3 as the mid-point, in case of the Jharkhand village the distribution is mesokurtic, whereas in case of Bengal village, the distribution is quite different, notably flatter/ platykurtic. Thus their social compositions are considerably stratified, only shapes are different. Their standardized entropy is 0.8452 and 0.9822 respectively. The oral histories of settlement of caste/communities in different villages also support such differentials in shape of stratification (Choudhuri and Jana, 2013).

Stratification by Source of Livelihood Categories and Ownership of Land

From the standpoint of occupational affiliation, all the villages show a significant level of stratification. From Panel-C of Table 19.1, it is seen that the villagers of both villages are mostly dependent on agricultural activities—more than 50 per cent of the households depend upon agriculture, cultivation in particular.

Table 19.2: Panel-A: Distribution of households by caste/community categories in Jharkhand village and West Bengal village [% in first bracket]

Caste/ community category	*Jharkhand Village*	*West Bengal Village*
	Mc	*Rp*
(1)	(2)	(3)
H1	0 (0.00)	1 (0.58)
H2	28 (31.46)	44 (25.29)
H3	51 (57.30)	56 (32.18)
S.T.	0 (0.00)	64 (36.78)
CC2: H3+S.T.+M	61 (68.54)	129 (74.14)
Muslim	10 (11.24)	9 (5.17)
Total	89 (100.00)	174 (100.00)
CC1: H1+H2	28 (31.46)	45 (25.86)
H1 + H2	28 (31.46)	45 (25.86)
H3	51 (57.30)	56 (32.18)
ST +M	10 (11.24)	73 (41.96)
Total	89 (100.00)	174 (100.00)
Standardized entropy*	0.8452	0.9822

* St. En. (J) ? ?? pk log (pk) / log k, [0 ? J ? 1], where k = No. of categories; pk = proportion value of the per cent of the k-th category; logarithm with base 10.

Panel-B of Table 19.3 shows that both the two villages are steeply stratified with respect to occupational class and the distribution of households across the occupational classes is more polarized in cultivation than others. In West Bengal, agricultural developmental measures of the State Government and land reforms have strengthened the farming activities of particularly

Table 19.3: Panel A: Distribution of households by family principal source of livelihood (SL) in Jharkhand village and West Bengal village [% in first bracket]

Source of Livelihood	*Jharkhand Village*	*West Bengal Village*
	Mc	Rp
(1)	(2)	(3)
Farmer+cultivator+share cropper (FC)	50 (56.18)	101 (58.05)
Profession +Service (PS)	8 (8.99)	4 (2.31)
Trade & Small business (TB)	0 (0.00)	20 (11.49)
Petty business+Craft & Artisan (PB/ CA)	5 (5.62)	7 (4.02)
Labourers (L)	26 (29.21)	37 (21.26)
Others (O)	0 (0.00)	5 (2.87)
Total	89 (100.00)	174 (100.00)

Panel B: Standardized Entropy

Source of Livelihood	*Jharkhand Village*	*West Bengal Village*
	Mc	Rp
(1)	(2)	(3)
Farmer+cultivator+share cropper	50 (56.18)	101 (58.05)
Profession+Service+ Trade & Small business	8 (8.99)	24 (13.79)
Petty business+ Craft & Artisan+Labourers+Others	31 (34.83)	49 (28.16)
Total	89 (100.00)	174 (100.00)
Standardized entropy	0.8264	0.8609

the middle and lower rung of the farmers. On the other hand, in Jharkhand village, the non-availability of good transport communication and absence of suitable governmental measures have stabilized the people as agriculturists.

Table 19.4 exhibits that, in case of ownership of land, there lies a great degree of stratification. However, on the whole, the distribution of households by land ownership is more skewed in Jharkhand village than Bengal village.

Table 19.4: Panel-A: Distribution of households in two villages by class on land ownership (in bigha) (% in bracket)

Landholding in bigha (L)	*Jharkhand Village*	*West Bengal Village*
	Mc	Rp
(1)	(2)	(3)
Nil	4 (4.50)	21 (12.07)
0< L ≤ 1.5	43 (48.32)	37 (21.26)
1.5 < L ≤ 3.0	30 (33.71)	45 (25.86)
3.0 < L ≤ 7.0	8 (8.98)	53 (30.46)
7.0 < L ≤ 15	4 (4.49)	12 (6.90)
15< L	0 (0.00)	6 (3.45)
Total	89 (100.00)	174 (100.00)
L ≤ 3.0	77 (86.52)	103 (59.19)
3.0 < L ≤ 15.0	12 (13.48)	65 (37.36)
15.0 < L	0 (0.00)	6 (3.45)
Total	89 (100.00)	174 (100.00)
Standardized entropy	0.3599	0.7231

3. *Findings from SNA*

In measuring reciprocity, Rao and Bandyopadhyay (Rao and Bandyopadhyay 1987) have studied different measures of reciprocity. It is also available in several studies (Rao and

Bandyopadhyay 1987; Jana, Bandyopadhyay and Choudhuri, 2013) that the s3-measure with given out-degrees is more suitable for standardizing the observed reciprocal pairs of a social network. Hence, for standardizing the number of reciprocal pairs, we adopt the s3-measure of reciprocity. Besides, the other measures adopted here have been discussed in details by several researchers (Rao, Bandyopadhyay and Sinha 2010; Jana and Choudhuri, 2013). Now we start the network analysis by giving summary measures of the relevant characteristics of the social networks of the two villages as shown in Table 19.5.

Table 19.5: Summary measures of the social networks of the two villages

Measure	*Jharkhand Village*	*West Bengal Village*
	Mc	Rp
(1)	(2)	(3)
No. of hhs. (n)	89	174
No. of ties inside village in %	53.92	65.50
No. of ties going to outside village in %	46.08	34.50
Total Ties (inside vill. + outside vill.)	100.00 (n1=217)	100.00 (n1=458)
Ties within castes (inside vill.) in %	70.09	48.00
Ties between castes (inside vill.) in %	29.91	52.00
Total Ties (only inside vill.)	100.00 (n2=117)	100.00 (n2=300)
Ties within castes (outside vill.) in %	62.00	39.87
Ties between castes (outside vill.) in %	38.00	60.13
Total Ties (only outside vill.)	100.00 (n3=100)	100.00 (n3=158)
Average out-degree: within village	1.3	1.72
Total	2.44	2.63
No. of reciprocal pair	9	10
s3- measure of Reciprocity (in %)	15.52	6.67
No. of isolates (within village ties)	13.48	4.02
No. of isolates	3.37	0.57
Percentage of reach. Pairs (dir.)	15.67	4.34
No. of strong components (p)	68	159
Size of largest strong comp.	16	4
Average finite distance (dir)	4.49	2.37
Maximum finite distance (dir)	14	9
Percentage of reach. Pairs (undir.)	69.40	92.14
No. of weak components (q)	14	8
Size of largest weak comp.	74	167
Average finite distance (undir)	4.86	4.33
Maximum finite distance (undir)	13	11
Connectedness: strong [(n-p)/(n-1)] in %	21.00	8.67
Connectedness: weak [(n-q)/(n-1)] in %	85.23	95.95

The details of relevant mathematical exercises are described by Jana and Choudhuri (2013).

It is already mentioned that, as per selection scheme, the two villages in both Jharkhand and Bengal are far from town. What Table 19.5 says is described now. In case of both villages, the interaction among the people inside the respective village is greater (more than 50% in each village) than the people outside the village. It indicates that the people of the two villages have less tendency of establishing connection to their outer world. In Jharkhand, ties within a village are more concentrated to within the same caste than between the castes, whereas, in West Bengal, ties within a village flow between the castes little more than within the same caste. It shows that caste-based interaction for getting help is more in Jharkhand village and, on the other hand, its base is secular in case of West Bengal. Even the same picture is observed in case of articulation of ties going to outside village(s). The settlement pattern of the Jharkhand villages may be one of the reasons for becoming caste-based ties (Choudhuri and Jana, 2013).

Table 19.6: Percentage distribution of inside village ties of help by class in each village

Class	*Jharkhand Village*	*West Bengal Village*
	Mc	Rp
(1)	(2)	(3)
Panel A: Class by source of livelihood		
Within class	57.26	42.33
Between class	42.74	57.67
Total	100.00 (n_2=117)	100.00 (n_2=300)
Panel B: Class by land ownership		
Within class	48.72	20.67
Between class	51.28	79.33
Total	100.00 (n_2=117)	100.00 (n_2=300)

Again, when we go through the distribution of inside village ties across the classes, by family main source of livelihood or land ownership, the almost similar picture is observed (Table 19.6). Here also, in case of Jharkhand village, ties have higher tendency to be distributed within same class, whereas it is greater between the classes than within class in case of West Bengal village. It indicates that people of Jharkhand village depend more on the people belonging to same class for getting help, whereas, in West Bengal village, it is higher on the people belonging to other classes. The average out-degree indicating individual expansiveness or the percentage of isolation reflecting the self-dependence of households is not high throughout the two villages. Even the measure (s3) of reciprocity illuminating the solidarity/ cohesiveness among the households is not also high. On the other hand, reachability (i.e. possibility of a household approaching another, either directly or indirectly through intermediaries for getting help) is not high, but moderate. If we ignore directions (i.e. if we assume that A can go to B and B can go to A whenever at least one of them goes to the other), reachability becomes increased tremendously—69.40 per cent and 92.14 per cent in Jharkhand and Bengal villages respectively. It shows the high connectedness (when direction is ignored) representing the intensity of becoming tied up each other and it is also reflected by the values of the measures of weakly connectedness. In this context, the articulation of the ties across the different caste groups as mentioned earlier is presented in Appendix A.

Now, to make an in-depth analysis, we concentrate to the collected data on: to whom (i.e. relation) people go for help; the amount/quantity and type of help sought; and what purposes served by help received.

From whom help was sought?

Sources to which requests for help at different times of emergency were made by the villagers and received, were gathered and classified. This is shown in Table 19.7. It is clearly understood from the Table 19.7 that non-formal help from kin, neighbours, employers etc. are much in abundance in village society under our study. However, in the village of Jharkhand, the kin's (hence, "caste") provide the bulk of informal support while in West Bengal village, the neighbours give the lion's share of informal support.

Table 19.7: Percentage distribution of ties by sources of help in each village

Sources of help	*Jharkhand Village*	*West Bengal Village*
	Mc	Rp
(1)	(2)	(3)
	Panel A: On inside village ties	
Kin	72.25	18.67
Neighbour	20.06	70.67
Friend	5.13	6.00
Employer-Employee	1.06	2.33
Others	1.50	2.33
Total	100.00 (n_2=117)	100.00 (n_2=300)
	Panel B: On outside village ties	
Kin	68.00	19.62
Neighbour	0.00	62.97
Friend	14.00	8.80
Employer-Employee	11.00	4.27
Others	7.00	4.34
Total	100.00 (n_3=100)	100.00 (n_3=158)

Amount/Quantity and Type of Help Sought

We have classified the requests for help by its type, as financial, material, and physical (man-power, advice etc.) in Table 19.8. It is obvious from this Table that non-formal help ties for money are much in the village of Jharkhand, whereas, this is high for material exchange in case of West Bengal village. Again, there is, in Jharkhand village, non-formal advice or man-power help to some extent, but it is almost nil in West Bengal villages.

The distribution of the monetary ties according to the total amount (in rupees in a whole year) is shown in Table 19.9. In case of Jharkhand village, such ties are more than 60 per cent, whereas, in West Bengal, these are less than 35 per cent. In this context, we mention here that the monetary help is not necessarily a loan, because it is in most cases without interest and the borrower generally repays at his convenience. The group discussions among

Table 19.8: Distribution of ties (inside + outside vill.) by types ("at all") of help in each village [% in bracket]

Type of help	*Jharkhand Village*	*West Bengal Village*
	Mc	Rp
(1)	(2)	(3)
Financial	144 (66.36)	156 (34.06)
Material	51 (23.50)	305 (66.59)
Physical	88 (40.55)	4 (0.87)
Total	100.00 (n_1=217)	100.00 (n_1=458)

the people of the respective villages give possible reasons behind such difference of monetary help between two provinces. Cash income generated from out-migration in non-agricultural jobs is more in the Jharkhand village than in West Bengal village. Again if we look at help taken in the nature of food (mainly rice) in Table 19.9, such requests are more in West Bengal village than in Jharkhand village. Due to comparatively less land ownership of the households in Jharkhand village, such requests become low.

Purpose of Help

Table 19.10 shows that the purpose of help in Jharkhand village poses a great level of difference with that of the village of West Bengal. Medical facilities are poorly shaped in the village of Jharkhand. At the same time, the villagers in Jharkhand spend lavishly in order to perform their rites in a pompous way. The village of Jharkhand very frequently requires help for medical treatment and also for performing family rites and coping with urgent consumption requirements. The village in West Bengal does the same mostly for their maintenance of "sudden" consumption needs for social reasons. Therefore, help becomes very much essential there.

Table 19.9: Percentage distribution of ties (inside + outside vill.) of help on cash and kind in each village

Cash in Rs. (C)/ Kind in Kg. (K)	*Jharkhand Village*	*West Bengal Village*
	Mc	Rp
(1)	(2)	(3)
	Panel A: Cash (in Rs.)	
0 (noncash)	33.64	65.94
0< C ≤100	10.60	5.90
100< C ≤250	11.06	7.21
250< C ≤500	15.21	11.14
500< C ≤1000	12.44	5.24
C>1000	17.05	4.59
Total	100.00 (n_1=217)	100.00 (n_1=458)
	Panel B: Kind (in Kg)	
0 (non-kind)	77.42	33.62
0< K ≤20	12.44	45.41
20< K ≤60	5.07	7.86
60< K ≤200	4.15	7.64
200< K ≤500	0.46	3.71
K>500	0.46	1.75
Total	100.00 (n_1=217)	100.00 (n_1=458)

Table 19.10: Distribution of ties (inside + outside vill.) by purposes ("at all") of help in each village [% in bracket]

Purposes of help served	*Jharkhand Village*	*West Bengal Village*
	Mc	Rp
(1)	(2)	(3)
Survival	17.51	32.10
Medical	27.19	4.80
Family rites	42.40	17.03
Family crisis & household requirements	5.53	25.55
Production	16.13	20.31
Others	0.00	1.09
Total	100.00 (n_1=217)	100.00 (n_1=458)

Conclusion

As a way of conclusion, we would discuss about different aspects on the basis of SN data what we have presented in various ways.

In Jharkhand the ties—both inside and outside—have developed mainly among the members of the same kin group, hence the same caste. Ownership pattern and principal sources of livelihood have not produced any impact on the pattern of articulation of relationship. But contrary to ties being formed within the kin group in Jharkhand, the same is articulated among the neighbours and others in Bengal. In Jharkhand, kin-group (caste) based social networks have developed owing to social compulsion in the direction of strengthening a social safeguard or insurance on the part the weaker sections of the village against the manifold sources of vulnerabilities in life and living, particularly aggression and exploitation by land owning caste groups, in a situation where there is no effective structural remedies to ameliorate the condition of their life and living. In fact, this raises the level of social depth of social network analysis to a higher dimension.

In fact, unlike structure-function based methodology of study, SNA does not begin with any a priority given boundary. Being able to identify empirically its boundary, parameter remains quite amenable to respond to the variations in social reality.

Our SN based findings give both "no" and "yes" as answer. In Jharkhand, ties still circulate mostly by kins (caste/community), but connect closely the section in the village with their village and with their counterpart in the larger society. Thus, kinship or caste groups provide instrument of communication and contacts for linking the village with the far away job market.

This is one side of the coin. The other side, the internal one, is as follows. The economic situation of the village may not be changing in the near future. The more is un-industrialisation or de-industrialisation over time, as it is happening in Giridih region of Jharkhand, the sharper will be the competition/conflicts over ownership of land and the more forcibly one will drive to mobilise support. A readily available effective instrument in this regard is to depend upon their kin or caste groups as a matter of strategy. We note that earlier land productivity in the village around Giridih, on average, was very low and that, too very much subject to uncertainties of rainfall. The region was rain fed. However, now-a-days, prospect of irrigation has opened up, though it needs individual investment, since public programme of irrigation is almost absent. Because of lack of cash income, private investment in irrigation also was lacking earlier. But since migration has resulted in flow of cash income, this has made investment possible for agricultural development. The above means "yes", but with a new meaning.

In Birbhum of West Bengal, on the other hand, usual structural-functional categories come out as rather residuals. The concept of social group, rather, appears to be more appropriate unit for understanding social structure. In rural West Bengal, presently the prime issue is of reducing the level of unevenness in development, i.e., which villages have moved far ahead and which ones are lagging behind. Implementation of land reforms and the Panchayat Raj have been instrumental in shifting the political and social power to the down-to-the-soil villagers, and consequently the villagers are coping up with the problems of their life and living by getting them identified as a social class or group. This has brought about a noticeable qualitative difference in socio-economic base of networks support among the villagers in Birbhum. It comes out from our study that the savings of the villagers in West Bengal, which are generated internally, are being invested insight the rural areas in both agricultural and non-agricultural sectors, ensuring thereby a sort of recycling of the internal resources in the state.

On the basis of the study, it is suggested that in the planning and decentralization process, some mechanism needs to be developed to provide some sort of institutionalized avenues for help which should be available without much botheration and at short notice. In this regard, Panchayat and / or any other Local Body can perhaps play an important role to some extent. The study may be replicated in case of the people of North-East India.

Appendix-A

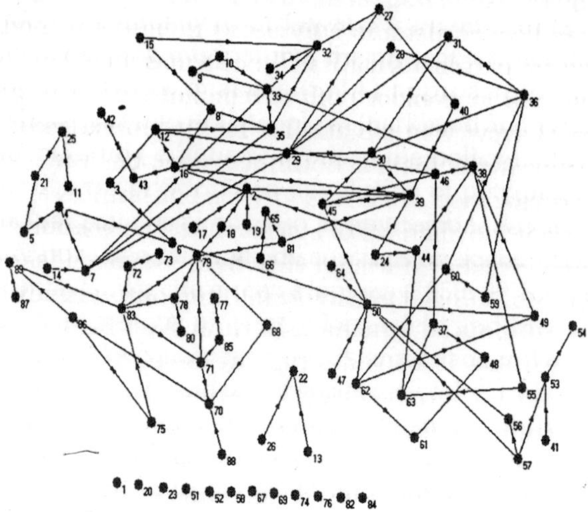

Fig. 19.2: Social network for Mahacho all

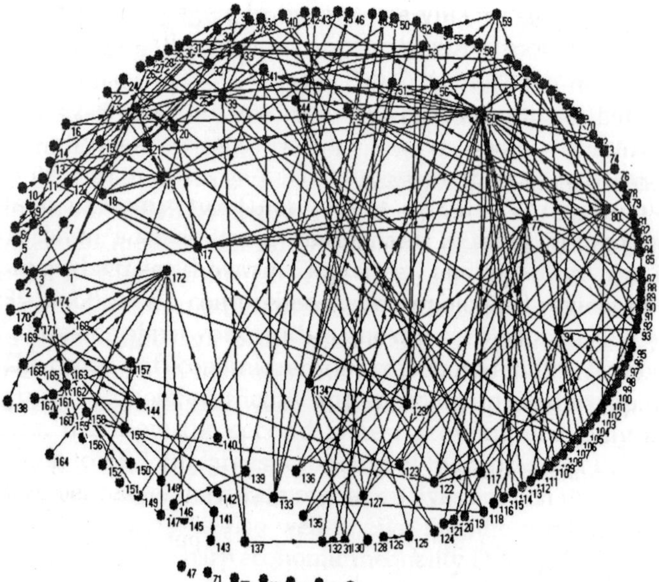

Fig. 19.3. Social Network for Raspur All

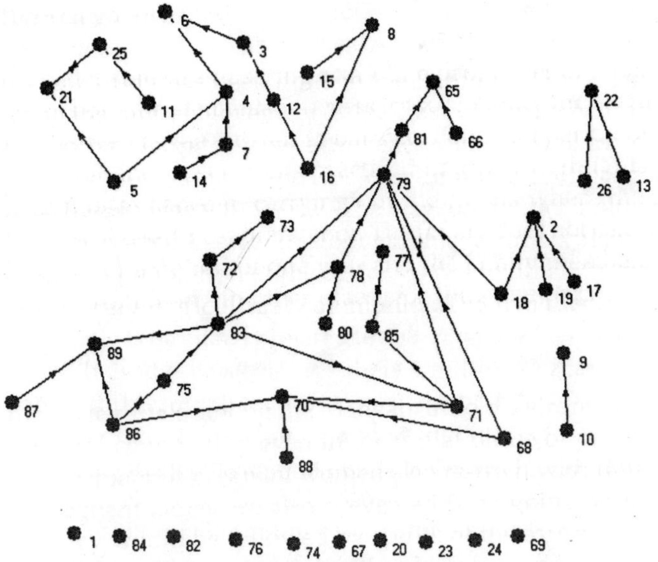

Fig. 19.4. Social Network of Hindu Low of Mahacho

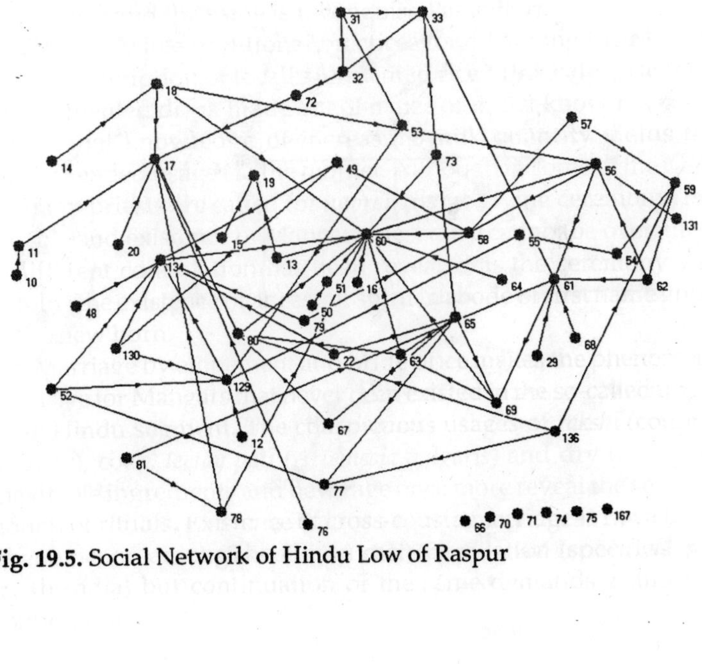

Fig. 19.5. Social Network of Hindu Low of Raspur

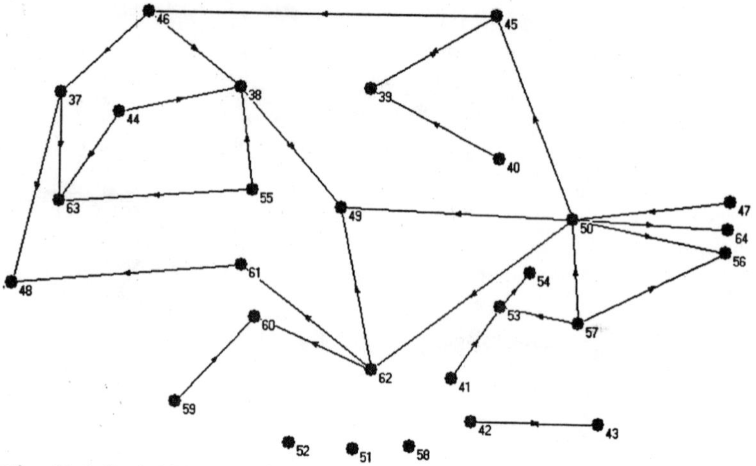

Fig. 19.6. Social Network of Hindu Middle of Mahacho

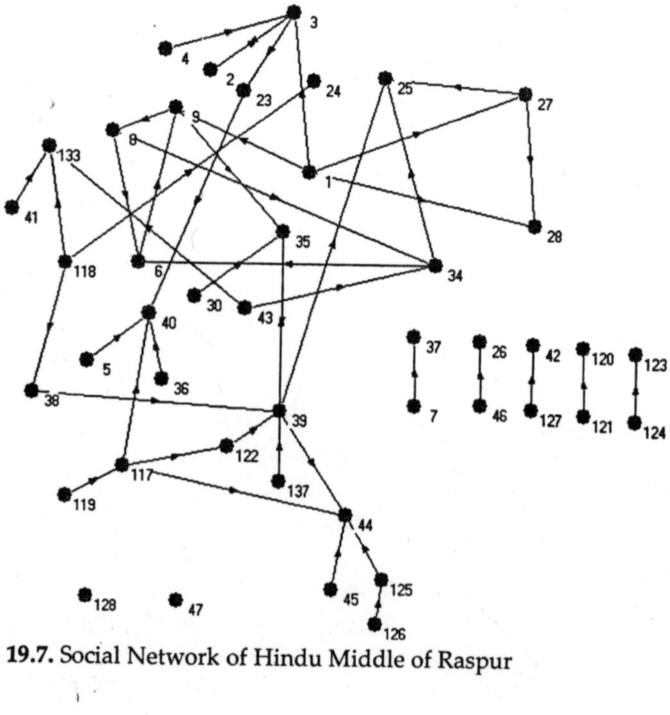

Fig. 19.7. Social Network of Hindu Middle of Raspur

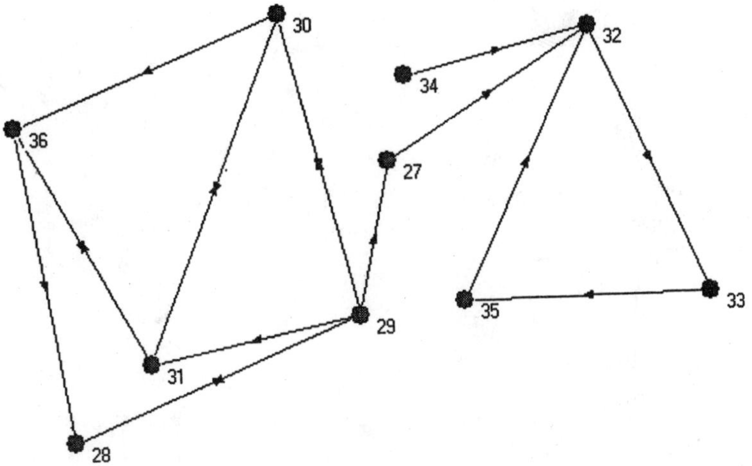

Fig. 19.8. Social Network of Muslims of Mahacho

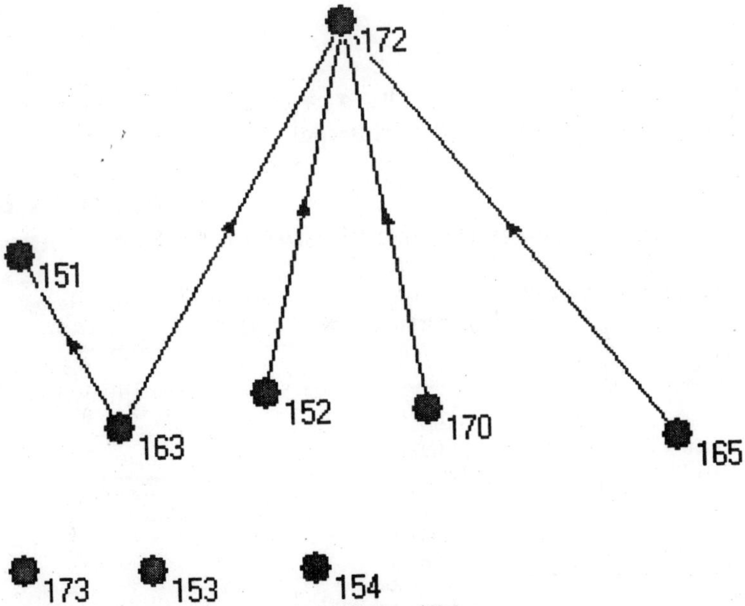

Fig. 19.9. Social Network of Muslims of Raspur

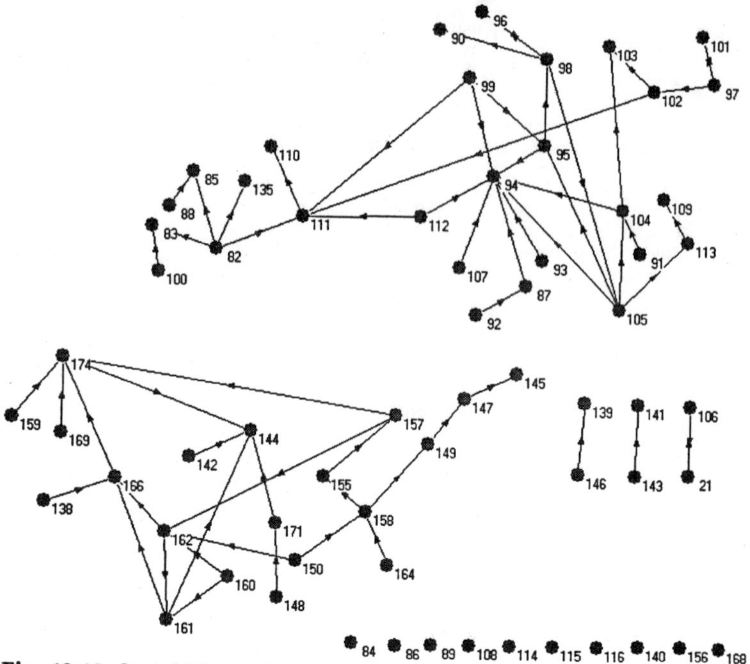

Fig. 19.10. Social Network of ST of Raspur

Appendix B

Caste/communities Distribution of the Two Villages

Ritual status Category	*Caste/ community*	*Jharkhand Village*	*West Bengal Village*
		Mc	Rp
(1)	(2)	(3)	(4)
Hindu High Castes (H1) **	Rajput	-	1
	Total	-	1
Hindu Middle Castes (H2)	Koiri	8	-
	Lohar	-	13
	Gowala	20	13
	Baishnab	-	3
	Sadgop	-	15
	Total	28	44

(*Contd.*)

Ritual status Category	*Caste/ community*	*Jharkhand Village*	*West Bengal Village*
		Mc	Rp
(1)	(2)	(3)	(4)
Hindu Low including Scheduled Castes (H3)	Chamar	25	-
	Dusadh	26	-
	Bhuia	-	10
	Hanri	-	7
	Sunri	-	39
	Total	51	56
Scheduled Tribe (ST)	Santhal	-	16
	Orang	-	44
	Kora	-	4
	Total	-	64
Community	Muslim (M)	10	9
Village total		**89**	**174**

* Mc = Mahacho, Rp =Raspur

** H1 = Hindu High, H2 =Hindu Middle, H3 =Hindu Low, ST =Scheduled Tribe, M = Muslim

References

Bandyopadhyay, S., A.R. Rao and Sinha Bikas K. 2010. *Models for Social Networks with Statistical Applications*. London, Sage Publications.

Bandyopadhyay, S. 2003. Introduction to Social Network Analysis. *Proceedings of Workshop on Network Analysis with Applications,* funded by Department of Science and Technology, Government of India, and organized by Theoretical Statistics-Mathematics Unit, Indian Statistical Institute, Kolkata.

Bandyopadhyay, Suraj and Donald Von Eschen. 1980. "The conditions of rural progress in India", A report to the *Canadian International Development Agency*, Ottawa.

Berkowitz, S. D. 1982. *An Introduction to Structural Analysis*. Toronto, Butterworths.

Burt, Ronald S. and M. J. Miror (Eds.) 1983. *Applied Network Analysis: A Methodological Introduction*. Beverly Hills, Sage Publications.

Chatterjee, A. K., Suraj Bandyopadhyay and A. R. Rao. 1993. Relative importance of different factors for boundary of reciprocity: An illustration. *Connections: Bulletin of the INSNA,* 16: 15-22.

Collins, Randall. 1988. *Theoretical Sociology*. San Diego, Harcourt Brace Jovanovitch Publishers.

Holland, P. W. and Leinhart, S. 1979. *Perspective on Social Network Research*. NewYork, Academic Press.

Homans, George C. 1950. *The Human Group*, Harcourt Brace.

Jana, R. 2005. Statistical and Graph Theoretic Analysis of Social Networks of Rural Farmers in Different Agricultural Activities. Ph.D. Thesis, Burdwan University, Burdwan, West Bengal.

Jana, R. and Choudhuri, A.K. 2013. "Studying various aspects of social networks with socio-economic changes in a rural area: A case study from West Bengal", *Guru Nanak Journal of Sociology*. Vol 34 (1 and 2), 1-29.

Jana, R., S. Bandyopadhyay and A.K. Choudhuri. 2013. "Reciprocity among farmers in farming system research: Application of social network analysis", *Journal of Human Ecology*. 41(1): 45-51.

Knoke, D. and J.H. Kuklinski. 1988. *Network Analysis*. USA, Sage Publications.

Laumann, E.O. and F. U. Pappi. 1976. *Networks of Collective Action*. New York, Academic Press.

Lazarsfeld, P. F. and H. Menzel. 1962. "On the relation between individual and collective properties". In: *Complex Organisations–A Sociological Reader*. ed by Holt Reihart and A. Etzioni, pp. 422-440. Winston Inc.

Martindale, Don. 1960. *The Nature and Types of Sociological Theory*. Cambridge, USA, Houghton Mifflin Company Boston, The Riverside Press.

Mitchell, J. 1969. "The concept and use of social networks." In: *Social Networks in Urban Situations*. Ed. by J. Mitchell, pp. 1-50. UK: Manchester University Press.

Moreno, J. L. 1934. *Who shall survive? Foundations of Sociometry, Group Psychotherapy and Sociodrama*. New York, Beacon House.

Moreno, J. L. 1956. *Sociometry and the Science of Man*. New York, Beacon House.

Moreno, et al. (Eds.). 1960. *The Sociometry Reader*. Illinois, The Free Press of Glencoe.

Rao, A. Ramachandra and Suraj Bandyopadhyay. 1987. "Measures of reciprocity in a social network." *Sankhya, Ser. A*, Vol. 49: 141-188.

Srinivas, M.N. and Andre Beteille. 1964. "Networks in Indian social structure." *Man*, Nov. December, 2012–2013: 165-168.

Wasserman, S. and K. Faust. 1999. *Social Network Analysis: Methods and Applications*. Cambridge, Cambridge University Press.

Weisberg, H.F. 1993. "Central Tendency and Variability." In: *Basic Statistics*, Vol.1. ed by M.S. Lewis-Beck. London, Sage Publications.

Wellman, et al. 1991. "Integrating individual, relation and structural analysis." *Social Networks*. 13: 223-249.

Wellman, Barry. 1997. *The Network Community: An Introduction*. Boulder & Co., Westview.

Wolff, K.H. (Eds.). 1964. *The Sociology of Georg Simmel*. New York, Free Press.

20
Revisiting The Lepcha Tales
The Lungten Sung

Prerna R. Lepcha and Nil Ratan Roy

Introduction

The Lepcha people are believed to be the aboriginal inhabitants of the Eastern Himalayas comprising Sikkim, Darjeeling district of West Bengal, Ilam district of Nepal and the Samtsi district in south-western Bhutan. The homeland of the Lepchas is known as 'ne mayel lyang' 'hidden paradise' or 'ne mayal maluk lyang' or land of eternal purity or mayel lyang. The Lepchas call themselves mutanchi rongkup 'children of Rong or God' or simply rongkup 'children of the rong' in their native language Rong-aring or Rongring which falls under the Tibeto-Burman family of language. Among the three ethnic groups of the Eastern Himalayas namely the Bhutia, Lepcha and Nepali, the Lepchas are the most primitive and indigenous tribe. Earlier the Lepchas were animist and as they were born naturalist, they were well acquainted with their surroundings. However, the origin of the Lepchas is still held under controversy. Some of the anthropologists believe that they emigrated from various parts of Mongolia and Tibet. However, the various folklores suggest that they are the original sons of the soil of Mayel lyang.

Objectives

- To explore the age old folktales that has been imbibed in the minds of the tribal people.

- To highlight the relevance of the different oral narratives in the form of folktales, folklores and myth.
- To examine the relationship between folktales and the life of the people.
- To study the impact of the folktales on the tribal community as a whole.

Methodology

In the present study the investigator has used historical research method which is qualitative in nature. The source of information has been collected from the books, journals and various articles to give a clear perspective of the past experiences of the tribal people.

The peace loving Rongs possess a very rich culture. Their language, their songs and dances, custom and tradition, practices tells us a story. These stories and folklores have been embedded in the minds of the Lepcha people. Their daily activities like hunting, fishing, agriculture, cooking etc. have their own uniqueness and practices which have been followed for years. Every aspect of their life, be it social, economic, cultural, conjugal and sacred beliefs have been represented in their folktales, legends, myths etc. The folktales are the oral representation of the tribal way of life. Like any other tribal practices, after the hard day work when no other forms of entertainment existed, the elders used to sit down and tell stories which were considered one of the most favourite pastimes. They used to reward themselves with a little intoxication in the form of *Chee,* the tribal drink and sit down together to share their daily adventures. It is remarkable to see how intoxication works in making men great story tellers. Lepcha elders are known to be very good narrators and story-tellers. Some of the important and absorbing Lungten Sung tales are presented and discussed in the following lines.

The Lungten Sung

Stories of the Lepchas or the Rongs from the ancient mythology, legends and other folklore which included stories of animals, birds, insects and also fairytales is known as Lungten Sung. These stories have a very important place in the heart and mind of the Lepcha people. These stories have influenced the very existence of the listeners be it in their behaviour or in their daily activities. These stories always carry a moral view so much so it creates awareness among the listeners to do well in life and live according to the will of the Almighty Creator. Apart from the stories shared at home, the Rongs get reminders about the legends while walking through, working in the fields, collecting firewood, hunting and so on. Every aspect of their surrounding tells a story which makes them so attuned to the nature around. It has been pointed out that the Lepcha Shamans, the Mun and the Bongthing, are acknowledged experts in telling stories. These stories form an essential part of rituals, funerals, wedding etc. The art of story-telling has been practised for ages, so in the hands of story-teller, most of the stories are either spliced up or clubbed together or narrated in chained sequence. The customary practice of narrating Lungten Sung is dominant in almost all the gathering.

Tales of the Creation

There are many theories and folklores about the origin of the Lepchas. Itbu-moo, the Mother creator, created everything on earth and in the heavens. She created and shaped Kongchen-Konghlo and other 'Chyu bee' or mountains, and called them males. Then as companion to these mountains, she created the 'daa', the lakes and called them females. After what she thought was completion of her work, she stopped to reconnoiter her creation and realized there was something lacking in her creation. Thus she created the first man Tukbothing who later came to be known as Foodoongthing or Fudongthing. K.P. Tamsang in his book "Unknown and Untold Realities of Lepchas", writes, the Lepcha tradition says that in the beginning, the first primogenitors of the Lepchas, Foodoongthing and Nazaongnyo were created by God from the pure and virgin snows of Kingtsoomzaongboo (Mt. Kanchenjunga) Choo's or mountain's pinnacle and sent them down to live, prosper and spread all over Mayel Lyang that lies in the lap of the mountain Kanchenjunga. Therefore, the Lepchas' first parent were created at the summit of Kingtsoomzaongboo by God himself, the Lepchas thus proudly proclaim themselves as Rongkup that is the son of the snowy peak and Rarnkup, that is son of God or simply Rong.

However, John Morris in his book "Living with the Lepchas"

has written, "Itpumu, the man, Kumsiting, the woman were born from the two peaks of Kanchinjunga. They had two children, a boy name Tashay Thing and a girl named Nazong Nyu. These two married and because they were brother and sister all their children were devils and for this reason their mother refused to suckle them. Eventually they gave birth to a child who was not a demon and named it Ril Bu Shing. And because it was their first real child the mother treated it tenderly and suckled with loving care. When the demon children saw this they got very angry and they decided to do away with Ril Bu Shing. Then they did, he was buried near a certain peak on the right bank of Taluk River. The parents got very upset and separated, Tashay Thing going towards Tibet and his wife towards Sikkim. Prior to this, the grandmother, Kumsiting, called all their demon grandchildren together and addressed them. She told them that in future there would be no objection in their 'eating the souls' of human being; but, on the other hand when offering were made to them on the behalf of these same humans by Bongthing, Munnor Rumfat Bu, they must accept them and that when they did this they must leave the humans alone. This is said to be the origin of making sacrifices to various demons. After this Kumsiting created man, the first man was called Tarbong Pu; the first woman Nari Pu. They lived on the twin peaks beyond Seniolchum; and from there all the races of man, including the Lepchas, descended.

The Sun and the Moon

Itbut-moo, the Great Mother creator, created two suns in order to give light and warmth. The younger of the two was to come out in the morning and the elder one in the evenings. So in presence of suns without any break, the people of world were in great confusion as they did not know how to divide time between work and rest. Even all the other creatures were in great confusion. So at last after many discussions they decided that one of the sun should be killed. Volunteers were called with the view of killing one of the Sun. "Takblo Taluk", the big Green frog, seeing no one coming forward offered to kill one of the suns. So it made a bow from 'Katname', a kind of red-stemmed vegetable plant, it shot and killed the elder of the two because it was bigger and more ferocious in its heat. The younger brother seeing his dead brother mourned and the whole world turned into darkness. The mortars that were kept in the garden turned into tigers and the pestles into serpent and snakes. They started attacking and eating up the mankind. It was dark everywhere and it was impossible to do any work. So the humans and other creatures were forced to meet again and they decided to coax the younger sun back to activity. But after many failed attempts to coax the younger brother sun, the little bat tried to volunteer. The bat then made a small bow, bending it, caught one end of the bow with his hands and the other end he stuck up to his nostrils, leaving the feet free to hang on the twig, near the face of the sun. Now he went and hung himself upside down, right on front of the covered up face of the mourning sun. The bat started talking and pleading. The sun had already heard such pleadings from humans and other creatures but that day the voice sounded uncommon and strange. Getting curious the sun peeped out a little wanting to know the unheard voice belonged to. Seeing the funny creature dangling upside down and talking, the sun could not help but smile. As soon as the sun smiled there was sunshine. The poor bat who was too near to the sun got charred and fell down. That is the reason today we see all his hands and legs broken up and the body a dark roasted shade, complete with its upturned nose, due to effects of the bow. So the humans and the creatures pleaded the sun to come out completely. The sun thus came out reluctantly that too on certain condition. These were, firstly, to give proper punishment to the culprit who killed his brother. Secondly, to do something so, that the dead brother would be remembered always. In order to approve the first condition Takblo taluk's thumbs were cut off so that that he would not be able to shoot arrows again and banished to a freezing place. As the fulfilment of the second condition, it was arranged that the months would be calculated from the phases of the dead sun itself. The Dead sun became the moon, we call it 'Lavo', because the younger brother during the crucial time, kept crying and saying, 'Kasu anum labo', 'give back my brother'; 'labo' became 'lavo'. The sun is called Su chok originally meant the one who succeeded in warding off the Su, the evil designs of the conspirators.

The Lepcha Clan

Helen Plaiser has written, "The Lepcha are divided into various clans or families known as putsho and each clan has its own dâ 'lake' and cú 'mountain peak'. The cú are regularly honoured in cú rumfát 'mountain worship' ceremonies." The origin of the clan names is traditionally explained as follows: when the evil king Laso mung 'Lhasa Devil' was killed by Támsáng thíng 'Lord Támsáng', then Lord Támsáng expressed his gratitude to 108 men by bestowing upon each of them an honorary title, as well as placing each of them under the protection of a specific lake and mountain peak. When the devil was slain the Lepchas and Tamsangthing moved the place called Tarkaol Tam-E-Tam (Valley of deliverance), then Tamsangthing give the title to Lepcha according to their role in the war. The Lord Tamsangthing conferred honours and titles like Tamsangmoo, Simikmoo, Sangdengmo, Adenmoo, Sampumoo etc. and each clan was allotted a snowy peak. Foning has listed few examples of how some of the clan got their names after slaying of the Laso Mung. The one who first ventured out to see if the body of the demon was breathing was called 'Luck-som' because luck derived from 'Ahlut or lut' means heart and 'Asom or Som', means breathing. The brave who broke the eyeball was called 'Samik" since "amik or mik' means eyes, the next who cut off the limbs was called Sangut, meaning to cut and next who pounded the bones was called Sandyang, dyang means pounding. The person who helped in making weapons like, sword, spears etc. was called 'Karvo', meaning blacksmith. The ones who fed the warriors are called 'zoreeboo', 'Zo' meaning rice and 'Reebu' means distributor. Some people who arranged seats for the feast were called 'Adenmoos', 'aden' means carpet seat. Some people who offered thanksgiving to the Almighty was called 'Manlonmoo,' Manlom means thanks.

Origin of Bongthing and Mun—'The Keeper and Custodian'

From the very first day of creation, Itbu Debu Rum, 'the great creator and sustainer' has made necessary arrangements to face the earthly obstacles and difficulties. The institutions of muns and bongthing have been devised to do so. They have originally been ordained and have the power to communicate with Gods as well as the Mungs or the devils or the demons. They have the power to intercede with the Gods on the behalf of people, and also exhort or appease the different mungs or devils so that humans may be unharmed. Foning in his book "Lepcha My Vanishing Tribe" has written, "according to our folklore, Tukbothing, also called Fundongthing, the male, and Nazong Nyo, the female, our very first ancestors, were brought into existence by Itbu-moo, the great mother creator, and they were placed separately in Naho and Nathor lakes, in the sacred region where the Gods lived." They were not supposed to live together, but later this two disobeyed the command of the Creator. As a result of disobedience, Nazong Nyu started giving birth to various mungs—the evil spirits, the devils and the demons. Thus, later in course of normal human propagation in our world, these very mungs, started to pester and trouble mankind. When the Great Good mother saw this, she had compassion on us humans, her favourite creation, and created a bongthing who she sent down to us. He was commissioned not only to control these troubles making mungs, but was also to do everything for our welfare.

Accordingly, the bongthing came down to earth and summoned these mungs to a conference. There he agreed to a certain proposal and had a covenant with them. According to the agreement, the bongthing promised to offer animal and bird sacrifice to them, and they in turn promised to leave human beings unmolested after receiving the same. This is the reason why, in sickness, disease and other troubles which are caused by these mungs, our bongthings offer these sacrifices. The only mung that the Bongthings do not attempt to appease is the Dom Mung, the devil of dreaded disease leprosy. It is said that in the conference called by the Bongthings, this mun kept him away, and therefore the bongthing could not get hold of him. Hence, this disease is considered incurable and the bongthings never undertake the appeasement work for it. The word bongthing is the derivative of the two words abong and athing. Abong means 'the trunk', 'the main' or 'the original', and 'athing' means 'honourable and highly respected one.'

Soon after the agreement, true to their evil and dark nature, the mungs started giving more trouble. More and more offering had to be made by the bongthings which consumed more and more time in preparing the offering of the sacrifice. The bongthing thus had to work relentlessly full time. As he didn't have time to attend to the human welfare, he picked up a woman amongst the mortals and with due ceremonies delegated his other function that of welfare work to her. He confined himself to the appeasement of the muns for which he was particularly sent, and attended to only some works related to welfare. He assigned the work on the incorporeal and spiritual side wholly to the female, who, later on came to be known as 'mun'.

Origin of Chyee

Chee (Chyee) is often referred as the holy drink of the Lepchas. To use the supernatural powers bestowed upon Nyolik Nyosongmun by Eetboo-Deyboo Rum, she revealed that the medicine for the restoration of lost morale of the Lepcha soldiers lay in the form of Buth (ferment). Buth was in possession of matlimanyoo and Tungdyer Palyung a Cockroach agreed to bring the Buth from Matlimanyoo. On the way back while tired Tungdyer Palyung was resting, pamaol Bu, a pure Black Cobra snake stole a bit of Buth from tungdyer Palyung and tested it and became mad and very poisonous. A honey bee (hu) tested a little Buth, developed sharp needle to prick with seemingly negligible string, like this sum large birds became carnivorous, a tree (kantek) develop sour taste. Finally kundong koonge a plantain tree touched it and it fruit became sweet. Lepcha people believe, in this process, Buth became poisonless and got ready for them. Tungdyer Palyung finally arrived with Buth and gave it to priestess who cooked millet, mixed Buth to prepare Chyee, fermented beverage the ultimate power potion, and distributed it among Lepcha soldiers to raise their morale in the war against Laso Mung-Pano, the devil. With their high morale the Lepchas fought gallantly.

In another legend of Chi, H.G. Joshi in his book-Sikkim: Past and Present", p.187, has written, 'this intoxicating drink according to the tradition of the Rong is of heavenly origin. Tradition has it that at the very outset the ferment used in the manufacture of the intoxicant was brought to mankind form the other side of the world in a cunning manner by a special messenger. Birds have special part to play with the drinks. The quail is considered to have performed the chi sacrifice after the deluge. Two birds have said to have brought the drink of immorality from the land of Gods. Then a two-fold effect which causes merriment is described. When the snakes drank Chi, they went mad. To quote Stocks, "you have stolen my ferment, if you only know how to use it, you would be able to offer the chi to the Rum, but now you will find that it always excites you it will cause you to quarrel, it may even kill you." There is a general belief among Lepchas that ferment was stolen from a woman 'Matli Mun' who put a curse on it saying, "Chi Thong Yong Gong Mon, Chi Thong Mayon Gong Nyung" meaning, "if you know how to drink, it is medicine, and if you don't know then it is poison."

Folktales and Festivals of Lepcha

Tendong Lho Rum-fat: Foning is his book "Lepcha—My Vanishing Tribe" on page 91 describes it as folloes: "Rongfolk, the children of Fudongthing and Nazong-Nyu, according to the plan of Itbu-moo, prospered and multiplied. Mayel Lyang, or the country, the original utopian land of our tribe, was fertile, fruitful and prosperous. But a time came when they started forgetting Itbu-moo, the mother creator and became negligent in offering sacrifices and prayers. So, the great mother was hurt. The big black shiny Pamolbu, the very embodiment of evil in a serpent form, took that as a cue. This cursed creature, true to its evil nature, now went and blocked the flow of the two main rivers, Rongit and Rong Nyu, flowing through the prosperous Mayel country. The flowing of the two rivers has been dammed, started rising till at last, a time came when all the land was submerged under the great flood.

Forest, hill and mountains started disappearing; there was commotion among the Rongfolk. They started running here and there; they climbed up the trees, and climbed up high mountains; and yet the water kept rising up and up. At last the whole of the prosperous land became a mass of water, destroying everything. Seeing the fast destruction caused by the flood many realized their mistakes and set about appeasing Itbu-moo's wrath by offering special sacrifices, incense burning and prayers; it was of no avail. Animals, birds and all other earthy creatures also tried their very best to soften the Mother's hurt feeling. Till at last, 'Kahom Fo', the partridge reached the topmost part of a mountain, started oblation of 'Mong Chee', the brewed millet seeds, which it had brought wrapped up in big 'Tangfyumnyum', the huge leaf of a bing-leafed plant. Facing towards Kongchen-Konghlo, it started tossing the Chee grains towards the sky, praying and pleading for mercy. This fervent appeal, and the prayers of Kahom Fo on the behalf of the creatures of the earth, had its desired effect. Itbumoo softened and she thought of her beloved Mutanchi, the mother's loved ones, an endearing appellation by which we Rongfolk call ourselves. The flood started abating. Now the few who had followed the partridge also succeeded reaching the top and they were saved. It is said they are the ones who are responsible for the continuance of our tribe in this world". Thus, the Lepcha tribe was saved.

This mountain from which the Kohom Fo made Chee offering is the Mount Tendong, meaning 'upturned', which can be seen above Namchi in Sikkim. Tendong has come from Lepcha word 'tun rong', tun, means 'upgoing or upturned', 'rong' from 'arong', means horns. It means that the mountain went up like horns to save the people. Every year during the monsoon season, the mount Tendong is worshipped by offering Chee and other sacrifices by the Bongthing and the occasion has been declared as a holiday in Sikkim. This festival is called Tendong-Rum-fat.

Another legend about the great flood has been mentioned by R.P. Lama in his book "Across the Teesta" is based on a love story between Rongnit (male) and rongnue (female). The lovers decided to meet at a rendezvous place now known as Teesta, but Rongnit led by a bird roamed many places before arriving at the destination and find the lover Rongnue led by the snake had already arrived. Rongnit, his pride hurt, feels dejected and after exclaiming 'Thee stha' meaning 'already arrived' starts going back to the Himalayas, causing the great deluge and flood. To save the rongfolk the Tendong Mountain went up and up. Only by the prayer and Chi sacrifice made by 'Kahom Fo' the flood abated. That is why river 'Rongnue' is known as Teesta. It is said that even at an altitude of 7000 ft above sea level on the slope of Tendong with an altitude pf approximately 8000 ft, sand and polished river-bed stones are still available.

Chu Rum Faat and Lyang Rum Faat: 'Chu Rum Faat' is the worship of the mountains. This is observed during the autumn season before the onset of winter, with the main purpose to plead the God for adequate snowfall in winter to feed the rivers below and also for the protection of Rongfolk. It has already been stated that Phang Lhabsol in Sikkim was started by great Lhatsun lama as a thanksgiving ceremony to the Lepcha deity Kanchenjunga and other mountains. 'Lyang Rum Faat' is the worship of the land

and Lepchas celebrate it èvery year during the monsoon season. The purpose of the ritual is to pray to God for harvest.

Tale about the Aspiration of Lepchas

After the creation, with the advent of time the world became full with men, women and children. Men took up heavy manual work and took the role or provider and the women folk did the household work and other choruses. They all lived happily. However, the human developed an aspiration to go right up to Rum Lyang, the place of Gods, to see and meet the Great Mother creator. So they decided to build a structure going right up beyond the clouds through the sky. For this purpose they started searching for a suitable site. At last they found a flat piece of land in the heart of their Mayel country, in a place known as 'Tal-om-partam', 'plain of the way up', in present day west Sikkim. They decided upon constructing the structure with 'Fat fityok' earthen pots. So many workers got busy. Some started shaping the earthen pots, collecting firewood to burn and harden them while the others got busy with the construction by piling up the burnt up pots upside down. When the structure had almost reached the ceiling of the firmament, the ones who were there on the top, to hook it to the sky ceiling, shouted down, 'Kokveem yang tal', pass the hook stick up. The ones below heard, "Veen chyek tel!", smash down on the left side!. Since there was considerable distance between the workers at the top and those working at the base of the construction, they failed to hear the words correctly. Both side repeated the message several times but they hear the same reply. At last the top was being disgusted shouted down nodding vigorously, "Ak, Ak", "Yes, Yes". So the ones at the bottom smashed down the left side at the bottom and then came the inevitable crash and fall. Thus, this ended the foolish aspiration of the Lepcha people to have a face to face encounter with the Almighty Creator. This attempt served as a lesson to the Rongs or the Lepcha people that they cannot make a physical contact with Itbu-moo however the Almighty Creator can be approached through prayer, sacrifices and offerings.

Today considering this act of the early Lepchas, a person who shows lack of intelligence and common sense is known as 'Na-ong'.

Observation and Discussion

All the stories which have been discussed above have a moral insight. The first tale about the creation has great similarity with the Biblical reference about the creation. It talks about the destiny of the wicked and how their evil works can never go unpunished. The second tale about the sun and the moon, remarkably talks about the love that exists between the siblings. It teaches the humanity about the power of brotherhood. The secret jealousy and the plans of the wicked always lead to destruction of the humanity. Any cold war or feuds can always be resolved through talks and collaborative effort of both the parties involved. The third tale about the origin of keepers and custodian, enlighten one about the deep insight of the custodian of a belief and custom that exists in a society. It talks about their importance as a guide and as well as their self-less effort to maintain peace and harmony in the community as a whole.

The fourth story about "chee" the intoxicating drink teaches humanity about the ill effect of using beverages. The stories about the origin of the clan give a historical account of various incidents and the birth of different clans. The tales about the various festivals gives an account of the physical and geographical impact on the community in the past. Furthermore, the story about the aspiration and inquisitiveness of the Lepcha people teaches one to focus on things which a person is capable. Foolish decision often leads to failure which may impact the entire community as a whole.

Educational Implication

The above oral narratives have greatly influenced the tribal community as a whole. It has been able:

- To educate the tribal community to understand the difference between the good and evil.
- To help the children who have been continually listening to these tales to become a responsible and morally sound person.
- To generate interest among the tribes towards their ethnicity, their cultural values and their custom.
- To live in harmony with the surrounding without harming

the environment. To acknowledge and appreciate the gifts of nature and use it wisely.

Conclusion

The Lepcha have some more tales about the origin of year, creation of Lepcha priest and Priestess, the two brothers etc. which has been passed on from generation to generation. After the entire day's work, the Lepcha elders used to gather around the hearth and tell stories. These assimilating stories have been imbibed so deep in the minds of the Lepchas that it has been capable to influence the very behaviour and attitude of the Lepcha people. These folktales mythological and legendary stories and parables are thus reciprocally related to the life of the Lepcha of Sikkim and Darjeeling. These stories which are tales for children seem to have a deep and long lasting effect on the Lepchas. Folklore shows indication to construct the history of Lepcha. The folktales, folklores and myths carry a vivid picture of the Lepcha way of life. Every inch of the Lepcha land or Mayelyang is associated with a tale, the mountain peaks, lakes, the rivers, the springs, plants are named accordingly. The Lepchas, close association with nature can be derived from the well-described folktales. It is simply impossible to detach the history of the Lepchas and the myths, the folktales and the folklores.

References

Donaldson, F. 1900. *Lepcha land or six weeks in Sikkim Himalayas*. London, Sompson LowMarsten.

Foning, A.R. 1987. *Lepcha—My vanishing Tribe*. Delhi, Sterling Publishers Private Ltd.

Gorer, G. 1938. *Himalayan village: An account of Lepchas of Sikkim*. New Delhi, Gain Publishing House.

Plaiser, Helen 2005. "A brief introduction to Lepcha Orthography and Literature." *Bulletin of Tibetology 7*.

Roy, D.C. 2012. *Lepcha—Past and Present*. Siliguri, N.L. Publishers Siliguri.

Tamsang, K.P. 1982. *The Unknown and Untold Reality about the Lepchas*. Kalimpong, Lyángsóng.

Thakur, R.N. 1988. *Himalayan Lepchas*. New Delhi, Archives Publishers and Distributers.

21
Indigenous Knowledge, Conflict and Practices of Indigenous Communities of North East India and Surroundings

Nabajit Das

Introduction

The North East region of India is a land of diverse people each with their own cultural tradition and nature-linked celebration. India's North East consists of Assam, Arunachal Pradesh, Manipur, Meghalaya, Mizoram, Nagaland, and Tripura. Of late, Sikkim is also considered to be a part of this region. The North East India is a strategically important location sharing international boundaries with Bangladesh, Bhutan, China and Myanmar. The region is characterized by distinct ethnic, cultural, religious, and linguistic pluralities. North East India is the homeland of large number of ethnic groups who came to the region from different directions at different historical times. These groups belong to the different racial stocks, speak different languages, and have varied socio-cultural tradition. As a result the region has become the epicenter of numerous ethnic nationalities. Especially the society in the hills of North East region reflects high degree of diversity as each community living therein has its distinct characteristics. The North Eastern region of India is home for rich cultures, nature-friendly traditional technologies and enduring social institutions. These have been shaped and nurtured by many tribal and non-tribal social formations inhabiting different parts of the region. Among the indigenous communities, there are more than 120 Scheduled Tribes, most of whom are traditional inhabitants of the hill regions, which make up over 70 per cent of the total area. Despite impressive social and economic changes, the indigenous communities, tribal and others, still retain a great deal of the pristine elements of their age-old lifestyles. Nearly every indigenous community can be considered as a repository of a distinctive body of knowledge, cultural traditions, social institutions and technologies, which have evolved over a long period of time. Wisdom and knowledge embedded in the socio-cultural life of the folk people of this region is often astounding.

According to the 'People of India' project sponsored by Anthropological Survey of India out of 5,633 communities living in India 635 are categorized as tribals, of which 231 are residing in India. The project had listed 325 languages of which 175 belonging to the Tibeto-Burman group and Mon-Khmer group are spoken in North East India. (Bhaumik S., 2005).

The isolated areas of the region are among the most enchanting land rich in natural resources. The geographical features of the region present the complexities of the sub-Himalayan ranges, the Indo-Burmese hills of Nagaland, Manipur and Mizoram and the eroded surfaces of the Meghalaya plateau. The Brahmaputra Valley and the Hills differ physically and culturally but are interdependent. The altitude of Manipur and Naga hills varies from 900 to 2,100 meters, the Mizo hills rarely rise above 900 meters, the Shillong Plateau and the Garo, Khasi and Jaintia Hills are 1,200-1,800 metres and parts of Tripura and Imphal Valley represent areas of low relief. The Assam valley is an alluvial expanse created by the Brahmaputra and its tributaries. The mountain range to its north is high in Arunachal Pradesh, loses height towards the south and ends in the low hills of Mizoram (Fernandes *et al.*, 2008: 6).

The North East falls in the distinctive part of Indo-Burma hotspots. The region ranks 6th among the 25 biodiversity regions of the world. The region is a treasure trove for herbs, plants, animals and microbial resources. Nearly 54 per cent of the geographical area is recorded as forests and that accounts for 7 per cent of India's dense forests. The region is rich in biodiversity and contains more than a third of the country's biodiversity. Its forest system ranges from the tropical ecosystem in the plains to sub-tropical, temperate and alpine forest ecosystem in the Hills

(FRI 1999). Its biodiversity depends on its unique climatic and topographic conditions.

The State-wise Population of North East India

The following figures for Manipur, include sex, the estimated population, 0-6 population and literates of Paomata, Mao Maram and Purul sub-divisions of Senapati district of Manipur for Census 2001 and 2011. For Census 2011, the population of "others" has been clubbed with the "Males" for working out population, 0-6 population, literates and related rates and ratios.

State	*Total Population*	*Males*	*Females*	*% Decadal Growth 2001-2011*	*Sex Ratio*	*Density (Persons Per SQ. KM)*	*Child Population (0-6 Years)*	*Child Sex Ratio (0- 6 years)*	*Literacy Rate Persons*
Sikkim	607,688	321,661	286,027	12.36	889	86	61,077	944	82.20
Arunachal Pradesh	1,382,611	720,232	662,379	25.92	920	17	202,759	960	66.95
Nagaland	1,980,602	1,025,707	954,895	-0.47	931	119	285,981	944	80.11
Manipur	2,721,756	1,369,764	1,351,992	18.65	987	122	353,237	934	79.85
Mizoram	1,091,014	552,339	538,675	22.78	975	52	165,536	971	91.58
Tripura	3,671,032	1,871,867	1,799,165	14.75	961	350	444,055	953	87.75
Megha-laya	2,964,007	1,492,668	1,471,339	27.82	986	132	555,822	970	75.48
Assam	31,169,272	15,954,927	15,214,345	16.93	954	397	4,511,307	957	73.18

Source: Series-1, India, Provisional Population Totals, Paper-I of 2011, Census of India 2011.

The Traditional Tribal Culture of Land Use In North East India

The traditional tribal systems are based on the concept of nature in general and land in particular as community sustenance that has come down from the ancestors and has to be preserved for posterity. Because of this close link between the identity of their community and land and other natural resources, they have for centuries managed the resources according to their unwritten customary laws that treat them as renewable. The community that was the legitimising factor in their land use and management systems, built a culture and an economy based on their sustainable use (Shimray 2006: 10-11). Land, in this system was a resource which is an asset that is meant to be used according to need but not destroyed or exploited for profit.

The tribal traditions of land use in India, in the North East in particular, were based on a culture that had three main traits. The first is the sustainable or renewable use of their resource composed of forests, land and water sources that were also their sustenance. Basic to them being renewable was Common Property Resources (CPRs) and community ownership. They did not reject individual ownership completely but combined it with community control. In the North East, for example, some like the CPR dependent Aka tribe of Arunachal Pradesh lacked the very concept of individual ownership and had only usufruct rights over the CPRs. In the *jhum* season every family cultivated as much land as it required for its sustenance. After the harvest or the three-year cycle that plot reverted to the community (Fernandes, Pereira and Khatso 2007: 8-9). Others like the Angami of Nagaland combined individual with clan and village ownership but all of it was within a community ethos. A family managed its assets according to the tribe's community-based customary law (D'Souza 2001: 11-12).

In these as well as other tribes, the community included not merely the present but also the past and the future generations. That goes with the second feature of the resource being renewable. That too is linked to the community. The belief that guided the resource management for a renewable sustenance was that it had been handed over to them by their ancestors. They had, therefore, to be used according to present needs and environmental imperatives and preserved for posterity (Sachchidananda 2004: 141-143). That belief itself emanated from the basic principle of sharing and intra and inter-generational equity. Within each generation, their customary law ensured that every family had enough to eat according to its need. The Aka custom of land reverting to the community after using it for *jhum* is one of its examples. Such control ensured that the resource was used according to need and preserved for posterity. That was inter-generational equity (Fernandes, Pereira and Katso 2007: 38-39).

The third feature is the relatively high status of tribal women compared to that of women in caste societies. That too is true more of the North East than of other regions. However, while attributing a relatively high status to them no tribe treated women as equal to men. The relatively high status too is based on CPR management. As long the resource is community owned, women exercise partial control over it because of the gender-based division of power between the family and social spheres. In most tribes, the village council, made up of men alone controls the resource and political power. In most tribal traditions, the woman was in charge of the family and controlled its economy and production. The man represented the family in his society. In matrilineal tribes both descent and inheritance are through the woman but their tribe too is patriarchal and man controls society (Nongkynrih forthcoming).

The working of all these principles is visible in the tribal land ownership and management systems, especially in *jhum* cultivation on which some 25 per cent of the tribals in India as a whole and 90 per cent in the North East sustain themselves (Roy Burman 1993: 176-177). Equity is seen in its decision-making process. Traditionally, the village council decided which plot to cultivate in a given year, determined the amount of land to be allotted to each family according to the number of mouths to feed and decided which family with an excess of adults would assist which one with a deficit of workers. After it the man of the house chose the plot his family would cultivate and performed religious rites to mark the beginning of *jhum*. At this stage, the woman took charge of cultivation and organised work. As a result, the division of work was more gender friendly in *jhum* than in settled agriculture (Menon 1995: 101-102).

The technology used and the spacing of various crops ensured that land was preserved for the future generations. *Jhum* was practised on slopes of up to 20-degree gradient. To ensure soil preservation, no plough was allowed to be used on it. Only a hoe could be used. The crops planted were spaced. Before the rains began they sowed root crops that protected the soil on the slopes. They sowed paddy and other crops after the rains began. Weeding too was graded. Some weeds that could preserve soil were left behind. Because of spacing in sowing crops, food was available from October to March since also harvesting was spaced. After March summer fruits became available (Gangwar and Ramakrishnan 1992).

Administrative Structure of the Region—Past and Present

The North East has been added to political India only in recent times, though India itself was rarely been unified for most of its history. Assam, which included at independence, Nagaland, Mizoram and Meghalaya was rarely part of political India for most of its history. Manipur and Tripura were princely states also rarely a part of political India. Arunachal Pradesh was beyond the outer line of British India at the beginning of the 20th century. These areas were incorporated into mainland India during the British Raj when British colonial authorities annexed traditionally separate countries after the Yandabu Treaty of 1826 and joined them to the Indian Territory. After the treaty the colonial rulers divided the region into the hills and that their status of development and accessibility. Restrictions were put on the people from the plains going to the hill or buying and owning land in such areas (Kumar 2005: 199).

The political boundaries of the British Empire in the region left many tribes divided. This division continued in the post-independence state formation. The same tribes were divided between different states. At independence, Arunachal was the North East Frontier Agency. Later it became Union Territory and finally a full-fledged state on 20th February 1987. Tripura officially became part of India on October 15, 1949, a Union Territory on 1st November 1956 and a state on January 21, 1972. Manipur too became a Union Territory in 1956 and attained statehood in January 21, 1972. British rule was established over the Naga Hills in the 1890s. In the post-Independence era Assam witnessed several divisions of its territory. The Government of India established a single Naga administrative unit in 1957. In 1960, in the face of civil unrest, the Indian Government agreed to make Nagaland a self-governing state within India. The state was officially inaugurated in 1963. The present States of Meghalaya and Mizoram were with Assam till Meghalaya was separated as a full-fledged state on January 21, 1972. The formation of Mizoram State took place on 20th February 1987.

Types of Administrative Structure for the Tribes of North East India

State	*Special Constitutional Provision*	*Administratve Structure*
Arunachal Pradesh	Art. 371H	No Autonomous Councils, the state has adopted the Panchayati Raj.
Assam	Sixth Schedule Read with Art. 371B (for Schedule	Three Autonomous Councils: (i). Karbi-Anglong, (ii). North Cachar Hills, (iii). Bodo Territorial Council.
Manipur	Art. 371C	The Manipur (Village Authorities in Hill Areas) Act, 1956
Meghalaya	Sixth Schedule	Three Autonomous Councils: (i). Khasi Hills, (ii). Jaintia Hills, (iii). Garo Hills
Mizoram	Sixth Schedule Read with Art. 371G	Three Autonomous Councils of Pawi, Lakher, Chakma, and other areas without the Autonomous Council.
Nagaland	Art. 371A	No Autonomous District Councils.
Tripura	Sixth Schedule	Tripura Tribal Area Autonomous District Council, Khumulwang.

Source: Nongkynrih, forthcoming.

Each state of the North East has a different administrative structure under the Constitution of India. Some areas are under the Sixth Schedule and or under special constitutional safeguards. The Sixth Schedule is applicable to the three Autonomous Councils in Assam, namely North Cachar Hills, Karbi Anglong and Boro Territorial Council, the whole of Meghalaya and the hill areas of Tripura. The Constitution of India was amended in 1963 to introduce Article 371A to bring civil affairs in Nagaland under the tribal customary laws. Article 371G introduced in 1986 conferred the same powers on Mizoram. It is stated in Article 371A of the Constitution:

Notwithstanding anything in this constitution–no Act of Parliament in respect of (i) religious or social practices of the Nagas; (ii) Naga customary law procedure; (iii) administration of civil and criminal justice; and (iv) ownership of land and its resources shall apply to the state of Nagaland. Safeguards, like exemption from the Land and Land Revenue Act Manipur, 1960 are made for the tribal population of Manipur under Article 371C without the Sixth Schedule. The tribes of Arunachal Pradesh run their civil affairs under their customary laws without constitutional recognition. The State is the absolute authority in land related and other administrative matters. As a result, Arunachal Pradesh opted for the *Panchayati Raj* institution established in 1969 and not the District Council system as it prevails in most tribal areas of the North East (Nongbri 2003; Hansaria 2005). The administrative structure has serious implications on the land relations. Each structure has its own land laws and land relationship. The concept of CPRs is very important in this structure of power both at the community and at the State level. The following section will try to see the CPRs from this perspective.

Illegal Immigration from Neighbouring Countries

For the past several decades the North East has received a continuous flow of economic migrants from neighbouring countries and as a result of that in the states like Tripura and Assam demographic imbalance has been tilting against indigenous population. The waves of refugees and migrants besides causing demographic change also causing displacement of indigenous population from their ancestral land. In such cases displacement generally takes place quietly without direct conflict. Only when indigenous people realizes the danger to their existence, they begin to express their grievances through mass protest and social movement and only then the displacement drew public attention (Dutta, 2008). This had happened in the states of Assam, Arunachal Pradesh, Tripura and Meghalaya.

The Case of North East India

The North Eastern region of India is often described as the cultural mosaic of India consisting of diverse tribal communities, linguistic, and ethnic identities. Often these identities transcend the territorial and social boundaries drawn by the Indian state and the larger community respectively. The region, connected to the mainland India with the 22 km long "Chicken-Neck Corridor", consists of eight states and has international border with neighbouring countries, namely Bangladesh, Myanmar, Nepal, China, and Bhutan. In the international scene, it is a strategic location linked to South and South-East Asia. From internal security point of view, the region is known for the 'problem states', experiencing law and order problems, inter and intra-tribal conflicts and human rights violations by the security forces. The politics of North East India is marked by ethnicity and extremism for a long time. The assertion of various ethnic identities and the attitude of the state in containing ethnic extremism make the region distinct from the rest of India. The root cause of ethnic assertion can be found in the identity crisis of various tribal communities who extend over the territorial boundaries drawn by the Indian nation state. Most of the ethnic assertions are due to ethnic groups' desperate attempts to protect their identity, culture and language. For instance, it is argued that "claims to ethno-nationalism of the Bodos can be interpreted as closely intertwined with issues of institutional and social exclusion based on language politics" (Saikia, 2011: 60). In other words, the basis of ethnic assertion can be seen in two contexts. Firstly, the tribal communities' subjective consciousness of being excluded, oppressed and marginalized. Secondly, the process of development failed to address the legitimate concerns of the people. Though after independence, the Indian state tried to integrate and assimilate various ethnic communities in the mainstream national identity, the development process generated a feeling of alienation among them. Moreover, development led to the unequal distribution of resources across the communities and regions. Thus, both non-economic (subjective consciousness) and economic (material) factors created a sense of exclusion among the some ethnic communities. In North East India, the fear of exclusion started even before Independence. The Nagas foresaw the possibility of exclusion in post-colonial India in the event of their integration with Indian Union, and started mobilizing Nagas for a separate nation free from the clutches of the Indian state. Moreover, they also felt that their community life and values would be threatened with the increasing number of the majority communities from other parts of India. The sense of social exclusion in the North East was articulated with the emergence of new social forces–educated elite, students and youth groups, etc. The reasons for the emergence of social forces in the North East include: the impact of Christianity on the socio-cultural life of the people, spread of education, etc. Oommen identified three major agents of change among the tribes of North East India the state, the civil society (of which the Church is the major element) and the market forces. (Oommen, 2009: 10). Ethnic identity provided the grouping ground for their mobilization. Like Dalit mobilization started among the educated sections of Mahars in Maharashtra, these social forces articulated the grievances of the communities. It is argued that the Youth who feel alienated from society and excluded from job opportunities and decision making may turn to ethnic mobilization. Karna argued that the process of ethnic identity formation in the North East region was based on the idea of large group formation (Karna, 1991).

Moreover, the social exclusion of ethnic communities has a dialectical link with psychological exclusion of the tribal communities of the region. These include exclusion from deliberative institutions due to their lack of cognitive orientation and the epistemological inequality due to lack of access to epistemological resources. The impersonization of their social, cultural, economic and political life by people from other communities or modern state further accelerated this process.

Conclusion

The above analysis has explored the status in the states of the North East. Ethnic tension in North Eastern region in most cases is a byproduct of land alienation owing to demographic change as the people are fighting for natural resources in the same geographical space. Therfore, it is obvious that peace can be restored in the region by land restoration, poverty alleviation, education and development especially in rural areas. Each state of the North East has a different administrative structure under the Constitution of India. Some areas are under the Sixth Schedule and/or under special constitutional safeguards. However, with the changing dimension of time and influence of globalization, a number of social and cultural changes can be noticed among the indigenous communities and their cultural heritage is facing a major challenge, which is ultimately creating an identity crisis for them.

References

Baruah B. 1998. *Sonowal Kacharis of Assam*, Assam Research for Tribals and SC.

Baruah, Apura Kumar. 1991. *Social Tensions in Assam: Middle Class Politics*. Guwahati, Purbanchal Prakashan.

Bhaumik, Subir. 2005. "India's North East: Nobody's People in No Man's Land." In: *Internal Displacement in South Asia*. ed by Paula Banerjee, Sabyasachi Basu Ray Chaudhury and Samir Das, pp. 144-174. New Delhi: Sage Publications.

Biswas, Prasenjit and Chandan Suklabaidya. 2008. *Ethnic Life-Worlds in North East India*. New Delhi, Sage Publications.

Brass, Paul R. 1991. *Ethnicity and Nationalism: Theory and Comparison*. New Delhi, Sage Publications.

Hazarika, S. 2000. *Rites of Passage: Border Crossing, Imagined Homelands, India's East and Bangladesh*. New Delhi, Penguin Books.

Roy, Sanjay K. 2005. "Conflicting Nations in North East India." *Economic and Political Weekly*, Vol. XXXX, No. 21, May 21-27: 2176-2182.

Saikia, Pahi. 2011. *Ethnic Mobilization and Violence in North East India*. London, Routledge.

Sen, Amartya. 2006. *Identity and Violence: The Illusion of Destiny*. London, Penguin Books.

Sengupta, S. 2003. "Thengal." In: *People of India, Assam*. ed by K. Singh 2003, pp. 830-835. Calcutta: Seagull Books.

Sharma, Manorama 1990. *Social and Economic Change in Assam: Middle Class Hegemony*. New Delhi, Ajanta Publications.

Singh, B.P. 1998. *The Problem of Change: A Study of North East India*. Delhi, Oxford University Press.

SECTION-IV
Folklore, Oral Narratives and Interaction Between Great-Little Traditions

22

Goalpariya Culture from Myth to Modernity

An Investigation from Emic Perspective

Subhajit Choudhury and Joydeep Chakraborty

Introduction

Geographical location of Goalpara region, mostly associated to the historical undivided Goalpara district, is a region that is associated with the people and culture of Goalpara. It is bounded on the north by Bhutan, on the east by the Kamrup region, in the south by Meghalaya and in the west by Cooch Behar and Jalpaiguri in West Bengal and Rangpur in Bangladesh. The natural landmarks are: Sankosh and Brahmaputra rivers on the west, the Manas river on the east in the north bank, and a corresponding region in the south bank; the Garo Hills in the south and Bhutan Hills in the north. The then Goalpara District is now divided into six districts of Assam namely Dhubri District, Bongaigaon District, South Salmara District, Goalpara District, Kokrajhar District and Chirang District.

The *Goalpariya* has been coined as people do speak common dialect known as *Goalpariya*. The history of *Goalpariya* language is not known just like other languages of the world, but as per the classification it belongs to Indo-Aryan (or Indo-European) broadly.

The history, pre-history and mythologically the rich Goalparain are well known which are reflected in various facets of Indian History, Culture and Ethinicity.

Sanskriti—Culture: *Goalpariya Sanskriti*

"Sanskriti" is the Sanskrit term for culture. It comes from the term "Sanskaar". *Sanskaar* means impressions made on mind, reason and ego. Expression of these impression in form of values and principles of life and thus evolved life pattern is *Sanskriti* i.e. culture. It is also used to mean refinement. (Even the name of language "Sanskrit" means "refined"). It is also used to mean what it means in the term "Tissue-culture" i.e. nurtured, refined (Mukund Hambarde).

However, Sadguru Yogi Vasudeva defines *Sankskriti* as "the Science of developing human mechanism of exploring life up to the fullest possibility".

According to Hofsted, cultural differences manifest themselves in different ways and differing levels of depth. Symbols represent the most superficial and value the deepest manifestations of culture, with heroes and rituals in between.

- Symbols are words, gestures, pictures, or objects that carry a particular meaning which is only recognized by those who share a particular culture. New symbols easily develop, old ones disappear. Symbols from one particular group are regularly copied by others. This is why symbols represent the outermost layer of a culture.
- Heroes are persons, past or present, real or fictitious, who possess characteristics that are highly prized in a culture. They also serve as models for behaviour.
- Rituals are collective activities, sometimes superfluous in reaching desired objectives, but are considered as socially essential. They are therefore carried out most of the times for their own sake (ways of greetings, paying respect to others, religious and social ceremonies, etc.).
- The core of a culture is formed by values. They are broad tendencies for preferences of certain state of affairs to others (good-evil, right-wrong, natural-unnatural). Many values remain unconscious to those who hold them. Therefore, they often cannot be discussed, nor can they be directly observed by others. Values can only be inferred from the way people act under different circumstances.
- Symbols, heroes, and rituals are the tangible or visual

aspects of the practices of a culture. The true cultural meaning of the practices is intangible; this is revealed only when the practices are interpreted by the insiders.

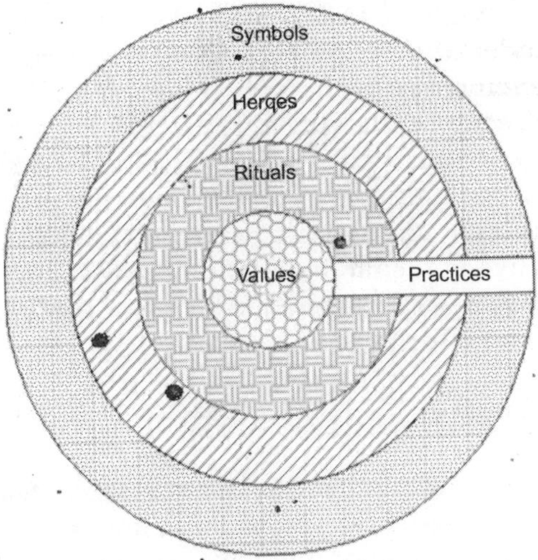

Fig. 22.1: Manifestation of Culture at Different Levels of Depth
Source: Hofstede, 1997.

The importance of preservation of cultural heritage is a great matter of concern in today's multifaceted fast moving economy. In this regard, Sekler observed that, "tangible cultural heritage has the great advantage over its intangible counterpart, such that with proper care it will remain authentic over centuries. As long as historic monuments remain without falsification and misleading imitations, they will, even in a neglected state, create a sense of continuity that is an essential part of cultural identity."

The preservation of cultural heritage is central to protecting a sense of who we are, a meaningful reference in our culturally diverse world. However, Sekler (2001) states that "there are many ways in which a cultural identity is formed and maintained. Much of the process has to do with the intangible cultural heritage of a body of traditions and usages, rites, poetry, song, and dance. A great deal of all these are passed on orally through generations. Consequently, its survival is always threatened...".

World Bank is also very serious and has warned that: "Cultural matrixes contain elements of the human collective memory–lánguage, beliefs and transmitted from generation to generation. Cultural references and signs are essential to the formation of national, group, and individual identities."

Further, UNESCO (1995) argued convincingly that the prevalent model of development based solely on the narrow yardstick of economic growth is outmoded... the report concluded that, above all, cultural diversity is here to stay. It is a manifestation of the limitless creativity of the human spirit. Its aesthetic value can unfold in multiple ways and stimulate the production and marketing of new and unique products. UNESCO has been extremely active in identifying world heritage sites all over the world. These sites are considered to be important for the world's cultural or natural heritage.

Goalpariya Sanskriti

Here in this chapter, *Goalpariya Sanskriti* as it is recorded by various scholars, Archeological Survey of India and also information recorded through scheduled interview are discussed.

a. Mythology and Goalpariaya Sanskriti (Culture)

(i) The story of *Manasa* Mangal of Padma Puran, Chandsadagar related to this undivided Goalpara (i.e. Dhubri district, Kokrajahar district, Boangaigaon district, Goalpara district, Hatsigirimari-South Salmara Districts, Chirang district) The waterways of Brahmaputra were once popular trade-routes. It was through these routes that the ships of Chand-saudagar (a famous trader) passed, bringing him great fortune. Chand-saudagar was a serious worshipper of Lord Shiva. Goddess *Manasa* tried to get him worship her but in vain!!! Annoyed at his stubbornness, the goddess finally cursed him. As a result, Chand-saudagar lost his wealth, his ships sank, six of his children died after birth and his hardships continued. While he was going from one place to another, his seventh son, Lakhindar, was born. Luckily, this child survived and went on to marry *Behula*.

Chand-saudagar was alerted by Lord Shiva about the imminent death of his son. So, he ordered a room made of iron where no one could enter for the newly married couple of *Behula*-Lakhindar. Lord

Viswakarma was asked to build this iron-castle. However, goddess *Manasa* was able to convince Viswakarma to keep a small hole in the otherwise solid structure, almost impossible for anyone to enter. The newly married couple entered this castle to spend their first night, quite oblivious of the fact of what lay ahead. As the couple was tired, they went to sleep. The bride, *Behula,* slept with her hair open (she had long and beautiful hair) that touched the floor. While *Behula*-Lakhindar slept, a snake slipped into the room and was trying to reach Lakhindar, who was sleeping on a specially-made bed that was inaccessible by a snake from the floor. Suddenly, the loose ends of *Behula*'s hair offered an easy route. Thus, the snake made its way to the bed and bit Lakhindar, thereby draining his life from the body. (People say this is one reason why women are asked not to sleep with their hairs open at night). Next morning, when *Behula* woke up, she found her husband dead from the snake's poison. As the news was passed on, the merry scenario changed to a gloomy one in a few seconds. Chand-saudagar was at a loss, thinking where he went wrong in his construction of the iron-castle. At the same time, the inability to save his last heir was breaking his heart. Goddess *Manasa* appeared at this moment and asked Chand-saudagar to offer his prayers to her. She promised that if he did so, his son would be blessed to live again. But Chand-saudagar was adamant. He had been a devout devotee of Shiva and couldn't change sides, even if it meant losing his son forever. So, on a boat, the body of Lakhindar was placed and made to float on the river. *Behula* accompanied her husband on this last journey. When the boat was passing the bank of what is now called Netidhopani, *Behula* saw an interesting thing. A woman was washing clothes and a child was continually disturbing her. Annoyed, she sprinkled some water on the boy. The boy became lifeless. The woman finished her laundry and then again sprinkled some water on the boy, chanting some mantras, to bring him back to life. *Behula* decided in a flash that this was the person who could bring her husband back to life. She rowed the boat to the bank and asked the lady (Netidhopani) to teach her the verses. The lady asked *Behula* to be her maid and serve her with diligence. Only then would she grant her wish. Many months passed-by as *Behula* served her unquestionably. Finally, one day she put her foot down and asked Netidhopani to tell her the secret verses by which she could bring Lakhindar back to life. At this, Netidhopani told that her verses don't have the capability to do so as Lakhindar died due to the curse of a goddess. However, she offered to take *Behula* to heaven instead. *Behula* agreed and came to heaven. There, she prayed to Lord Shiva for Lakhindar's life. Shiva said, "*Manasa* is my daughter. I can't do such a thing to insult her. It's better for you to return and find your father-in-law. Ask him to offer his prayers to the goddess. Only then will your husband be alive again." *Behula* came back, found her father-in-law after much difficulty and finally persuaded him to worship *Manasa*. However, Chand saudagar agreed only on the condition that he would offer his prayers by left hand (to show his displeasure and as a mark of protest). Thus, Lakhindar defeated death and lived happily ever after with *Behula*. This whole story is mentioned in *Manasa- Mangal of Padma Purana*. In this way, Netaidhopani has a connection with the famous legend of *Behula*-Lakhindar.

Now, again, the word *Dhuburi* (name of a place, Dhubri, the then headquarter of undivided Goalpara District) comes from a legendary lady named Netai-Dhubuni. It is also evident that on the bank of the river Brahmaputra, clothes of God and Goddess were washed by the Netai-Dhubuni. The stone on which clothes were kept to wash have been fortified by the Archeological survey of India located in Dhubri.

(ii) Surya Pahar (Hill)

The Gateway: ***Surya pahar***

Sri *Surya pahar* is located about 132 km north-west of Guwahati, nearest city is Bongaigaon and nearest town is Goalpara which is around 12 km in south-east.

This is a significant archaeological site in Assam, India. The site is a hilly terrain where several rock-cut Shivalingas, votive stupas and the deities of Hindu, Buddhist and Jain pantheon are scattered in an area of about one km (Religiousportal.com).

The name of 'Sri *Surya pahar*' implies that the site was perhaps associated with the cult of sun (Surya) worship. Literary accounts corroborate that among other Hindu deities worshipped in ancient Assam, 'Surya' (or the Sun God) occupied a prominent place in its cultural history. References are found in the *Kalika-Purana* (c. 10th century) about two seats of sun worship in ancient Assam. One of the centres has been identified as Sri *Surya pahar* which bears the iconographic significance of the cult as well (www.holidayiq.com).

According to archaeologists a carved stone slab, now housed in the Sri Surya Temple and worshipped as 'Surya', may be the detached part that formed the ceiling of the temple of Surya. The central figure in the circular carvings of the slab has been identified as *Prajapati*, which is carved inside an inner circle while the outer circle of the surrounding is in the form of twelve lotus petals, each seated figure of an Aditya. Again these Adityas are described as twelve solar divinities namely Dhatri, Mitra, Aryaman, Rudra, Varuna, Surya, Bhaga, Vivasvan, Pushan, Savitri, Tvastri and Vishnu.

Remains of Hinduism at *Surya pahar*.

Shiva Temple at *Surya pahar*.

The name of 'Sri *Surya pahar*' implies that the site was perhaps associated with the cult of sun (Surya) worship. Literary accounts corroborate that among other Hindu deities worshipped in ancient Assam, 'Surya' (or the Sun God) occupied a prominent place in its cultural history. According to *Kalika Purana* of the 10th century CE, Bhrahma created Pragjyotishapura, as a city equal to the city of Indra the King of the Gods. The word *Prag* refers to the Eastern region and *jyotisha* refers to the word star- astrology. Pragjyotisha is also said to mean, 'eastern city of astrology'. To the east of Guwahati, there is a hill temple known as Citracala, dedicated to the Navagrahams or the nine celestial bodies (www.templenet.com).

Stone Carvings

Besides the numerous stone carvings of Shiva Lingas and the 'Prajapati' slab, there are many rock carvings of the Hindu deities which can be seen at the foothills of Sri *Surya pahar* and its adjacent areas. Notable among them are the sculptural panels of Shiva and Vishnu. The twelve-armed Vishnu with a seven-hooded canopy over its head stands prominent. It is worshipped as Dasabhuja Durga. Adorned with necklace, *kundalas*, armlets, garlands, etc., the deity stands erect on a lotus.

There are differences among scholars about the identification of the twelve-armed 'Vishnu' sculpture. According to Baruah, (1988), the sculpture is of *Ma* (mother) *Manasa* while the Archaeological Survey of India has identified it as a male deity which was tempered with thick plaster into a female one subsequently. "The image of *Manasa* goddess, also identified as Durga by some, is a twelve-armed deity cut out of a single rock. She holds weapons of different kinds in each of her hands. She is standing on a lotus with seven snakes spreading their hoods like a canopy over her head." This is perhaps "the singular instance of a 12-armed goddess hitherto discovered in Assam." There is a series of rock carvings on either side of this prominent figure. The notable remains are the Ganesha, Hari Hara (or Harihara), Vishnupadas, etc. Most of these carved figures are assigned to circa 9th century AD. Similar to the Surya Chakra, there also exists a 'Chandra Chakra', but the natural vagaries have eroded it badly (www.hindubooks.org).

Remains of Jainism at *Surya pahar*.

As far as Jain remains are concerned Jainism could not get any remarkable footing in the North-East region of India throughout its long history. Except for the solitary example existing inside the natural caves at Sri *Surya pahar*, hardly any other Jain remains have been found so far in the region. It was probably the followers of Rishabhnath whose foot prints are also at Sri *Surya pahar*. The iconography of jain images found here is little different near their hands, but are found naked as per jain's traditional iconography.

On the southern slope of Sri *Surya pahar*, there is a natural cavern made of piled stones. Within the natural caves, there are Jain carvings. Remains of these Jain affiliations in the form of inscription and rock carvings are assigned to the 9th century AD. There are two figures carved in a big granite boulder which are in low relief. The figures are shown in standing posture with their hands hanging down to the knees and their cognisance are shown below the figures in low relief. Another figure carved at the top of the hill is identified as Adinath. The figure is carved in sitting posture in the rocky outcrop and two bulls are marked at the base, the mark of cognisance of the first Tirthankara. These figures are also believed to be of the 9th century AD.

Remains of Buddhism at *Surya pahar*

On a vast area right from the extreme northwestern slope of the Sri *Surya pahar* hill up to one kilometer further south, there are found as many as 25 votive *stupas* of different shapes and sizes cut out of granite boulders. These *stupas* are significant for it shows two points: firstly, there was Buddhist influence in ancient Kamarupa. It is in contrast with the commonly held belief that Buddhism was not prevalent in the cultural history of ancient Kamarupa. Secondly, the Buddhist influence in ancient Kamarupa was much earlier than in the rest of the country.

On the extreme north-east corner on a higher altitude, a huge fallen granite boulder was selected for carving three giant *stupas*, carved in one row, facing the east. The structural feature of the *stupas* consist of *Vedi, Medhi Anda & Harmika* which are distinct. The *stupas* are archaic in shape with three gradually receding rings round the base. The topmost ring that supports the dome is almost semicircular in shape with flattened top. On the top of the dome there are the remnants of a square 'harmika' with groove in the centre to hold the shaft of 'chhatra' or 'chhatravali' (parasol). The crowning element is, however, missing. The three monolithic *stupas* are representative of either *Dharma, Sangha* & Buddha or they could be termed as *Uddeshika stupa* carved in the memory of Lord Buddha.

According to the Archaeological Survey of India, the archaic shape of the carvings shows that the *stupas* at Sri *Surya pahar* were hewn during the Hinayana phase of Buddhism of early Christian era. Further development of the faith in the later phases is not yet seen at the site. Later phases of Mahayana and Vajrayana esotericism were seen in the neighbouring territories of Bihar and Bengal.

An interesting feature of the *stupa* complex is that in the 9th-10th century A.D., when the area was pre-occupied by the followers of Hindu pantheons, attempts were made to carve Siva Lingas along with Younipith and channel spout on fallen boulders. Altogether half a dozen Siva Lingas exist there.

One Elliptical *stupa* was also carved on a smaller boulder lying within two huge boulders is an interesting piece of Art, as this elliptical shape is very rare in Eastern India. One of such *stupa* found at Langudi in Jaipur district of Orissa dates back to the 1st A.D.

The *stupas* and also the terracotta plaques with figure of Buddha found in regular excavation indicate that Buddhism flourished in lower Brahmaputra valley, especially in and around *Surya pahar* during the early part of the Christian Era and continued up to the 10th Century A.D. In the 9th century A.D. the Pala Dynasty (who were followers of the Mahayana and Tantric schools of Buddhism) stretched to a large part of India including Assam resulting in spread of Buddhism throughout the length and breath of Brahmaputra Valley (undivided Assam). Buddhist remains found in some nearby areas like Pancharatna, Barbhita village and Bhaitbari (now in Meghalaya) in the southern Bank of the lower Brahmaputra valley also strengthen the fact.

Archaeological Survey of India (ASI) started excavation works in Sri *Surya pahar* in1993. But the initial works were carried out for brief periods annually which, however, exposed startling relics including heads of deities with Karanda Mukuta, Kirtimukha, vestiges of *stupa*, terracotta mortar-pestle and vessels used in rites, designed tiles, Apsaras, Purnaghat, etc. Excavations carried out in 1996 and 1997 hit gold when archaeologists discovered a Buddhist *stupa* along with monastery (vihara) which were estimated to belong to the 8th-9th century AD (contemporary to Paharpur *stupa* now in Bangladesh).

Excavations carried out in later years also yielded two temple complexes one of which was a brick temple complex aligned in north-south directions. These rectangular enclosure walls enclose the remains of several brick structures including the sanctum sanctorum and porch built in three substructural phases. The excavators also found a number of antiquities at the site most of which were terracotta tiles and plaques. Remarkable discoveries from the temple complex near the ancient tank include sculpture of Ganesha and Mahishasuramardini. In the southern foothills of Sri *Surya pahar*, excavators found a stone-paved water *kund* with revetment walls. This type of ancient *kund* which can control the natural flow of water has been found at many archaeological sites spread over India. This *kund* found at Sri *Surya pahar* was probably used to take bath and to perform other daily ablutions by the devotees and monks before going to worship the Jain god which was carved in the natural cavern.

ASI founded a museum at the site to exhibit most of the antiquities unearthed from the excavation. Some of these 96 collections displayed at the site museum include stone sculptures of Gajasimha, Mahishasuramardini, decorated lion head, moulded fish, plaques of human figure, mythical animals, kiritimukhas, amalaka fragment, decorated tiles of floral and geometric designs, etc. (Shri Shri Suryapahar 1992-93). Gurudwara (Sri Guru Tegbahadur Sahibji) as witness of place of pilgrimage for Sikh people in undivided Goalpara as a mark of *Goalpariya* culture:

In the heart of the Dhubri Town and on the bank of the river mighty Brahmaputra, this famous Gurdwara is situated. Sikh Guru Nanak visited this place in 1505 A.D. and met Sri Sankardeva during Guru Nanak Devji's way from Dhaka to Assam. Thereafter, the Ninth Sikh Guru Teg Bahadur came to this place in the year 1666 and established the Gurdwara during 17th century accompany of Raja Ram Singh. Sikh devotees from all over India and abroad assemble in this Gurdwara every year in the month of December to mark the Martydom of Sri Guru Teg Bahadur with due solemnity and ceremony. Sikh devotees call it reverence of Sahidee-Guru-Parav. Pachpeer Dargah: it is a Mazar Sharif of the five Sufi saints who accompanied Raja Ram Singh during Mughal fight with the Ahom regime of Assam.

Mahamaya Dham (temple) which is located at Bogribari which is 30 kms away from Dhubri town is also another milestone to record the part of *Goalpariya* rituals. Mother Goddess Mahamaya of Parvatjowar was worshipped by the local people like Kacharis, Koches and Naths. It was the presiding deity of the Jaminder of Parvatjowar.

Rangamati Mosque: Rangamati Mosque or Panbari Mosque was built during 17th century by Hussain Shah, the Governor of Bengal belongs to pre-Mughal period which can be recognised from its typical architectural design. It is about 25 km from township of Dhubri. Rangamati area was once a very prosperous during the reign of the Koch rulers as a frontier post. During

Mughal regime Rangamati was a great fort of the invading Mughal Army. This unique Mosque was used as a prayer place by the Mohmmedan soldiers. There is also an *Idgah* and a deep well which were also constructed during the same period.

Folk Song as Epitome of *Goalpariya* Culture

Goalpariya Folk Art (Kuhila Silpa) Photo: Punam Barua

Regional folk songs or "Desi" songs (as it is referred by the people of western Assam) have a special position in western Assam of undivided Goalpara District. Prior to 1958, Goalparia folk songs are known as 'Desi' songs or 'Bhawaiya Geet'. In 1958, Pratima Barua Pandey and Dr. Bhupen Hazarika changed the name from 'Desi' to 'Goalparia Lokageet' or Goalparia folk songs (Ajir Axom).

Goalpariya Lokgeet is one of the popular folk songs of the state of Assam. It is a folk music of undivided Goalpara district of Assam, sung to traditional lyrics. Love and devotion are the primary theme of these songs. There are various subgenres of this music that differ in the musical mood and themes, of which the *bhawaiya* and *chatka* are principal forms, beside *moisal* and *maut* songs. These songs are often sung in chorus, but they are suited as solos sung to the solo accompaniment of the *dotara* (a traditional musical instrument). In this section, the various images of the society as found in folk-song (i.e. *Goalpariya Lokgeet*) are discussed (Chakraborty, *Goalpariya Lokgeet).*

Nature in *Goalpariya Lokgeet*

In *Goalpariya Lokgeet* nature is worshipped like anything. It covers river, pond, other water bodies, rain, sun, windy days, cold days, hot summer, various seasons and its changes. The description of various birds due to change in weather is well mentioned. The nature is often compared with lovers and love in nature gets depicted. It is nevertheless to mention that the relation between human being with river is depicted in many songs, fisherman totally depend on river and the farmers are found in proper justifications through these songs. Few of them have been discussed for example:

"Dhu Dhu Kashiyar Ful Nadi
hail hulusthul
Mor Bandhua Kemone hoibe par"

Here flower as depicted as dominance in the region (one type of flower which is grown on the bank of the river) and river (i.e Nadi) (which is pregnant and restless), under this condition it is not possible to cross the river.

Some more songs related to river are as follows:

Torsha nadir pare pare
Didilo raida nadir pare O ki
sonar bandu gan Gaya jay

Here one song which depicts one fish called magur:

Bura Maril re.
Dangeya komrer hara bhangailre Aure
mok marili bhale korili Chaoa roil
kandiya;
Magur mach enga diya Kay
dibo randhiya

Here this song is narrating various fishes which are available in this area with a title called Marriage of Fish:

Makrar jale fandil dura bhai
Kakilar khal khali hashi Chengti
machor betir biya Tenga machok
diya
Dorkina mache uthia koi Chengtis
hoim mui kamali
Puthi mache uthiya koy Tengar
hoim mui bairati Bhedai mache
uthiya kaoy Chengtis hoi mui
shashuri Soul mach uthia koi
Biyar hoim mui maroadari Singi-
magur re uthia koy
Chengthir hoim mui mondopdhari
Boayali mache uthia koi
Chaynar hoim mui Dhapulidhari
Bangi mache uthiya koi Chinar
hoim mui kabari Tepa mache uthiya koi
Chengthir hoim mui
dhulidhari Kursha mache uthia koi

Chenthir hoim mui shainaidhari Shal
mach uthia koi
Chingthir hoim mui kashidari.

Here one song which tells about the monkey. It is very interesting to mention that only in this region there is taboo related to monkey is found such as Monkey killing is prohibited. Name of monkey should not be uttered before the young preferably before children below certain age, it is also believed that if monkey is uttered then the face of child will look like monkey.

aler Bandar dal-fal khay
Matir Bandar gu khay Daler
Bandar dalat Paytha kubang galat

Further, amongst all, song related to elephant is integral part of this culture. The life of a *mahut* has been narrated in various ways such as; withstand sun and rain while driving the elephant leaving their near and dear ones for the sake of livelihood.

Are O mor Hastir Kanya re Tok

sundarir lagi ghuriya berang re
Aji tor hastir karene o
Ashichung ai baner
Tok hastik dharibar bade Rahilam
sei kanane
O mor hai hastir kanaya re
Khanik daya nai tor Mahutak
lagia
O mor dental hatir mahut re Jedin
mahut chikare jay Narir mon mor
jhuriya rayre.
"Tomra Gailey Ki Aaseeben, O MorMahut
Bondhu Rey, Hastir Naran Hastik Charan,
Hastir Golaay Dhori Mathay Niya Tam Kalashi
O
Hathey Sonar Jari............................"

Similarly, there is mentioned about wild cat in this song, one of this given below:

Bagheswari paharat bara bag
dihiray Pariche Basantare kal
Garjan sunia
dauriya palaite
Kamor bhakar
komor khangil

In another song, due to fear of wild cat, parents put their children in between them.

Ashiwan-Kati bhagher bhoy
Chowa chot majot thoy.

In addition to *mahut* (elephantman) there is also mentioned about the *Maishal* (Buffalo man). When they go out the only companion of a buffaloman is a flute and a *dotora* (double string musical instrument).

Champa nadir pare pare maishal Ken
bajan bashi

Bhashia nile champa nadi Mor
kangkher kolshi.

Love (both *prem* and *biraha* (tragedy)) in *Goalpariya* in *Lokgeet*

***Biraha* (Tragedy):** Goalparia *Lokgeet* (folk songs) are full of tragedy revealing the feelings of human emotions due to separation of the wives from their husbands when husband moves out of home for business purposes are beautifully expressed in the sentimental feelings of women.

O pran Sajani-

Kar age kabo dukher
katha Kisher mor randhan,
kisher mor
baran
Kiser mor
haldi bata; O
re moro
praner nath
Anner bari jai
sai Barir
angina diya
hata
Aor jadi kedhung aro jadi
sunang Annya janer sange
katha;
Ore
bharajoiban
mor Sare
bhashabo
Pashane
bhangabo maha
Aitaay mor pati
hoi Anneyr bari
jay, moi
Kar age Kabo dukher
katha Ninder alishe hat
pare balishe Mone
bhabung pati achche

kache, Ore chetan paya
dekhung mui Pati nai
mor kache sai
Pati mok geiche saria.

Similarly, songs related to love affairs in different stages of life are to be found in such songs. For instance, union, separation and extra-marital affairs of a woman/man have been highlighted.

Madhu mahajan mach mare Basher pal
diya re;
O re mui Sundari Dekhia
Hasung Mukhe anchal
diya.
Sambandhe hoi mama shashur Koi kiba
fushur fushur
Mui hashing mukhe
Anchal diya

Further another song which reveals the inner urge due to separation of life partner:

Oki Pati Dhan—
- Pranbachena Joiban
Jalay Mori Chariya
Geche praner nath mor
Moe nay jay kaya

Bhara joiban kamane
rakhim moi Anchale
bandhiya re.
Jeman Dala matir kalar
gach Agala dalmal kare
Oi Mot narir
joiban more Dine
dine barere.
Ar chariya geche mor praner
pati mor Ruiya geche kala
O re pat katiya nai khang
bhat mui Juyan Boisher
balare

Aar Akashate naire
Chandra Taraye ki gun
kare
Je narir Swami nai re
Rup ki Gun kare re.

Aar je narir swami ache Randhe
bare khay
Jaro bhagey swami nai Parar mukh chayre
Aar Sati narir pati jemon
Parbater chura
Asati narir pati hayre
Bhanga nowkar gurare.

Songs Related to Mysticism, Spiritualism, Dehattata etc.

Songs related to dehattata (human body) did not carry any particular religious ideology. These songs are based on the ancient ideals of devotion to 'Param tatta' i.e., immortal soul which is in destructive. Human beings are mortal and shortlived. It is full of expression of human body, human life, wealth and property, relatives, friends, etc.

Kachur pater pani
jeman Talbal talbal
kare
Sei moto manusher
jibon Kundin dhulia
pare

Another song related to dehattata is very popular and common too as follows:

Aai deher bharasha
naire Bhaber bajare
Akbar haribala mon
rashana Manab deher
Gairab kairo na Manab
deho eek matir bhanda
Bhangile hoibe
khandare khanda

Bhangile deha jor.:libe
na.

Songs related to worshipping by offering sacrifice of animals and human being such as:

Nila nadir tire aak srifal
taru ache Satyapir bashe
tate sannyashir beshe Daiba
joge sehi din Shishupal raja
Narabali diya kare Astakali puja.

Songs related to *Ramayana* known as Kushan song of *Goalpariya Lokgeet* are also very common and popular. Songs which depict confluence of two religions (Hindu and Muslim) are as follows: Satyapir (Here Satya-Narayan for Hindu and Pir saint for Muslim).

Kali kale abatar mui satya-narayan
Hindur devata mui
musalmaner pir Ghare
ghare mor nashe bharil
jikir

Songs related to Krishna are also very common, one of them is as follows:

Pakhi haya
jabe tumi
Tir diya
marmu
aami
Shymere chikan galar bashire

Songs related to Lord Krishna, Manasha (Snake God) other God and goddess: These songs are having full of devotion towards god from Aakar to Nirakar.

Hari (Lord
Krishna/Narayan):

Harir nam bine annya
gati nai Aai na
bhabar bajare
Hari bine
bandhu nai Ari
bine kay achche
bhai Bharja-putra,
dhan-jan Sabe haila akaran
Hari bine bandhu kaha nai.

Devoted to Lord Shiva:

Shiva nache durga nache
Nache
maheswar Hate
kharga dhari
nache
Parbati Shankar.

Devoted to Goddess Durga:

Kar gharer devi
mao Tumi
mandire
bashiya Tomar
charan ma mui
Pujibo ki diya

Song related to Goddess Manasha which further related to *Manasha Mangal* of *Padma Purana* is well reflected in *Goalpariya Lokgeet,* few of them are given below:

How to Perform *Manasha Puja*—

Ahin kati mahat saneka devi puja
kare Dhak-dhol bajay sanekar
prati ghare ghare Magï jachi
sanekar rang hoila mon.
Bahura pujibak lagi karila

jatan. Kala-dhala patha
lale gale jari diya Bahura
mandop lagi jay re chaliya
Dudhure pukhuri dila
sendurer ali
Dhup-dhuna naibidya patile shari shari
Agaru chandane thai
pabitar karil Homshala
jagyashala anande patil.
Chandi-khara dhal lol
hatat kariya Bahurar
name bali dil re katiya.
Akon kene kanda aai tui gun
sumariya Nedile kolar chaya kay
nibo kariya
Bhar khaicha bheti khaicha bhokra
chagol Chando gharer dhan dekhi
hoicha pagol
Bhar khaicha bheti khaicha danger danger
mach Chando gharat jhi diba nachail ag
pach
Uni dhaner chira khaicha, bannidhaner
khai Khan charek gua khaicha, aro
tenga doi.
Dui tinibar barta lao
bahire Dukhi sukhi jei aishe
khuao tahare.

Descendant of Sri Chaitanya Mahaprabhu in Bongaigaon (a place of undivided Goalpara district):

The author have visited the site and recorded the information which have been narrated below:

The site where this Chaitanya Dham/Satra (temple) is situated around 3 kms from Baongaigaon Town (now it is separate Bongaigaon District) place called Gosaipara. This place is surrounded by three small hills and on western side there is one river called Tunia. Other places which are near to this Dham are Barshan gaon on south and Jel kajhar in north.

The photograph of Chaitanya Dham, Bongaigaon:

150 years worshipping of tools

সত্ৰৰ ধাৰা

শ্ৰীশ্ৰী৺চৈতন্যদেৱ
তৎপত্নী ৺লক্ষ্মী দেৱী
৺বিষ্ণুপ্ৰিয়া দেৱী
|
৺বিষ্ণুপ্ৰিয়াৰ আজ্ঞাপাত্ৰ
৺গদাধৰ
পত্নী ৺খন্তেশ্বৰী
|
আজ্ঞাপাত্ৰ ৺শ্ৰীশ্ৰীমাধৱদেৱ মিশ্ৰ
পত্নী ৺জম্বুৱতী দেৱী
|
মাধৱদেৱৰ পত্নী জম্বুৱতীৰ ভায়েক ৺জয়নাথ
৺কান্তেশ্বৰী
|
তৎপুত্ৰ ৺জনাৰ্দ্দন
৺আদ্যেশ্বৰী
|
তৎপুত্ৰ ৺চন্দ্ৰনাথ
পত্নী ৺জয়ন্তী দেৱী
৺পৰশমনি দেৱী
৺দীনেশ্বৰী দেৱী
|
তৎপুত্ৰ ৺ভূতনাথ
পত্নী ৺ৰূপেশ্বৰী দেৱী

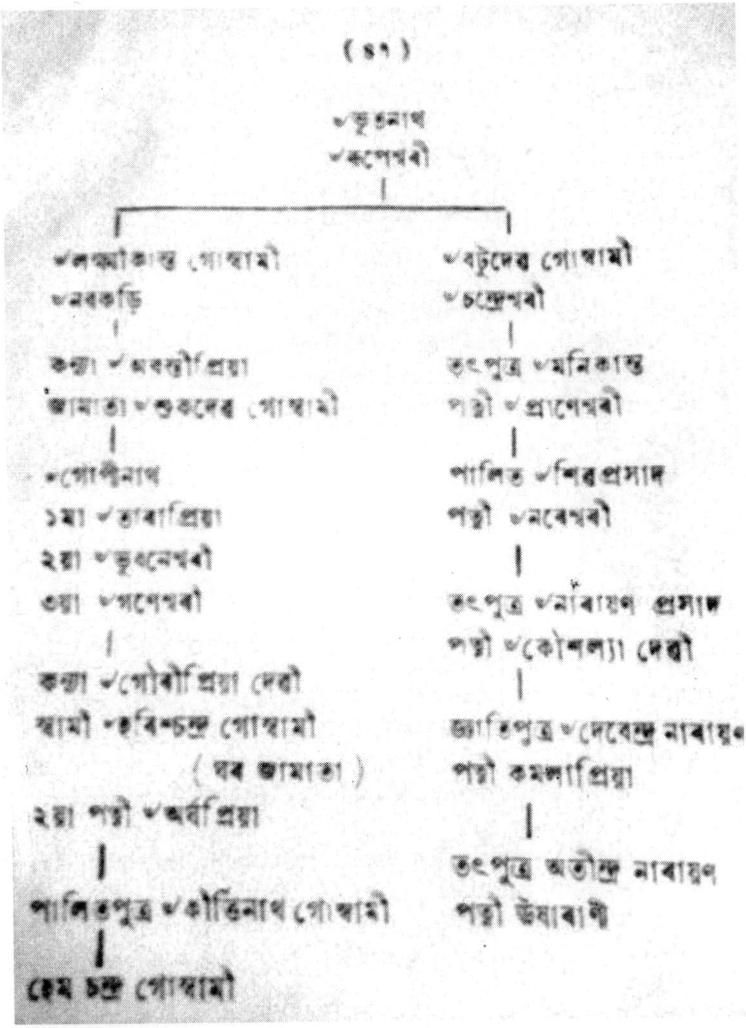

(৪৭)

৺ভূতনাথ
৺ৰূপেশ্বৰী

৺লক্ষ্মীকান্ত গোস্বামী
৺নবকড়ি
কন্যা ৺অবন্তীপ্ৰিয়া
জামাতা ৺শুকদেৱ গোস্বামী
৺গোপীনাথ
১মা ৺তাৰাপ্ৰিয়া
২য়া ৺ভুৱনেশ্বৰী
৩য়া ৺গণেশ্বৰী
কন্যা ৺গৌৰীপ্ৰিয়া দেৱী
স্বামী ৺হৰিশ্চন্দ্ৰ গোস্বামী
(ঘৰ জামাতা)
২য়া পত্নী ৺স্বৰ্ণপ্ৰিয়া
পালিতপুত্ৰ ৺কীৰ্তিনাথ গোস্বামী
হেম চন্দ্ৰ গোস্বামী

৺বটুদেৱ গোস্বামী
৺চন্দ্ৰেশ্বৰী
তৎপুত্ৰ ৺মণিকান্ত
পত্নী ৺প্ৰাণেশ্বৰী
পালিত ৺শিৱপ্ৰসাদ
পত্নী ৺নৱেশ্বৰী
তৎপুত্ৰ ৺নাৰায়ণ প্ৰসাদ
পত্নী ৺কৌশল্যা দেৱী
জ্ঞাতিপুত্ৰ ৺দেৱেন্দ্ৰ নাৰায়ণ
পত্নী কমলাপ্ৰিয়া
তৎপুত্ৰ অতীন্দ্ৰ নাৰায়ণ
পত্নী ঊষাৰাণী

Right now, the daughter of Late Atindra Narayan Goswami Mrs. Manjumala Chakraborty (Goswami) and his grandson Mr Joydeep Chakraborty provided all the information related to this unique Dham.

1. Plan for preservation of Cultural heritage to protect this culture for future:

A plan has been laid out considering all the facts and figure of this culture which is not only the treasure of Assam but integral part of Indian culture and Civilization.

(a) The Central Government

The centre should work for development of national strategies and practices for management of the cultural heritage sector. The Central Government should take proper initiative to bring these places under the ambit of conservation of this site. Of course Archeological Survey of India and Anthropologist along with the researcher of History of the country and the region are doing well. Further directives should be issued to all the departments and institutions to take proper care of these sites and culture as well. Special financial provision in Annual Budget to invest for preservation and promotion of this *Goalpariya* culture.

(b) State Government

It is the responsibility of the State Government (i.e. Assam) to provide all information to the Central Government and highlight the importance of this culture. Further, the state must execute the directives of the Central Government.

(c) Educational Department and Organization/Institutions

UGC should take necessary step to strengthen the qualitative study on the subject matter. Further, the department of folklore, history and Anthropology as it is available in the Gauhati Unviersity, Assam University Diphu Campus, Dibrugarh University should be provided PhD scholarships to investigate on this culture by the UGC under the consent of the MHRD. This is possible through special drive programme of the UGC to uplift of the *Goalpariya* Culture.

(d) Creation of Knowledge Hub for this Culture

The online database of cultural heritage to be made by the Government of India in collaboration with Governemnt agencies/ organsiations/institions/private agencies etc. A retrospective conversion of the treasure which are already there with ASI and other education institutions and libraries.

The libray and information centres to be given the assignment to collect the information and archive them in their library then after the same will be deposited to the State library and finally national library will have the treasure of this knowledge for dissemination and distribution as and when required.

(e) Tourism and Excursion towards Promotion of the Culture amongst the People

The department of tourism should make proper documentation on this mythological *Surya pahar* and other site. As an alternative to survival of *Goalpariya* culture from its ethnicity and economical point of view. The tourist who are visiting other sites of Assam just like Kaziranga, Pabitara etc. to be made aware about the place like Dhubri for its Netaidhupuni ghat on the bank of the river Brahmaputra. Proper infrastructure to be developed for this tourism.

Further excursion programme to be made as part of the curriculum for the young school children to encourage to know about the cultural heritage.

Concluding Remarks

The factor which is responsible for socio-cultural development is culture. Cultural heritage is based on the aspects of our past that we cherish, want to keep and pass on to future generations and outside world. The protection and conservation of cultural heritage contributes to social cohesion and to the preservation of history for future generations.

The chapter narrates the various aspects of social cultural milieu of the region. Firstly, the *Goalpariya Lokgeet* (folksong) is unique in its subtleness and creativity. The matter mostly presented in a very straight forwardly unlike in other folksong. The fellow feelings of the songs are well interwoven. Even extramarital affairs are projected through this song in very clear way there is no hesitation to unlock heart, a sense of open and free flow of thought amongst the dwellers prevail is also another striking characteristics of these folk songs. Social taboos related to monkey is another feature to be worth mentioned. Further, these songs are the reflections of Indian cultural diversity and unity as part of one India.

Here again, Hindu God known as Vishnu or Satya-narayana and in contrast Pir is regarded as equivalent saint for Muslim known as Satya-Pir for this region. As evidence to it Panch (five) Pir Dargah is there in Dhubri where Hindu and Mulsim community people do visit for fulfilment of their desire/wish. Anyway, the blend of two religions was prevalent for the region which marks an unique place of peace and tranquility. Moreover, a place called Dhubri (Headquarter of undivided Goalpara district) where Srimanta Sankardev and Guru Nanak met on the way to Assam from Dhaka for their religious deliberation which again the blend of Vaishnavism and Sikhism in *Goalpariyan* culture is well evidence of mutual respect amongst two different believers. Beyond all this, Sri *Surya pahar* tells the story of three religions in one place is itself an unique and well mentioned in the history of Indian cultural heritage. The conglomeration and confluence of Hinduism, Jainism, Budhism, Sikh and Muslim mark the land of rich culture and a strong bondage of humanity which is exemplary for the world. However, this cultural heritage needs to be protected and equally to be disseminated not for the protection of the *Goalpariya* culture but for the other parts of the country and the world as well.

References

Buruah, B.K. 1988. *Temples & Legends of Assam*. Bharatiya Vidya Bhavan.

Nath, D. 2008. *Goalpariya Lok Sanskriti*, Banalata Press, Guwahati, pp. 1-360.

Hofstede, G. 1997. *Cultures and Organizations: Software of the mind*, New York, McGraw Hill.

Sanghamitra Choudhury and Pratima Neogi. 2013. "Folk Music as a Voice of Marginalized Society: A Comparative Study of Goalparia Folk Music of Assam and Phleng Phue Chiwit of Thailand." *The Eastern Anthropologist*. 66: 279-291.

Sekler, E. 2001. "Sacred spaces and the search for authenticity in the Kathmandu Valley." pp 16-20, In: *Historic cities and sacred sites: Cultural roots for urban futures*. ed. by Serageldu, I., Shluger, E., & Martin-Brown, J. Washington DC: The World Bank.

Templenet on Surya Pahar http://www.templenet.com/Assam/suryapahar.html> accessed on 2/01/2016 at 7.03 pm accessed on 02/01/2016 at 7.18 pm.

UNESCO, 1995. *Our cultural diversity*. World Commission on Culture and Development. Paris. UNESCO.

World Bank. 2001. *Historic Cities and Scared Sites, Cultural Roots for Urban Futures*. Washington DC: World Bank.

23

Narrative Construction of Womanhood

A Socio-Cultural Perspective of *Along The High Road*

Merry Baruah Bora

"...what peculiarly signalizes the situation of woman is that she–a free and autonomous being like all other creatures–nevertheless finds herself living in a world where men compel her to assume the status of the Other" (Beauvoir, 29). Beauvoir's reading of the peculiar condition of woman situated within the specificities of her socio-cultural predicament is proof enough of the fact that society and culture exercises tremendous influence upon the 'autonomy' of a woman, considered most of the time as the 'second sex', as all societies and cultures tend to be predominantly patriarchal. Within the socio-cultural givens of a patriarchally structured worldview, it is only natural that a woman finds herself constantly under the disciplinary strictures of patriarchy. A conformist ideological construction of womanhood therefore would engender an understanding of femininity along the lines of hegemonic impositions of patriarchy. Thus constructed as the 'Other', a woman appears to find herself, generally at the peripheries of socio-cultural institutions such as family and marriage notwithstanding the relationships sheltered therein. Under such a predicament it would be almost impossible to visualise a woman as an individual with an autonomous self, capable of action and a party to decision making strategies within her situational context.

Bina Barua's *Along the High Road* published way back in 1944, narrates the lived lives of a society that was witness to the reformist culture of Indian freedom movement. The myriad of social and cultural experience of living at such a time and the anticipation of a progressive society that was supposedly being given shape has been captured by the narrative universe in a manner that moves the reader even today. It is perhaps understood that all narratives intend to give expression to the complexities involved in the process of living and the manner in which the society of the times too, is moulded. The socio-cultural realities may be read as a convention adopted by the people subjected to a certain ideological construction of the space within which they are situated. The spatial construction of people and the allocation of power therein are to a large extent determined by the societal and cultural construction of the lived experience of the people. Such constructions, on closer examination would reveal that they are the products of an ideology, a culture which appears predominantly patriarchal. Patriarchal ideological constructions are very often saturated with values that intend to produce the society and culture in a manner that serves to propagate and legitimise patriarchy within the situational context. Given such a worldview, it is imperative to examine the constructedness of the notion of womanhood, embedded within a particular socio-cultural context to reach at an understanding how various elements of culture, especially myth and folklore, serves to discipline and produce the female body through cultural conditioning.

The focus of this chapter would be to examine the socio-cultural disciplining of the female body through patriarchal conditioning that aims to produce the docile body which imparts an apparently unified and coherent meaning to the shared experience of living. It goes without saying that within a given socio-cultural milieu, the values that give shape to the lived lives and the worldview therein are products of the ideological operations of patriarchy. Such ideological exercises are directed at the human body which is not only the nucleus of culture but also appears to be the text where through various signifying systems culture is discursively produced and legitimised. As said earlier, society is predominantly patriarchal and therefore it would be interesting to examine how such a cultural practice engendered the idea of womanhood achieved through a disciplined body, as expressed in the narrative universe of the novel by Bina Barua. While referring to Mary Douglas in her essay titled "The Body and the Reproduction of Femininity", Susan Bordo has stated in context of the female body that it "is a powerful symbolic form, a surface on which the central rules, hierarchies, and even metaphysical commitments of a culture are inscribed and thus reinforced through the concrete language of the body"(2362). It would be interesting to note how the narrative of *Along the High Road* 'narrates' the woman represented through several female characters especially that of the central protagonist Tagar through the lens of patriarchy "reinforced through the concrete language of the body."

The novel opens in a rural setting ushering in the ethos of a society that is steeped in traditional conventions revealed through the rituals and customs carried out on the eve of the impending marriage of the Mauzadar's daughter Aaideo. Mauzadar's son Krishnadatta studying in the town visits his home for the auspicious occasion along with his friend Kamalakanta, the son of Mahikanta, a clerk with rather high ambitions for his son. Kamalakanta meets Tagar here and falls in love with her instantly. He presents her with a ring as a mark of his love and loyalty towards her. Although there was initial agreement on this marriage from both the families eventually Kamalakanta's father plans his son's marriage with Suprova, the accomplished daughter of Rai Bahadur Manik Hazarika through whom Kamalakanta's appointment to the post of Sub-Deputy Collector is ensured. In due course of time Tagar gets married to Dharani, a weaving instructor from Roha. Her marital life with Dharani is devoid of peace as she is not only under her mother-in-law's scrutinising eyes but also being observed by the womenfolk of the village. Dharani later joins the Freedom Movement, is put behind the bars and succumbs to tuberculosis after his release from imprisonment. Tagar has a daughter named Kamali to look after and so she joins the weavers' guild in her village started under the initiative of a benevolent doctor. As fate would have it Kamalakanta who no longer remembers Tagar, is now appointed as the local revenue official. Incidentally his wife acquaints herself with Tagar without the latter knowing her identity. The narrative culminates rather tragically when Tagar is accused of a theft at Kamalkanta's house and when her house is searched by the police for recovery of Kamalakanta's possessions, they find a ring with the latter's name embossed on it. It is now Kamalakanta's turn to be surprised as all events of the past and his association with Tagar comes back to his mind; he falls into a trance like state being unable to endure the emotional stress.

The storyline in general is rather uncomplicated and may be said to be truly representative of the lived lives of the Assamese people in all its simplicity. However, a deeper analysis would reveal how the social and cultural values appear profoundly embedded in the narrative universe that make possible not only the corporeal conditioning but also facilitate the internalisation of such conformist values to such an extent that the fact of their constructedness remains masked. The patriarchal society and cultural values embedded therein act as ideological apparatus which serve to legitimise "an oppressive hierarchy, [in which] women are trained for and given access to only certain "service" positions (mother, nurse, teacher...sentimentalised roles) it is chiefly women who find themselves facing, in the actual presence of living individuals...the consequences of the cruelty and indifference of powerful males who control the professions and institutions. It is women who are supposed to absorb the anger, the hunger, the unmet needs, the psychic and physical pain of the human lives..." (Rich, 302) Rich's argument may be applied to an understanding of how the narrative of *Along the High Road* perpetuates patriarchal hegemonic worldview which is reflected in the manner in which the storyline unfolds right from the start. Through the use of myths and folk values, the narrative establishes the contemporary society—it is a society where women wait eagerly to get married, for the Lord who would come to them in the guise of their husbands. It is through their husband that their lives shall attain fulfilment as Tagar sings:

Lord Krishna is my
husband My life will
be fulfilled
There is no one more fortunate than I. (3)

Marriage occupies a significant place in a girl's life, rather it appears to be the only important task in a girl's life through which she would reach at a sense of fulfilment. However, it is within the institution of marriage that she shall be positioned as the other since patriarchal structure establishes the Man as the absolute. Thus within marriage she is conditioned to receive a "service position" that of a wife, a daughter- in-law or a mother, which would relegate the fact of womanhood into a "service position". Women thus deprived of agency, in turn become devoid of action and being culturally trained to measure themselves against powerful men find themselves continuously lacking. Patriarchal culture thus "gave purpose to the social system, and ensured its equilibrium" (Rapport and Overing, 95), an idea that is conformed to when in a particular moment in the novel the Mouzadar's wife converses with Kamalakanta regarding Tagar's education and states, "Her father wanted to teach her English. We prevented it...What is the gain by giving a girl too much of education? She should learn to manage the household perfectly...If a marriageable daughter is in the house, there is no end to the worries of her parents. A young girl is like the flood in the summer. The quicker you can get rid of her, the better for all." (25) It is perhaps the consequence of patriarchal hegemony that such a predestined fate awaits a girl's life within such a society where the accomplishment of a girl's life is considered only in terms of her marriage; an unmarried girl becomes a liability—a value engendered by patriarchal cultural worldview. Women thus relegated to peripheral otherness become the recipients of social and cultural dominance and subordination masked under the disciplinary codes within their situational contexts. It is significant that within this peripheral spatial existence, a girl like Tagar is seldom considered to have a mind of her own, a fact that comes to fore when we notice her father Bapuram Bora conversing with the Mauzadar and his wife after receiving the letter of rejection from Kamalakanta's father. Mauzadar's wife says: How many girls get the husband they seek after? Has she been concentrating on him all the time like Parvati did for Lord Shiva?... Girls should be content wherever her parents marry her!...[t]he people in the village have seen what have you done by giving much education to your daughter....(68)

Patriarchal construction of womanhood in a traditional society often appears to be influenced by the myths which act as a buffer to legitimise the socio-cultural framework of a given ideology. However, on close analysis it would be revealed that myths "refer to a fabulous, or untrustworthy, non-rational, and even deceptive set of ideas, story or discourse—to be found within the domain of religion, or held by a given class of society. Myth seems related to the notion of ideology, when the latter is used to mean false consciousness, and the ideas that are mistaken, wrong-headed, deceptive." (Rapport and Overing, 272) Thus understood, the attempt by the Mauzadar's wife to spell out a rational decision regarding Tagar's peculiar situation may be looked upon as the consequence of socialisation within patriarchy where women are conditioned into silence and acceptance. Silence being an integral part of socio-cultural imagination of womanhood has been imposed upon woman and therefore all paths that lead to knowledge and rationality appears difficult for a woman to achieve within a society that creates and establishes a kind of false consciousness regarding femininity and silence through what we may call myth. Thus, the Mauzadar's wife referring to the Parvati Shiva myth and her objection to Tagar's education may very well be interpreted as the conformist voice of a woman who has herself been disciplined within that very worldview to the extent that she becomes an agency of the hegemonic patriarchy.

The institutionalisation of patriarchal values through women may be seen throughout the narrative in the manner in which marriage and family relationships work within it. The opening of the second section of the narrative puts a pertinent question "How long does it take to be a daughter-in-law?" This question may be understood to have initiated the discourse of patriarchy as Tagar now moves on to a new phase of her life—as a wife and a daughter-in-law Tagar now is situated within relationships where her marginalisation appears absolute. Similar to the wife of the Mauzadar, Tagar's mother-in-law Ahini too, becomes the mouthpiece of institutionalised patriarchy—"[p]owerless within the institution of marriage", these women through internalisation of patriarchal ideology gained an almost absolute sense of "power over another human being, [their] only outlet for rage and frustration being the control she had over that person" (Rich, 283). The narrative is replete with instances where Tagar is subjected to mental pain and agony inflicted upon her by women through their gossip and day-to-day conversation regarding the former's performance in the role of a daughter-in-law. The women in the novel talk about her in a rather negative light a fact that may be attributed to Rich's understanding of the "rage and frustration" that every woman has to bear within the institution of marriage which leaves them powerless. Thus women who come to Tagar's house "did not shrink from lashing her with their tongues on her very face, others more vain pointed her many shortcomings to her mother-in-law...[s]till others carried tales to the neighbours..."(107). Always subjected to Ahini's powerful dominating nature who "was keeping a sharp eye on her daughter-in-law all the time"(109), Tagar is taunted even by Jetuki, a woman from the same village for putting an apparently small vermilion mark on her forehead:

Oh, god! Your mark is so small. Should it be so? Is there any shortage of vermilion in the house?... What would people say if they find the new bride with so small a mark on her forehead? Our sister-in-law is just sticking to her old manners inherited from her native place....(109)

It is interesting to observe Ahini's response to Jetuki's outburst against Tagar. Ahini's exercise of power over Tagar and her attempt to dictate the latter in terms of body and space in their lived lives is made evident in the manner in which she reacts to Jetuki's words against Tagar. Ahini angrily states:

Why don't you give her a good thrashing and teach her? She would have been a mother of three to four children had she been married in time. She pretends not to know how to put the vermilion mark on her forehead? Do you want to take another husband? (109)

Later in the narrative one comes across several moments in which Tagar had been persistently making efforts to condition herself to appease her mother-in-law according to the latter's instructions only to be thwarted every time; Ahini would be provoked at the slightest opportunity as she "liked to exercise strong control on her daughter-in-law"(113). In instances such as the ones cited, primarily Ahini and other women who appear in opposition to Tagar seem to act as the agencies of patriarchal ideology; the internalisation of patriarchy in these women seem almost absolute—within patriarchal strictures that form their lived lives they may be seen as bodies "worked over by culture...in its most radical formulation...*constructed* by the forces of culture."(italics in original, Barker, 130) Thus, the conformist notions of womanhood may be attributed to the operation of patriarchal culture within which women are situated—Tagar too is subjected to such patriarchal conditioning through the strictures laid down by her mother-in-law. She becomes a subject constructed through the discursive formulation of womanhood in patriarchy and a product of power—power exercised over her by not only the men but also the women around her who are now constituted within the discourse of docility and conformity. Thus, Tagar's womanhood may be considered as a reflection of a self that lacks in autonomy being subjected to "determinate social and cultural conditions" (Barker, 233) that inform her socio-cultural situational context. Eventually although Tagar-Ahini relationship improves, it may be attributed to the birth of Ahini's grand- daughter Kamali through whom Ahini begins looking into the future and for Tagar being elevated to the coveted status of a mother—her womanhood thus achieves completeness and she moves forward within the hierarchy of women.

The concluding section of the novel focuses on relationship between Tagar and Dharani, Ahini being dead by this time; it is both the husband and wife who move across the terrain of domesticity. Dharani wishes for a male child when Tagar is expecting for the second time but unfortunately, Tagar delivers a still born child. In the ensuing moments we witness a defined spatial demarcation of the feminine space of domesticity within which Tagar remains confined and Dharani carves a special niche in the public domain with his persistent engagement with social issues and the ongoing freedom struggle. He became more and more indifferent to the needs of his wife, household responsibilities as "[h]e liked to spend most of the day outside the house" (140). With the passage of time Dharani becomes more active in the public sphere, contributing in his own way to the cause of the freedom movement and is eventually sentenced to two years of imprisonment. After being released from imprisonment, Dharani suffers from bad health and dies leaving Kamali and Tagar to face life alone in a society that possess little sympathy for women. At a cursory glance Tagar's predicament would make one recall Hardy's heroines—women tormented by fate that has an overimposing presence in the lives of these women that one would rather forget that they are autonomous individuals capable of independent action; Tagar's life may be seen as representing the predicament of a woman in whose life the role of a housewife has taken precedence while she "suffer[s] from more monotony, social isolation and pressure of time ..."(Oakley in Haralambos & Heald, 388).

What emerges central to the reading of *Along the High Road* is perhaps not its underlying theme of idealism and patriotic zeal; rather, even at time that is far removed from its days of conception, the novel would appeal one now, through its narrative construction of womanhood that attempts not only to provide a conformist representation but a critique of the existing socio-cultural paradigm achieved in a quiet and nuanced tone. The narrative universe deals with the fabric of social life with realism while creating for the reader subtle moments of introspection which would make one realise that Tagar's life would have perhaps been different had she been not subjected to the hegemonic conditioning of patriarchal culture. The internalisation of patriarchal values render all women in the novel perpetrators of the hegemonic culture as they go about performing their mundane tasks with the false consciousness of having self sufficient, autonomous existence–through their conformity to the socio-cultural construction of womanhood, they remain as the 'other', relegated into a position of marginality stripped off their very personhood and self.

References

Barker, Chris. 2003. *Cultural Studies: Theory and Practice*. London, Sage.

Barua, Bina. 2013. *Along the High Road*. [Translated by Lalit Kumar Barua, Jorhat, Assam Sahitya Sabha.

Beauvoir, Simone de. 1953. *The Second Sex*. London, Vintage.

Bordo, Susan. 2001. "The Body and the Reproduction of Femininity." In: *The Norton Anthology of Theory and Crititcism*, ed. by Vincent Leitch *et al.*, pp. 2360-2376. New York: Norton.

Haralambos, Michael and Robin Heald. 2000. *Sociology: Themes and Perspectives*. New Delhi, Oxford University Press.

Rapport, Nigel and Joanna Overing [eds.] 2004. *Key Concepts in Social and Cultural Anthropology*. London, Routledge.

Rich, Adrienne. 1979. *On Lies, Secrets and Silence: Selected Prose*. Norton, New York.

24
Folklore, Proverb and Riddles of the Karbi People

Jushna Beypi, Bamonkiri Rongpi and Rengmini Tokbipi

Introduction

Folklore is the traditional art literature, knowledge and practice that is disseminated largely through oral communication and behaviour in the society. Further folklore is the body of expressive culture, including folk-tales, folk-songs, folk-music and dance, legends, oral history, proverbs, jokes, popular beliefs, customs, and forth within a particular population comprising the oral traditions of the culture, and their anaesthetic life which is noteworthy to mention. Various aspects of tribal life such as their economic life, social life, conjugal life, sacred life, their thoughts, their cattle and poultry, vegetable and fruit are also amply represented in their folklore. The folklore of the tribals contains in itself their unwritten record of cultural life. In other words, the folklore is the mirror of the tribal culture.

Further the most distinction of the folk art is the repetition of a particular act whether it is the working of a song, a dance or a material tune, and so on. Another remarkable characteristic of folklore is its great persistence with respect to form. Contents may vary, but its form is relatively stable. There may be new riddles or new ballads, but the riddle form and the ballad formula remain the same.

In tribal communities of India, myths, folk-takes or folk-songs in general are not an idle speculation about the origin of things of institutions, nor are they the outcome of the contemplation of nature anrhapsodical interpretation of its laws. The function of myths is neither explanatory nor symbolic. It is a statement of an extraordinary event, the occurrence of which had once and for all established the social order of a tribe or some of its economic pursuits, its arts and crafts or its religious or magical beleifs and ceremonies.

The folklore of a particular tribal community is part of the entire culture of the people. It reflects the culture of the people and also brings solidarity, continuity and consistency in a culture group. A sacred tribal tale, for example, told in justification of a ritual or to illuminate religious mysteries, is of the greatest importance of that it systemises belief and regulates conduct. Again a legend; or an incident in tribal history may also contribute to the building up of morals.

The folk-art among the tribal people is the traditional handing from generation to generation of stories and folk-songs, of riddles and puzzles, of dramatic games and dances, depicting their failure and success, the importance of religion and magic, of totems and taboos, of discipline and customs, the roles of work and games, of hunger and work, of tribal sentiments and aspirations.

The feature common to different folk-arts of the tribal society is very simple in nature. The patterns present in folk-music may also be found in other forms of folklore. For example, the pattern departure and return is found in folk-music, exemplified by the melodic or harmonic technique of ending where one began: on the initial note or in the initial tonality. The same pattern is manifested in games by leaving and returning safely to home base; in folk-dance by leaving and returning to the initial position; and in the folk-tale by the hero's leaving and a quest and his returning. Also, some of the patterns in folk-art may be found in non-folk artistic materials. Folk-art, one must remember, is after all just one part of human culture. If there are formula laws which govern it, there is no reason why these laws could not regulate other aspects of the culture.

The tribal people sit at a place in the village for chatting dancing, singing and ever talking serious matters of the village. In many of the tribals, there is an institution of youth dormitory, a place where all the unmarried youth of the village assemble at night. This regular assembly of boys and girls, which is embodied in the tribal institutions of youth dormitory, is helpful in many ways in the origin, development and transmission of tribal folklore in an institutionalized form. For the tribals, the functions of folklore are more important than its form.

The Karbis are one of the major tribes in Assam, mostly inhabiting in the district of Karbi Anglong. The Karbi folklore mentions that they originated from a place called Hogpilar and from there to a place described as Lambejung, an area between present Diphu and Dimapur. Some Karbi still believe that they originated from the range of hills near present Kaziranga National Park, section of Karbi people still consider that they originated from the present Khasi hills of Meghalaya to lower altitude for various reasons. In the traditional Karbi society folklore plays a vital role in day-to-day life. Different types of folklore can be shared similar if not identical, functions. In a verbal dwelling situation, one can use tales, riddles and proverbs.

The Present Study and Methodology Applied

The present study is done on the Karbi tribal group of Karbi Anglong district. In this region, most of the people have an animistic religious faith. In the daily livelihood of the Karbi people, religion bears a special resemblance and it is intimately associated with their well-being. However, if some uncanny happens then they had a fear about the malevolent effect of evil spirits and the adequate remedy became a prime matter of concern for them. The present study is primarily focused on to know about the folklore, riddles and proverbs of the Karbi people.

The livelihood of the Karbis has a deep correlation with surrounding forest and environment from multidimensional perspective. In this regard, supernatural forces, spirits and souls are intimately associated in their religious faith. Related to the present study, is conducted on the Karbi tribe group of Karbi Anglong district in Assam. The prime focus is on folklore of the Karbi people. Origin narrative is intimately associated with the Karbi oral traditions. Their way of life lie in the state of verbal communication and here the folklore reflects their land, ecology and cultural setting more faithfully. It is focussed on the human groups or the process of social interaction and knowledge is built through the collection of secondary source like Books, internet, etc. On the other hand, the data has been collected from personal interview from Mr. Sikari Tisso, President, *Karbi Lammet Amei,* Diphu, and are also from Mr. Dharamsing Teron, who is a Karbi Cultural Activist, in October 2015.

Further it can also be noted that the purpose of data is based on primary sources as well as secondary sources by applying Anthropological method. The prime focus is done on Karbi folklore, proverbs, and riddles that is associated with the community identity and socio-cultural life.

Karbi Folklore

Folklore is the integral part of the Karbi folk culture. Folklore have a diverse function in the traditional social-life, it is associated with the contextual function. In traditional Karbi society folklore is learnt through singing songs or verbal communication process. Stories are used in the discipline of very young children, and lullabies sung by mother and may describe her own frustration through the song that the babies to sleep. "*Hemphu* is the creator and there is a creation myth of the creator himself. Myth making in these sense that man's attempts at rationalizing the powers of the supernatural beings *vis-a-vis* his real existence". Such exercises in the development of a culture would imply that human is constantly trying to find a suitable context for a proper meaningful relationship between themselves and the powers surrounding him, and at times to harness these powers for himself. The 'Myths' as they tell of both creation and origin of things and are represented in the narrative mode of traditional tales.

Creation of the Earth

In the Karbi folklore, there is mention of a universe god (Songsar-arnam), such god is considered to be the almighty and all powerful one and is considered to be the creator of the universe along with mountains, rivers, plants and all the creatures inhabiting in it. The myth elaborated how the world in a systematic and almost leisurely way, by chanting:

Pirthekimnang g, Mindarkimnang g
Pirthe do lo, Mindar do lo Longpuipo,

Kampuipo
Englong ne pui, arlok ne pui La inglongdolo,
La arlokdolo Be-siri, E-sir

Lang-jeng ne b, Lang-roi ne b Sim
a-mu, Bon a-um
La Pirthe a thak, Mindar a tha Sim
k-rik, Bon k-riks

An origin narrative deals with the idea of *Keplang* or creation myths. The origin of myths can be categorized as follows:

Hemphu Keplang: origin of Hemphu
Lunke Klang: Origin of singer and song
Karbi Keplang: Origin of Karbi
Rong-Kim: Origin of the first village
Sok Keplang: Origin of Rice
Bong Keplang: Origin of Bottlegourd
Thap Keplang: Origin of Fermented Rice caked
Vo Keplang: Origin of Fowl

There are many numerous other origin myths which deal with songs and they are very rich in composition. In order to understand the people, it is necessary to know their stories how world is created. These myths delineate the processes by which the Karbis define the nature of the universe in which they exist. In these contexts, the Karbi worldview is constructed around these origin narratives which dominate the Karbi oral traditions.

Hemphu Keplang (Origin of Hemphu)

In the Karbis folklore *Hemphu* is considered to be the supreme deity, *Hemphu* along with his sister *Ra-sin-ja,* made his first appearance in the presence of two brothers *Long-Mukrang* and *Bang-Mukrang* on the banks of the river *Kulang*. He was eventually accepted as part of the village and given a place in the village by the headman and father of the two brothers, *Rang Mukrang. Hemphu* has been variously addressed as *Langmangpo* or *Langmingpo* (once who glanced sideways) or *Vo- Hangpo* (once who asked for a red flow) or also as *LangmingpoVo-Hang.*

Lunse Keplang (Origin of Singer and Songs)

In the Karbi folklore, how the God of universe (*Songsarpo*), knowing that the Karbis do not had songs as well as singers, so and there *Songsarpo* sent a divine personality named *Rangsina*, who assumed in a human form and appeared in a Karbi village in the bank of river *Telehor.* Two other divine personalities in the guise of brothers *Sing Mirjeng* and *Long Mirjeng*, a couple of snotty kids, also accompanied *Rangsina.* The leader and his deputy of the youth dormitory, *Longbi* and *Chedu*, received them. Through this way the lessons in song and singing started immediate under the supervision of *Rangsina* and the two *Mirjeng* brothers.

Karbi Keplang (Origin of Karbi)

Karbi origin narrative called *Karbi Keplang* has a lengthy verse called *Mosera Kihir* (recalling the past), through these tale of migration of the community is considered to be part of origin myth of the Karbi. "In this origin of myth, the Karbis trace their origin to the 'Navel of Earth' *(Longle a-chete)* through the 'white mountains'*(long-le kelokabui)* and the land of the Burmese *(Barmipiakengri/Barmipoakengri)* to the present habitat. In this version of the origin myth, a mythical bird *Plakvutpilays* thousands of eggs and the Karbis are born from the biggest one of them. There is no divine intervention in this narrative as in the case of *'HemphuKeplang'.*

Rong-kim (Origin of First Village)

There has since a dominated folklore about *Rong-Kim*, how village had origin in *Karbi. Rongkim-lun* is the song (lun) how the first village (Rong) was build (Kim) by a village elder or *Kasen*, addressed as *Ru* the grand oldman. By the banks of the river *Kopili*, the village of a thousand households is built in a place called *Nongkula.*

Sok Keplang (Origin of Rice)

Rice being the staple diet of Karbi, there is the story of its origin. According to a version of the legend, *Harbamon*, the headman of the village of *Teronrongsopo*, had a dream that the daughter of sky-god (*sining Recho*) called *Kathipi* was residing in a banyan tree (*chiri*) in the middle of the river *Kuleng*. *Harbamon* declared that he would give his youngest daughter in marriage to the man who would succeed bringing *Kathipi* to his home. The only person to achieve success was a young man called Ronsingpo with whom *Kathipi* agreed to come in the form of a banyan seed. However, while on the river, the seed slipped and was swallowed by a fish. The fish was captured by Chindaipo, who decided to plant the seed that he found in his garden. Soon enough, he had a golden harvest of paddy. It so happened that *Harbamon* was a friend of *Chindaipo* and one day, he visited *Chindaipo* with his grandson. The little boy was attracted by the golden harvest and started to cry for it. *Chindaipo* plucked a bushel and give it to the crying child in order to pacify him. Later, *Harbamon* planted some of them in his own garden and when he realised that the new crop was tasty to eat, it was shared by all the villagers with as much joy and fervor.

Bong Keplang (Origin of Bottlegourd)

Bottle-gourd is bong (lagenariasicerariastandl) and it has a very significant ritual usage besides being an unavoidable part of a Karbi wedding (*adamasar*) without which the ceremony cannot be performed. According to the legend, bottlegourd first grew from the tooth of *Rang-Mukrang,* a Karbi chief about whom mention has already been made above. The creeper bore two fruits; one was named 'Bong *chim*' and the other 'bong dam'. These bottlegourds are compulsorily offered to the wife givers.

Thap Keplang (Origin of Fermented Rice Cake)

Thap is fermented rice cake for preparation of homemade brew (*Hor* in general), which is extensively used in Karbi social and religious rituals including the *Adam-asar.* Origin of *thap* in a way is the origin of *hor* and without *hor,* no Karbi ritual can be accomplished. The myth narrates that droppings of *vo-kongching* (a species of bird) led to the first discovery of *thap* by two sisters, *kareng* and *kading,* who later devised the fermentation and prepared the magical brew as explained to them in their dream. They found out that the brew was energizing and refreshing.

Karbi Folktales

Tales, on the other hand, are those narratives which are of chronologically subsequent observations of man about life in general and about the life of nature around him. There are numerous folktales in the Karbi societies. As it is said "The Karbi life of yore come alive in the folk-tales which include stories of creation, totem tales, animal tales and tales of demons and supernatural beings. There are swan-maidens and fairy-wives and of course tales of the mischievous, adorable, valorous and amorous trickster heroes, *Jangreso,* the orphan is a dominant character in Karbi folklores who begins as a destitute, living with his poor and often blind grandmother, goes on to marry a beautiful princess and becomes rich and famous, defeating all his adversaries as a standard trickster tale".

The Karbi possesses a large body of heroic ballads and epic poetry preserved in oral tradition, in their local language. One such oral epic, telling the story of 'Sabin Alun' the Karbi Ramayana and the tragic story of 'Ha-I', it is a long poem in the indigenous way of creating a folk story. Both 'Sabin Alun' and 'Ha-I' are the epic ballads in a Karbi tradition. 'Sabin Alun'(Song of Sabin), committed to text in 1986, contains 2775 lines with 7 syllables each. These are the popular and lengthy story in the Karbi folk.

Proverbs and Riddles of the Karbi People

The Karbi people are also fond of riddles and proverbs, which is a part of expressive culture. Proverbs are regarded as "wise man's words" or *'sarlamthe'* among the Karbis and they form part a rich oral art of the community. Riddles served to 'amuse and instruct' in various social situations among the Karbis, are equally important oral art forms. Riddles are short and are designed to puzzle the listeners. The first line begins like a story, probably to impress the listeners and hence riddles are called *'tomo-patar'* or 'story-puzzles'. Riddling among the Karbis also reflects that expressive culture, just as they do in the expressive cultures of many other societies throughout the world.

Some example of Karbi proverbs and riddles—

Ave ongtechehe ta ok. Lit. When there is no fish, a crab is. For a non-vegetarian Karbi in those days of plenty, having to forego a meal without a piece of meat or fish is an unimaginable torment. In such a situation, even a crab is as good as fish or meat. (English equivalent–Something is better than nothing.)

Sining le ingthokteemahangchero. Lang alilethutekengarkonngchhero. Lit. Spit to the sky, spit on one's own face. Cut the water current, cut one's own skin. The adage is used when quarrels or differences arise among relatives. If you speak against your daughter in-law, it is also like speaking against your own soon. If I speak against my in-laws, it is also like speaking against my parents. (English equivalent–He who spits towards the sky spits upon his own face. He who blows in the dust fills his own eyes with it.)

Tam le arju un te, rongta do un. Lit. Stay idle at home if you can bear the scolding. The adage speaks about a lazy or idle person who would rather prefer to be rebuked to stay in the comfort of a home than go out to the field and work. (English equivalent–Let the lazy starve.)

Karbi Riddles-

Ingnamkii-ikpiajo
Vo-ikpi pen vo-ikpo
Langke-erjunbomra do La ke kopi lo oso?-Rek.

(In the shadow of a thick black forest/ A pair of black birds Drinking red water/ What is that little one? –Louse.)

Hem tibinpiies Sarpiapokkesolivoi Kopilo?-PheloBisir.

(In the shadows of a house/ An old granny is down with loose motion. What is it?.- Bamboo strainer producing eatable alkali.)

Langroitibinpi le Seratarsoahiathak
Mithongkrangbikok. Kopilo?-Chehe.

(In the shadowss of a big river/Over the gold-woven mat lies a spinning wheel. What's it?-Crab.)

Pirthetebinpi arum Apiphutapjap
Asohaimunak, Kopilo?-Birik.

(In the shadows of the earth, what is a mother with unruly hair sitting idle and her offspring so offensive?—Chilli.)

These are examples of typical Karbi riddles. Generally, the riddle starts with words like–*'pirthe/ hem tibinpi le....'*, or *'ingnamtibinpi le...'* etc., which translate to 'in the shadows of a house earth....forest' etc., etc.

"Karbis riddles are instructive, as they may mention ecological names or contain references to historical events. Certainly they develop a sense of observation and often certain elaborate and rich linguistic forms."

General Observation

Folklore in Karbi society is narratives and very rich in oral tradition. The Karbis have numerous cultural folklore in narrative. In the origin of folk the dominant personalities of the Karbi legend—*Hemphu, Kasen, Rang Mukrang, Harbamon, Rangsina, Mirjeng* brothers, etc., had discovered an 'expressive culture' of their own long before the appearance of 'print culture'. Folktales, Epic of ballads are also very important part in their folk society. It is to be noted that riddles and proverbs are the expressive culture in the Karbi tradition. It can be observed that within the limited circle of experience, Claude Levi-Strauss spoke of the primitives' peoples not as "peoples without history" but as "peoples without writing". Karbi orality is the unwritten tradition, still remaining outside print culture. Oral tradition are some of the most vital means of building, preserving and transmitting knowledge, values and collection of memory which plays a very significant role in cultural vitality.

References

Philip, V.B. 1988. *The Study of Folk Music in the Modern World,* University Press, Indiana.

Vidyarthi, L.P. 1973. *Folklore Research in India, Essays in India Folklore* (ed) Indian Publications, Calcutta.

Tisso, L.C. 2004. *Karbi Proverb, Art and Cultural Department*, KAAC, Guwahati.

Teron, D.S. 2011. *Karbi Studies vol-2*, Assam Book Hive, Guwahati.

Teron, D.S. 2012. *Karbi Studies vol-3*, Assam Book Hive, Guwahati.

Datta Ray, D. 2015. *Oral Tradition of the North East: A case study of Karbi Oral Traditions*, Assam Book Hive, Guwahati.

www. New world encyclopedia/Folklore of India, Dated: 25/12/2015.

25
Socio-Cultural Significance of Bihu in Assam
An Ethno-ecological Observation

Joyshree Bora

Introduction

Culture consists of the abstract values, beliefs and perceptions of the world that lie behind the people's behaviour and that are reflected by their behaviour. These are shared by members of a society, and when they are acted upon, these elements produce behaviour that is intelligible to the other members of that society. Human being acquires their culture both consciously through formal learning and unconsciously through informal interactions. Culture includes all the elements in man's mature endowment that he has acquired from his group by conscious learning or by a conditioning process—technique of various kinds, social and other instructions, beliefs and patterned modes of conduct. The relation between life and environment is extremely intimate. The daily livelihood activities and the cultural aspects of human being are closely related with the surrounding environment. In the context of Indian culture and civilization, there are two distinctive but inter-related cultural traditions, one was formal, written, literate and reflected few while the other is informal, oral, illiterate and unreflected many. In this context, the simple society culture has its own importance. The daily lives of the people in simple society are closely related with their surrounding environment. The simple society culture has its own heritage and it is nourished in the lap of nature. Their folk cultural elements are nothing but the reflection of interaction between the concerned people and surrounding environment.

In the context of multiculturalism in India the culture of Assam and Assamese society has its own importance. The most important social and cultural celebrations of the Assamese people are the three Bihu festivals observed with great enthusiasm irrespective of caste, creed and religious affinity. It is celebrated in three different seasons of the year. The Bohag Bihu, celebrated in mid-April, is the most important one. It is also known as Rangaali Bihu ("rang" means merry-making and fun). It is observed by dancing and singing in open spaces as well as in the houses. The second important Bihu, Magh Bihu, is a harvest festival celebrated in mid-January. It is celebrated with community feasts and bonfires. It is also known as the Bhogaali Bihu ("bhog" means enjoyment and feasting). The third Bihu festival is observed in mid-October. It is also known as the Kangaali Bihu ("kangaali" means poor) because by this time of the year which is before the harvest is brought home, the stock of foodgrains is low in a common man's house.

Prior to conduct the study among the major literature surveys it can be noted that, Dickens (1992), emphasized mainly on the interaction between society and its functional aspects along with the natural and environmental circumference. Gait (2010), discussed about the historical formation of Assam and its phases of development related to art, cultural tradition and customs. Subba and Ghosh (2003), focused on the rich ethnic and cultural diversity of North East India. Barua (2003), stated about the phases of development in the cultural tradition of Assam in the historical perspective. Gogoi (2012), analyzed about the cultural tradition of Assam with a special reference to folk and material cultural aspects associated with Bihu. He analyzed in detail about the different material cultural implements in Bihu with their significance. Gondhia (2012), stated about the cultural tradition and customs associated with Bihu. Further, he analyzed about the significance of Bihu song and their importance in Assamese folklore. However, all of the above studied works are still to focus a detailed analysis about the Bihu from the ethno-ecological and cognitive cultural perspective and the present study will try to focus on it.

The Present Study

The present study was conducted in three districts of Assam viz., Nalbari, Nagaon and Tinsukia. It was done primarily focused on to know about the origin as well as socio-cultural, socio-economic and socio-religious significance and tradition of the Bihu festival celebrated by the Assamese people. The livelihood of the studied people was intimately related to soil, river and allied natural resources. It was the core part of their traditional agricultural occupation and resource for sustenance. All of their folk-cultural performances reflected the affection and devotion to nature. It was done in the Sataibari village of Nalbari, Kasorigaon village of Nagaon and Dubbspara village of Tinsukia district in Assam. It was done on 300 families with a total population of 1637, where there were total 850 male and 787 female, with a sex ratio of 925.

Significance of the Study

The correlation between cultural cognition, ethno-ecology and festivals as reflected through the musical performances of Bihu songs especially the role and significance of women folk in Assamese culture. All of their folk cultural performances reflect the affection and devotion to nature.

Objective of the Study

The present study is primarily focused on three important aspects—

1. To know about the particular customs, traditions and rituals associated with Bihu.
2. To know about the socio-cultural significance of Bihu.
3. To know about the interaction between human livelihood, nature and culture as reflected through Bihu through ethno-ecological and cognitive cultural perspective.

Methodology

The present study is primarily focused on to know about the socio-cultural, socio-economic and socio-religious significance and tradition of the Bihu festival celebrated by the Assamese people.

A pilot survey in the studied area was done during December 2012. The concerned filed-work was conducted into various phases. It was started from the above mentioned time and extended up to April 2013. There were four divisions of the total field-work.

Division-1: Foremostly, the general observation of the village was done along with the completion of Preliminary Census Schedule (PCS). The details of that form are discussed in the forthcoming sections of this chapter.

Division-2: Case studies were taken focussing on the issues of their historical background, early settlement, traditional occupational pursuit, present economic pursuit, function of social organization. It was mainly focused to know about the folk-cultural heritages, religious festivals and allied material and non-material cultural aspects associated with Bihu.

Division-3: Detailed open structured interviews were taken from the key informants and village elders on the significance of Bihu in the Assamese society.

Division-4: During this phase the qualitative primary data was analyzed.

Findings and Discussion

Bihu is the most important festival of Assam. Though its inclination is more on the agricultural side than the religious, it nonetheless is celebrated with much joy and abundance by all the tribes and other people, regardless of what their faith or beliefs may be. Historically, it is believed that the festival of Bihu originated in the pre-Aryan days around the 3500 century BC is the most important non-festival of the Assamese people.

Bihu festival is observed with great enthusiasm irrespective of caste, creed and religious affinity. There are three such festivals in Assam: in the months of *Bohaag* (Baisakh, the middle of April), *Maagh* (the middle of January), and *Kaati* (Kartik, the middle of October). The Bihus have been celebrated in Assam from ancient times. Each Bihu coincides with a distinctive phase in the farming calendar. The *Bohaag Bihu* marks the New Year at the advent of seeding time, the *Kaati Bihu* marks the completion of sowing and transplanting of paddies, and the *Maagh Bihu* marks the end of the harvesting period. *Bohaag Bihu* is also called the *Rongaali Bihu* or the Festival of Merriment, *Maagh Bihu* is also called *Bhogaali Bihu* or the Festival of Food, *Kaati Bihu* is also called *Kongaali Bihu* or the Festival of the Poor. The folk songs associated with the *Bohaag Bihu* are called Bihugeets or Bihu songs.

Importance of *Kati Bihu*: Kati Bihu or Kongali Bihu, signifies the relocation of the rice crop, which is an important phase in the life of the paddy crop. This day is also considered auspicious because it is believed that the spirits of the ancestors visit to give blessings, and so the Assamese peasants light lamps called Akaxbonti on top of bamboo sticks to show these spirits the path to heaven.

***Bhogali Bihu*:** It all starts on the eve of the Bhogali Bihu day when young men move into the fields and set up Mejis: structures made of thatch, firewood, and hay, which are burnt on the following morning. Around these Mejis, temporary hut-like structures called Bhelaghars are also set up. People, especially the agrarian community, spend the whole of the night in these Bhelaghars, guarding the Mejis through the night and partaking in community feasting, fun, games, music and dancing to Bihu geets. In the night, a grand feast is prepared and the whole community partakes in it. In the morning at sunrise, people move out from Bhelaghars, take a bath, and then return to light fire to Mejis. Edibles like coconuts and betel nuts are thrown into the fire which is like symbol of thanksgiving for the harvest that has been collected. People also pray to the Agni Devta and seek his blessing for the next harvest season.

During the time of Bihu dance performers or *Nassonis* (dancers) wear different kind of Assamese traditional jewellery like Lokaparo, Keru, Golpata, Satsori, Jon biri, Bena, Mukuta Moni, and diversified rings including Senpata, Horinsakua, etc. Gamosa is a unique identity of Assamese society. This small piece of cloth has high esteem and wide usage in Assamese culture. Gamosa is also known as 'Bihuwaan', as it is an essential part of Bihu festival of Assam. Significantly, the gamosa is used equally by all irrespective of religious and ethnic backgrounds. At par with gamosa, there are beautifully woven symbolic clothes with attractive graphic designs being used by different cultural sub-systems and ethno-cultural groups as well. Jaapi, the hat-like head gear, keeps significant importance in Assamese culture and society. It's being placed together with Gamosa as a traditional symbol of Assam.

A number of traditional musical instruments and natural products are used in Bihu like—

1. ***Dhol***: Dhol is considered to be the most important musical instrument of Assamese Folk culture. Once, the Dhol players are considered best life partners for girls, which indicate that it was the symbol of masculinity. Dhol was also linked to human fertility.
2. ***Pepa:*** One of the most important and charming musical instruments of Assamese Bihu is the Pëpa. The Pëpa is made from buffalo horn. Traditionally it is an instrument discovered and used by the Buffalo keepers and later on in the hands of the folk artists it was developed to a full-fledged musical instrument.
3. ***Toka***: Toka, is a very popular and easily available musical instrument used in Assamese folk music. Toka is made of Bamboo, and bamboo being the most common produce of the forests of Assam, it is used abundantly by Assamese folk musicians. The primary beat of Bihu music was kept by clapping hands, which finally led to development of instruments like toka.
4. ***Taal***: Taal is a percussion instrument used in a pair, is made of bell metal. Taal has a widespread and varied use in Assamese folk music. Taals of different sizes and shape are used in almost all forms of folk music of the region.
5. ***Gogona***: Gogona is an instrument primarily used in Bihu of Assam; this is a type of harp. It is held in the mouth to play, Gogona imitates the sound of a frog. Being a very melodious instrument, Gogona is very popular among the Bihu dancers.
6. ***Xutuli***: This instrument looks like the half moon. It try to imitate the sound of animals and birds and produce the sound of a flute. In the Assamese folk culture, people believe that the sound of Xutuli invites rain. In Bohag Bihu, Xutuli has importance of its own.
7. ***Kopou* Flower and *Bihu***: In Assam, it is popularly known as Kopou Phool. Its scientific name is *Rhynchostylis retusa* and is an integral part of a Bihu dancer's attire. Bihu *nassoni* uses this flower to decorate their hair knobs. Among the

youths, this orchid is regarded as symbol of love, fertility and merriment.

8. ***Jetuka***: During Bohaag Bihu, Bihu nassonis decorates or paints their palms and hills by using jetuka. The paintings are looking like tattoo. Jetuka is also a medicinal plant which prevents many skin diseases.

Bihu is associated with a number of special food items like—

Til Pitha; Ghila Pitha; Narikol Pitha; Hutuli Pitha; Tekeli Pitha; Bhaat Pitha; Sunga Pitha.

Recipe of Hundred and One Vegetables During *Bohag Bihu*

The first day of Bohag Bihu is called Goru Bihu. In that particular day, people make recipe of 101 traditional vegetables, locally known as *Ekho Eta Sak*. They believe that this special recipe has some medicinal values which are good for health for the next year too. Bihu represents the beautification of Nature and its significance in livelihood and culture. The month of Bohaag in which the springtime Bihu is held, is the pre-monsoon period and marks a gradual transition from a relatively dry winter to a hot, wet summer. It is thus an appropriate time for festivity, because the reproductive cycles of most plants are renewed and the tropical landscape is still penetrable and conducive to human activity. Songs sung during the festival directly refer to Bihu as the time of year when "the progeny of trails radiate", meaning that the dense evergreen forest and grassland habitat become more open and accessible at that time. This lyrical description of the landscape has a deeper meaning in terms of the environment as it reflects a lived cultural experience of people in the landscape that plays host to the Bihu festival. Birds and animals commonly found in the surrounding environment are often described in the Bihu songs. Many of the songs illustrate observations of natural history in a lyrical and intense manner. Descriptions of birds in the everyday landscape of the Brahmaputra flood plain are also found in the festival songs. A host of other birds like the river tern, shikra, barbet, spotted dove, ruddy shel duck, Asian koel, Indian cuckoo etc. are also mentioned in the Bihu songs. Several types of fish (xal, xol, xingi, senga, bami, borali, balisonda, eleng, dorikona, naro, bato, rou, and cital) are also referred to in the songs, thus emphasizing the influence that the landscape has on the particular cultural form. They help in defining the landscape that influences the culture and the space from, and into which, the cultural phenomena unfold.

An Overview

In the context of North East India, Assam is regarded as the richest zone of ethnicity and cultural diversity. Among them the Assamese culture is a core part of greater Indian civilization and the most precious great traditional element of North East India. Bihu is regarded as the most important social and cultural festival of Assamese society. The lyrics of Bihu represent the reflection of their mind about the beauty of colourful flower, beauty of sky and sunlight that makes their mind colourful and gracious. Further, Bihu are performed in different season which represents different climatic condition and correlated economic situation. It symbolizes the variation of crop production on different climatic period. Through the tune of music and dance the beautification of nature is represented through the dress, ornament, colours, musical implements which are being performed by the male and female folk of the Assamese society. So it may be summarized that Bihu is the cultural festival representing the cognitive aspect of ecology and natural resources in which the people are dwelling in. Thus, it can be recognized that through Bihu the worship of Nature is expressed through describing the beautification of the female folk and the contemporary climatic situation. In this festival, the cultural cognition about the colour, natural objects become integrated with the concept of ethno-ecology among the concerned people. Again it metamorphically signifies the combined role of male and female in a society or the combined representation of the *Prakriti* and *Purusha,* which sustains the livelihood of an individual within the said society as well as surrounding environmental milieu. It is recognized that Bihu is the festival of tradition, culture, social structure, and kinship based-social interaction as well as to get beloved. So it may be summarized that Bihu is the cultural festival representing the cognitive aspect of ecology and natural resources in which the people are dwelling in.

References

Barua, B.K. 2003. *A Cultural History of Assam (Early Period)*. Kolkata, Ajanta Printers.

Basham, A.L. 1975. *A Cultural History of India*. Oxford University Press.

Choudhury, K.N. 2003. *Society and Culture of the North East*. Kolkata, Punthi Pustak.

Deogaonkar, S.G. and S.S. Deogaonkar. 2003. *Simple Society Dance and Songs*. New Delhi, Concept Publishing Company.

Gait, E. 2010. *A History of Assam*. Delhi, Surjeet Publication.

Gogoi, L. 2012. *Asomor Sanskriti*. Guwahati, Banalata Publishers [Assamese].

Gogoi, L. 2010. *Bihu-Eti Samikhha*. Guwahati, Banalata Publishers [Assamese].

Gondhia, J. 2012. *Bihu-Bidhi aru Badhi*. Guwahati, Ank BaK Publishers [Assamese].

Haviland, W.A. 1970. *Cultural Anthropology*. London, Harcourt Brace College Publication.

Herskovits, M.J. 1955. *Cultural Anthropology*. Calcutta, Oxford and IBH Publishing Co.

Hoebel, E. A. and E.L. Frost. 1976. *Cultural and Social Anthropology*. New York, MacGraw Hill Book Company.

Hussain, A. and S.N. Deka. 2012. *Husori: Bihu Nachor Niomabali*. Guwahati, Banalata Publishers [Assamese].

Kessing, F. M. 1958. *Cultural Anthropology: The Science of Custom*. New York, Holt Rinehart and Winston.

Mahanta, K.C. 2008. *North East India: The Horizon of Anthropology*. Delhi, Singal Print Media.

Sarkar, A. 2000. *Ethnoecology of Indian Tribes: Diversity in Cultural Adaptation*. Jaipur, Rawat Publications.

Sen Gupta, S. 1964. *An Outline of Folklore Research in India*. Calcutta, Indian Publications.

Shirokov, Y. 1975. *Man Society and The Environment*. Moscow, Progress Publishers.

Subba, T.B. and G.C. Ghosh. 2003. *The Anthropology of North East India*. New Delhi, Orient Longman.

Vidyarthi, L.P. 1973. *Folklore Researches in India, Essays in Indian Folklore (ed.)*. Calcutta, Indian Publications.

26
Cultural Historiography, Gender and Manipuri Folktales

Yaisna Rajkumari

Introduction

The term 'folklore' was coined in 1846 by the British scholar William Thoms. From the 19th century, folklore has come a long way. Today a folklorist is concerned with myths, tales, ballads and sometimes with interpreting the beliefs of the cultures that they are studying. Folklore, as defined by W.R. Bascom, "comprehends all knowledge that is transmitted by word of mouth and all crafts and techniques that are learnt by imitation and example as well as the product of such crafts" (2002: 14). It, therefore, also includes folktales, folk art, folk dance, folk songs, folk gestures and even folk beliefs, recipes, songs, myths, ritual, performances, proverbs and riddles. These components collectively form the culture of a society. Folklore hence, is also a part of unrecorded tradition of the culture of a people and it is transmitted by word of mouth from one generation to the other. There are notable features unique to folk literature such as its orality, its fluidity, its relationship to mythology and its didacticism.

While Folklorists such as William J. Thoms believed in studying folklore as a subject connected to the distant past and not connected to lived, historical reality. Other scholars in the field have tended to view the discipline as intricately linked to the dynamic culture of a people. According to Soumen Sen, "Folklore in its totality is a conscious, rational and ideological construct in a distinct cultural context" (1985: 7).

The orality and fluidity of folklore are features that are particularly significant when dealing with a cultural construct such as gender in a reading of folktales. Stith Thompson argues that the "origin of folk literature is hard to trace"(1977: 2). Folklorists assert that the oral tradition is kept alive by some of those groups who were not accustomed to reading and writing. In the process of this oral tradition being passed on from one group or generation to another, folklore undergoes numerous transformations. A study of these changes in individual folktales would alert us to the fact that these changes are culturally and historically determined, reasserting the idea that folklore studies can no longer ignore the lived reality that it engages with. Soumen Sen talks about the "paradigm shift" in re-defining the whole concept of folklore; he points out that it is no longer considered as a dead past or a past history (1985: 1). Sen quotes Melville J. Herskovits' argument against seeing 'folk' as a quaint idea. He points out that in fact this 'folk' is in a state of constant flux and is hence dynamic in nature. Instead of considering folklore as related only to a distant past, he points out that folklore studies can be looked at in terms of its ever-evolving dimensions.

Written literature can be preserved in manuscripts and books, a practice which is less likely given the orality of folk literature. Hence, folktales are kept alive through songs, story-telling, performances etc. Memory therefore plays a definite role in this transmission; again transformations or changes and additions or omissions are inevitable. For example, in the Manipuri folktales of North East India, the name of the protagonist called Chaoba or Tomba which are common Manipuri names, can be changed when a new narrator tells the story. In another Manipuri folktale which deals with the Burmese invasion of Manipur, the tribals and the Meiteis' version of the story is very different. While the thematic concerns remain unchanged, details are not similar. For example, in the Meitei version, a rebellious Manipuri prince goes to Burma and he becomes the king whereas in the Tangkhul tribal version of the story, the person who goes to Burma is an orphan who fled from Manipur. The second instance given above is directly related to a historical event—namely the Burmese invasion of Manipur in the 19th century. The factuality of history notwithstanding, the tale has multiple versions. Such changes sometimes compel placing folklore studies in opposition to historiography as the latter is concerned with 'unchangeable' documented facts.

Folktales are closely connected to the ethnic tradition and culture of the area from which they arise and can hence be seen as representing many of the folk cultures and beliefs of these cultural spaces. India is generally understood as having a rich source of folktales but folkloristics in India largely remains a relatively new area of study. A.K. Ramanujan's essays and the publication of his *Folktales of India* (1987) did provide a much-needed impetus to folkloristics in the subcontinent. A number of bodies such as the National Folklore Support Centre (NFSC) based in Chennai, Indian Folklore Congress (IFC) and the establishment of folklore departments in various universities such as Manipur University have helped in the promotion and popularisation of folktales as well as folklore as a discipline.

Nevertheless, tales from the northeastern frontier region continue to remain unmapped or underrepresented. Vinay Lal mentions in Soumen Sen's book that in the Indian publication of *Folktales of India*, "some areas are vastly overrepresented, others underrepresented or even ignored" (1985: 2). He also argues against A.K. Ramanujan's idea of representation by saying that his "dismissal of this important question of representation seems somewhat cavalier" (1985: 2).

Findings and Discussions: The seven North Eastern states of India—namely Assam, Manipur, Arunachal Pradesh, Meghalaya, Nagaland, Tripura and Mizoram—are largely left out in anthologies like the "Folktales of India". Lal states that "the tiny states of Nagaland and Manipur, which scarcely mark their presence in the consciousness of most Indians supply one-fifth of all the tales, and in general the vast majority of the tales" (1991: 118). In fact, the folktales from these frontier regions can help in redefining the mainland Indian culture. By including tales from these states, there could be a broader understanding of the country as a whole.

An anthology of the folktales of Manipur titled "Folktales of Manipur" compiled by Dr. Haobam Bilashini has mentioned in its introduction that "perhaps the most popular and most frequently overriding of all concepts one can come across in the studies of folktales on a world-wide basis is that of fairy tales" (2009: np), echoing Stith Thompson's idea that the term folktale is often used in English to refer to the "household tale" or "fairy tale" (1977: 2). Apart from household tales, the people of Manipur also have tales which are based on legends and tradition. Sometimes they can even include historical characters, leading us to the relationship between folklore, history and historiography.

Historiography can be defined as the writing of history based on critical study of the sources and careful selection of materials from the given authentic sources and finally forming, according to Datta, a "synthesis of those particulars into a narrative that will stand the test of critical methods" (2002: 12). It is a well-known fact that the study of historiography started only about two and a half centuries ago. Especially in Indian context, writing of history has not been given a center-stage. Though history has become a mandatory subject in schools and colleges, history has always been concerned with conquests, wars, fights between two or more ruling classes without giving much importance to the lives of common people. The focus of historiography has always been on the ruling class and those who hold power.

Eminent historians have showed a deep interest in folklore. "Datta talks about the earliest historian Herodotus, also known as the father of history, who had included travellers' accounts of the strange ways of exotic peoples in distant lands including amusing stories" (2002: 14). However, the general tendency to see folklore as related to a mythic time and history as dealing with 'historical' time has tended to place historiography and folkloristics in opposing categories. Given that Manipur as a frontier state is grossly under-represented in studies of Indian and Indian folklore and that folklore itself is marginalised in historical studies, we can see that cultural historiography can be studied along with folkloristics in dealing with issues and aspects which are themselves historically situated. We can identify gender as one such issue as women and sexuality are themselves marginalised.

In the northeastern region of India, folklore studies is crucial in that it helps in preserving the cultural heritage of the indigenous peoples. According to Meena Deka, "As an alternative source, folklore is significant to explain and understand societies in the context of preserving cultural diversity and protecting minority cultures, especially those of indigenous people and marginalised social groups like peasantry, labour, ethnic tribes and women" (1985: 1). It also provides ways to reinforce socio-cultural and ethnic identity. Various ethnic communities contribute to north-eastern folklore and many of them are oral in nature. Soumen Sen and Desmond Kharmauphlang argue that "oral traditions express self-identity and upholds social organizations, religious practices, ethical values and customary laws" (1985: 5).

This chapter will focus on seven selected Manipuri tales—all the tales are from the Meitei community which is the majority ethnic group in the state and will highlight gender division and inequality in the tales.

In the 1980s and 1990s, gender emerged as an important approach in the study of folklore. This collaborative study of gender and folklore led to the questioning of existing patterns of authority and domination. Gender can be viewed as a social construct that affects both the sexes. Judith Butler's *Gender Trouble* (1990) claims that gender is constructed and enacted by people in the society which "proves to be performative—that is constituting the identity it is purported to be" (1990: 22). According to her theory of performativity, gender depends on the cultural and social framework within which it is being performed, and it is constructed continuously like a performance. Butler defines gender as a social role performed or enacted by the individuals, and validated and accepted by society largely depending on the societal framework within which it is enacted or performed. This social framework she continues is controlled and administered by patriarchy. Kate Millet in her *Sexual Politics* (1969), argues that the socialisation of both sexes to the ideals of patriarchy is needed for the formation of divisions in terms of masculinity and femininity. The qualities which are fixed by the societal or patriarchal norms denote either male or female and people are often evaluated on the basis of those qualities. Millet writes that, "patriarchy's chief institution is the family" (1995: 33). It is a smaller unit of the larger patriarchal society and it also acts as an agent of the institutionalised law of the society.

According to the *Theory of Sexual Politics*, "... patriarchy as an institution is a social constant so deeply entranced as to run through all other political, social or economic forms, whether of caste or class, feudality or bureaucracy, just as it pervades all major religions, it also exhibits great variety of locale" (1995: 25). Millet explains patriarchy as having a fold pattern—males dominating females and elder men dominating younger. It also affects women, as they start improvising the rules imposed upon them by patriarchy. This can be seen in many Manipuri folktales. In "UchekLangmeidong", the step mother takes on the role of a dominating male and discriminates between the daughter and son. In "My Beloved Doll", Tampha's mother-in-law, accuses her of being a witch. "The mother-in-law got petrified and came home to discuss the matter with her husband and son. They all came to the conclusion that Tampha could be a cannibalistic, possessed woman and decided to send her back to her mother's place".

In folk narratives, there is often a clear distinction between male and female roles. Lalita Handoo argues that, "folklore production, transmission and analytic processes, seem to be conditioned by gender" (1999: 147). Bottigheimer argues that gender "as a community category provides pre-defined and pre-ordained spheres of activity, modes of dress, forms of deference, expectations about behaviour, and even parameters of design, for even architecture is subject to fundamental divisions of space into gender-defined areas" (1999: 2). The society acts as a system which controls and defines the necessary roles to be played and enacted by both the genders. The particular "roles of men and women in this system do not come about by accident, rather they are learned and internalised both in practice and through concepts and images. Practices such as the division of labour and its associated tasks, as well as images, the concepts and ideals linked to female and male, are all part of the traditional culture of any society" (1999: 21). In "The Story of an Old Man and Woman Who Settled Down on the Moon", one can notice a gendered division of labour. The husband's work is to plough the fields and the old woman's work is to manage and clean the house. In "UchekLanagmeidong", Haiyainu's father goes far across the land to earn more money for the family: "One day, Hayainu's father had to go far across the land to earn more money for the family. So he told his wife to take care of Hayainu to be good to her". Day to day activities are defined by gender distinction in society. The bread winner of the family is generally a man and the role of a home-maker is taken on by woman. Women are expected to be meek and feminine but do not necessarily become so just because they play the role of a house wife. In "The Story of an Old Man and Woman who Settled down on the Moon", while there is division of labour, the old woman isn't meek or feminine, instead she performs hard physical labour such as husking rice using mortar and pestle. A supposedly powerful male god such as Indra finds it impossible to descend because of the old woman's pestle thereby defying the notion of women being the weaker sex. The pestle can be viewed as a phallic symbol but in this folktale it is handled by a woman and ironically has prevented a male god from entering into her domain.

While on the one hand, these folktales can be read as merely representing the inequality between the sexes, we can also see that the tales may act as a space where such inequalities are subverted. The tales can be seen as offering an insight into various ways in which women have dealt with gender inequality.

Human personalities and their outlook are formed along gender categories as society has endowed values for each gender. According to Kate Millet, ...temperament, involves the formation of human personality along stereotyped lines of category, based on their needs and values of the dominant group and dictated by what its members cherish in themselves and find convenience in subordinates: agression, docility, "virtue", and ineffectuality in the female (1995: 26).

In the stories selected here, women who do not conform to the societal norms are either termed as witches or evil women. In the story "The Witch", the witch can be looked at, using Bottigheimer's idea, in terms of "manly hearted woman" (1999: 2). She does not fall into the category of womanly women and is neither meek nor docile. The witch in the story is differentiated from the boy's mother. Both are widows and are portrayed differently in the story. The witch is shown as a monster-like figure who does not fit in to the society whereas the boy's mother is docile, vulnerable, a supposedly good mother and a meek woman who does not go against the society. She knew that something terrible has happened to her son. "She even imagined her son's condition in distress. She was roaming aimlessly with teary eyes"(translation mine). She patiently waits for her son to come home. The 'witch' on the other hand, is shown as active (itself a prototype of a 'bad' woman) and is also shown as eating meat. The inclusion of meat-eating and its correspondence with 'bad-ness' can help us place the text within a particular cultural context—namely the arrival of Vaishnavism in Manipur. Vaishnavism and pre-Vaishnavite religio-cultural beliefs therefore work along with gender in categorising women as 'good' and 'evil.'

In "My Beloved Doll", Tampha becomes an outcast and is branded as a witch by her family just because she communicates with the other living beings. Feminist scholarship often discusses the heirarchisation of the 'virgin' and 'whore' categories; on the other hand in folktales these caterigorisations are in terms of 'fairy' and 'witch' with the witch becoming a symbol of a woman who does not fall into the stereotypical categories. In *The Madwoman in the Attic* (1979), Gilbert and Gubar discuss the portrayal of women in terms of either an "angel" or a "monster" (596). They argue that throughout literature, these two images have been constantly created and women are subjected to these categories. It is also argued that Wilhelm Grimm's years of editing and filtering led to the creation of evil witches and evil stepmothers in western fairy tales. The issues about witches and stepmothers are questioned by women folklorists. This dichotomy is elaborated by Simon de Beauvoir in her *Second Sex* (1949). She mentions that this "the duality is a constructed framework" within which the society functions (1995: 5). Duality functions in terms of the "Self" and the "Other", in which the male is the self and female is the other. The father figure in the story "Laikhutsangbi" is a manly male who destroys the monstorous Laikhutsangbi. He is the ideal manly male celebrated by the society. Shashima the wife is witty but also vulnerable without the male figure in the family. She would have been defeated by the monster if Shashipa hadn't arrived on time. Chivalrous males are celebrated in folk narratives and some female figures are continually ignored or left out. Bottigheimer argues that—Historical folk narrative was subject to much the same processes that affected the disciplines of history, literature, and the sciences. In the nineteenth century when an influentially enormous amount of folk narrative was collected, it was simultaneously edited and re-written to conform to nineteenth century male standards of conduct so that primary material imperceptibly incorporated secondary, masculine views, which in turn both steered and hobbled analysis of tales treated in that manner (1999: 4).

The story-teller plays a significant role in the gender conditioning of the story. When a male narrator presents the story, certain instances or situations are altered according to the societal norms. Whether the narrative voice is female or male depend largely on prevailing societal patterns. Bottigheimer states that "voicing within tales depends to a great extent on the gender of the voice that tells a tale. Does the heroine speak? What does she say? Is there a heroine at all? Is there a hero? What does he do? Each of these narrative acts depends on social patterning of the society" (1999: 5). In the story, "The Witch", the real mother is passive whereas the witch is fearless and active. The two female figures are constructed according to the societal norms. Finally, the witch is eliminated to serve the purpose of the society. In another story titled "My Beloved Doll", the female protagonist Tampha has received a superhuman powers but she is branded as a possessed woman by her family. The angel-monster or the witch-godmother dichotomy is obvious in the stories.

Bottigheimer argues that "as in other disciplines, the study of folk narrative has been deeply coloured by the gendered views of its theoreticians" (1999: 26). Women characters are either portrayed as a supplementary character to the male protagonist or "women's courage becomes a help for a man" (1999: 7). This can be seen to operate in the folktale titled "Laikhutsangbi", the wife helps the husband who was trying to save the whole family but her contribution is not clearly emphasised in the story.

Bacchilega analyses the "fairy tale metaphors that tie suffering women to nature represent immasculization, the assimilation of patriarchal ideals of feminity which here include female suffering as 'natural', with folk narrative as both the process and the product of a power struggle which constructs gender" (1999: 8). Female perspectives are sidelined and physical experiences such as childbirth not given emphasis in male-centric folktales. In the story "The Old Wolf":

The old wolf without any sign of doubt or hesitation, said to her, "Alright wife! Let us go to our new house". He led her to a large tiger cave and told her, "wife! See, this is our new house, come come! You can go in and give birth to our babies". On seeing the big cave, the female wolf exclaimed, "wow! I am feeling happy". After saying this she went inside the cave and gave birth". (translation mine)

Lalita Handoo argues that "man's action is applauded as sacrifice and martyrdom and rewarded appropriately, but woman's death in action while giving birth is not considered a heroic act (1999: 148). The wolf's wife does not die in the process of giving birth but her experience is not mentioned in the story. Woman becomes a child bearer as well as a caretaker and "nature produced the fundamental inequality—half the human race must bear and rear the children of all of them—which was later consolidated, institutionalised, in the interests of men" (1995: 247).

One of the most significant Manipuri folktales which can be analysed in terms of gender perspective is "How the Tiger became Panthoibi's Mount". The story is a part of Manipuri myth in which goddess Panthoibi is considered as an independent spirit and at times worshipped as Shakti. This equation with Shakti could be because of the heavy influence of Hindu tradition among Meiteis. In the story, Panthoibi is self-willed and strong and her unconventional ways are conveyed to the readers.

Now Panthoibi was married to TaramKhoinucha and she also fulfilled her parent's wish yet the love she had for NongpokNingthou remained unshaken and intact inside her. She was independent and did not care for the society or her marital status. Panthoibi was, in other words, rebellious and she did not do any of the duties she was expected to do in her husband's home (Translation mine).

Her attitude towards society is not perceived in a positive light in the story. Despite her devotion, her love is tested by her lover NongpokNingthou. He wanted to test her love but ended up taking a tiger form which became her mount, thereby asserting the victory of the women over masculine attempts to subjugate or question her.

It can be seen from the above analyses that gender perspective in folktales has opened up new dimensions, with particular reference to the Manipuri folktales. A study of more folktales from the Meitei community or of folktales from other tribe in Manipur using gender a matrix within the framework of cultural historiography would offer a fruitful area for further research.

References

Bhogeshor, O. 1985. *Manipuri Lok Sahitya: Meitei KhunairolPhungaWari.* Imphal, Manipur State Kala Academy.

Bilashini, Dr. Haobam. 2009. *Folktales of Manipur.* Imphal, RS Publication.

Bhattacharya, Sabyasachi. 2011. [Eds.] *Approaches to History: Essays in Indian Historiography.* New Delhi, Primus Books.

Butler, Judith. 1990. *Gender Trouble: Feminism and The Subversion of Identity*. London, Routledge.

Datta, Birendranath. 2002. *Affinities between Folkloristics and Historiography: Some Theoretical Implications in the Context of Medieval and Modern History of North-East India*, India, NFSC.

Handoo, Lalita and Ruth B. Bottigheimer [Eds.] 1999. *Gender and Folklore*. Mysore, Zooni Publications.

Lal, Vinay. 1991. "Literature from Below", Review of The Folktales of India. *Indian Literature* 34, No. 3: 111-118.

Schneir, Miriam. (ed.) 1995. *The Vintage Book of Feminism*. London: Vintage. London.

Sen, Soumen. 1985. *Folklore in North-East India*. New Delhi, Omsons Publications.

Subadani, Kshetrimayum. 2010. *Illustrated Folk Tales of Manipur*. Imphal, Linthoingambi Publication.

Thouyangba Meitei, Thokchom. 2011. *EshuShaPupuWariLibigae*. Imphal, Golden Publication.

Thompson, Stith. 1977. *The Folktale*. US, University of California Press.

27

Bardowa *Than* of Nagaon District, Assam and Its Socio-cultural Perspectives and National Cultural Heritage

Contemporary Issues in Present Scenario

Mon Mayur Bora

Introduction

Bardowa *Than,* centre of Vaishnavite art and culture, the birthplace of Jagat guru srimanta Sankardeva, the great Vaishnavite personality and social reformers of Assam. Sankardeva, the greatest Vaishnava saint of Assam was well-known for his religious reform activities. He preached a new religious ideology known as *Ek Sarna Nama Dharma*. His contributions not only made the foundations of Assamese literature, culture and social structure but also established the super structure thereupon. All contributions of Sankardeva bear his remarks distinctively. Srimanata Sankardeva's greatness as socio-religious exponent has to be found in his idea of establishing the *Satra* and *Than*. It is kind of Monastery where everything centers around the *Namghar* and the dwelling huts for his disciples. During his life time the *Thans* became not only the centre of religious discourses, recitation of sacred texts, congregational prayers and dramatic performances but also places for mass education and courts for dispensation of justice. Sankardeva started a revolutionary movement to reform and reconstruct the society. With this aim he established two powerful institutions, *Namghar* and *Than*, which later came to be known as *satra*. His dearest disciple Mahapurusha Madhavadeva systematized the *Than* system. But unfortunately the *Satra* institution started diverting from its original path just after the departure of Srimanata Sankardeva. The structural pattern of a *Satra* is marked by the factors as a *Namghar*, a *Monikut*, a *Karapat* and four rows of *Hatis*. *Namghar* is the center of all religious activities of a *Than*. The *Than* institution plays a major role in the spiritual and cultural life of Assam. As the state is famous for its diverse ethnic groups these institutions are playing a key role to enhance the cohesiveness among different ethnic groups of the area. As like as other part of Assam, Bardowa was influenced by the wave of Neo-Vaishnavisim movement and Bardowa *Than* was established in the area for spreading the spiritual and cultural values of the movement. Religious and cultural in origin there is the institution for guiding the whole Assamese society. They are fulfilling the spiritual and cultural necessities of Assamese people. The role of the *Than* in the propagation of spiritual and moral education and organizing religious cultural activities is confined not only to the boundaries of the *Than*, it extends far beyond into the villages lying far and wide. Villagers came to *Than* to attend religious ceremonies and also to attend the religious and moral discussions organized in *Than*. "Although the word *Than* is used loosely to mean any place of public worship, it has a special connotation amongst the Vaishnavite circle. Therefore those *satras* which have been preserving some relics of the saints are also called *Than*. In Kalasamhati the places of cremation of religious heads are also called *Than* by the disciples." (Sarma, 1996: 140)

Satra and *Than* Institution

The abode of the two Gurus (Sankaradeva and Madhavadeva) is known as *Than* (Skt. S*Thana*). There is a difference however between *Satra* and *Than*. In the post-Sankaradeva period, the holy places where some saints passed came to be called *Than*. Sometimes, a prayer-hall is erected at such a place and this is called *tha-ghar* (*sthana-grha*). The places where Sankaradeva stayed—even for a few months—are also called *Than*, e.g. Bardowa *Than*, Belaguri *Than*, Barpeta *Than*, etc. instead of Bardowa *Satra* etc. In early Assamese literature, Bardowa is referred to as a *Than*. Certain biographers however use the term *Satra* synonymously for *Than*.

Description of the Place Bardowa

Bardowa has one degree college, one higher secondary school, one High school, one mini health centre and a police station. The place Bardowa situated at the distance of 15.42 km towards north-east from the district headquarters of the central Assam district of Nagaon in the state of Assam. As per the 2011 census, Bardowa has 1442 number of households with 6891 population, which comprises 60 per cent Hindus, 40 per cent Muslims approximately.

Bardowa's administrative setup is discussed below:

Village-Bardowa, Mouza-Bardowa, Block–Bardowa, District–Nagaon, State-Assam.

Demographic Profile: Demographic Feature of Nagaon District

Demographic Aspect	*Total*	*Rural*	*Urban*
Population	2826006	2457906	368100
Male	1440307	1252756	187551
Female	1385699	1205150	180549
Percentage of decadal growth	22.09	20.70	32.27
Sex ratio	944	948	912
Child Population (0-6)	446238	408476	37762
Child sex ratio (0-6)	958	958	968
Literate	1755838	1461302	294536
Literate Male	947986	791020	156966
Literate Female	807852	670282	137570
Literacy rate	73.78	71.30	89.16
Literacy rate Male	78.19	75.76	93.23
Literacy rate Female	69.21	66.67	84.93
Population density	711 per km^2		

Source: Provisional Population Totals Assam, 2011, Paper 2, Volume 1-Data on Rural & Urban.

The Bardowa *Than*

The present study has been done in the Bardowa *Than*, Nagaon district, in the mid of November 2015. This primarily focused on some important facts to know about the origin as well as socio-cultural, socio-economic and socio-religious significance of Bardowa *Than* in Nagaon district. The Nagaon district is situated in the central part of Assam. The topographic feature is plain land in nature. The population of the district is predominantly simple society and rural agricultural community. The livelihood of the studied people is intimately related to soil, river and allied natural resources. It is the core part of their traditional agricultural occupation and resource for sustenance. All of their folk cultural performances reflect the affection and devotion to nature. Related to the present study, a field-work was conducted in the Bardowa *Than* village of Nagaon district. Bardowa *Than* is a beautiful tourist place with its various historical places and objects like—

(i) *Daul Mandir*, where Sankardeva's first drama "Chihna yatra" was staged at the present site of *Daul Mandir*, which was built by his disciples as high stage as per his direction,
(ii) *Silikha* tree where Sankardeva wrote his books in simple language of his time, which are the base of Assamese literature,
(iii) *Padashilla*, where Sankardeva wrote his books, sitting on the stone under the *Silikha* tree.
(iv) *Aakashi Ganga*, the devotees believed that it was the place where the saint Chyavana got back his youth.
(v) *Sanskrit tol*, the Sankardeva's school, which was also known as Mahendra Kandali's tol is now located near Doul Mandir.
(vi) *Chari hati* and *Kirtana ghar*, Sankardeva established it in 1509 and built the *Than*. The congregational prayers are regularly held in the *Kirtan ghar* by the devotees (fourteen Prasanga).
(vii) *Manikut*.
(viii) *Shantijan*, which is famous as "*Santi Radhika Shantijan*".

The *Than* has two major divisions: (i) *Naruwa Satra* and *(ii) Salguri Satra*.

The Major Issues Faced by The Bardowa *Than*

Srimanta Sanakradeva's greatness as socio-religious exponent is to be found in his idea of establishing the *Than*. During his lifetime the *Than* became not only the center of religious discourses, recitation of sacred texts congregational prayers and dramatic performances but also places for mass education and courts for dispensation of justice. The *Than* institution is unique feature of the cultural environment of Assam. No definite data can be ascertained to the origin of the *Than* institution. Bardowa *Than* as an institution have continued till today indicate the importance although its contemporary status in Assamese society is a poor shadow of its status in previous centuries. The *Than* institution spread to various parts of the Brahmaputra valley and several geographical factors were important in their location. *Than* is the place where devotional prayers are offered to the lord Krishna. It is the place where reside the Vaishnavas engaged in the religious and cultural performances like *nam kirtan* and *nam prasanga* of lord Krishna. This holy place is called as *Than*. Villages are made up of families from a number of distinct castes. The caste system, although it exists, is not as major as in other parts of India. Cultural life of Bardowa is interwoven with the activities of two important cultural and religious institutions, *Than* and *Namghar*. The Bardowa *Than* have been in existence for more than 500 years and no doubt Sankaradeva was the founder of the *Than* institution.

For the survival of a religious institution, a strong economy is needed. In this regard an interview schedule was prepared for collecting requisite data in the field for first hand information. Bardowa *Than* was visited for personal observation and for getting an insight into the working of this *Than*. The schedule was so prepared so as to cover only the economic, social and cultural aspects of Bardowa *Than*. Further information was collected through some discussions with the *Than* committee and *Bhakats*. The managing committee is working very seriously for all-round development of the *Than*. But the committee as well as the *Bhakats* are facing various kinds of internal and external problems. Some major issues facing the Bardowa *Than* are—

1. The conscious people of Bardowa *Than* and disciples of the *Than* fear about the safety and the security of its

properties, as well as the historical records of the *Than* as there is no strong security system in it.

2. On the other hand Bardowa *Than* have gradually lost honour, deep respect and the moral influences. This is because of some other *Thans* and Satras are themselves responsible for working under modern social atmosphere and is partly responsible due to the influence of westernization.
3. In present days some people have began to criticize the even Sankaradeva and his birth place and on the other hand lack of awareness and consciousness among the young generation of the area is an emerging issue.
4. The traditions of the Bardowa *Than* failed to attract the young generation towards its fold due to the day by day influences of modernization.
5. The *Than* did not receive any strong financial support from the government also. Most of the trained *Bhakats* are under an unconvincing situation to leave the *Than* for livelihood. Therefore, the training that was traditionally imparted in the *Thans* received a setback.
6. Lack of guest house facilities in this *Than* is one of the vital problem faced by the pilgrims as well as the tourists and specially for the foreigners.
7. Monikut of the *Than* has addition of certain valuable traditional property. In this regard lack of strict security system is the major issue.

Suggestion

The *Than* should start some kinds of activities which can attract the young generations. Along with the government should formulate some new set of rules regarding the *Than*. The people associated with the *Satra* should change their outlook towards the rest of the society and lastly the scholars of the Sankaradeva studies should encourage the coming generations to follow and maintain the *Sankari* culture and tradition.

Conclusion

The *Than* is one of the most important cultural institutions of

Assam. Assamese society has acquired its strength over the years from the vast contributions. The *Than* have made to the cultural variety of the state. Nowadays there is growing awareness in the world about the need of preserving animals as well as heritage sites that are facing extinction. The *Than* are also in the process of extinction. It is not too late that the problems of this institution may be taken seriously that it finds the new ways to solve the problems. *Than* and *Satra* institution is gradually facing so much attack on its cultural and activity especially from western culture and civilization yet it is still relevant to maintain our social identity and national character. So in this regard mandatory attention is required towards the multifarious activities of *Satra, Than* and *Namghar*.

References

Baruah, M.M. 2009. *Srimanta Sankardevar JanmasThan*. Dibrugarh, Kaustrubh Prakashan.

Bora, K. 1991. *Borduwa*. Guwahati, Pocket Book Center.

Borkakoti, S.K. 2006. *Unique Contribution of Srimanta Sankardeva in Religion and Culture*. Guwahati, United Printers and Publishers.

Chetia, B. 2013. "Role Played by Sattras in Disseminating Vaisnavite art and culture and its influence on the youth of Nagaon district." *Neo-Vaisnavite Sattras of Assam in 21st century*, 67.

Chakrabarty, A. 1996. *Pracya-Pranja*. Guwahati, Bani Prakash.

Goswami, K. and Goswami, T. 2013. "Ankiya–Bhaona of Srimanta Sankardeva and Madhavadeva Performed in The Satra Institution of Assam: A Study." *Neo- Vaisnavite Sattras of Assam in 21st century*, 90.

Nath, J. 2013. "Role of Satra and Namghar in Assamese Society." *Neo-Vaisnavite Sattras of Assam in 21st century*, 143.

Phukan, B. 2010. *Srimanta Sankaradeva Vaishnava Saint of Assam*. Guwahati, Kaziranga Books.

Rajkhowa, J.P. 2003. *Sankardeva: His Life Preachings and Practices*. Guwahati, B.S. Publication.

Sarma, S.N. 1996. *Neo-Vaisnavite Movement and The Satra Institution of Assam*. Calcutta, Sreekanta Press.

Sharma, K. 2013. "The Satras of Assam: Its Present Scenario." *Neo-Vaisnavite Sattras of Assam in 21st century*, 34.

Index